The Coca-Cola Sampler

The Most Often Asked Questions

—How many people know the secret formula of Coco-Cola, including the mysterious ingredient No. 7X? *see page 40.*
—Did Coca-Cola ever contain cocaine? *see page 41.*
—What's the significance of the traditional Coca-Cola bottle design? *see pages 83ff.*

A Quiz for the General Reader

—The inventor of Coca-Cola also named it. True _____ False _____ *see page 6.*
—Who first bottled Coca-Cola? *see page 54.*
—Does The Coca-Cola Company also bottle the beverage, Coca-Cola? *see pages 65ff.*
—How did Coca-Cola change America's image of Christmas? *see page 151.*
—Is Coca-Cola sold behind the Iron Curtain? *see page 196.*
—What is the most valuable Coca-Cola collectible? *see page 285.*

A Quiz for the Genuine Coca-Cola Buff

1. Is Coca-Cola the same drink today as when it was invented by Dr. Pemberton? Yes _____ No _____ *see page 23.*
2. Was Coca-Cola ever considered an aphrodisiac? Yes _____ No _____ *see page 15.*
3. Heating the syrup is still a part of the manufacturing process, as when Dr. Pemberton heated the first batch in a brass kettle. True _____ False _____ *see page 107.*
4. Frank M. Robinson designed the famous Coca-Cola trademark by writing it out in his fine Spencerian hand in one sitting. True _____ False _____ *see page 15.*
5. Archie Lee wrote the famous slogan, "The Pause that Refreshes." True _____ False _____ *see page 228.*
6. Asa Candler sold the bottling rights for Coca-Cola at a price of $10 million _____ $1.00 _____ $50,000 _____ None of these _____ *see page 57.*
7. What was the title of the first novel about Coca-Cola? *see pages 74ff.*
8. Who invented the original Fanta drink and under what circumstances? *see page 170.*
9. After Robert W. Woodruff's retirement in 1955, who was the "Boss" of Coca-Cola? *see page 202.*

Favorite Anecdotes in the Coca-Cola Story

—How did carbonated, rather than plain, water come to be added to the syrup? *see page 16.*
—How did the term "soda pop" originate? *see page 56.*
—What was the message sent from Coca-Cola's German bottler immediately following the end of World War II? *see page 176.*
—What has been the relationship between U. S. Presidents and Coca-Cola? *see pages 240ff.*
—What about the long-time love affair between bees and Coca-Cola syrup? *see pages 267ff.*
—What is the all-time favorite anecdote? *see page 198.*

One of the early "pretty girl" posters, a major element in the early 1900s advertising campaigns.

Other books by *Pat Watters*

The Angry Middle-Aged Man
Down to Now: Recollections of the Civil Rights Movement
The South and the Nation

Trade-mark ®

An Illustrated History

—————

PAT WATTERS

DOUBLEDAY & COMPANY, INC.

GARDEN CITY, NEW YORK

1978

Acknowledgments

The author and publisher express their appreciation to the following for permission to include excerpts from the material indicated:

Atlanta magazine for "Coca-Cola's Project Alpha" by Bill Diehl (May 1963); reprinted by permission of *Atlanta* magazine.

The Atlanta *Journal and Constitution* for *The Atlanta Constitution* (May 13, 1886); The Atlanta *Journal* (April 22, 1891; December 10, 1908; November 23, 1908; December 11, 1913; December 21, 1910; September 8, 1920; July 28, 1930); and The Atlanta *Journal-Constitution* (September 11, 1977).

The Coca-Cola Company for the following publications:

"The True Origins of Coca-Cola: Additional Facts Relating to Its Early History" by Charles Howard Candler. Unpublished article. 11 pp. (1932). This is an uncopyrighted piece produced for The Coca-Cola Company.

The Coca-Cola Company: An Illustrated Profile of a Worldwide Company. Copyright: The Coca-Cola Company. 1974.

Opinions, Orders, Injunctions and Decrees Relating to Unfair Competition and Infringement of Trade-Mark. The Coca-Cola Company. 3 volumes. Vol. I (1923); Vols. II and III (1939). An uncopyrighted work produced by the Legal Department of The Coca-Cola Company.

Thirty-three Years with Coca-Cola, 1890–1923 by Charles Howard Candler. Only four bound copies of this publication were printed. 1945. This booklet was produced for The Coca-Cola Company and is an uncopyrighted piece.

The Coca-Cola Bottler

What is it? What it is: Interesting History of Coca-Cola . . . From May, 1886 to January 1901. This is an uncopyrighted piece produced for The Coca-Cola Company.

Twenty-Second Annual Report of President to Stockholders. January 22, 1914. This is an uncopyrighted piece published for the stockholders of The Coca-Cola Company.

Sixteenth Annual Report of President to Stockholders. January 23, 1908. This is an uncopyrighted piece published for the stockholders of The Coca-Cola Company.

Robert Winship Woodruff by E. J. Kahn. Published in 1969. Copyright is held by The Coca-Cola Company.

Annual Report to the Stockholders for the Year 1928. February 5, 1929. This is an uncopyrighted piece published for the stockholders of The Coca-Cola Company.

Coca-Cola in World War II by James M. Kahn. Unpublished manuscript commissioned by The Coca-Cola Company in 1946. This piece was never copyrighted but was produced for The Coca-Cola Company.

Ichauway Plantation by Charles Elliott. This volume was published in 1974 and the copyright is held by Mr. Robert W. Woodruff.

The Refresher. This is a Company publication for The Coca-Cola Company.

Excerpts from the above publications were reprinted by permission of The Coca-Cola Company.

Library of Congress Cataloging in Publication Data

Watters, Pat.
Coca-cola.

1. Coca-Cola Company—History. 2. Atlanta—Industries. 3. Atlanta—History. I. Title.
HD9349.C62U58   338.7′66′3620973
ISBN: 0-385-13499-1
Library of Congress Catalog Card Number 77–16954

Drug Topics for "How I Won and Lost an Interest in Coca-Cola" by Dr. Joseph Jacobs (July, 1929); reprinted by permission of *Drug Topics*.

Emory University for "Atlanta and the Automobile" by Herbert T. Jenkins and *Asa Griggs Candler* by Charles Howard Candler; reprinted by permission of Emory University.

The Emporia *Gazette* for material quoted from an article by William Allen White; reprinted by permission of The Emporia *Gazette*.

Esquire magazine for "Coca-Cola" by Jean Stafford (December 1975) copyright © 1975 by *Esquire*, Inc.

Fortune magazine for "To Pause and Be Refreshed" (July 1931); "Bob Wodruff of Coca-Cola" (September 1945); and "The Competition That Refreshes" (May 1961); reprinted by permission of *Fortune* magazine.

Juris Doctor for "King and Spalding" by Larry Woods (May 1977); reprinted by permission of *Juris Doctor*.

Miami *Herald Tropic* magazine for a story by Anthony Haden-Guest (August 26, 1973); reprinted by permission of author.

Prentice-Hall, Inc., for *Up Against the Corporate Wall* by S. Prakash Sethi, copyright © 1971 by S. Prakash Sethi; reprinted by permission of Prentice-Hall, Inc.

Simon and Schuster for *Soda Pop* by Lawrence Dietz, copyright © 1973 by Lawrence Dietz; reprinted by permission of Simon and Schuster

Southern Exposure for "Journey to the White House . . ." by Bob Hall (Vol. 5, No. 1, 1977); reprinted by permission of *Southern Exposure*.

Time magazine for "The Sun Never Sets on Cacoola" (May 15, 1950); reprinted by permission from *Time*, The Weekly Newsmagazine; Copyright Time, Inc. 1950.

To our great city of Atlanta

Contents

A Preface of Appreciation

This is to say "thank you" to an extraordinary group of people who not only helped me with research on this book, but who also—by their courtesy, generosity of spirit, and geniality—made this work the most enjoyable I have ever experienced.

First the pleasant and impressive people of Coca-Cola:

Archivist Wilbur G. Kurtz, Jr., tireless and wise in the sharing of his knowledge of Coca-Cola lore and materials. Harold Terhune, photographer and ever-helpful friend in locating and printing archives photographs. Mrs. Janet Pecha, also very helpful in finding archives lore. Philip F. Mooney, who as manager of the corporate archives has gotten off to a good start in the formidable job of filling the recently retired Mr. Kurtz's shoes.

Vice-president J. William Pruett, Jr., John B. White, Kenneth Baldowski and others of the public relations department. Pope E. Brock and John A. Sibley, retired but still active former legal chiefs of the company. Retired executives J. H. (Red) Hall and Ezekiel S. (Zeke) Candler (great-nephew of Asa G. Candler, founder of the company), both of whom told some of the secrets and adventures of the extraordinary fountain sales successes. E. Delony Sledge and Hunter Bell, retired advertising department executives, who shared their memories of the promotional wizardry and their knowledge of Coca-Cola history, and went the extra mile trying to guide a fellow writer.

Executive vice-president Claus M. Halle and retired executive H. Burke Nicholson who shared their knowledge and recollections of overseas operations. Retired executive John Talley who told of both overseas and wondrous World War II Coca-Cola adventures. Retired executive John C. Staton, equally eloquent about his overseas work but reticent regarding his development of the first Coca-Cola cooler.

Lynn LaGarde, chuckling over the inventiveness-out-of-necessity when he headed the engineering department. Dr. Orville May, quietly telling astonishing things about being in charge of quality control before his retirement. Marshall Lane remembering his days as art director during some of the great promotional years.

Arthur L. Montgomery, genial chairman of the board of directors of The Atlanta Coca-Cola Bottling Company, telling bottling lore back to the days when his great-uncle pioneered in the Atlanta plant. Jerry E. Clack, corporate production manager of the Atlanta bottling company, explaining filling-line operations, among other intricacies.

J. Paul Austin, chairman of the board of directors and chief executive officer of The Coca-Cola Company, and company president J. Lucian Smith, both of whom took time out from internationally busy schedules to discuss today's operations.

Charles Howard Candler, Jr. (grandson of Asa Candler) and George Woodruff (brother of the retired leader Robert W. Woodruff), both members of the board of directors, whose memories of Coca-Cola go far back.

Boisfeuillet Jones, in charge of various Woodruff and Coca-Cola-related foundations, who explained the vast philanthropic undertaking. Mrs. Lucille Huffman, secretary to Robert W. Woodruff, giving guidance toward better understanding of her boss. Vice-president J. W. (Joe) Jones, assistant and close-associate of Mr. Woodruff, whose insights and courteous, efficient helpfulness were invaluable.

Finally, Robert W. Woodruff, retired board chairman and president, still chairman of the finance committee, the mythic figure who saved the company and then built it into an international giant, who was gracious and helpful to me, and entirely human, during a visit to his office.

Then, the other ladies and gentlemen who gave of their time for interviews and/or guidance toward better understanding of the intertwined history of Coca-Cola and our great city of Atlanta:

Franklin M. Garrett, historian of the Atlanta Historical Society, whose help was invaluable, and Richard Eltzroth there, whose patience in finding photographs was infinite; David Estes, curator of the Special Collections of the Robert W. Woodruff Library at Emory University, and Henry M. Bowden, chairman of Emory's board of trustees; former Atlanta mayor Ivan Allen, Jr., and present mayor Maynard Jackson; retired Atlanta police chief Herbert T. Jenkins; Georgia representative John W. Greer; Georgia secretary of state Ben W. Fortson, Jr.; Mrs. Catherine Candler Warren, granddaughter of Asa Candler; Cecil Stockard, grandson of Coca-Cola pioneer, Frank M. Robinson; Ed Forio, Jr., son of a memorable Coca-Cola figure; Sinclair Jacobs, Jr., whose grandfather owned the drugstore where Coca-Cola first was sold; my uncle, John Bookout, whose memory of Atlanta goes far back; Carroll P. Jones of the Trust Company of Georgia; Dr. Marvin Roberts, Jr., and Dr. Carroll Hitchcock who told about past glories of the soda fountain; Claud and Margaret Almond, representatives of the genial and happy Cola Clan, collectors of Coca-Cola memorabilia.

Trade-mark ®

An Illustrated History

Wherever you go you will find

AT ALL FOUNTAINS Coca-Cola 5¢

to refresh the parched throat, to invigorate
the fatigued body, and quicken the tired brain

I

Dr. Pemberton's Beverage

The breezes that waft about the sprawling complex of buildings on Atlanta's North Avenue, which comprise the world headquarters of The Coca-Cola Company, are laden with a pleasant, confectionery odor, as though the air were cotton candy. It is the smell of sugar and water in mixture to make Coca-Cola syrup, and that smell is the sweet smell of an extraordinary success.

From the most humble of beginnings in Atlanta, Coca-Cola moved out of the South, across America, and then over the world to become, as company publications like to point out, the best-known trademark on earth, served in more homes than any other, consumed by more people.

The Coca-Cola success story is a southern one, and Southerners do not sit too easy with success. Hence, the almost self-deprecatory tone of one of the many company publications as it speaks of "the modest role" of Coca-Cola in the affairs of the world: "Mankind would not perish or be notably inconvenienced if Coke were not around. But mankind is better off with it. For a universal common denominator of all humans is alternate rest and activity. The role of Coca-Cola has always been to make the rest periods more pleasant—to insure that any pause can be the pause that refreshes."

This "modest role" involves sale of Coca-Cola and other company products in 135 nations, give or take. (The figure keeps varying.) The products are advertised in eighty different languages.

The basis of the business is simple, and this is one of the secrets of its success. The company manufactures the Coca-Cola syrup and syrup for other carbonated beverages and sells them to franchised bottlers. The bottlers in turn sell the products to the public. (Syrup is also sold by the company to soda fountains and other dispensers.)

Consolidated net sales by the company in 1976 were three billion, thirty-two million, eight hundred twenty-nine thousand and fifty-six dollars. That was an all-time high, as was the consolidated net profit for the year: $284,959,120 or $4.76 per share.

Coca-Cola stock went public in 1919 at $40 per share. One of those shares today is worth $11,000.

Foreign consumption accounted for 40 per cent of those total sales in 1976 and 55 per cent of profits. In nations other than the United States, Coke and other company products are consumed daily by more than a million people, who buy from more than four million retail outlets. Overseas bottling plants, owned for the most part by indigenous citizens, number 770, including one twelve feet below sea level in Amsterdam, Holland, and another thirteen thousand feet above sea level in La Paz, Bolivia.

Great is the lore of how Coca-Cola signs have penetrated to the far reaches of the earth, people having espied them deep in remote jungles, on hard-to-reach mountaintops, on pyramids and humble native huts. The story is told about a United Nations official who made an inspection trip of combat zones during a civil war in the Congo. It was a terrifying experience. He traveled in a jeep painted light blue and bearing the UN symbol, but was shot at many times. Nobody, he said, seemed to have heard of the UN. But everywhere about were Coca-Cola signs. Next time, the official declared, he would paint his jeep bright red and plaster it with Coca-Cola signs.

To deliver what the signs advertise, Coca-Cola bottlers operate the largest commercial fleet of trucks on earth. In all, there are 1,331 franchised bottling plants which employ several hundred thousand workers. The Coca-Cola Company itself, though, has only thirty thousand employees, fourteen thousand of them overseas.

The company ranks in "The *Fortune* Directory of the 500 Largest U. S. Industrial Corporations" (1976) 69th in sales, yet 121st in number of employees. It takes relatively few people to achieve the pinnacles of Coca-Cola success, and we shall see again and again that this is largely due to the unusual method of the manufacture of the drink.

Ah, the sweet smell of Coca-Cola's syrup of success. The tenth billion gallon of Coca-Cola syrup was produced in March 1976. It took fifty-eight years for the world to consume drinks made from the first billion gallons. But now the world swigs drinks made from nearly a billion gallons each year. That's a lot of gooey, sweet Coca-Cola syrup. The company has compiled analogues to dramatize how vast is the sea of drinks of ice-cold Coca-Cola made from all that syrup. They go like this:

If all the Coca-Cola ever produced were—

***Poured into one big bottle, that bottle would be 6,356 feet tall and 1,930 feet wide—more than a mile high.

***Put in regular-size bottles, those bottles placed end to end would reach through outer space to Mars, Venus, or Mercury.

***Put in cases of twenty-four regular-size bottles, there would be eleven cases for every living soul in the world.

***Flowing over Niagara Falls, the Falls would flow at their normal rate for eight hours and fifty-one minutes.

***Loaded in regular-size bottles on average-size Coca-Cola trucks, and those trucks were to pass a given point, bumper to bumper at ten miles per hour, it would take eight years, seven months, three weeks, and two days for all the trucks to pass that point.

And so on . . . Company people call these "gee-whizzers." Maybe even whizzier is the thought that the people of this earth drink two hundred million of the drinks produced by Coca-Cola every day. That means that at any given minute in any twenty-four-hour period, *138,888 human beings are enjoying the pause that refreshes.*

And, at an average of eight ounces per drink, they are consuming a total of one billion, six hundred million ounces a day, or twelve million, five hundred thousand gallons. That means people are guzzling down eighty-six hundred gallons of Coca-Cola drinks *every minute that passes.*

A cosmic amount of Coca-Cola! But Coca-Cola people look upon such by-the-minute guzzling from a global perspective and think of what yet might be. At present, their drinks are available to 1.1 billion people where they live on the planet. That leaves nearly three billion yet to be offered the pause that refreshes, a splendid market for expansion, a continuing challenge to the company.

And after that? A company publication reports: "During the space missions of the sixties and seventies, The Coca-Cola Company received a number of applications from would-be entrepreneurs requesting that they should have first options when the company began to grant Coca-Cola bottling franchises on the moon."

So a uniquely flavored concoction came forth from a small Atlanta beginning to encircle the earth and reach to the stars. At company headquarters, the man who can tell us about the beginning and is among the most enthusiastic seers of future successes, archivist Wilbur G. Kurtz, Jr., sits amid Coca-Cola memorabilia worth several fortunes—trays, pretty girl posters, the Tiffany-style chandelier, porcelain urns, Coca-Cola clocks, and much else, in sparkling red-and-white and green-and-yellow happy hues.

Mr. Kurtz, serving out the last few months before his mandatory retirement at age sixty-five and having spent virtually all his working years with the company, is a bald and benign, thickset gentleman who knows everything worth knowing about Coca-Cola. His eyes twinkle (they really do) as he leans toward his guest and, in a courtly voice, edged with exquisite humor and irony, asks:

"Would you care for a glass of Dr. Pemberton's beverage?"

The irony and humor are peculiarly southern, built upon the Southerner's intimate and inherited familiarity with defeat (by cotton and the Union most notably), the Southerner's philosophical acceptance of defeat, and his attitude of amazed amusement over the rare joy of victory. ("Sheet," Jody Powell is said to have exclaimed after his boss, Jimmy Carter, had won the 1976 presidential election. "I still don't believe it.") Mr. Kurtz's intoning of his question reflects that kind of amusement, common to old-timers of the company, over the spectacular success Coca-Cola has known through the years. And it expresses eloquently the philosophical acceptance of the fate of the inventor of Coca-Cola, Dr. John Styth Pemberton, whose whole life may be said to have been one of endless defeat.

Elsewhere in the headquarters building, Coca-Cola people move through an exhibit of the 1977 Technical Conference ("product quality through technology"). Here, they watch the Lasermark 901 system print a code (telling time and place of bottling) on a Coca-Cola bottle cap in one-millionth of a second, 125 bottles a minute, with a "burst of infrared energy" that "forms the image by burning off a surface layer on the closure, exposing a contrasting colored surface below." There, they see models of the machines of Coca-Cola-owned Aqua-Chem, including one which "turns seawater into fresh, polluted water into clean." And over here, a closed-circuit television flashes one commercial after another showing fresh-faced young people of all the earth's races singing in dozens of different languages that Coke is the real thing, against accompaniments ranging from the twang of oriental stringed instruments to the thumping of British rock to the squeal of bagpipes.

Upstairs, in his office in the executive suite for active officers, the present board chairman, J. Paul Austin, tells his views on the role that international business can play to prevent the world's being blown up. (There is another executive suite for retired president and board chairman, Robert W. Woodruff, who still serves as chairman of the company's finance committee, and his staff.)

Outside, Mr. Pope T. Brock walks a sedate old man's walk to the bus stop in front of the International Building, with a Coca-Cola flag flying alongside the American one, both outsize. He is a short, squat figure in a dark summer suit with a 1920s-style, round sailor straw hat level on his head. "We know it's spring when Mr. Brock puts on his sailor straw," a young associate says. "And we know summer's over when he takes it off and puts on his black fedora." He is eighty-nine years old, his memories of the company, for which he was legal counsel, going back as far as anyone's. He appears at his office each morning, on hand as a legal consultant—usually the telling of "ancient history" that might be needed in a lawsuit. Every few years, he requests the board of directors to pay him less since he has been doing less work. Now he waits for his bus to the fashionable Northside where his daughter will meet him at the bus stop and drive him home. Often he gets off blocks ahead of the stop to enjoy walking to it.

He can hear from next door the loud noises of construction of a new building complex, which will include a twenty-six-story office tower. It will contain the continuously expanding international and national operations of The Coca-Cola Company in the franchise marketing of its soft drinks and the sale of other beverages, including coffee, frozen citrus juices, and, most recently taken on, powdered-flavor drinks and wine.

Back upstairs, another executive describes with enthusiasm a display, in several of the windows of Tiffany's in New York City, of Coca-Cola bottles contrived to look like people, with round balls for heads and clothes painted on, the work of artist Vicki Romaine. "It would be worth your time to go up there and see them," he says to an associate, such a trip to the two of them, with the whole world their territory, being no more than a drive across town.

Downstairs in the technical conference exhibit, another display is of the three-valve, mechanically refrigerated, postmix dispensing machine for low-volume office accounts, with a capacity in its one-by-two-foot frame of 1,250 six-and-a-half-ounce drinks. The capacity of that one little machine is almost one half of the total amount of Coca-Cola sold during the first year of its existence, some 3,200 soda-fountain glasses of it.

COURTESY OF THE ARCHIVES, THE COCA-COLA COMPANY

Dr. John Styth Pemberton.

Coca-Cola Story Highlights: 1873–89

From that small beginning by Dr. Pemberton to the mind-boggling bigness of Coca-Cola today—how did it happen? Who the people, what the skills, how the strategies, which the crucial decisions?

The Coke commercials from around the world, flashing on the closed-circuit television set, employ the technique of quick-shot sequences and abrupt scene shifts developed for that medium. See, then, the small beginnings of Coca-Cola in the same quick, abrupt way:

Early in 1873: Asa Griggs Candler arrives in Atlanta and spends the day going from one drugstore to another in the rough-and-tumble railroad town asking for a job. He has served out his apprenticeship as a pharmacist in Cartersville, Georgia, a small place of even smaller opportunity, and he has $1.75 in the pants pocket of his homemade suit. At nightfall, he finds a job and works until midnight in George Howard's drugstore. One of the pharmacists who turned him down is Dr. John Styth Pemberton, partner in the Pemberton-Pulliam Drug Co.

May 8, 1886: By melting sugar mixed with water in a brass kettle heated over an open fire, in the back yard of his home at 107 Marietta Street, and adding certain ingredients of his choosing, the same Dr. Pemberton perfects the syrup for a new concoction to add to various proprietary medicines he has invented and marketed.

(Among these is French Wine of Coca, sometimes called French Wine Coca, a better draught, which he sells for a dollar a bottle.) He plans to market this new one in a novel way, by the drink at soda fountains for five cents a glass. Unlike his other nostrums and those common to the day, this one tastes good.

The Origin of the name "Coca-Cola"

One of his four partners, Frank M. Robinson, a bookkeeper, comes up with the best of several suggested names for the stuff. Mr. Robinson says call it after two of the ingredients in it, the coca leaf and kola nut, and spell kola with a *c* to make it look better in advertisements. Then, as legend has it, the redoubtable Mr. Robinson sits himself down and proceeds to write the trademark in his fine, bookkeeper's Spencerian script, virtually as it appears today, as familiar as the landscape the world over. He actually writes out "Coca-Cola Syrup and Elixir," but it is decided not to use the descriptive labels. Shortly afterward, Mr. Robinson, this remarkable man, puts together the slogan, "Delicious. Refreshing" (the and was added later), equally familiar around the globe.

May 1886: Some Atlanta person becomes the first ever to pay five cents for and drink down a glass of ice-cold Coca-Cola. He does this at the soda fountain run by Willis E. Venable along the right-hand side of Jacobs' Pharmacy at the corner of Peachtree and Marietta streets, known then as Norcross Corner, later as part of Atlanta's Five Points. Attendant on this first selling of the drink, Dr. Pemberton or one of his associates hangs up an oilcloth sign on the awning of Jacobs'. In red letters on a white background, it says: "Drink Coca-Cola."

Atlanta's Jacobs' Pharmacy, where the first glass of Coca-Cola was sold in 1886. In 1887, this became the company's second "home."

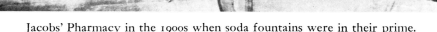

Jacobs' Pharmacy in the 1900s when soda fountains were in their prime.

May 29, 1886: A small, one-column advertisement appears in the Atlanta *Journal,* the first in the printed media for the drink. In bold black letters, it says: "Coca-Cola, Delicious! Refreshing! Exhilarating! Invigorating! The new and popular soda fountain drink containing the properties of the wonderful Coca plant and the famous Cola nut. For sale by Willis Venable and Nunnally and Rawson."

The soda-fountain season (spring and summer only) of 1887: Dr. Pemberton and his associates may be seen on the streets of downtown Atlanta, approaching the gentlemen in derby hats and the ladies in their long dresses with bustles, proferring tickets entitling the bearer to a free-sample drink of Coca-Cola at one of several soda fountains. Tickets are mailed to lists of people compiled from the current city directory. The tactic, once again the brainchild of Frank M. Robinson, was based on the assumption that once a person tried the drink, he or she would like it enough to keep on buying it.

July 1887: Dr. Pemberton, his health failing and his new product not bringing in the money he needs to meet his obligations, begins selling part of his interest in the Coca-Cola enterprise. He eventually sells two thirds to Willis Venable and George S. Lowndes, a prospering Atlanta businessman. The equipment for manufacturing and advertising Coca-Cola is moved from Dr. Pemberton's home to the basement of Jacobs' Pharmacy.

April 14, 1888: Asa G. Candler, by now owner of his own wholesale and retail pharmaceutical company, becomes a partner (in the ownership of the two-thirds interest in Coca-Cola) with Woolfolk Walker, a former salesman for the Pemberton

The Venable Family, 1890s. The man seated on the left, Willis Venable, served the first glass of Coca-Cola. Seated next to him is Ed Venable, owner of a famous Atlanta restaurant.

Chemical Company, and Dr. Joseph Jacobs, proprietor of the drugstore, along with Mr. Walker's sister, Mrs. M. C. Dozier. They have purchased it from Mr. Venable and Mr. Lowndes. A short while later, the corporation buys the remaining one-third interest from Dr. Pemberton.

August 16, 1888: Dr. Pemberton dies of the ailment, possibly cancer of the stomach, that had plagued him during the short life of his new product. He was never to know what a mighty thing he had wrought.

May 1, 1889: A full-page advertisement appears in the Atlanta *Journal* proclaiming Asa G. Candler and Company as sole proprietor of Coca-Cola. (Though the familiar script trademark had appeared in most of Dr. Pemberton's newspaper ads for the drink, the name for some reason is in regular block type in this one.) "Delicious/Refreshing/Exhilarating," it says. "The new and popular drink containing the tonic properties of the wonderful coca plant and the famous cola nuts/On draught at the popular soda fountains at 5 cents per glass." The ad also commends Mr. Candler's drug company and another of his products, Delectalave, "the great tooth-wash." The announcement is premature; some of the stock is still outstanding.

April 22, 1891: After a series of transactions with his partners, Mr. Candler does become sole proprietor of Coca-Cola. In all, he has paid out a grand total of $2,300 to acquire it. The paraphernalia of Coca-Cola had already been moved from the Jacobs' store basement to the store of Asa G. Candler and Company, 47 Peachtree Street, in 1888, the entire inventory hauled in a one-horse wagon driven by Mr. Candler's nephew and employee, Samuel Candler Dobbs.

INTERNATIONAL EVENTS DURING COCA-COLA'S EARLY YEARS

On that momentous day when Dr. Pemberton stirred the first batch of Coca-Cola syrup, General Nelson Miles was pursuing the Apaches in the American West. The Statue of Liberty was unveiled in New York Harbor, and the Eiffel Tower was under construction in Paris, France.

It had been, and would continue to be, a tumultuous decade for America. In 1881, Charlie Guiteau shot down President James A. Garfield and was hanged for the assassination the next year. In 1884, a New York associate of Republican James G. Blaine, candidate for President, declared, in a speech in the candidate's presence, disdain for the party of "rum, Romanism, and rebellion," and the affront to Catholic voters was said to account for the victory of Democrat Grover Cleveland. In 1886, a bomb was thrown during an anarchist's meeting in Haymarket Square in Chicago, setting off a riot and subsequent witch hunt. On May 31, 1889, an abandoned reservoir gave way and its waters destroyed Johnstown, Pennsylvania, killing some three thousand people.

The Brooklyn Bridge, one of the great engineering achievements of the century was opened in 1883. That same year, the Civil Service Act was passed with the intent to destroy the spoils system. In 1886, the American Federation of Labor was formed to join the Knights of Labor in battle against such conditions as twelve-hour shifts and child labor. In 1890, Congress passed the Sherman Antitrust Act after John D. Rockefeller had set up the Standard Oil Trust with its threat of monopoly in the manufacture of a consumer product.

Progress was rolling right along. In the last year of the previous decade, Thomas A. Edison had given the electric light to mankind's nights. The mechanical typewriter made its first orderly mark during the 1880s and Herrs Benz and Danzler were combining their energies toward construction of a practical internal-combustion engine automobile.

ATLANTA

The modern age was in its beginnings. But a perusal of the Atlanta *Constitution, on a typical day of Dr. Pemberton's big month of May 1886, reflects how the old and the new were blended in the town of Atlanta.*

COURTESY OF THE ATLANTA HISTORICAL SOCIETY

Atlanta, 1882, at Whitehall Street.

The Constitution *readers were told that the Methodist Episcopal Church South was in convention in Richmond, Virginia.*

The United States Senate had passed a measure to regulate interstate commerce—a "fraud" and "Utopian scheme," the Constitution *asserted in its news account.*

The State Sunday School Convention was in session in Macon, Georgia.

A railroad was under construction to connect Macon with Quitman, Georgia.

The game of marbles was reported popular in Barnesville, Georgia.

A prohibition election was to be held in Atlanta.

In its advertising columns, the Constitution *offered Dr. Haines' Golden Specific for the cure of drunkenness, two different cures for morphine addiction, and Dr. Francis' Tonic and Blood Pacifier at forty cents a quart. At George E. King and Company Hardware Store, 47 Peachtree Street, there was available the latest improved fly fan: "It drives all flies away by the shadow and movement of the wings." When wound up with a thumbscrew, it would run for an hour and a half.*

Former Confederate General John B. Gordon made a gubernatorial campaign speech in Americus, Georgia, and the Constitution *described the effect on his "lady hearers": "In his feeling allusions to the period of bitterness, there were very few dry eyes among them."*

A large and enthusiastic audience enjoyed the Huntley-Stark Company's performance of A Celebrated Case *at DeGive's Opera House (its successor, DeGive's New Grand, fifty-three years later, as the Loew's Grand, housed the world premiere audience for the film version of* Gone With the Wind).

DeGive's Opera House, 1891.

Jenne Lawshe, a colored girl, was gored by an angry cow she was trying to milk on Alabama Street near the ice mill.

A meeting of the Fulton County Confederate Veterans Association was scheduled for the evening. The "Black Maria" police wagon had made five calls after ten o'clock of the previous evening.

A miscreant was sentenced to ten days on the rock pile for drunkenness.

And on the sports page, the headline on the previous day's baseball activity flatly stated that "Unfair Umpiring Causes Atlanta to Lose Another Game." (Shades of the Braves!)

It is hard to believe, but Atlanta had a sophistication and worldliness unusual for the South of those times. In the words of one of Asa Candler's four sons, Charles Howard Candler, author of Asa Griggs Candler, *a biography, it was a "goods-selling, money-making, business-minded town."* Built as a railroad center, only as long ago as 1837, along tracks ultimately coming from all directions, burned to the ground by Sherman in 1864, out from under military rule*

---

* The words may not actually be those of Charles Howard Candler, after all. He was assisted in the preparation of the biography, which was published by Emory University in 1950, by Bradford Ansley, then public information officer at Emory. (Mr. Ansley in more recent years was associated for a time with Royal Crown Cola, bless us.) The terse description of early Atlanta may well have been his handiwork; Charles Howard Candler's style, as expressed in other writings in which he was unassisted and in most of the biography, has a stately rhythm and precision of diction that are a joy to behold.

by 1868, rebuilt by 1870, it was an economically reviving, bumptious town of some forty thousand souls in the 1880s. Its railroads freed it from dependency on the struggling southern agrarian economy of evolving sharecropperism, and the influx of people from over the country to work for the railroads freed it some from the southern provincialism of the time.

Asa Griggs Candler

But we have seen in the *Constitution* how the grip of the past was not altogether loosened. Notions of gallantry and chivalry were not gone yet with the wind, and religion, the old-time revivalist religion, was a strong influence. So the little city partook of the old as it grasped for the new. It was a blend of the Old South and of Victorianism with go-getting modernism. And if ever a man embodied that blend, it was Asa Griggs Candler, and Mr. Candler put the stamp of that upon The Coca-Cola Company.

He was a pious man (one of his eight brothers, Warren, a Methodist Bishop), a man of stern moral principle, and he was a devoted member of the Atlanta Horse Guard whose bugle calls faintly echoed the shrill blasts that hurtled the chivalrous Confederate troops to their doom.

But he was also the epitome of a shrewd and hard-driving businessman, as suggested by the short span of years it took for him to move to prosperous druggist and sole proprietor of The Coca-Cola Company from that day when he first came to town as a nearly broke jobhunter. He had started out living over Howard's Drugstore in an attic room with ceilings so low that he, a man of short stature, had to stoop to get about. People in need of emergency medicine after business hours would ring a bell on the store's door and Asa Candler would rouse himself and get it for them. As soon as he could, he moved to Mrs. Richard Lochart's rooming house on Ivy Street.

Like a Horatio Alger hero, he had pluck and luck, working long and hard. Therefore, in 1877, four years after his arrival in Atlanta, he owned half interest in a wholesale and retail drug firm. Soon after that, he married Lucy Elizabeth (Lizzie) Howard, the daughter of his first employer, over the good gentleman's protest. And after that he bought half interest in his father-in-law's firm and later bought him out, setting up the Asa G. Candler and Company wholesale and retail drug firm in 1886.

Dr. John Styth Pemberton

However, fortune did not smile so kindly upon the enterprises of Dr. Pemberton. He seems to have been a dreamer, always putting together new products, but never seeming able to do much with them. He had lived in Atlanta for

COURTESY OF THE ARCHIVES, THE COCA-COLA COMPANY

This sign promoted the early 1880s forerunner of Coca-Cola, French Wine of Coca.

seventeen years when he mixed the one that made his name famous, and, during that time, had worked at, or been part owner of, nine different pharmaceutical firms. He came to Atlanta in 1869 from Columbus, Georgia, where, after service as a Confederate Home Guard officer, he had gained some renown for operating an imaginative and innovative soda fountain, as well as for his medical inventions.

Dr. Joseph Jacobs, owner of the drugstore, writing in *Drug Topics*, July 1929, characterized Dr. Pemberton as "a druggist of the old school, thoroughly versed in the manufacturing part of the business and . . . constantly experimenting with new preparations. He had successfully exploited Pemberton's Extract of Styllinger, Pemberton's Globe Flower Cough Syrup, and other proprietary medicines, all of which had a fairly good sale." (Extract of Styllinger is no mean feat of product-naming. It sounds like some god of antiquity. A dose of it would *have* to do you good—it was "for the blood.")

One of Dr. Pemberton's Atlanta firms, Pemberton, Iverson and Dennison, had been sold to Howard and Candler in 1885. At that point, he set up a chemical laboratory with one Ed Holland and went into the patent medicine business full time. His products included Indian Queen hair dye, Gingerine and Triplex liver pills. But his main fascination was the French Wine of Coca, "ideal nerve tonic and stimulant."

It was after formation of the chemical laboratory that the magic touch in the person of Mr. Robinson came to Dr. Pemberton. Hailing from Osceola, Iowa (having been born in East Corinth, Maine, in 1845), Mr. Robinson had set up shop in Atlanta as a bookkeeper for several firms a few years before. (He had been clerk of court in Iowa.)

Hunter Bell (a retired vice-president and manager of The Coca-Cola Company's advertising department), who has delved deeply into Coca-Cola lore and history, says that Frank M. Robinson's finding of the life work for which he was so uniquely suited occurred quite by chance. Mr. Bell says that Mr. Robinson and a man with the anonymous-sounding name of D. D. Doe called on Dr. Pemberton to try to interest him in a pioneering process they had developed for printing color in newspapers and that, evidently, Dr. Pemberton was able to get them more interested in his enterprises than they were able to interest him in theirs. The upshot was that the two joined the doctor and Mr. Holland in a partnership in 1886 to establish the Pemberton Chemical Company, which produced and marketed Dr. Pemberton's potents, including the French Wine of Coca.

The Origin of Coca-Cola

We have it on the authority of Charles Howard Candler in an unpublished manuscript, "The True Origin of Coca-Cola"† written in 1952, that the Coca-Cola syrup formula was evolved from French Wine of Coca. Charles Howard Candler wrote of Dr. Pemberton and his partners, "This group of adventurers decided to include caffeine in their syrup blend to make it a headache remedy, starting as they did with Dr. Pemberton's Wine-Coca which had in it the stimulating Extract of Coca leaves; by eliminating the wine and increasing the sugar in the formula and adding an acid for zest, they probably got a medicine which . . . had a far from pleasant taste. They contributed to the bitterish taste of their concoction by including in the formula some fluid extract of Kola."

(Dr. Pemberton had studied up on kola and on the basis of his research made subsequent claims that Coca-Cola would relieve exhaustion, was exhilarating, and would relieve dyspepsia, including that caused by alcohol. Commented Charles Howard Candler: "Though this medicine might relieve the results of intemperance, the good doctor apparently believed it would promote

† Based on matters "which I many times heard my father, Asa G. Candler, and Mr. Frank Robinson discuss at length."

temperance and replace alcoholic drinks." The "good doctor" also read that African Negroes highly valued the kola nut as an aphrodisiac, so he and his three partners were "intrigued" with the popular-appeal possibilities of that. There is no record, however, that they ever found a way to communicate this particular claim to Atlanta's soda-fountain clientele when eventually they put the brew on sale.)

But before they could do this, the four had to do something about that bitter taste. "In order to disguise the unpleasant taste," Charles Howard Candler went on, "the product was flavored with a relatively large variety of essential oils which imparted the delicious aroma that was sought. Some of these oils had similar characteristics and some antagonistic and masked others when used together."

At last, it was right. The great day of May 8, 1886, had come and there in the back yard of his two-story, brick antebellum home at 107 Marietta Street, between Spring Street and Bartow Street (now Techwood Drive), Dr. Pemberton made the big stir of his life. And Mr. Robinson offered his great contributions—the name, the trademark, the first slogan. Ah, that naming and labeling! An account produced by the archives of The Coca-Cola Company quotes Mr. Robinson on the feat of the naming: "It had no name in the beginning. It was experimented upon—Dr. Pemberton compounded a preparation . . . and after they had made various changes in the compound, it seemed to be satisfactory. . . . I just took Coca-Cola as a name, similar to other advertising names, thinking that the two C's would look well in advertising."

On the matter of Mr. Robinson's having sat down and written out on the spot the world-famous trademark (which some have called the most valuable bit of calligraphy in the world), Cecil R. Stockard, his grandson, an Atlanta attorney, remembers that his mother told him that Mr. Robinson worked for a year perfecting his masterpiece, getting it just right.

But on that day in May, they marched forth with Coca-Cola to market, bearing a rudimentary trademark, the name, and a jug of syrup. Archivist Wilbur Kurtz has recreated the scene for us: "Dr. Pemberton stepped out of his house to the street and began walking east. In his hand was a gallon jug containing the syrup.

"The day was warm, but the trees lining the street protected him a little from the morning rays of the sun. But he had no protection from the swirling dust and the pungent smell of horse-droppings. He walked as far as The Girl of the Period Saloon where he turned to cross to the south side of the street. Jacobs' drugstore was located on the southwest corner of Marietta and Peachtree.

"As he crossed the street he stopped to allow the Marietta Street horse car to pass. It was making its morning trip out Marietta Street on its track and was pulled by two mules ambling along seemingly without any appointments to keep.

"From the opposite direction, Dr. Pemberton saw approaching Mrs. Captain English in her Victoria drawn by a pair of beautiful horses. Just following her was a Landau occupied by George Adair and Patrick Calhoun. Dr. Pemberton waved a greeting to the three.

"Soon Dr. Pemberton reached Jacobs' drugstore and walked in. At the soda fountain was its proprietor, Willis Venable, who was leasing from Dr. Joseph Jacobs, owner of the drugstore.

"After mutual greeting and some small talk, Dr. Pemberton placed the jug of syrup on the counter and explained what he had done. Meanwhile, they were joined by Dr. Jacobs who had been working at his desk in the back of the store.

"Pemberton suggested to Venable that he mix some ice and plain water with the syrup in the proportions of one ounce of syrup to five ounces of water. He made three drinks and placed them on the counter. The three of them stood smacking their lips and nodding their heads in approval. However, on the second go-around, by accident, Venable put carbonated water into the glasses instead of plain water.

"After tasting the contents of the second glass, the three men became excited, all talking at once. Their delight and pleasure was obvious on discovering what a delicious drink was produced by the combination of carbonated water with Dr. Pemberton's syrup.

"Later Dr. Pemberton was to declare that it was this mixture of carbonated water with the syrup which actually brought Coca-Cola into being."

There are other versions of how the carbonated water got in. The informal corporate history, *The Coca-Cola Company, An Illustrated Profile*, has Mr. Venable making the happy error later on—in early 1887. Charles Howard Candler in his manuscript on the origins says the "epochal event" occurred even later—in the spring of 1887. Prior to that time, he wrote, the syrup was packaged in secondhand pint beer bottles with these instructions on the label: "Take a tablespoonful in wine glass of water for the relief of headache and nervous affections, neuralgia, hysteria, melancholia, etc. A brain tonic and nerve stimulant."

Then, according to this version, "a customer, a man whose name was soon forgotten, suffering with a headache stepped into a drugstore and asked the druggist for a bottle of Coca-Cola, about which it appears that he already knew, and as the bottle was handed him, asked the druggist to open it, pour out a dose, add water and let him take it there at once in order to hasten relief. The shelf from which this bottle was taken was nearer the soda fountain than it was to the hydrant located behind the prescription case and also a glass for the dose was readily available at the fountain. The druggist suggested soda water instead of tap water. When the customer drank the bubbling dose he enthusiastically proclaimed that it really tasted fine and that this was a vastly superior method of taking the medicine over the prescription by the label. The word got around among the few druggists who stocked Coca-Cola, and it wasn't long before these druggists were administering this remedy in soda water to customers who casually called asking for something to relieve headache."

Charles Howard Candler went on to maintain that it was only after this that Dr. Pemberton and his associates seized on the salability of Coca-Cola as a refreshment, maintaining that they had hitherto considered it no different from the other medicines they peddled. But there is the contrary evidence of that first newspaper ad, which appeared the same month that Coca-Cola was concocted, proclaiming it delicious and refreshing as well as exhilarating and invigorating. People in the company today, ever conscious of image, cite that as proof that the intent from the beginning was, at least partially, refreshment.

The first newspaper ad for Coca-Cola.

Production, Marketing, and Promotion of the First Soft Drink

Probably, the first marketing objectives were mixed. Certainly, Dr. Pemberton and his associates had a mind-set on medicine only. But then their efforts to sweeten up French Wine of Coca produced something that tasted spectacularly good. If, indeed, carbonated water replaced tap water later, then there they were with something that tasted even better. And what they had was something that nobody had ever had before, a new thing for which there was then no name, something with a new, distinctive taste—a soft drink.

Soda fountains dispensing flavored carbonated beverages had existed in America since the 1830s (with ice cream sodas added in 1874). But these were marginal, seasonal enterprises doing little business with the masses. The work ethic then was universal and stern. You went to the drugstore to get something for what ailed you. Never mind that much of the medicine, whether distributed by commercial patent medicine companies or concocted by the individual druggist or sold as snake oil from medicine-show wagons, contained generous quantities of alcohol and/or narcotics of one kind and another. The working man and the respectable housewife could get a lift or a soothing down from these potents without incurring the opprobrium that Victorian society held for imbibers of John Barleycorn. But one didn't say anything about that in an advertisement.

So Dr. Pemberton and his men had ahold of something unprecedented, a medicine that possibly gave a little bit of a cocaine lift to its imbibers—but, more importantly, a beverage that had a unique, entirely pleasing taste: *the first such new beverage taste since the discovery in antiquity of tea and coffee*, as Coca-Cola people like proudly to point out.

The Pemberton advertising and, indeed, that of Asa Candler through the 1890s exhibit a profound ambiguity on whether to extol Coca-Cola's taste or its curative powers, as shown on this label on a Pemberton syrup jug from company records of 1887: "This 'intellectual beverage' and Temperance Drink makes not only a delicious, exhilarating, refreshing and invigorating Beverage (dispensed from the soda water fountain or in other carbonated beverages), but a valuable Brain Tonic and a cure for all nervous affections." The label also included the same list of afflictions that had appeared on the earlier label—sick headache, neuralgia, hysteria, melancholia, plus: "The peculiar flavor of Coca-Cola delights every palate; it is dispensed from the soda fountain in the same manner as any fruit syrups."

The ambiguity probably reflects nothing more than the effort of men accustomed to one kind of selling to move into an entirely different one, all the while cautious not to offend Victorian and work-ethic sensibilities.

For all of that, the Pemberton operation did not thrive. It is legend that the group, during the first year, spent $73.96 for their schizophrenic advertising and took in only $50 from sale of the syrup. (At a dollar a gallon, the fifty gallons provided the base for the 3,200 drinks sold that first year.) Business was little better for the group in subsequent years. Sniffs Charles Howard Candler in his "Origin" manuscript: "They must have believed that it had little value and no potential assurance of subsequent success," remarking that this was typical of Dr. Pemberton's Atlanta career.

Daniel B. Candler, a nephew of Asa Candler (later dispatched to Texas to establish the product out there), described in an archives document the desultory scene at 107 Marietta Street when, in late 1886, he went to Dr. Pemberton's home to buy a quart of syrup to fill an order for a customer of the Candler drug firm: "I went around to the back of the house. There I saw Charlie Pemberton, son of the doctor, working with a three-legged pot, capable of containing fifteen gallons; with an instrument he stirred the contents of the pot containing the product that he was compounding. When the contents in the kettle, which was over a fire, had reached the proper consistency, the fire was withdrawn and with a ladle the contents were transferred to a barrel. This was the first Coca-Cola factory. As primitive as it was, I presume the *daily*‡ capacity of the factory was equivalent to the actual *annual** demand for the product they manu-

‡ Italics added.
* Italics added.

Early "pretty girl" calendar promotion.

factured. I bought the Coca-Cola, paid them sixty-five cents for it, and sold it to my customer. This was possibly the first quart of Coca-Cola that was ever distributed through the wholesale trade."

Interim Ownership of Coca-Cola Between the Pemberton and Candler Eras

With his last dream come to a dismal end, Dr. Pemberton sold the two-thirds interest in Coca-Cola to Willis Venable and George S. Lowndes. The syrup factory was transferred to the basement of Jacobs' Pharmacy, as was the other property of Pemberton Chemical Company. The inventory accompanying the transfer,† written in Dr. Pemberton's rather scrawling hand, tells its own version of the sad story of high hope come to naught.

First the factory: *1 Brass Kettle $50.00; 1 Grate $4.52; Brick $5.68; 1 Perculator $1.50.* Then the advertising department: *1 Stencil Plate Coca Cola (no dash used); 500 Street Car Signs $6.50; 1 Street Car Sign wood engraved $12.00; 1600 posters $6.00; 1 Large Poster $14.00; Wood Cut $8.00; 14 oil cloth signs at Fountains $14.00; 1 wood cut $1; 5 Coca Cola cards $15.00.* Then the ingredients (suggestive of how much blending and brewing went on in that kettle): *8 lbs Phospho Atnc Acid and (illegible) $2.20; 5 oz oil nutmeg @ 40¢ $2.00; ½ lbs fluid extr nutmeg $1.30; 40 lbs Fld. Ex. Coca Leaves $40.00; 45 Coca Tin (illegible) $4.60; 5 oz oil Spice $1.05; 15 oz oil Lemon $2.80; 1 oz oil (illegible) lime $1.20; 10 oz Ex. Vanilla .60; 5 oz oil nutmet 2.00; 5 lbs citric acid $2.70; 1 lb Elix. Orange .80; 20 oz (illegible) Caffeine $18.86; ¾ oz oil neroli $3.37.* Apparently, Dr. Pemberton had run out of cola-nut extract. Net worth of the inventory was $283.29.

Some of the details of the decline in Dr. Pemberton's dreams and fortunes are recounted in Dr. Joseph Jacobs' article in *Drug Topics,* "How I Won and Lost an Interest in Coca-Cola." Also described was a sale by him of Coca-Cola stock to Asa Candler that is not well known and may have been (he does not tell the date it occurred) Mr. Candler's first acquisition of the stock.

Dr. Jacobs wrote that his fountain was doing a large business, $150 a day, when Mr. Venable agreed to vend Coca-Cola. "It did not have a large sale, but was being talked about, especially by friends and acquaintances of Dr. J. S. Pemberton."

After the transfer of the inventory to Dr. Jacobs' store, he acquired some of the stock that Dr. Pemberton had sold to Willis Venable, but Dr. Jacobs was unhappy about the whole situation. Dr. Pemberton, he wrote, was receiving a royalty of five cents per gallon of Coca-Cola syrup used in the store, and: "He seemed to be pressed for money pretty much all the time and was having money advanced, based on the potential royalty. This did not please me."

† Reproduced in the original handwriting in *Opinions, Orders, Injunctions and Decrees Related to Unfair Competition and Infringement of Trademark,* published by The Coca-Cola Company, 1923. The inventory was part of the company's proof of ownership.

Dr. Jacobs and Asa Candler were friendly competitors and got together once or twice a week to talk about, among other things, their business difficulties. Mr. Candler was upset about Atlanta and Macon competitors in the wholesale drug business giving long credit and was preparing to make a change, according to this account. He had acquired a preparation known as BBB or Botanic Blood Balm, along with the dental preparation, Delectalave. Dr. Jacobs told Mr. Candler of his frustration about the advances to Dr. Pemberton. The upshot was an agreement that Mr. Candler would take over the Jacobs' Coca-Cola stock in exchange for some stock in a glass factory on South Pryor Street, along with some "odds and ends" from the Candler inventory. The two haggled over who should pay the one-mule drayman, whose post was at the northeast corner of Peachtree and Edgewood, for hauling the supplies a block from the one store to the other. And as it turned out, the glass factory burned up with its insurance lapsed. Dr. Jacobs subsequently spoke "in a jocular manner" to Mr. Candler, saying he thought he should be recompensated for the "worthless glass stock."

However, the late Sinclair Jacobs of Atlanta, Dr. Jacobs' son, recalled that the argument over paying the drayman was in regard to the later transfer of a considerable portion of Mr. Candler's inventory, $1,800 worth, to Dr. Jacobs when Mr. Candler bought out his partners.

Regarding the record of the first transaction, Dr. Jacobs wrote that he lost it, and it was not recorded in the company's line of title to the stock. "This transaction, however, may be covered by the instrument showing the sale to Mr. Candler by Walker, Candler & Company, temporarily formed, and of which I was a member. There is no record . . . of the Venable sale to me, nor of my interest thus acquired to Mr. Candler."

But, Dr. Jacobs went on, he and Mr. Candler talked about the first transaction on several occasions. ". . . Mr. Candler (who was not given to reminiscing) discussed the matter with me at one time in his own home . . . [and] at another time in his office."

Those sales of stock by Dr. Jacobs provided his son, Sinclair Jacobs, with the material for a wryly jocular Christmas greeting to his friends in 1968, entitled: "How I lost ⅓ of ⅓ of Two Billion, Forty-Four Million, Three Hundred and Eighty-one Thousand, Four Hundred and Eighty-Two Dollars"—this being the amount his father's shares would have been worth in 1968. "Ah me," the greeting ends. "I at age 80 still have a bottle of Dawson's Scotch, one of Hennessy's Cognac—why not come by of an evening—Let's relive the early days of our great city of Atlanta."

Sinclair Jacobs, Jr., in an interview at his father's picturesque apartment, with the old gentleman ill in the next room (soon to die), told his own wry memory regarding his grandfather's spectacular miss-out. He worked at Jacobs' in the 1930s and one of the products in stock was Golden Belle Toilet Water in a bottle with rounded beads on the glass, a magnificent container it seemed to him as a boy. His father told him the product was one of those gotten in exchange from Asa Candler for the Coca-Cola stock. It had been on the shelves that long. "You think about it," Sinclair Jacobs, Jr., said. "Trading the formula of Coca-Cola for some Golden Belle Toilet Water!"

There is hardly an old family in Atlanta which doesn't claim an ancestor who had the priceless opportunity to buy into Coca-Cola early and cheap and didn't take it. But the truth is that Asa Candler offered stock to very few people, mostly family members and close friends.

Sinclair Jacobs, Jr., said that the reason his grandfather relinquished his stock and subsequently said no when Asa Candler would urge him to buy some —to get in on a good thing—was that Dr. Jacobs didn't believe in Coca-Cola. "He thought it was belly-wash," Mr. Jacobs said. "He was a very serious pharmacist who believed that products should be efficacious, should help people. He didn't focus on its commercial value as a refreshment. He saw it as a tonic."

In his magazine article, Dr. Jacobs said, "After disposing of my Coca-Cola stock to Mr. Candler, I never owned any more of it, which evidences my poor judgment."

Frank M. Robinson "Sells" Coca-Cola to Asa Candler

When Dr. Pemberton began selling off stock (highly embellished certificates, according to Charles Howard Candler) to the people at Jacobs', Frank M. Robinson, of the name and trademark fame, was understandably outraged. According to Hunter Bell, Mr. Robinson stormed over to Judge John Candler's (another of Asa's brothers) and sought legal aid in getting his share of the proceeds. Judge Candler went out to Inman Park, the northeast neighborhood where Dr. Pemberton by then resided, and talked with him. He returned sadly and told Mr. Robinson he had no case. Dr. Pemberton would soon die. (Inman Park was also the neighborhood where Asa Candler and various of his kin had homes, as did Ernest Woodruff and his family, including son Robert W. The fine old Victorian homes located there became rooming-house slums during World War II, but nearly all have been restored in recent years by energetic young Atlanta families.)

We have it on the authority of Hunter Bell again that Mr. Robinson then got a job with Mr. Candler and set about to interest him in buying and running the Coca-Cola business. Mr. Candler once told how he became interested in the drink. It may well be he was referring to Mr. Robinson when he said, during a speech to a Coca-Cola sales meeting in 1913 as reported in the Atlanta *Journal:* "One day there came along a friend of mine with a gallon of Coca-Cola. He wanted me to buy it, but not having any soda fountain, I didn't take much stock in it then. One day he suggested to me that we buy the drink and finally, some sort of way, we did get to own it. I asked him what did he expect me to do with Coca-Cola? He replied: 'See that wagon going by with all those empty beer kegs? Well we are going to push Coca-Cola until you see the wagons going by with Coca-Cola just like that.'"

And so, of course, they immediately began to push Coca-Cola with a vigor and variety unparalleled back then in business and advertising annals. But first they set about to improve upon Dr. Pemberton's formula. Company publications, probably because Coca-Cola people like to say as little as possible about the formula, make scant mention of this, and neither does most other published material about the drink. But it is clear that considerable change was made in the formula by Mr. Candler and his associates, to an extent that no one, since 1888 or 1889, has known the taste of the original Pemberton Coca-Cola, and it is lost to the world today. But knowing what we do about both Dr. Pemberton and Asa Candler, it is safe to agree with Charles Howard Candler that the beverage his father gave us is far superior to the old one. An account in the Atlanta *Journal* in December 1908, by Samuel Candler Dobbs, Mr. Candler's nephew and his first salesman, said that when Mr. Candler acquired some of the Coca-Cola stock in 1888, he heard from fountain owners, starting up the season for the year, that the Pemberton syrup they had left over from the previous season had spoiled. Pharmacist Candler set about to correct that without harming the taste, indeed with a thought to making it better. Further improvements were made the next year, Mr. Dobbs said.

"The Pemberton product did not have an altogether agreeable taste; it was unstable; it contained too many things, too much of some ingredients and too little of others," wrote Charles Howard Candler in his "Origin" paper. "Mr. Candler's pharmaceutical knowledge convinced him that the formula had to be changed in certain particulars to improve the taste of the product, to insure its uniformity and its stability. . . . Several needed materials, one notable for its preservative virtue, were added. The first thing he did was to discontinue the use of tin-can containers for shipping. On account of the inclusion of a very desirable constituency in the formula, the use of tin cans was dangerous."

While Mr. Candler was carrying on negotiations to buy up the rest of the stock, he, a pharmacist, a chemist, and a prescriptionist (who all worked for him) continued to tinker with the formula. Finally, Charles Howard Candler wrote, "Mr. Candler and Mr. Robinson originated and adopted the splendid formula" that has come down to the present.

And at this juncture, Mr. Robinson revealed another of his many strong virtues for such a company. "Mr. Robinson's sense of taste and smell were remarkably keen and reliable. By a sniff and a sip of any fraudulent imitation or substitute for Coca-Cola, he could immediately brand it as a fraud. Mr. Candler's perception of flavor and savor could always be relied on," as well. From the beginning of their making the syrup, one of them, and usually both, sniffed and tasted a small sample from every batch to be sure it was up to standard. Charles Howard Candler, when he was later president of the company, continued to have them perform this service "as long as either of them was able to afford me the benefit of his expert ability."

Cecil R. Stockard, Mr. Robinson's grandson, spoke of the warm relationship that existed to the end between his grandfather and Mr. Candler. They lived next door to one another in the Druid Hills section of Atlanta (developed during the teens by Mr. Candler and others as the "best" neighborhood into which many of the Inman Park dwellers moved). Mr. Candler's mansion was at 1428 Ponce de Leon Avenue. The only memory Mr. Stockard has of Mr. Candler is of seeing him once in his back yard feeding his flock of chickens.

He said that, in his family, they would refer to various members of the

COURTESY OF THE ARCHIVES, THE COCA-COLA COMPANY

Frank M. Robinson.

Candler family by their first and last names (and title)—Bishop Warren Candler, Judge John Candler—but when they spoke of the founder of Coca-Cola, it was always just Mr. Candler.

Of his grandfather, Mr. Stockard had only a few memories from boyhood. He was muscular and quite short, five feet four (which most likely endeared him to Mr. Candler who was not taller than many people). He might come to the dinner table without a tie on, but never without his coat. Once when Mr. Stockard was a boy, he was in the car with his grandfather, leaving for somewhere from his home; they saw a hired man swinging a scythe on some oats and he was not doing it properly. Mr. Robinson ordered the chauffeur to stop the car, whereupon he got out, went over, took the scythe from the fellow, and showed him how to swing it correctly.

It is interesting to note that none of the early associates of Coca-Cola, with the exception of Mr. Robinson's brief experience with Dr. Pemberton, had any knowledge of what they were setting about. Indeed, there was no model for it. They would contrive and innovate to establish the first national soft-drink sales and distribution system, learning as they went, and leaning on instinct. The instinct they had at the very beginning—to tinker with the formula, to improve the product—was to prove probably the best of all they had.

Ever after, quality of product was to be a foremost preoccupation of Coca-Cola people. And another was promotion of the product. How it happened, the great growth from Dr. Pemberton's back-yard brass kettle to the globe-encircling supercorporation today—all that the people of the company did through the years—will tell itself largely in terms of those two preoccupations.

The Death of Coca-Cola's "Originator"

Alas, Dr. Pemberton and his back-yard brass kettle. Upon his death on August 16, 1888, all of the Atlanta druggists closed their stores and sat in a body at his funeral. They also held a meeting in Asa Candler's store to pay tribute to their departed colleague. There, Mr. Candler spoke in memory of the man who invented the drink that was to make Mr. Candler wealthy beyond whatever wild dreams he might have had growing up in the impoverishment that settled on nearly every southern family after the Civil War. Charles Howard Candler tells us in his "Origin" paper that Mr. Candler spoke of Dr. Pemberton's "lovable nature and many virtues," and said: "Our profession has lost a good and active member."

Descendants of Dr. Pemberton were to litigate with The Coca-Cola Company until World War I, claiming they had been deprived of rights to the ownership of the drink, according to archivist Kurtz. But they were up against an airtight chain of title records documenting that Dr. Pemberton did indeed sign over his rights to Mr. Candler and others and that Mr. Candler bought all that the others owned.

Dr. Pemberton was buried in Columbus, where he grew up. (He was born in Knoxville, Georgia.) His grave was unmarked for more than seventy years. Then public-spirited citizens of Columbus erected a monument, identifying Dr. Pemberton as "the originator of Coca-Cola."

Some of these good citizens of Columbus maintain that the good doctor made his great invention while working as a pharmacist there. They cite a prescription book in which there is a formula involving coca leaves and kola nuts. (Could this have been the beginning of French Wine of Coca?) "We have never accepted this," Mr. Kurtz said. "If he invented it in Columbus, why would he have waited eighteen years before marketing it in Atlanta?" It is a reasonable question. "I like all my friends there," Mr. Kurtz added. "So I don't argue with 'em about it. They are amused at my tact and diplomacy about the matter."

The good citizens there have also, through the Historic Columbus Foundation, restored one of the two houses (the better one) in which Dr. Pemberton lived as a boy and have set up in the yard a totally authentic reproduction of an early apothecary shop. It is the only real shrine for the growing numbers of Coca-Cola collection enthusiasts in the land. Jacobs' pharmacy was torn down in the late 1960s (it operated until then, but closed its fountain in the early 1960s) to make way for a bank and office skyscraper. None of the other early seven homes of Coca-Cola (the place where the syrup is manufactured) exists today. No one has seen fit to put up any kind of memorial to the important business history Coca-Cola has made in Atlanta.

The Columbus restoration is located not on the land where Dr. Pemberton's home was, but on land near other beautiful restorations, the building having been picked up and hauled with care to the spot. The house and original lot cost $33,000, the restoration $30,000, and the apothecary shop $10,000. Columbus people contributed all but the $33,000 for the house and lot which was donated by The Coca-Cola Company, and thereby, as is so often the case where Coca-Cola is concerned, hangs a tale.

Abbott Turner of Columbus—a member of the company's board of directors since 1923 and the son-in-law of the late William C. Bradley of Columbus, who also had been a member of the board and something of a Coca-Cola patriarch—approached J. Paul Austin in 1969 about the company's buying the Pemberton house and lot. After having the matter checked out, Mr. Austin, as president of the company, authorized the donation.

At a subsequent meeting of the board of directors, Mr. Austin informed Mr. Turner that the chairman of the finance committee, one Robert W. Woodruff, the retired great leader of the company who took over after Mr. Candler, had expressed displeasure about the donation. And to this day, when Mr. Woodruff expresses displeasure about a matter, Coca-Cola people, right on up to the president and chairman of the board, are anxious to rectify matters. On this occasion, Mr. Turner told Mr. Austin not to worry; he would handle things.

He strode into Mr. Woodruff's office and, after the amenities, said he understood that Mr. Woodruff was upset about the donation for the land. Mr. Woodruff said yes, he couldn't see any purpose in it.

And, as the story is told, Mr. Turner pointed his finger at Mr. Woodruff and said, "See here, Bob. If it hadn't been for John Styth Pemberton, you wouldn't be sitting there in that chair behind your desk."

There was a long pause. Then Mr. Woodruff chuckled and said: "Yes, I guess you're right." The chuckle was, very most likely, in much the same spirit as was Wilbur Kurtz's, when offering his guest a glass of Dr. Pemberton's beverage.

II

Wars Have Raged ...

Coca-Cola executives during the years of the company's great growth liked to end their speeches at sales meetings and the like with a little rhetorical flourish celebrating the uninterrupted progress and success that Coca-Cola had known. They would recite a list of important happenings in the big world, and then say that, all the while, Coca-Cola had endured and, indeed, prospered. A typical one of the flourishes: "Wars have raged, thrones have toppled, nations have risen and perished, the map of the world has been recast since the one-horse wagon rattled down Marietta Street in Atlanta carrying all there was of the infant enterprise in a single load on a lonely journey to a basement home. Through all those years, the business has progressed. Now, few places in all the world are foreign to its product, its trademark, or its trucks."

The point seems to have been that, come what may, Coca-Cola would keep on succeeding. In a world of uncertainties, the company was something you could count on. Those Southerners who started it all and the Southerners who through the years have imparted a distinct southern tone to the company, amid the defeats ever haunting them (that greatest one only twenty years past when Coca-Cola was born), had at last found themselves a winner.

INTERNATIONAL EVENTS DURING COCA-COLA'S EARLY YEARS

The decade during which the company scored its first victories—1890–1900 —had its share of those dire kinds of events listed in the speech. In 1892 strikers against the Carnegie Steel Company battled Pinkerton detectives in Homestead,

Pennsylvania, resulting in seven fatalities. The panic of 1893—inspired by European selling of American securities and withdrawing of gold—wiped out many investors, lowered wages, heightened unemployment, and revived the silver issue in national politics. To restore economic health, Jacob S. Coxey proposed in 1894 that the federal government issue $500 million for road construction. On May 1, he led his hundred-man Coxey's Army in a march on the Capitol where the leaders were arrested for trespassing on the grass. Caught up in the silver controversy, William Jennings Bryan cried out at the Democratic convention of 1896 about how "You shall not press down upon the brow of labor this crown of thorns; you shall not crucify mankind upon a cross of gold," and won the first of his several nominations in his unsuccessful attempt for the presidency.

Electric street lights illuminated the World's Fair in Chicago in 1893; gold was discovered in the Klondike in 1896, precipitating one of the grandest gold rushes ever. The sinking of the battleship *Maine* in Havana harbor on February 15, 1898, set off the Spanish-American War with attendant carnage and yellow-fever fatalities. Cuba was freed from Spanish rule; Hawaii became an American territory.

ATLANTA

If Asa Candler and his small staff were blind to these events and all else but the fundamentals of manufacturing and marketing the syrup formula they had got from Dr. Pemberton, so too were the people of the railroad-entranced town of Atlanta blind to the big things that were getting underway right under their noses in the three-story, gabled, brick business building of Asa G. Candler & Company, on the east side of Peachtree Street at number 47, two doors south of Wheat Street (now Auburn Avenue). The factory had been moved back to Dr. Pemberton's fine old antebellum home during the time of the two-thirds-owning partnership, and thence to 47 Peachtree with acquisition of the sole proprietorship in 1888.

From within that brick building, and three other "homes" of Coca-Cola (the volume of business kept outgrowing the "homes") during the 1900s, one of the most spectacular national sales organizations and campaigns in the history of business was to emerge and spread Coca-Cola in all directions across the land and into the minds of millions of Americans.

There was no mention in the Atlanta *Journal* of April 22, 1891, of Asa Candler's purchase, for a relatively small sum of money, the drink which would be the object of that mighty sales effort. The event was to be, of course, newsworthy only in retrospect. What there was of news for the *Journal* to print that day didn't amount to much, but it is suggestive of the milieu in which Mr. Candler and his small crew set out on one of the biggest business adventures of all time.

Four Gay Nineties young ladies in Atlanta.

Plans for the annual May Day festival were well underway, with promises of "sports and pleasure for the children." There would be three different Maypoles. "Professor F. C. Nott, the well-known dancing master, has the Maypole dancers in charge."

Opposition had risen to the placing of surface railroad tracks on North Peachtree Street. And, the Journal asked, rhetorically, will the residents of West Peachtree accept double-track on their street? "They already have electricity and have become accustomed to it," the report went on, for whatever relevancy this fact had back then.

A black man was on trial for murder of a white, and the reporter covering the case lavished his descriptive skills on the defendant in a manner to depict him as a fiend incarnate.

The annual meeting of the Girls High School alumni would be on the morrow.

The "monthly divorce matinee" had closed its curtain in Fulton County Superior Court, with 246 unopposed cases decreed upon.

In the advertising columns, and in a manner acceptable to the times, the front page was given over entirely to these:

H. L. Wilson, real estate agent, touted an auction sale of "some of the finest private residences in Georgia" in Inman Park. "Atlanta is growing so rapidly in wealth and population, choice lots are increasing in value daily," his advertisement exulted, and then warned that "Inman Park is building up remarkably fast." (Population of Atlanta had increased from forty thousand in the 1880s to sixty-five thousand in 1900.)

Readers were urged to visit the Civil War battlesite at Chicamauga in north Georgia, "the National Park, the state encampment."

Carter's Little Liver Pills were commended for the cure of sick headaches. Coca-Cola, sometime maker of that claim, was not represented that day in the Journal. *But the Old Doctor's Cotton Root Pills for Ladies was right in there to rectify "errors of youth," as was the Nervous Disability Pill designed to restore lost manhood and cure mental depression, irritability, palpitations of the heart, and lack of confidence—a devastating set of symptoms for any gentleman.*

Back to the news, President Benjamin Harrison, on an extensive trip that had included the South, was due to arrive in Los Angeles that day.

An Atlanta audience, displeased with a performance by a traveling drama troupe, hurled wienerwursts, cigarettes, cigar stumps, and green bananas at the hapless cast. Mr. Scott Thornton, the tragedian, said sadly that he was quitting the stage as a result. News accounts of the episode, he said, "have ruined me throughout the South."

Members of the Women's Christian Temperance Union announced that they would soon open a restaurant that would serve "no stimulant stronger than coffee."

Coca-Cola Story Highlights: 1892–99

The Gay Nineties were underway, and the Coca-Cola Company was ready to begin its delicate dance into the consciousness of the gentlemen in top hats and cutaway coats and the ladies in their bell-shaped evening gowns with their breathtaking dip of décolleté and cascades of lace descending from the bust (with, underneath all their lace overbodices and lace petticoats, their "health corsets" which were boned in a manner to throw the hips back and the bosom forward). Skirts were smooth over the hips, a revival of the bustle in the previous decade having been short-lived. (The 1880s bustle stuck out like a shelf and was constructed of wire netting and sometimes steel springs.) The New Woman of the 1890s, breaking away from Victorianism, wanted none of that.

In more of a broadside manner, Coca-Cola would also, during the decade, bombast the consciousness and change the buying habits of the more numerous working people in the country, becoming a deliberately planted, unconscious symbol of

Coca-Cola canvas-sign promotion in front of an 1890s drugstore.

their gradual move toward a more bearable existence. And Coca-Cola promotion would not overlook the white (stiff, detachable) collar man and his secretary in her floor-length dress with a tight collar, nothing of her flesh showing but face and hands. Again, with the abrupt scene-shifts of a Coke commercial, the onward march led by Asa Candler and his stalwarts:

January 29, 1892: Judge Marshall J. Clarke of Fulton County Superior Court grants a charter to The Coca-Cola Company, a Georgia corporation. (Dr. Pemberton had never incorporated.) The capital stock is $100,000 with shares valued at $100 each, Asa G. Candler holding nearly all of it. Messrs. Robinson and Dobbs have small holdings, as do favored retailers like J. H. Nunnally. Mr. Candler had, two years before, sold his drug company in order to devote his entire attention to Coca-Cola, and, presumably, paid for the stock with proceeds of the sale. That year, 1890, a total of nearly 9,000 gallons of Coca-Cola syrup had been sold compared with 1,049 in 1888, Dr. Pemberton's last year.

December 6, 1892: At the first annual meeting of the company, an advertising budget of $11,401 is adopted. Earlier in the year, jobber rights for the sale of Coca-Cola in the six New England states for a period of twenty years had been granted to Seth W. Fowle & Sons of Boston.

January 31, 1893: The trademark "Coca-Cola," in constant use since 1886, is registered in the United States Patent Office.

COURTESY OF THE ARCHIVES, THE COCA-COLA COMPANY

Joseph A. Biedenharn, the first person to put Coca-Cola in a bottle

December 6, 1893: Though the nation is in the grips of economic panic, the Coca-Cola Company declares, at the company's second stockholders' meeting, the first of an unbroken line of annual dividends. The directors set it at $20 a share which is 20 per cent of par value, phenomenal in the second year of any company's existence. The dividend is ordered paid "provided that such payment will not cripple the financial status of the Company," which it doesn't.

The spring of 1894: The first plant outside of Atlanta for the manufacture of Coca-Cola syrup is established in Dallas, Texas.

The summer of 1894: A soda-fountain operator and confectioner named Joseph A. Biedenharn, of Vicksburg, Mississippi, is upset because local bottlers, having run out, couldn't supply wholesale soda pop for him to fill an order for a picnic being held for workers on a nearby plantation. Soon after the picnic he sets up his own bottling operation and includes Coca-Cola made at his soda fountain among the drinks that he bottles. He thus becomes the first, though unofficial, Coca-Cola bottler of all time.

December 4, 1895: Asa Candler stands before the stockholders in annual convention and proudly announces: "Coca-Cola is now sold and drunk in every state and territory in the United States." Branch syrup-manufacturing plants have also been established in Chicago and Los Angeles.

December 9, 1896: At the annual meeting, President Candler, the lips of his broad mouth curled and his voice icy, tells the stockholders: ". . . The unscrupulous pirates often found in even the most respectable trade positions find it more profitable to imitate and substitute on the public than to honestly avail themselves of the profit and pleasure which is ever the reward of fair dealing and honorable competition." Whereupon, the board votes to request President Candler to consult an attorney in reference to the advisability of bringing a suit or suits "against such scoundrels."

A December day, 1897: President Candler begins the annual meeting on a happier note: "Our salesmen have become known everywhere in this union as gentlemen in every respect, and have not only maintained the good name of the corporation, but have succeeded in making Coca-Cola a familiar and gracious name in all the land."

January 13, 1898: President Candler in his annual report for 1897 has another proud announcement: "Coca-Cola is now sold . . . in some of the cities in Canada, and in the city of Honolulu. . . . Arrangements are on foot for its introduction into the Republic of Mexico. We are firmly convinced that wherever there are people and soda fountains, Coca-Cola will, by its now universally acknowledged merit, win its way quickly to the front rank of popularity."

December 13, 1898: The manufacture of Coca-Cola syrup, along with the business of the company, is carried out in a brand-new triangular-shaped building at the corner of Edgewood and College (now called Coca-Cola Place) avenues, the first building specifically designed to accommodate the needs of the burgeoning business. Asa Candler stands on its steps before marble columns and, with shoulders reared back, his voice reedy, declares to an assemblage on hand for the dedication: "This building is sufficient for all our needs for all time to come." (Less than ten years of time to come were happily to prove him wrong.)

July 21, 1899: Asa Candler and two snappy young lawyers from Chattanooga, Tennessee (with given names embedded in history), Benjamin Franklin Thomas and Joseph Brown Whitehead, complete negotiations on a proposition the two young men, whom Mr. Candler had never seen before, put to him. The three of them sign a contract granting Messrs. Thomas and Whitehead the rights to bottle and sell Coca-Cola throughout the United States, with the exception of most of Mississippi (reserved for Mr. Biedenharn), the five states of New England (reserved for S. W. Fowle & Sons), and Texas where negotiations with another party were going on. Mr. Candler makes no secret of the fact that he doesn't think much of the future of the bottling proposition.

In this year of 1899, a total of 281,055 gallons of Coca-Cola is sold at a gross price of $393,477. During the first ten months of 1892, the first year of the great Candler sales effort, it had been a total of 35,360 gallons at $49,676.50 and that compares with the 9,000 gallons sold in 1890 under the partnership, only two years before.

COURTESY OF THE ARCHIVES, THE COCA-COLA COMPANY

An early, banner-covered delivery wagon used by a Coca-Cola bottling plant.

Asa Candler's Development of the Syrup and Soda-Fountain Business

Wars have raged . . . but what a ten years those were. In that one decade of the Gay Nineties, the basic themes of Coca-Cola's existence were established. Ever after, the history and legend of Coca-Cola would be but variations on these themes:

The ever-increasing manufacture of syrup. The ever-increasing sale of it over the entirety of the United States. The move of it into foreign lands. The ever-growing, ever-more-skillful advertising and promotion of the product; the gentlemanly and gracious impression made by salesmen, a key characteristic of this effort. The ever-increasing profits and wealth of the company. The ugly rearing of the heads of the imitators and substituters, defilers to be fought down with eternal vigilance and deadly precision by the best of lawyers. The expansion of the sale of it from soda fountains only to bottlers through the middlemen, Messrs. Thomas and Whitehead. The subsequent packaging and selling adventures of individual franchised bottlers, beginning with Mr. Biedenharn.

During that crucial first decade, Asa Candler put his stamp on each of these basic themes of the business, and his early influence, if only unconsciously and not much acknowledged, lingers today.

Charles Howard Candler in the biography wrote with nostalgia of the formative years of the company: "As I remember those days in my boyhood, the company was a happy one. There was much to keep everyone busy. The business was expanding rapidly and my father managed to instill into all those who worked with him a pride in their accomplishments and in the growth of Coca-Cola."

Asa Candler involved himself vigorously in the manufacture of Coca-Cola, concerned with the control of quality from the crude start. He was at home in the place of manufacture; it was an extension of his profession as pharmacist. The biography gives us a picture of him at his best in his work, practicing the art of "free-hand cutting": "He would hoist a twenty-pound, wicker-covered demijohn full of [skin-destroying] carbolic acid to his left shoulder (he was left-handed) and pour some of its contents into a glass graduate held in his right hand in line with his eyes to be certain that the correct quantity was taken. Such casual handling of carbolic acid took a strong arm, a steady eye, and somewhat steadier nerves."

The manufacture of syrup was carried out during 1889 into 1891 in the basement at 47 Peachtree Street. The equipment was hardly more sophisticated than Dr. Pemberton's brass kettle. It consisted of a crude furnace for heating in a kettle the batches of Coca-Cola (along, at that time, with the Botanic Blood Balm). Asa Candler, in that 1913 sales-meeting speech of rare reminiscence, described the factory in these words: "We had a large copper kettle for boiling the syrup and one big-footed Negro to handle the paddles. Boys, it was some equipment."

The Fifth "Home" of Coca-Cola

The factory and offices were moved in 1891 to the fifth "home," on the second and third floors of 42½ Decatur Street, a block east of Pryor Street. Located on the north side of the street, it was a befitting, bright red brick building that had been erected in 1891 on the site of the original Trout House, a leading antebellum hotel to which General Sherman did his customary bad thing. The first floor of the brick building was occupied by a clothing store, a pawnshop, and a saloon. The latter could not have been pleasing to Asa Candler, a staunch foe of alcohol, when he confronted it each day.

The factory here was only a little less crude, but in its small way was the prototype from which, with only slight adjustments, the giant ones of today evolved. Not the least of Coca-Cola's advantages through the years has been the simplicity (not to mention the cleanliness) of its manufacturing process. Operation of the factory on Decatur Street illustrates this. (The description that follows of the manufacturing process and others herein were gleaned from the various writings of Charles Howard Candler.) The Decatur Street factory consisted of a square brick furnace with a brick smokestack. On the furnace sat a couple of forty-gallon copper kettles. On a platform around three sides of the furnace, workers rolled barrels of sugar on skids (the sugar bought from the

Revere Sugar Refining Company of Boston) and dumped them into the kettle which contained the required amount of water.

The workers at this site for some time to come were Sam Willard and George Curtright, a black handyman. After pouring in the sugar, they used a wooden paddle to stir the water and sugar and to prevent the solution from scorching. Then they dipped the finished syrup out with a five-gallon measuring pot and poured it into fifty-gallon barrels.

At this juncture, Mr. Candler and/or Mr. Robinson performed the crucial function of mixing in the other ingredients. Then, after the batch cooled, it was put in containers ranging from pint and quart bottles (which were retailed by druggists for home consumption) to one-gallon earthernware jugs and five- and ten-gallon kegs. These were secondhand whiskey barrels put, certainly in Mr. Candler's view, to better use by Coca-Cola and painted a bright red to disguise their ignoble origin. They had to be clear, not charred, clear, clean, white oak. Barrels that had contained gin could not be used because they were paraffined. Later, methods were found to clean out the char, glue, and paraffin. Still later, the company required so many barrels it had to have some of them manufactured.

William Curtright, brother of George in the factory, delivered the bottles and jugs and barrels to drugstores in a one-horse dray. The horse was named Ol' Bird. Sam Willard is quoted in the biography as saying: "I often reminisce over the thrill we all got when Bill Curtright got his first set of brass-mounted harness and how he spent most of his Sunday mornings polishing it."

The crew chuckled together over the time a druggist ordered a barrel of syrup and said to "put a good head on it." Sam Willard put soap bark foam in it. And there was the time when there was no syrup on hand, and a druggist came in to order a gallon. Mr. Candler set to and made him up the single gallon, saying afterward to his employees: "A sale of Coca-Cola lost today is not a sale that may be made tomorrow."

. . . *Thrones have toppled*, but not to be toppled was a company led by such a man, guided by such principles. No problem was insurmountable in the ongoing life in that little building at 42½ Decatur Street.

Well, almost none. One of the difficulties during the two years the company was there was that, despite the best efforts of Mr. Candler and Mr. Robinson, the crude method of manufacture just did not make for uniformity of product. Another problem was the recurring misfortune of a batch boiling over and oozing through the floor, to ruin stock in the clothing store below.

The Sixth "Home" of Coca-Cola

These were the main reasons for the move in the fall of 1893 to the sixth "home," a rambling and elaborate old mansion at 77 Ivy Street. It had been built in the early 1860s and, like Dr. Pemberton's old house used on Marietta Street, somehow escaped war's holocaust in 1865. It had just previously been the worship place of the Wesley Memorial Methodist Church which must have endeared it to Methodist Sunday school superintendent Asa Candler.

It was a two-story, with basement, building. Offices and storage space for advertising material were on the top floor. Sugar and the barrels of finished syrup were on the ground floor. And in the basement was an improved factory.

It consisted of the same kind of furnace as in the previous plant, plus a one-hundred-gallon copper kettle. The top of the kettle was even with the floor above, which facilitated the dumping in of the sugar. But the big innovation in the basement was a rectangular wooden tank capable of holding 1,500 gallons of syrup. The syrup was siphoned from the kettle into the wooden tank, and Sam Willard would measure with a graded gauge stick to determine each batch at 1,250 gallons. After the vital ingredients had been added, Mr. Willard would get on a ladder or box at one end and another of the workers would similarly position himself at the other end, then they would push the sugar and water toward one another, back and forth, with wide wooden paddles, for one hour, stirring and agitating the mix. "This large volume as mixed insured uniformity of product," Charles Howard Candler wrote with satisfaction in yet another publication, "*Thirty-three Years with Coca-Cola, 1890–1923*."* He went on to describe the division of labor in the new and improved plant.

Sam Willard and one or two blacks did all the work of receiving, manufacturing, drawing off, and shipping. George Reed and Charles Howard Candler (working then during summer vacations from Emory at Oxford [Georgia] College) would do light tasks like packing advertising matter, glasses and the like, rolling the sugar barrels and moving them back, painting the barrels bright red (the paint the product of the Samuel H. French Company of Philadelphia), preparing shipments, and riding them in the dray to the freight depot.

Another Willard, J. J., joined the company in 1894 at the Ivy Street location as an office boy at "$3.00 a week and lots of Coca-Cola." He wrote in a company publication of his experience at the same sort of jobs, including labeling and shipping kegs and barrels. If he mis-sent any of them, as once to Oxford, North Carolina, instead of Oxford, Georgia, he had, under Mr. Candler's parsimonious hand, to pay the freight himself. It was "geography learned with a vengeance." And all the while, there was Sam Willard in charge, becoming "caustic," in Charles Howard Candler's word, when a worker failed to keep the fire going under the kettle.

The Seventh and "Sufficient for all Time" "Home" of Coca-Cola

Adequate for only five years, 77 Ivy Street was replaced when Mr. Candler constructed that triangular building with three spacious stories and a basement on Edgewood Avenue which, he thought, would be sufficient for all time.

---

* Only four copies, a handsomely bound typewritten manuscript, were produced. One remains in the company archives.

The seventh "home" of Coca-Cola.

George E. Murphy was the contractor in charge of the construction. He found dealing with Asa Candler a disastrous experience. He contracted to erect the building for $11,100. It ended up costing double that—$22,368—with him having to pay the difference. The poor man went into bankruptcy. The canny Mr. Candler evidently made no effort to help him out, but did, according to the biography, "more or less" take him into employment. He was later to build a new home for Mr. Candler in 1903 and one for Charles Howard Candler in 1907, hopefully under a better contractual agreement. When The Coca-Cola Company sold the building in 1910, it got $49,000—double again what it cost to build.

The factory that was installed in the basement of the new building must have been a thing of joy, a beauty to behold for Sam Willard and his crew. First, there was a hydraulic elevator for the barrels of sugar and syrup and other heavy equipment, replacing the old method of rope-hoisting them by hand. And there was a steam boiler and the copper kettle was steam-jacketed and equipped with a stirring apparatus, powered by a steam engine. And that wasn't all. The simple syrup made in the kettle was piped to square, copper-lined cypress cooling tanks suspended from the ceiling and, from these, was piped to a cylindrical cypress mixing tank with steam-driven paddles. A platform around the kettle facilitated loading in the sugar.

That task, along with loading the finished syrup into barrels and one other activity, remained the only work to be done by hand in the whole process. *The Coca-Cola factory was close to full automation two years before the turn of the twentieth century*, another benefit of the simplicity of the method of manufacture.

The Secret Coca-Cola Formula: "Merchandise 7X"

That one other step in the manufacturing process still done by hand was, of course, the crucial one—still performed by Asa Candler and/or Mr. Robinson—of mixing in the vital ingredients after the simple syrup had cooled. Here now we confront the mystery of mysteries, the secret of the formula with its *ultimate* mystery, "Merchandise 7X," and now, too, we stand at the door of the holy of holies, the laboratory in which the formula is mixed. We may penetrate some the veil of mystery and secrecy through the various writings of Charles Howard Candler again.

In the new building, the laboratory was located in one of the triangular rooms at the front, this one fireproof with a sheet-iron safe door with a combination lock. Only Mr. Candler and Mr. Robinson knew the combination. Only they and a black helper were allowed in the room.

Mr. Candler was in charge of ordering the ingredients and checking to be certain the correct quality and quantity were received, and then making certain they had the proper care and preservation. It was his frugal duty, too, to see that nothing was wasted, not only in the Atlanta factory but in the three branch factories that were opened during the decade.

The shipments of the essential oils, seed kernels, and other ingredients, including bales of dried coca leaves and bags of kola nuts, were unpacked in the laboratory. Mr. Candler and Mr. Robinson would then immediately scratch the labels and any other identifying marks from the tin cans and bottles. Invoices for these were not sent to the bookkeeper, but kept under lock and key. Mr. Candler would write out a memo to the bookkeeper requesting a check for the amount needed to pay for each shipment. (Later, the bookkeeper was to be trusted enough to receive the invoices.)

Mr. Candler and Mr. Robinson had to keep up with market conditions of the various ingredients and with political conditions in the countries from which they came. Mr. Candler refused to use any vanilla made by other than himself. This entailed his personal selection of the proper beans, his personal inspection of each bundle for quality and quantity when they arrived (Dr. Jacobs mentioned in his article helping Mr. Candler do this on occasion), and personally cutting them into small pieces. Charles Howard Candler remembered as a boy helping his father do this with large shears. Later, a vanilla mill was acquired. Finally, Mr. Candler would stir the vanilla mixture in a barrel with a paddle. It was his considered opinion that vanilla was not properly aged until it had stood in the wooden barrel for two years. This "tied up considerable capital," Charles

Howard Candler commented in his *Thirty-three Years* manuscript, "but was justified by the results." Mr. Candler also insisted for many years on using confectioner's sugar in the Coca-Cola syrup ("my father . . . stubbornly stuck to the grade of sugar he had always used") but was finally persuaded to change to the less moist granulated variety.

Mr. Candler also considered himself better at preparing the fluid extract of the coca leaf and kola nut than any manufacturer, and did so for all mixtures of the formula. He used two large galvanized percolators to produce what he called coca and cola tincture, brilliant light brown fluid with a biting taste. Workers around the plant called it "tea."

Charles Howard Candler tells both in the biography and the *Thirty-three Years* manuscript with proper awe of the day when, after deciding not to finish medical school and to give his life to Coca-Cola, he was told the mysteries and secrets of the formula. ". . . I was initiated into the secrets of the product which have passed down by word of mouth only to the most trusted employees. . . . The total number of persons who have known the secret formula since Dr. Pemberton's day can be added up on the fingers of one hand. . . ." (This written in 1950.)

"One of the proudest moments of my life came when my father . . . initiated me into the mysteries . . . inducting me as it were into the 'Holy of Holies.' No written memorandum was permitted. No written formulae were shown. Containers of ingredients, from which the labels had been removed, were identified only by sight, smell, and remembering where each was put on the shelf when it came in from the supplier or was made in the same locked room. To be safe, Father stood by me several times while I compounded these distinctive flavors to see that proper quantities were used of the right ingredients and in the correct order to insure the integrity of the batches and to satisfy himself that his youthful son had learned his lesson and could be depended upon. . . ."

And then: "My father explained in detail the various essential oils, et cetera, the amounts of each to be used and how best to assemble them, with particular reference to the order in which they should be measured out and mixed. He . . . showed me the measuring graduates and scales for measuring the heavier oils by weight, and I thereupon experienced the thrill of making up with his guidance a batch of Merchandise 7X."

Wars have raged. Thrones have toppled . . . but how many sons of man have known such a moment with a father? Who would not have dropped the pursuit of a medical career when there was to be had the high drama of the secret formula and the excitement of the ever-growing business? And what a feeling it must have been for Mr. Candler and Mr. Robinson to have that secret knowledge, with all that elaborate protection of it, the secret transcending even the other magic of the company.

After his father's retirement in 1917, Charles Howard Candler made all of the secret formula for a number of years. Even today, only a few people (the official company answer to the invariable question: "less than ten") know its contents and proper order and measure of mixing. One of them, who prefers to be nameless out of fear of extortion attempts, spoke of the terrible responsibility of the knowledge, the care he had always to take not to say something that might reveal part of the secret.

The formula is now reduced to written form. Archivist Kurtz said he has seen the box (but not what was in it) in the special security vault at the Trust Company of Georgia bank where it is kept. The company has a rigorous set of rules to follow when a qualified person seeks access to the box. One of the rules: The qualified person must call the bank and request to see the formula at a specific hour of the day he will come. If he is one minute late, he can't go in.

When readers of *Die Sterne* saw, accompanying an article on Coca-Cola, a photograph of Mr. Kurtz holding the box containing the formula, they were not really seeing that box, Mr. Kurtz confided. It was an empty one just like it. "The secrecy," Wilbur Kurtz said, "it's just part of the mystique."

"Merchandise 7X" and Cocaine

Inevitably, talk of the formula gives rise to the question of whether Coca-Cola does or ever did contain cocaine. The question has haunted the company and its sweet and pure, handsome and wholesome image almost since its beginnings, with rumors regarding its contents emanating from the various divulgences of the Pemberton formula. The November 1909 issue of *The Coca-Cola Bottler* reported that "fanatical reformers," including Tom Watson with his Populist magazine, *The Jeffersonian*, were calling Coca-Cola "dope" and charging that it was habit-forming. The term "dope" was to become its nickname in the 1920s and 1930s, despite anything the company could do. Nazis, during their era in Germany, spread the word that the Coca-Cola produced there contained cocaine and that the German bottlers "were poisoning the people." The question persists today, in the folk culture, the advent of the drug subculture perhaps having renewed interest in it. Invariably in a conversation about Coke, the question will be asked, often wistfully enough in the hope that the cocaine is there.

It is not, of course, as the company would have everyone know. But once it was, according to no less an authority than a pamphlet released by Asa Candler in 1901 titled *What Is It? What It Is.* The pamphlet was directed against "sensational and unfounded statements made by persons ('having zeal without knowledge') that constant use of Coca-Cola will cause the formation of the Cocaine habit." An analytical chemist, Dr. H. R. Slack, had analyzed the drink ten years previously and found only an infinitesimal trace of the drug, the pamphlet said. Pointing out that many coca leaves are required to make a small amount of the narcotic and that only a small quantity of the leaf went into Coca-Cola, the pamphlet says: "The quantity of cocaine is so small that it would be simply impossible for anyone to form the cocaine habit from drinking Coca-Cola. . . ."

Justice Oliver Wendell Holmes, in a celebrated opinion in 1920 which

A company ad to counteract the rumors that Coca-Cola contained cocaine.

upheld the validity of the Coca-Cola trademark, commented on there having once been a "very small" amount of the drug in the drink, but "after the Food and Drug Act . . . if not earlier . . . it was eliminated from the plaintiff's compound."

An advertisement in the Atlanta *Constitution* had also addressed the question back in May 16, 1892. It quoted Mr. Candler as saying, "I have offered to give up my business if it could be shown that a single case of the cocaine habit has been contracted from using coca-cola. If I thought it could possibly hurt anybody I would quit the manufacture of Coca-Cola instantly, although it is the whole of my business."

And knowing Mr. Candler for the churchgoing man (loving to sing hymns louder than everybody else) and teetotaler that he was, the statement is a true one. Nonetheless, he put a chemist to work soon after the 1901 pamphlet appeared to obliterate the offending trace of cocaine, and no more was found in it after 1905. Lawrence Dietz, in his book *Soda Pop* (Simon and Schuster, 1973), commends Mr. Candler for taking the action before enactment of the Pure Food and Drug Act of 1906, one of whose purposes was to rid patent medicines of the various narcotics commonly used in them to send good Americans on a drug jag of twenty years' duration through the 1880s and 1890s.

Mr. Dietz makes the point that more than probably any other large American corporation, The Coca-Cola Company has, when confronted with some charge of wrongdoing, avoided the all too common reaction of "intransigence, violence, political maneuvering and/or vote buying, and bitter grumbling." He attributes this to the example set by Mr. Candler in the cocaine matter.

The question continues to vex the company. To confront it head-on would be something like one's saying he has stopped beating his wife. The main concern is to put down the deeply rooted rumor of the stuff still being in there. As for its once being in there, "that was another company and another time," as one official put it. He added that there is no way today to know the accuracy of that trace-finding chemical analysis said, in the old pamphlet, to have been performed by Dr. H. R. Slack, or, for that matter, anything about Dr. Slack.

The question continued to vex Mr. Candler, too. John Bookout of Atlanta, who in the 1920s was something of a young man about town, tells the story about the time an injudicious friend of his who was employed in Mr. Candler's bank invited the good gentleman to join him at the soda fountain of the Candler Building "and have a dope."

Mr. Candler, in his cutaway coated suit and open-gate shirt collar, drew himself up and thundered at the young man: "It is not dope! There is no dope in it! It is Co-Ca Co-la!" And on that authority, we may let the matter stand.

Sales and Promotion of Asa Candler's Coca-Cola Syrup

Just as the production started small and crude from the first two homes, so did the sales force and promotion activities. But it is important to note what Charles Howard Candler says in the biography of the resources his father had to use to get Coca-Cola before the public.

Asa Candler was "not a struggling pharmacist who stumbled onto a gold mine." His net worth in 1890 was $17,326 before he sold for $50,000 the drug firm, which was doing $100,000 worth of business a year. With this as a start, he was to plow back the proceeds into the business over the years, keeping only enough for his living expenses. The Coca-Cola Company spent a lot of money in that first decade to build the consumption from 9,000 to 281,055 gallons; the advertising budget of $11,401 as early as 1892 is but one example.

Mr. Robinson headed up a sales force (he was also in charge of advertising) of three other men: the go-getter, Samuel Candler Dobbs, Mr. Candler's nephew; Daniel Candler, another nephew who was to be in charge of the Dallas branch when it opened; and Georgia W. Little. This was when the company was operating out of the 47 Peachtree Street building in the very first years. As early as 1891, they were moving the syrup far beyond Atlanta (the only place Dr. Pemberton ever marketed it), getting it in some drugstores all over the South, including Mississippi River towns.

The soda-fountain season in the South was from May 1 to November 1. The spring opening was a big event, with ladies and gentlemen, and probably greater numbers of nursemaids and their charges, drinking down the lemon, orange, vanilla, pineapple, strawberry, cherry, and chocolate sodas. It was the mission, of course, of these three first salesmen to provide them the alternative of an ice-cold glass of Coca-Cola.

It was not an easy mission, and Asa Candler was a hard taskmaster. George Little got as far on one of his early trips as a drugs salesman as Alabama, in a buggy drawn by Ol' Bird, the horse later to be used on the dray. When Mr. Little started to ford the Tallapoosa River, Ol' Bird foundered, and then wouldn't budge, standing in the middle of the river, while the drug samples Mr. Little was carrying floated off downstream. He finally got Ol' Bird onto the opposite bank and then waded out into the river as darkness began to fall, trying to retrieve his samples. He got a good many of them, and that was fortunate for him. Had he not, Mr. Little is quoted, with a chuckle, in the biography, "There wouldn't have been any use in going back to Atlanta."

Samuel Candler Dobbs wrote about the building of the Coca-Cola sales force during the 1890s in *Advertisers' Magazine*, the article having been reprinted in the Atlanta *Journal*, November 23, 1908. In 1890, advertising costs equaled, if not exceeded, total receipts. "Our faith in Coca-Cola, however," Mr. Dobbs wrote, "never weakened."

In 1891, the three men covered the entire South and began the heavy use of "handsome lithograph hangers," fountain signs, and the free-sample tickets Mr. Robinson had devised in the Pemberton days. The sales force and sales continued to increase. By 1899, there were fifteen salesmen on the road. The sales season had been lengthened to February 1 through November 1, and the territory included all of the nation. "There is so much territory and so few of you men to work it," Mr. Candler told his sales force, "that it seems imperative that we do a little work in a great many places."

Some of the most effective salesmen, while the season was still short, were cotton buyers who sold Coca-Cola during *their* off-season. They were used later on to augment the staff in the summer months when business was heaviest. It was Mr. Candler's idea to seek their services.

Early Coca-Cola promotion pieces.

Not always did success meet the sales effort. Ezekiel S. (Zeke) Candler,* a retired executive and former fountain serviceman in Atlanta who is the son of Daniel Candler, retold a story of his father's about the days when he was sent by

* Zeke Candler recalls Uncle Asa's visiting his family in Dallas when he was a quite small boy. He recalls it vividly because his mother gave him a whipping for asking his famous great-uncle for a dime to go to the picture show.

He told another story about his father. Daniel Candler was a great outdoorsman and every fall would head into the woods for long hunting trips. One fall during the Robert W. Woodruff era of Coca-Cola, Mr. Woodruff and Harrison Jones were on a business trip and decided to stop over in Dallas in order to inform Daniel Candler personally that he had been made a vice-president of the company. But Daniel Candler was off on one of his hunts, out in the wilderness where no one could reach him. The two executives waited around a couple of days in the hope that he would come back in, then gave it up and let him know the good news by mail when he did finally get back.

A syrup-sales and advertising truck.

Uncle Asa to open the Texas branch in 1894. There he not only made the syrup, but would take it out and try to sell it.

On one occasion, he made up a batch and took it to Oklahoma. In a little town, he called on a druggist who had never heard of Coca-Cola. Daniel Candler tried to sell him a fifty-gallon barrel. The man laughed at him. Then he tried to get him to take a ten-gallon barrel to no avail. So Daniel Candler said, "Well how about buying a one-gallon jug? Anybody can sell a gallon of Coca-Cola."

The druggist looked at him and said, "Well, mister, you ain't done it yet."

It was 1899 when Charles Howard Candler joined the company full time. In his writings, he goes into great detail about the early selling. By 1899 the company was holding training meetings each year for several weeks in late winter. Mr. Candler, Mr. Dobbs, and Mr. Robinson personally instructed the new men, emphasizing the importance of seeing to it that soda-fountain operators served quality drinks, and that they be made fully aware of what a profitable proposition Coca-Cola offered. They also instructed the new men on how best to use the outdoor and point-of-sale signs. And they told them how to handle such a delicate matter as a customer whose credit standing was less than good.

Each salesman was furnished with a metal-bound fiber trunk to carry the advertising on trains and a telescope handbag to carry it from the train station to the stores. The company paid travel expenses and a not overly generous salary.

Charles Howard Candler and Samuel Candler Dobbs.

(Charles Howard Candler was paid $12.50 a week in 1899.) Each salesman kept a trip sheet which had listed on it every drugstore in every town on the route. It included a column for explaining *why*, when a store did not place an order. Mr. Robinson kept an up-to-date card file based on these reports.

The company has been commented on through its history for its skillful prodding of the retailers' profit motive to increase sales of Coca-Cola. In 1899, customers were given a 2 per cent discount if they paid for an order within ten days. The company paid the freight costs of orders of thirty-five gallons of syrup and more. And at the end of the year it paid rebates of five cents a gallon to customers who had bought one hundred gallons, and five cents for each additional one hundred gallons on up to twenty-five cents a gallon.

The salesmen were by then also selling glasses (with straight sides; the curved, bell-shaped ones somewhat resembling a statuesque woman had not yet been created). "Coca-Cola" was inscribed on them. There was some sales resistance to these from soda-fountain operators who didn't like the idea of buying something with somebody else's advertising on it. But the glasses sold generally well. But not so the products of the company's early attempt to diversify, with salemen in the 1890s offering Coca-Cola cigars and Coca-Cola chewing gum.

The New York City Coca-Cola syrup-sales force in the early 1910s. Their satchels contain advertising materials.

The two products were soon dropped, and the magnificent distribution system being built in the 1890s was used to market Coca-Cola syrup exclusively until the mid-1950s when a more successful diversification began.

To further encourage customers to buy more gallonage, the company offered premiums of decorative advertising clocks, beautiful porcelain fountain urns, prescription scales, prescription cabinets, and showcases. A customer could earn one of these with a thirty-five gallon order, with a limit of one of each to a customer. Volume was increasing so fast, the company was hard-put to keep up with awards of the premiums.

Mr. Robinson's ticketing scheme was the ultimate enticement to the prospective customer. He was offered a five-gallon keg of syrup for his fountain for $8.75. Then to a mailing list he provided, the company sent $5.00 worth of the free-sample tickets—and when the customer returned them to the company, he got $5.00 for them. So his risk investment was only $3.75. Sometimes as many as $20 worth of tickets went out, assuring a neat profit on that first barrel. The arithmetic here is also interesting for what it shows of the amount of profit the soda fountains made from a barrel of Coca-Cola syrup. The $5.00 worth of cou-

This cani entitles you to one glass of
Coca-Cola
TRADE   MARK.
FREE.
Present this at fountain of

This card is worth 5 cents. It pays for 1 glass Coca-Cola, which cures your Headache, or wonderfully refreshes you when exhausted.

ASA G. CANDLER, PROPRIETOR,
ATLANTA, GA.

pons used up one gallon of syrup, which would mean the $8.75 five-gallon keg produced $25 worth of glasses of ice-cold Coca-Cola. Discounting shipping costs, that was still a nice piece of business.

Mr. Dobbs in his magazine article explained another dimension of the ticketing scheme as a profit-motive goad. He noted that by 1891, drugstore proprietors were beginning to sit up and take notice of Coca-Cola. "We were actually sending people to their places of business with nickels or tickets that were worth five cents each to spend, and they often bought something else in the store." This bringing in of people who would buy other things, as well as the highly profitable Coca-Cola, was to become the bond that kept the drugstores of the country loyal and faithful to Coca-Cola as long as soda fountains lasted.

The druggists couldn't understand, Mr. Dobbs wrote, how the company could sell the keg for $8.75 and redeem from $5.00 to $20 in free tickets for advertising. "In spite of this apparent extravagance, we kept coming back steadily improving our product and helping the business of the dispenser. The majority showed their appreciation by giving us their hearty co-operation."

The reason the company could do it, of course, was that after that first keg on which it lost money, it usually had a customer to buy more kegs for life. Mr. Candler's capital was there to finance the scheme. And once again, the mind of Mr. Robinson had proven invaluable to Coca-Cola.

A Coca-Cola salesman, when calling on a new customer, also showed the soda-fountain help how to mix a proper Coca-Cola, checked on the carbonated-water machinery (the stuff had to be cold for Coca-Cola to taste right), and put up display advertising about the store. Further, he had the duty of contracting with a local billposter in each town and selecting locations for him to put up advertising displays. A commentary on the billposting profession of that day was the anxiety salemen felt about whether the displays would stay up the full thirty days called for in the deal. The company contrived a method to get around that problem. It required the billposter to get the customer to write his approval of the billposting job on the invoice before Coca-Cola would honor it. The customers were urged to delay granting the approval until the display had been up at least thirty days.

Those early posters were thirty by forty inches. In the very beginning, they included the legend, "Asa G. Candler, Proprietor." That was when he was better known than the product. But such a circumstance was not to last long, not with those barrages of advertising that Mr. Robinson was letting loose upon the nation.

In addition to continuing the use of the Pemberton era point-of-sale signs (including the oilcloth awning ones), newspaper advertisements, and the ingenious tickets, Mr. Robinson added the outdoor posters, painted wall and barn signs, blotters, calendars, serving and change trays, Japanese fans, bookmarks and marble paperweights, and streetcar cards. All across the nation the red-and-white or red-and-green signs with the cursive trademark were becoming as familiar as—well, a Coca-Cola sign today.

There was so much advertising material and so many varieties of it that the salesmen often had difficulty hauling it and getting it all distributed. Charles Howard Candler, in his *Thirty-three Years* manuscript, tell of his own strenu-

From 1898, the oldest Coca-Cola tray known to exist.

ous efforts in 1899, in Kansas City, under orders to distribute a hundred boxes of Japanese fans in office buildings, restaurants, hotel dining rooms, barbershops, and other such places. He strung the fans on a cord like beads, slung one of these necklaces of fans over each shoulder, and proceeded to the first office building he could find. He started at the top floor and, office by office, worked his way down to the first, and then marched to the top floor of the next office building. "I thus got rid of a tremendous amount of bulk advertising material, as well as practically all of my energy."

Mr. Dobbs recalled in his magazine article how in 1899 the company put painted signs on barns all over the Midwest at a cost of $4,319.60. Returns were so noticeable that the company had some more done in the Midwest later in the year and started in on the barns of the South.

John Bookout, who was a boy when all this proliferation was going on, recalls the painted sign on the wall of Dr. Fitz's drugstore in the hamlet of Greenville, Georgia where Mr. Bookout grew up. It was a big sign. "The letters were as tall as you and I."

The biography gives us this tapestry of the people of the company at their work, engrossed in the crucial annual chore of selecting the painting of a pretty girl for the calendar: ". . . Mr. David Wolf would drive up in a horse-drawn cab from the Kimball House with several large portfolios containing proofs. . . . This called for a conference with Mr. Candler and Mr. Robinson, and on occasion, Mr. Robinson would invite employees to pass judgment. . . ." Sam Willard recalled: "If a particularly beautiful portrait was shown . . . a lovely and discretely gowned model, Mr. Robinson would say, 'I think Mr. Asa will like this one.' That always called for a general twinkling of eyes."

Ah, those days! *Wars have raged. Thrones have toppled.* . . . Who could worry when caught up in such moments, when beginning the most extensive advertising and promotion campaign for one product that the world had ever seen, "pounding," as Mr. Dobbs put it in his article, "everlastingly into the public mind through printed display, the words, 'Drink Coca-Cola, Delicious and Refreshing, 5 cents.'"

The Early Coca-Cola Imitators

With the great push of Coca-Cola production out across the land through a vastly sophisticated, for the time, sales organization and methodology, and an incredibly thorough advertising and promotion campaign thus well launched, it should come as no surprise that Mr. Candler had to consult that lawyer about imitators.

Charles Howard Candler wrote in the "Origin" manuscript that Dr. Pemberton himself and an associate (Mr. Doe?) made and sold imitations and claimed that they were based on the original formula. One was called Yum-Yum.

Asa Candler complained about these activities in a letter to his brother, Bishop Warren Candler, in June 1888: "We are doing moderately well with Coca-Cola. Its only obstacle is that Pemberton is continuing offering a very poor article at less price and the public who pay for 'Coco-Cola' and are not benefited decide that it is a fraud." Parenthetically, it is interesting to note that, at that point, Pharmacist Candler seemed to view his product as medicinal, something people would feel a fraud if they were not benefited by it.

But it was from people who claimed, after Dr. Pemberton's death, to have his formula that most of the early trouble came. Dr. Joe Jacobs, in his magazine article, wrote that after the death "alleged copies of the formula then appeared and were sold to various people at prices, as I understand, ranging from $1,000 down to a bottle of whiskey."

A post-Pemberton French Wine of Cola (*not* Coca) seems to have been the worst offender. In his various writings, Charles Howard Candler complained of how its producers imitated the ticketing scheme and often would not redeem the tickets, causing dispensers to be suspicious of Coca-Cola's salesmen. In 1891, a Coca Ree was advertised in Atlanta papers as an "ideal brain food."

There is a record of only a few court actions against these early threats. But Asa Candler stood ready (and soon had to) spend thousands in court to defend his drink's good name. From his druggist days, he had been known for securing the services of top-quality specialists when he was in need of one, whether it be chemist or accountant or whatever. He did not draw up his own legal papers as many businessmen did back then, but hired the best lawyer he could find to do it for him. So it can be counted on that whoever the lawyer was he consulted in 1896, he was a good one, just as were those in coming years who spent their careers battling down imitators, substituters, and bug-in-the-bottle claimants.

Charles Howard Candler, in his *Thirty-three Years* manuscript, gives the simple human explanation of why the tradition was established, back in the beginning years, of the fiercest copyright protection in business history. Here, he said, were these few men who were sacrificing their pleasure and their recreation, who were giving everything they had to make Coca-Cola a success, who were plowing back into the business everything it made, and who believed in Coca-Cola so deeply and were so proud of its quality. They were simply not going to stand for somebody else reaping the benefits of *their* sacrifices, or allow

An early imitator of Coca-Cola's trademark and product.

anybody to palm off an inferior product under a name sounding or looking like theirs. And who could blame them?

The First Coca-Cola Bottlers

With the soda fountain sale of Coca-Cola so well established that imitators were popping up, now was to begin the great adventure of the building of the bottling business. The foreshadower of that unique enterprise, Mr. Joseph A. Biedenharn, whose father had established the confections' business in Vicksburg, was introduced to Coca-Cola by Mr. Dobbs. Mr. Dobbs remembered the occasion because Mr. Biedenharn received him so hospitably, was so friendly, in contrast to many potential customers he called on.

In *The Coca-Cola Bottler*, August 1944, Wilbur Kurtz quoted Mr. Biedenharn on the rationale he shared with many others as a result of that first decade's sales and promotion campaign: "I found out that the more Coca-Cola I was able to sell, the more I made out of it. This is why I began to push Coca-Cola, and I pushed it as much as Asa Candler did."

He went on to say that he was a great believer in bringing a product to where people were. "I wanted to bring Coca-Cola to the country people outside the limits of the fountain. Even in the cities, the fountains were limited in number and scattered here and there. I could see that many townsfolk wanted Coca-Cola, but it was not easily available."

He would always offer Coca-Cola to country people who came in his store, and he had the notion of putting it in bottles for them. Then the picnic incident occurred. (See page 32.) "This provoked me no end," Mr. Biedenharn told Mr. Kurtz. He had to improvise with a box of lemons and a sack of sugar and some coloring to provide red lemonade for the picnickers. And then he bought himself some bottling equipment and just went to work and started bottling soda pop and Coca-Cola as well.

"I know it is a fact that I am the first bottler of Coca-Cola in the world," Mr. Biedenharn was quoted, "because when I began there wasn't anybody bottling it at that time. The soda water bottlers . . . were merely content to make soda water."

Mr. Biedenharn also told Mr. Kurtz how he and Mr. Candler always got along fine. "He was awfully nice to me. I liked him from the start. Whenever he would come to town . . . we would sit on boxes in my store and pass the time of day talking about Coca-Cola and other things. Mr. Candler always left a good taste in my mouth, and I was glad to do business with him."

This is but the first of several portraits we shall have of Asa Candler in different locales sitting on boxes or Coca-Cola crates talking about his favorite subject to one and another Coca-Cola person.

Mr. Biedenharn also said that he didn't inform Mr. Candler that he planned to put Coca-Cola in bottles. "But I did ship to him the first two dozen cases of Coca-Cola I bottled. Mr. Candler immediately wrote back that it was fine. He

COURTESY OF THE ARCHIVES, THE COCA-COLA COMPANY

A Hutchinson "pop" bottle used by early Coca-Cola bottlers.

made no further comment at all that I remember. You know, to this day he has never returned my bottles!"

Two others who, like Mr. Biedenharn, weren't content with mere soda water were R. H. Holmes and E. R. Barber, owners of the Valdosta (Georgia) Bottling Works. They began bottling the fountain drink on their own initiative in 1897, three years after Mr. Biedenharn's pioneering move. Mr. Barber confirmed that they did this, in a letter dated August 26, 1954. "The drink was well accepted on the trade and our customers requested larger shipments of Coca-Cola," he wrote. "However, we soon discovered that we were running into a great deal of trouble due to the fact that the rubber washer on the [Hutchinson] stopper caused a not-too-wholesome odor in the drink after it had been bottled for a period of ten days or two weeks." The crown cork and seal soon solved that, and Mr. Barber was able to attest to the fact that the Valdosta plant bottled Coca-Cola "continuously" from the spring of 1897 onward. James Freeman Holmes, a kinsman of R. H. Holmes, carried on their bottling business. When he died, his will contained a provision that a Coca-Cola bottle be carved on his gravestone. This was carried out and, according to archivist Kurtz, is the only gravestone in the world with the bottle on it. Somewhere in there, too, according to the biography, an upstate Pennsylvania druggist started filling citrate bottles with fountain Coca-Cola which his small son would sell to factory workers across from his drugstore.

Mr. Candler's restraint regarding those first two cases of bottled Coca-Cola sent by Mr. Biedenharn was likely due to the fact that Mr. Candler took a rather dim view of the prospects for bottling. The Hutchinson stopper, then the only thing available, was a cumbersome device; the cork stopper was attached to the bottle with a wire hook which kept it in the bottle after the imbiber had pushed it down the bottle's neck. (It snapped down with a resounding pop, hence the term, soda pop.) The stoppers made it difficult to clean the bottles and made the process of filling them tediously slow. A writer in the fiftieth-anniversary issue of *The Coca-Cola Bottler* suggested this was the reason for Mr. Candler's uncharacteristic reluctance to take advantage of an obvious opportunity to get his beloved Coca-Cola to vast numbers more of Americans—the country people Mr. Beidenharn mentioned and people in town who didn't have ready access to a soda fountain. Mr. Candler was also said to be concerned about the possibility of damage suits over bottles exploding, as they frequently did back then.

Coca-Cola Bottlers Nationwide

There is the legend (repeated in nearly every writing about Coca-Cola) about the man who approached Mr. Candler and told him he would tell him a secret that would vastly expand his business. He asked a sum of money for the secret, some say five dollars, some say fifty thousand. Since the story has it that Mr. Candler handed over the money, it must have been nearer the former than the latter sum. When the money was in hand, the man whispered to Mr. Candler: "Bottle it."

Maybe so, maybe not. The two men who did finally get Mr. Candler to consent to bottling it, Messrs. Thomas and Whitehead, were, from all accounts, eloquent persuaders. First, they had to persuade a cousin of Mr. Candler's, one Sam Erwin of Chattanooga, to accompany them to Atlanta and introduce them to Mr. Candler. Then, of course, they had to persuade Mr. Candler.

It probably helped that both were avid fans of Coca-Cola and extremely enthusiastic about their idea of bottling it. There are several legends about how they were struck with the idea. One has it that Mr. Thomas, while in Cuba, observed a drink named Piña Fria being sold in bottles and made the obvious mental connection. Another has it that Mr. Thomas and Mr. Whitehead would often have glasses of Coca-Cola sent up to their law office in Chattanooga from a nearby soda fountain. If a client happened to have come in and one or both were closeted with him, the Coca-Cola would be set down in the outer office and become stale before the business was done. A bottled one, of course, wouldn't. Yet another legend is that the two loved baseball as much as they did Coca-Cola and would wish for the latter while sitting in the stands enjoying the former.

Whatever, they took the idea to Mr. Candler and got from him a six-hundred-word contract that was to become one of the most important in business history. It provided that Messrs. Thomas and Whitehead would set up bottling plants at no expense or liability to The Coca-Cola Company, buying the syrup from the company and not substituting anything else for it. The company agreed to sell the syrup to them and no one else (excepting Mr. Biedenharn and the New England firm) for bottling purposes, to furnish labels and advertising matter, and granted them sole rights to use the trademark on bottles.

Most accounts hold that one dollar changed hands to make the contract binding. But Hunter Bell points out that nowhere in the contract is money mentioned. It is his belief that the dollar didn't change hands, that the consideration involved was the agreement by Mr. Thomas and Mr. Whitehead to get Coca-Cola into bottles.

The two young men walked out of Mr. Candler's office naturally elated and excited. Virtually the whole country was theirs for the bottling. Mr. Candler apparently remained dour. Charles Veazey Rainwater, who was an associate of Mr. Whitehead in his early bottling work and later an important bottler figure, wrote in the fiftieth-anniversary issue of *The Coca-Cola Bottler* how "Mr. Whitehead told me years later that when the contract was signed, sealed, and delivered, Mr. Candler said to him and Ben Thomas: 'If you boys fail in the undertaking, don't come back to cry on my shoulder, because I have very little confidence in this bottling business.'" (Later, Mr. Candler was to say to Mr. Rainwater, remarking on the large volume of his Athens, Georgia, plant: "Veazey, what are you doing with all that syrup, pouring it into the Oconee River?")

A new era for the company would start with the beginning of the bottling adventure in 1900. The sales to soda fountains would continue to build on the basis of the policy simply stated by Mr. Dobbs in his magazine article: "Persistent, permanent publicity backed up and followed by an energetic selling force."

Heady times were to come. *Wars would rage, thrones would topple, nations would rise and perish*, but what of that when you're engrossed in something bigger, something certain, when you're involved in building the best national selling organization around, or you're back home in Chattanooga with the whole country to conquer for bottled Coca-Cola?

Wars have raged. . . . That time when Benjamin Franklin Thomas was inspired with the bottling idea from having seen Piño Frio in Cuba, he just happened to be on the island as a member of the United States Army fighting the Spanish-American War.

III

A Happy Family

It is common at The Coca-Cola Company archives in the modern-day head-quarters for a Coca-Cola bottler from out in the hinterlands or across the earth to bring in his son or daughter, or a young employee, "to indoctrinate" (in Wilbur Kurtz's phrase) this young person about Coca-Cola. On one occasion, such a father and teen-age son gaze upon the different displays which include all the different bottles that have been used to contain the drink, from the ungainly Hutchinson one, with the stopper dangling from the wire in the neck, to the straight-sided amber or clear ones, with a diamond-shaped, pasted-on, paper label, with the trademark embossed on the glass, to the familiar shape of the good old six-and-one-half-ounce regulation one that we have known and loved so long. One of the bottles they see is the priceless prototype for the regulation bottle—fatter than the regulation one, with more of a bulge in the middle. (It had to be trimmed down in order to fit into the bottling line machinery during the time of its design.) William Samuelson, the son of Alex Samuelson, a man who helped achieve the triumph of the design of the bottle, presented this heir-loom to The Coca-Cola Company a few years ago. In return, the company sent a check in his name for $10,000 to the Newark, Ohio, Chapter of the American Cancer Society.

The man who has come to the archives with his son greets an old friend who has come in, E. Delony Sledge, a retired vice-president and director of the company's advertising department, and, after introducing his son, engages in rather esoteric Coca-Cola banter with Mr. Sledge, with much hearty laughter between them. Then the father and son disappear into Mr. Kurtz's office to hear Coca-Cola lore, surrounded as they are by all the memorabilia in there.

Mr. Sledge says that the father is a third-generation bottler, meaning that he inherited a bottling business from his father who in turn had inherited it from his. The teen-age son will be the fourth-generation owner. "And on it goes," remarks Mr. Sledge.

The son has a tranquil, pleasant face and a genial manner of speech. The father, in his fifties, has a bluff, happy face. And both of them should probably be happy. They are heirs not only to a happy tradition which has seen each succeeding generation more solidly entrenched in local business and civic leadership in the place of their franchise, but also to one of the most lucrative businesses in existence. In the 1920s and 1930s, the local Coca-Cola bottler in towns and cities of the nation was high among, if not the highest of, the power-and-wealth elite. This was particularly true in the South where World War I industry barely dented the region's economic desolation and where the depression of the early 1930s hit particularly hard. In southern towns, the Coca-Cola bottling plant was often the most splendid building in town, and the owner of it likely also to be involved in banking, real estate, and other matters of high finance—a strong element in an otherwise weak economy. Even amidst today's affluence, bottlers are somebody special, and their relative power and financial standing is little diminished, because the trend in recent years has been toward consolidations, buying up other territories and building larger, fewer, faster plants.

Mr. Thomas and Mr. Whitehead set the tone that characterizes the bottlers, or the bottling family as they call themselves. The company's *Profile* characterizes Mr. Thomas as "kindly, attractive, popular and jolly," and Mr. Whitehead as "a friendly man, easy to approach, affable, ambitious and considerate of those associated with him." He was also well educated, soft spoken. ". . . He enjoyed a good joke, but frowned upon vulgarity."

On the point of the bottlers being a family, Charles Howard Candler, Jr., who has lived in Atlanta all his life and serves on the Coca-Cola board of directors, recalled how his famed grandfather thought of his company as a family, too. Indeed, as Mr. Candler pointed out, in the beginning it was comprised mostly of brothers and cousins and nephews, but grew so much that real family ran out and Asa Candler had to take on surrogate kin. But, said his grandson, "I think that feeling of family has carried on through to today."

Similarly, when the genial and happy bottlers of Coca-Cola call themselves a family, it has more than metaphorical meaning. In the beginnings of the bottling adventure, when a franchise was there for the $5,000, or less, price of setting up a plant, it was quite common for one man to start a plant and then set up a son or brother or other kinsman in another from the proceeds of the first, the process repeating itself to geometrical proportions. Bottlers have been linked, then, through the years, in intertwined familial and business connections. Wilbur Kurtz commented on the complication of some of the family ramifications. He said he spent an hour and a half one time on the telephone establishing the kinship of one Lupton (a famous bottler name) to another.

The men who set up those early bottling dynasties had no easy task. It took time before whatever happiness and geniality they might by nature have had could be attributed to the particular work that consumed them. Just as Asa Candler and his staff had done, the bottlers started small, with crude equipment, and worked long hours at hard labor getting Coca-Cola into clean bottles and then hauling it about in crates trying to sell it. For them, the first two decades of the twentieth century were like the previous decade had been for Mr. Candler and the syrup company—a time of getting organized in a business for which there was no model and of building it to the point where spectacular success

The Tampa, Florida, bottling plant, typical of the earliest bottling companies.

would follow. But they also knew the comfort of having an all absorbing something certain to work at and hang on to.

INTERNATIONAL EVENTS DURING COCA-COLA'S EARLY YEARS

Of course during those first two decades, while they built, major events occurred. That period was the beginning of future shock, mighty events appearing with a rapidity that made the 1880s and 1890s—full, as we have been reminded, of important occurrences—seem tame and slow by contrast.

These included the defeat and demise in 1912 of such a grandly named political organization as Theodore Roosevelt's Bull Moose Party, as well as, most certainly, the adoption of the 1913 constitutional amendment imposing income tax upon citizens of the United States, followed by another amendment in 1920 imposing prohibition of spirituous liquors on the nation. The horror of April 18, 1906, was the San Francisco earthquake, with three days of ensuing fire, killing thousands. Then the sinking of the unsinkable *Titanic* on April 14, 1912, with one thousand casualties. And the sinking, on May 7, 1915, of the *Lusitania*, presumably by German submarine warfare trying to blockade England—the 114 Americans among the 1,153 fatalities served as an emotional cause that moved America much closer to entry into the barbed-wire and poison-gas carnage of that war.

But in the spirit of the Coca-Cola bottler family, let us look at the happy side of those times. In 1903, Americans were treated to the first motion picture with a plot (though no sound), *The Great Train Robbery*, produced by members of Thomas Edison's staff. The era of the picture show had begun, and the last one has not yet been made. In that same year, Orville and Wilbur Wright made their famous flight to begin the age of aviation. By 1908, enough Americans were bumping along in automobiles, variously powered by steam, electricity, and gasoline, to justify declaring that vehicle, born in the 1890s, to have come of age. On April 6, 1909, Commander Robert E. Peary succeeded where many others had failed and stood athwart the North Pole where he jabbed an American flag into the snow and ice. In the month of April 1910, Americans stood in their yards and fields and stared up with awe and wonder at that rare handiwork of God, Halley's Comet. On rising, its tail swept across the entire horizon. In 1915, vast crowds surged through the Panama-Pacific International Exposition in San Francisco to celebrate the opening of the Panama Canal. President Woodrow Wilson pressed a button in Washington to set the mechanical exhibits in far-off San Francisco into action, a mark of the advance of the age of electricity.

Coca-Cola Bottling Story Highlights: 1899–1920

During those twenty years, Americans would be introduced to, and instructed in, the joy of lifting an ice-cold bottle of Coca-Cola to their lips and letting it gurgle down their throats. In the early 1900s, Coca-Cola advertisements showed ladies in bell-shaped, still ankle-length dresses, so daintily lifting the bottle. Gentlemen of the period still wore stiff collars, those hard round yokes of linen. In the 1910s some of the women's dresses had a V neck, a shocking development deplored by some quarters of the American clergy. A gentleman in the 1910s still wore a top hat and frock-coat suit on formal occasions, but for more relaxed evenings, he set out in a lounge suit with a Homburg hat perched jauntily on his head.

Through those years from 1900 to 1920, the Coca-Cola bottlers were chalking up their own important date lines, absorbed as they were in their own history and the making of slow, sure progress. Again, we may follow them in Coke commercial quick takes:

July 22, 1899: The first in the line of men made happy, indeed euphoric, by the prospect of bottling Coca-Cola, Mr. Thomas and Mr. Whitehead, sit in their office in Chattanooga and exult over what they had been handed. But the first of a series of sobering thoughts then sets in. Mr. Whitehead realizes he has virtually no capital to put into the vast enterprise of providing bottled Coca-Cola for all the nation. He seeks out a more affluent friend, a Chattanooga lawyer turned businessman, John T.

1894	1899–1902	1900 ------ 1916	1915	1923	1937	1957	1961	1975
			Nov. 16	Dec. 25	Aug. 3 (D-105529)	Applied Color Label (ACL)	One-Way Bottle (OWB)	One-Way Bottle (Plastic)

(Left to right) (*1894*): Hutchinson-style bottle in which Coca-Cola was first bottled by Joseph A. Biedenharn, Vicksburg, Mississippi. (*1899–1902*): Hutchinson-style bottle used briefly by bottlers of Coca-Cola after November 1899 and before 1903. (*1900–16*): Straight-sided bottle with the trademark Coca-Cola embossed in glass, designed for crown closures and distributed with the diamond-shaped label between 1900 and 1916 inclusive. Both flint and amber bottlers were used by the bottlers of Coca-Cola during this period. (*1915*): The first glass package for Coca-Cola using classic contour design and introduced into the market in 1916. (*1923 and 1937*): Two successive designs with patent revisions used between 1923 (patent date: December 25, 1923) and 1951 when the 1937 patent (number D-105529) expired. In 1960, the contour design for the bottle was registered as a trademark. (*1957*): Applied color label, for Coca-Cola trademark on panels, introduced on all sizes of classic contour bottles for Coca-Cola in 1957 and continued thereafter. (*1961*): The no-return, or one-way glass bottle, first introduced in 1961; later modified for twist-top. (*1975*): Experimental plastic ten-ounce package for Coca-Cola in classic contour design with twist-top cap; tested, 1970–75. This package not in general circulation, spring 1975.

Lupton, and sells him one-half of his one-half interest in the bottling contract for something under $5,000.

Late fall, 1899: Mr. Thomas puts into operation the first Coca-Cola bottling plant in Chattanooga, producing the drink at first in Hutchinson bottles.

Early in 1900: Another of those sobering realizations dawns on the still ebullient partners. They face the reality that setting up enough bottling plants to satisfy their contract with Mr. Candler is beyond the physical, not to mention financial, resources of any two persons. So, with the approval of Mr. Candler, they set about to find good and honorable people with sufficient capital to establish bottling plants in towns and cities across the country, guaranteeing to each an exclusive territory in perpetu-

Benjamin Franklin Thomas and Joseph Brown Whitehead, both from Chattanooga, obtained exclusive bottling rights for Coca-Cola and established the unique franchise system.

ity in which to sell the bottled drink, along with other considerations. It is the beginning not only of the bottling family, but also of a uniquely advantageous franchising system.

A short while later in 1900: Mr. Thomas and Mr. Whitehead, after what has been described as "amicable" business disagreements, decide to split their vast territory between them. Mr. Whitehead takes a map of the United States and decides upon how it shall be divided, and Mr. Thomas chooses which half he wants. He picks the heavily populated middle-Atlantic and Eastern states plus California, Oregon, and Washington, leaving Mr. Whitehead the Southeast, Southwest, and Midwest.

A day in April 1900: Mr. Whitehead, with the money he got from Mr. Lupton, sets the crude machinery running in the second Coca-Cola bottling plant, located appropriately enough in Atlanta, on the southeast corner of Edgewood Avenue and Courtland Street near the triangular home of the Coca-Cola Company. He has also established The Dixie Coca-Cola Bottling Company in Atlanta, to sell syrup to not-yet existent franchised bottling plants at a price slightly higher than the partnership pays Mr. Candler. Mr. Lupton remains in Chattanooga where he is to be made happy over the years by bottling Coca-Cola. Mr. Thomas is in Chattanooga, too, having earlier established his company there in late 1899—later called The Coca-Cola Bottling Company (Thomas)—with the same purpose as Mr. Whitehead's company. These are, in effect, wholesale companies, but, in the Coca-Cola bottling family, they are referred to as "parent" bottling companies.

Another day in 1900 . . . and certainly one of the happiest yet for the pioneer

COURTESY OF THE ARCHIVES, THE COCA-COLA COMPANY

An early bottling-plant interior containing delivery wagon, promotion pieces on the wall, and all the equipment necessary at that time to bottle the product.

bottlers: The crown closure, much as we know it today, is introduced to the industry. By 1903, all Coca-Cola bottlers are using it for its efficiency and cleanliness. By 1912, the troublesome Hutchinson bottle is heard to pop no more.

A happy day in spring of 1901: Mr. Thomas sells his Chattanooga plant to James F. Johnston and William H. Hardin of that city. Thus, they become the first franchised bottlers—the beginning of that long line of people made happy by personally bottling Coca-Cola. Many others join the line during the two decades.

Another happy day in the spring of 1903: Mr. Whitehead sells one-third interest in the Atlanta bottling plant to Arthur L. Montgomery and relinquishes the management of it to him.

A sad day in mid-August 1906: Mr. Whitehead, exhausted from his endeavors and down with a bad cold, has sought rest on vacation at his wife's hometown of Thaxton, Virginia, and contracted pneumonia. He dies there at the age of forty-two, having known the excitement of the business adventure he started so happily only seven years before. He is succeeded in the presidency of his company by Charles Veazey Rainwater, his early associate.

The last day of December 1910: Coca-Cola is being busily bottled in a total of 379 plants across the country.

March 7, 1914: Twenty-five Coca-Cola bottlers gather in Atlanta to organize the Coca-Cola Bottlers' Association, a mark of the growth of their enterprise and the growth, also, of a number of common problems the organization will attempt, through united action and a joining of ideas and information, to solve.

Another sad day, June 25, 1914: Mr. Thomas dies at age fifty-three, having earlier suffered a stroke as a result of Bright's disease. He had been fifteen years into the great adventure of his life. Mr. Thomas is succeeded in the presidency of his company by a nephew, George T. Hunter.

An ad from the early 1900s illustrating the first use of a straight-sided, crown cork and seal bottle.

A day in December 1916: Perhaps this is the happiest day of all for the bottlers and a memorable one certainly for The Coca-Cola Company. The Root Glass Company of Terre Haute, Indiana, begins production of that celebrated curved bottle and soon will send it rattling along the filling lines of the still-growing number of bottling plants across the country.

The last day of December 1918: Those bottles are rattling down the lines at Coca-Cola bottling plants in towns and cities in every state of the Union and are happily carted to the ever-growing market of thirsty Americans who have learned—or better, been taught—that they, too, can find happiness, a moment of it, by heeding the signs that say drink Coca-Cola . . . *in bottles*.

The Enhancement of Coca-Cola's Success by the Development of Bottling Franchises

So much of Coca-Cola's good fortune was fortuitous. The humorous history of Mr. Thomas and Mr. Whitehead's getting back home to Chattanooga and coming down from the exhilaration of securing the bottling contract free, to face the sober reality of the enormity of fulfilling the job, led them, by chance and, of course, necessity, to the invention of Coca-Cola's franchise system. And that was as important a discovery for the future of marketing goods in this world as it was to prove one of the best things that ever happened to The Coca-Cola Company.

Not only did it augment the already excellent distribution system for the drink that Mr. Candler and his crew had put together to get it sold at the soda fountains. It also gave the company another kind of advantage which Charles Howard Candler described well in the biography. After confessing that he had no way of knowing why his father gave the bottling rights away, he went on to say: "As a matter of fact the system which evolved of allowing Coca-Cola to be bottled in hundreds of communities by persons native to and respected in those communities, who themselves profited greatly by the energy and initiative which they put into the promotion of Coca-Cola, is probably largely responsible for much of the success which the company has enjoyed."

The unnamed author of one of the more eloquent writings about Coca-Cola, an article entitled "To Pause and Be Refreshed" in *Fortune* magazine, July 1931, commented that some might think, if Mr. Candler had done the bottling himself, the company would have been making some $13 million *more per year* at the time of the writing. "The flaw in this otherwise excellent argument is that it interprets the past in terms of the present," the article asserts. "Simplicity of manufacture and distribution permitted the original Coca-Cola Company to concentrate, with phenomenal success, on sales and advertising. To have developed the bottling business as well could have produced a terrific strain on Candler energy and Candler capital."

The author further noted the advantage to the company of the bottler's having *a perpetual contract*—"something which made Coca-Cola bottling his business and not the business of some distant corporation—that he was willing to go out and sweat, not for The Coca-Cola Company, but for himself." Consider, the article continued, automobile dealerships. "The automobile dealer is usually overloaded with a sales quota of the manufacturer's devising; he goes out of business with disturbing frequency and marked ill will." Hence, the conclusion that "Mr. Candler's decision . . . may rather be applauded as a master stroke than deplored as an error."

Asa Candler established another company policy regarding bottling that has proved equally advantageous. Just as he had done with equipment for the production and sale of the syrup, he refused to have anything to do with manufacturing bottles or crates or any of the other paraphernalia connected with producing the bottled drink. It was his conviction, the biography tells us, that a single product, expertly made and marketed, was the best way to profits for all.

Thus the bottling arrangement enriched not only all those happy bottlers around the country, but also many manufacturers of equipment and supplies—such things as bottles, crates, coolers, and trucks. The bottlers eventually were to operate the largest commercial fleet of trucks on earth. Some bottlers have escaped unionization by the Teamsters Union, because, to organize that largest of all truck fleets, the Teamsters have to deal with each plant and plant owner individually. (The Coca-Cola Company, itself, has long and amicably been under contract to the Teamsters.) In some areas, the bottlers have again avoided unionization of plant workers by keeping somewhat ahead of union pay and fringe-benefit scales—a strategy that might be called southern since it is employed by other southern firms like Delta Airlines and some textile mills.

As we shall see, both the franchise system and Mr. Candler's single-product policy were to prove important in making Coca-Cola, when it began bottling in a big way in other lands, essentially and advantageously different from other multinational corporations. And it all came about by chance—that of the sale of the bottling rights to begin with and the manner in which the two young lawyers exercised them.

A Brief History of the Early Bottlers

Mr. Thomas and Mr. Whitehead wasted no time in getting started with the fantastic adventure of building the bottling business across the country. With the first two plants in Chattanooga and Atlanta running, they set about to find those upright citizens with the required cash to start other plants. That was not so easy in the beginning. The soft-drink bottling business was not highly regarded at the time; people of means shunned it. And those who engaged in it weren't much interested in taking on Coca-Cola, satisfied as they were with just selling soda pop.

But the two parent bottlers, the one, Mr. Thomas, operating out of Chattanooga, and the other, Mr. Whitehead, with his Atlanta headquarters, soon began to spread plants across the land. J. J. Willard (who learned his geography the hard way, as a shipping clerk for Mr. Candler) wrote that Mr. Thomas' skills of persuasion almost depopulated Chattanooga of young men, sending them forth on the bottling adventure to all parts. These were beginning railroad men, lawyers, bankers, people from all walks of life. Among them, he noted, was Crawford Johnson, who began his eventually flourishing business in Birmingham wearing trousers with a patch on the seat of them.

One of the very first persons to see the possibilities of bottling and aspire to own a plant was Frank M. Robinson, as might be expected. But, according to his descendant, Cecil R. Stockard, "Grandmother put her foot down," and just would not allow it. She had, Mr. Stockard said, been listening too much to Asa Candler and his dim views of the bottling enterprise.

Those who did get into the business made slow, but steady, progress. Mr. Willard wrote about how (presumably by purchasing secondhand equipment) "with a capital of around $3,500, a man was able to get started. When Saturday night came, the owner may not have had any money for Sunday school, but most of the employees had been paid off. One plant owner, who has subsequently given away sums of six figures to hospitals, colleges, and orphans' homes, frequently did not have carfare and was given credit by the streetcar conductors in his hometown."

Plants located in the South did best during the early years, proving Mr. Thomas faulty, at least in the beginning, in his first choice of other areas.

Bottlers in the North often ran out of money before they could build up a profitable trade. The plants up there changed hands frequently.

Proliferation of the plants in the South was so rapid that, by 1903, both Mr. Whitehead and Mr. Thomas had to split up their territories, establishing more parent companies to tend to the needs of the bottlers.

Mr. Whitehead had taken over the Texas territory in 1902. After the Seth Fowle contract had expired, The Coca-Cola Company took over the New England territory in 1912 and subsequently, in 1916, established the New England Coca-Cola Bottling Company as an independent parent company. In 1924, Mr. Thomas' nephew, George T. Hunter, set up the last of the parent companies, The Pacific Coast Coca-Cola Company in Los Angeles.

In recent years, The Coca-Cola Company has acquired all the parent companies and now sells syrup directly to the bottlers at the mark-up the parent companies employed. The last purchase was of the Thomas Company in 1975, for a total of $35 million in cash, a rather nice increase on Mr. Thomas' initial investment of nothing.

The early success in the South was marked by a 1906 parent company advertisement appearing in trade publications, announcing that all the southern territories had been taken, but saying that good openings were left in other realms. "Any bottler who will put Coca-Cola on its merits, in any latitude, and who will bottle it according to directions, will succeed in establishing a permanent paying business the year around," the ad promised. "Beware of imitations, substitutions and frauds."

One of the early bottlers, Arthur W. Pratt, conveyed the sense of the beginning struggle in his saga of "My Life with Coca-Cola" in the fiftieth-anniversary issue of *The Coca-Cola Bottler*. "During those early years," he wrote, "when I was trying to promote the sale of bottled Coca-Cola, I often became depressed. For a long time we maintained operations at a deficit, and at times this was discouraging. My inspiration and motivation to continue came largely from my two friends, Asa Candler and Ben Thomas. Whenever I became discouraged, the thought would come to me that I could not let them down—and so I continued.

"My first impression of Asa Candler reminded me of my father because he was such a lovable character. I came to regard him as a member of my family and called him 'Uncle Asa.' He used to visit me at the bottling plant in New York, and we would sit on a syrup barrel and talk about the future of Coca-Cola. When he left, I would be full of enthusiasm and eager to work for that future."

In the 1920s, Mr. Pratt headed up the Pacific coast parent company, doing such things as clearing out deadwood in plants, giving advice, financial aid on occasion, and often a pat on the back to struggling bottlers. A number of these were Southerners who had gone west to seek their fortune with bottled Coca-Cola.

The death in 1906 of Joseph Brown Whitehead, at the height of the early struggle, came as a blow. Charles Veazey Rainwater, in some "Observations and Comments" in the fiftieth-anniversary issue of *The Coca-Cola Bottler*, recalled how J. T. Lupton telephoned him in Augusta, Georgia, shortly after the fu-

John T. Lupton, who joined Mr. Whitehead as a partner, in his half of the exclusive bottling contract. They and Mr. Thomas are now called "parent bottlers."

neral, and asked him to come to Atlanta the next day for an important business discussion. Mr. Rainwater replied that this was not possible because he was to be married on that day in Anniston, Alabama. All right, Mr. Lupton said, make it day after tomorrow.

This Mr. Rainwater did. And Mr. Lupton at their meeting designated him to succeed Mr. Whitehead as secretary-treasurer of the Atlanta-based parent company. The position put him in charge of administering to the needs of five hundred plants. "I was only twenty-four years old," Mr. Rainwater wrote, "just a kid."

He had been closely associated with Mr. Whitehead in establishing the Atlanta bottling plant and presumably had impressed Mr. Lupton enough to place him, though just a kid, in the responsible position. His performance was to justify Mr. Lupton's faith. One of the first problems he inherited was Joseph Biedenharn's persistence in refusing to sign the standard bottler's contract which Mr. Candler had insisted that he have for Mississippi. Mr. Biedenharn had gone right along bottling as he had those years before the bottling companies were formed. He didn't see any need to get saddled with a contract which would require him to buy at least fifteen hundred gallons of syrup a year, and would also require him to invest sufficient funds in equipment to take care of the Mississippi demand. To heck with that, Mr. Biedenharn said. He was getting along nicely as it was. Finally after many trips to Vicksburg, Mr. Rainwater talked him into putting his name to the paper.

Mr. Biedenharn, incidentally, fit finely into the family tradition of the bottlers. He began setting his brothers up in the business, and soon all six were happily bottling away in Mississippi, Louisiana, and Texas.

Another early action that Mr. Rainwater took, suggestive of wisdom beyond his years, was to set up an advisory board. He said he studied how he might succeed and realized he needed the advice of older, wiser heads. So he named to the board the five most active bottlers in his territory: Arthur Montgomery of Atlanta, W. A. Bellingrath of Montgomery, Crawford Johnson of Birmingham, W. King McDowell of Charleston, S.C., and J. K. Croswell of Sumter, S.C., all names that live in bottling fame today.

One concern of the board was keeping abreast of, and spreading the word on, technological progress. The crown closure had come happily during bottling's second year. But until 1910, the bottlers had to pump a foot pedal to operate the machine that filled and capped the bottles. In that year, the Crown Cork and Seal Company brought out its "Senior" machine which eliminated the foot-pedaling. The bottles were placed in a little line to be filled with syrup and carbonated water and then shaked up and then closed with a crown and cork. But bottlers still had to wash the bottles in a hand-operated soaker and brush and rinse them. Soon, in the 1910s, came semiautomatic soakers capable of washing three thousand bottles an hour. A Dixie semiautomatic machine to perform the cleaning and filling chores came in 1920, and in 1927 fully automatic machines were available.

The first bottlers sent their goods out to be sold locally on wagons drawn by slow-plodding mules or horses. To get bottles to farther reaches, they used railroad express companies. But by the 1910s, trucks had just about replaced the wagons, with models coming, in those days of real competition, from White, Stewart, Mack, Federal Garford, International Harvester, Autocar, and Packard. The trucks and the nation's building of steadily improving roads ended dependency on the express companies.

Thus, route men could deal directly with all of a plant's customers, giving them, in Mr. Rainwater's words, "our profit story." He went on to say in his fiftieth-anniversary *Bottler* account: "Availability became a part of Coca-Cola's program of progress, supported by the greatest distribution service of any product in the United States."

But with the progress came problems. By 1909, there were enough of these that the advisory board elected to set up meetings of bottlers in which they might discuss difficulties and exchange ideas. The first such meeting was held in Atlanta on January 19 and 20 of that year, with one hundred bottlers and five wives in attendance.

Serious among the problems was the constant threat and continuing reality of court suits claiming that roaches and other repulsive items had been included with Coca-Cola in a particular offending bottle. One woman reportedly had as her vocation the bringing of such bug-in-bottle suits against one Coca-Cola plant after another. When the bottlers tried to buy insurance to protect them if a suit were lost, they were told no such policy existed. If one were able to persuade a company to cover him, he had to draw up the policy.

The litigation problem was a main impetus for organization of the Coca-

Cola Bottlers' Association in 1915. Ralph Beach, association secretary since 1924, was able, in the 1959 fiftieth-anniversary issue of the *Bottler*, to look back and report with satisfaction: "There was a time when individual bottlers would settle almost any kind of fantastic claim rather than risk going into court and suffering the attendant publicity. I am happy to say such is not the case today. We, on occasion, settle claims because we think they are just. But we refuse to submit to swindlers. If we suspect a fraud is being attempted, we let the courts decide." The bottlers' association helped engender such a healthy attitude.

Another chief concern of the association was the one Asa Candler was so fierce about—quality control. Charles Howard Candler wrote to Mr. Candler on August 7, 1913, about one aspect of this: ". . . Some of the bottlers have experienced some difficulty this year with the goods souring. I have been able to convince all of them that the trouble was local and not due to the coca-cola [sic] syrup. Dr. Heath of the Pratt Laboratory has shown a number of cases where their bottles were not thoroughly cleaned and sterilized in their washing and soaking process. This leaves a culture medium in the bottles for the development of bacteria which will cause fermentation."

The Dr. Heath he mentioned was Dr. W. P. Heath, chief chemist of the N. P. Pratt Laboratory in Atlanta. He was hired by the bottlers' association in 1914 to troubleshoot and supervise the bottlers' efforts to achieve more cleanliness and better and more uniform quality. Until Dr. Heath came along, the attitude of bottlers toward such an important matter as carbonation has been aptly described in Coca-Cola literature as "casual." A usual procedure for determining if the carbonator was working properly was to pour a little Coca-Cola out of a bottle onto the floor. If it fizzed, it was carbonated. Dr. Heath, after long study of the effect of temperature and pressure on carbonation, issued a chart which showed the degree of carbonation achieved by different combinations of temperature and pressure. This guide to a proper degree of carbonation was hailed by bottlers as a giant step forward toward uniformity of product. Posted on filler room walls, it is still in use today.

In 1923, The Coca-Cola Company took Dr. Heath on to direct an even more rigorous quality-control program, one of the foundation stones of Robert W. Woodruff's presidency of the company. Until his retirement, Dr. Heath worked at improving water and all the other ingredients of the drink.

Another concern of the association was standardization. Having been reminded at their 1924 business meeting by Mr. Rainwater: "Gentlemen, there is, as you know, a wonderful effect in the uniformity of things . . . ," the association members set about standardizing letterheads and bottle crates in 1925; trucks (yellow and red, black hood, radiator, and fenders) in 1927; plant specifications (three sizes) and uniforms for workers (white inside the plants, buff on the trucks generally, but not universally) in 1928. Through the years, the association has modified or changed the standardizations, particularly the uniform, to keep up with the times.

In the midst of the early years of struggle, of progress and problems, there came that other serious blow to the bottling enterprise, the death in 1914 of Benjamin Franklin Thomas. Yet again, another strong figure was on hand to step into his parent-bottler shoes. His nephew, George T. Hunter, took command in

Chattanooga in as strong a manner as Mr. Rainwater had in Atlanta. Mr. Pratt in his fiftieth-anniversary *Bottler* account tells us that Uncle Ben had trained Mr. Hunter in all phases of the business so he would be able to run it with competence when the time came. This Mr. Hunter did for many years. He has said that whenever he confronted a thorny problem, he would always say to himself: "I wonder what Uncle Ben would think of this."

And so the bottling adventure, with its ups and downs, its strong leaders and building of success, paralleled the early saga of Coca-Cola's beginnings. In all the different elements of the business, the bottlers had by 1920 gotten things organized and were ready, as The Coca-Cola Company with its syrup had been twenty years before, to move on to unprecedented sales and growth.

Just as Coca-Cola people like to say that they moved soft drinks from the saloon to the salon, they also boast about how the bottling of their beverage improved the general tone of the soft-drink business, moving its plants from obscure locations to prominent sites, indeed making them local show places. As we shall see, this same upgrading was to occur in each country around the world that Coca-Cola has gone into, bringing with it improvement in sanitation, technology, and tone.

The happiness of success was to endure through the generations in the domestic bottling family, not to mention contributions to the economic and civic betterment of the communities in which the members dwelled. As early as January 1911, Asa Candler had come around enough, in his thinking about the bottlers, to write the following of them in *The Coca-Cola Bottler:*

"I cannot refrain from expressing my cordial appreciation of the high character of men who represent the bottling department of this corporation through the country. Without exception they rank with the best and most respected businessmen of their communities. I find them actively associated with commercial bodies, lending their help toward building up the material and moral interests in their localities. Generally, they are officially connected with some church, and are depended upon for active, useful service in connection with church influences and purposes. . . ."

The Bottlers Get Their Own Publication

During the first decade of the bottling adventure, Asa Candler's nephew, Joe Willard, gave another kind of endorsement to the infant enterprise. He felt confident enough in its fiscal future by 1909 to establish as a private venture *The Coca-Cola Bottler*, a trade magazine devoted exclusively to the bottlers' interests.

From its start, the *Bottler* has been one of the means by which the large and widespread bottler family has been held together over the years. (Since it addresses itself to bottling-plant owners mainly, it is essentially different from The Coca-Cola Company's periodical publication, *The Refresher*, earlier called *The Red Barrel*, which is directed at company employees.)

In Mr. Willard's first issue of April 1909, full of timely information and much advertising of bottling equipment and other supplies, there was started a tradition that continues today of exhortations to the bottlers to follow sound business practices, with this: "Keep your eyes on all of your customers all the time. Do not let them get the idea that your interest in them ends with the landing of your customer. Make it a point to hold on to them, and make your goods and your advertising, as well as your company, just as attractive as possible. There is always another man just as anxious to get your customers as you were to make them yours."

The May issue was fatter and fuller of news of the trade, communicating across the years the feel of the early bottling endeavors and the texture of the times. Southern bottlers were reported getting good response from a spiffy promotion idea, providing cloth caps inscribed with the trademark to cotton-mill workers (presumably to keep lint from getting in their hair). Charles A. Matson reported problems with imitators in Canada. As in the States, he commented, "They spring up in the summer early and usually wilt with the frost." An advertisement warned: "If you are not bottling Solo Ginger Ale, you are simply not keeping up with the reputation of the Coca-Cola bottlers." (From the start and until The Coca-Cola Company developed its own line of fruit-flavored drinks, the bottlers often carried them as side lines. They had to, as one bottler pointed out, because bottled Coca-Cola didn't really "take off" until the 1920s.) "See your trade. Know your trade. Like your trade," Samuel Candler Dobbs exhorted in that issue.

In the July issue of 1909, there was indignant report of yet another form of unscrupulous competition, the pushing of a cheap cola syrup to bottlers with the recommendation that they mix it half and half with Coca-Cola syrup. In Ann Arbor, Michigan, an angry man, forced out of his livelihood as saloon-keeper by the state's adoption of Prohibition, was reported trying to establish a statewide boycott of Coca-Cola on the belief that the company contributed $25,000 to advance the local option movement in Michigan. His belief was not founded in fact, the *Bottler* contended.

An electric machine that would shine shoes for five cents was reported in operation on Market Street in Philadelphia. And under the heading, "A Zealous Salesman," there was an account of the arrest in Memphis of a pushcart operator given to blowing a horn on his cart late at night, "and after he has sounded a few piercing blasts he cries out, 'Coca-Cola' as loud as his rusty lungs will permit."

The First Novel About Coca-Cola

The bottling family looks back fondly and proudly to the first twenty years of successful struggle reflected in the early issues of the *Bottler*, and, as we have seen, even Asa Candler was won over to their side during those years, to the point where he extolled them as almost saintly performers of civic endeavors and the Lord's work.

But there are, of course, always those around who would dispute the claims of business virtue, who would chip with revisionist zeal at these versions of corporate history. Such a one is William T. Campbell, author of the first novel about Coca-Cola, *Big Beverage* (Atlanta: Tupper & Love, 1952). As befits a work of fiction, there is a disclaimer to representation of actual persons or events, but the principal character, Lonnie (Pop) Butts has been construed by some to be a representative type of early bottler. And the story of his being persuaded by two young city slickers to bottle the big beverage—Sola-Soda (dubbed a "kick" by the masses)—has an awfully familiar ring.

There are beautiful touches throughout the book, like the scene where Pop is beguiled by those two city slickers. He tells them how he has developed a stick candy to market along with his pop, but hasn't been able to think of a good name for it. Without a word, one of his visitors gets out a pencil and piece of paper and writes out: "Fantas-Stick." Before they are done, they have convinced Pop he thought the name up, and they have a contract wherein he agrees to bottle Sola-Soda.

Mr. Campbell's character delineation of Pop and his fellow bottlers is not created out of the stuff of Mr. Candler's eulogy. One of his characters, a lawyer, sums up Pop's colleagues as string-savers, little men incapable of thinking big.

Pop himself is a complex figure. Unschooled, the son of sharecroppers, he started out with the virtue of being devoted to his little pop-and-candy business. Sola-Soda made him rich beyond any sharecropper boy's dreams, but he never felt good about the drink, never liked it. It vexed him that it so outsold his little line of fruit-flavored drinks to which he remained loyal to the end. Sola-Soda bothered Pop because it was not of his own making, its syrup, an unknown quantity, the brainchild of someone else.

The wealth and power that Sola-Soda bring Pop do not improve his nature. He is depicted as crooked in business deals, miserly, brutally exploitative of underpaid workers, and disgustingly conspicuous in his *nouveau riche* consumption of things. His final act of treachery is to refuse to make a loan during the depression to the very man who years before loaned him money to save his little pop business. Instead he buys his old friend out in bankruptcy proceedings and, adding insult to injury, sets up an animal farm in the poor man's beloved old antebellum family home, acquired also in the bankruptcy sale.

Author Campbell was once associated with Coca-Cola bottling and, given artistic license and maybe axes to grind, he can be presumed to know what he wrote about. But a sense of reality suggests that the early bottlers were somewhere between the monster he presents and the paragon envisioned by Mr. Candler, and were of varying temperaments, degrees of sophistication and sense of business ethics.

Coca-Cola's overseas expansion provided the subject matter for a movie, *One, Two, Three*, starring James Cagney and produced by Billy Wilder. It is about a Coca-Cola man involved in Cold War intrigue in Berlin, and there is, of course, a lil ol' honey-chile female character from Atlanta.

The most recent fictional account based on the Coca-Cola story was the novel, *Members of the Tribe* by Richard Kluger (Doubleday, 1977). The drink is called Jubilee (the gen-u-one) in the book, and historical figures and events of the real-life, turn-of-the-century South are woven into the plot. For example,

Tom Watson, the Georgia Populist leader later turned race-baiter (and foe of Coca-Cola) is a major stockholder in the founding of Jubilee. Another tragic figure, Leo Frank, Atlanta pencil-factory manager who was accused of murdering a teen-aged girl and lynched in an ugly drama of anti-Semitism, also appears. In the novel, he is Noah Berg, manager not of a pencil factory, but the Jubilee factory in Savannah. Thus does art improve on real life.

The First Bottler in New Orleans

What were the early bottlers really like in real life? Somewhere between Mr. Candler's characterization and the negative one in Mr. Campbell's novel, they emerge in other accounts more simply as a hard-driving, determined breed, willing to start small and, with great faith in the product and much diligent effort, build to success.

A. B. Freeman, the first bottler in New Orleans, seems to have been a sort of superspecimen of the breed. He started out with not much money but, in the words of J. H. (Red) Hall, a retired fountain salesman who knew Mr. Freeman well, "He had a lot of guts and deep faith in the product." The July 1909 issue of *The Coca-Cola Bottler* carried an account of how Mr. Freeman was plying the bayous in a motor launch, *Josephine*, to supply the wild and otherwise unreachable South Louisiana Cajun country, with salesmen putting up signs on moss-festooned trees in the wilderness as they went.

Eventually Mr. Freeman built enough success and became so important a personage in New Orleans that one year he had bestowed on him the highest honor that city can offer, King of the Mardi Gras. A contemporary of his said that people who knew him and saw him standing in his fine robes on the majestic float, bowing first to one side and then to the other, knew that "he wasn't bowing to the people. He was counting the empty Coca-Cola cases stacked up in front of stores on the sidewalks."

The First Coca-Cola Bottlers in the Northeast

Benjamin Franklin Thomas had seen as his main chance, when taking that first choice of territories, the populous Eastern seaboard, and he was eager to prove that bottled Coca-Cola would sell up there. Almost as soon as he got his first plant running in Chattanooga, he took himself off to Philadelphia to set up, and personally run, a plant there during the summer months of 1901. He located the business in a grocery store at Nineteenth and Carpenter streets, using a stable in the rear for the bottling plant. He spent $2,500 getting set up, and then temporarily shut the plant down, when summer was done, to return to Chattanooga.

Back home, he soon encountered Earley W. Adams, private secretary to a

Chattanooga federal judge. Mr. Adams often had time on his hands and had formed the habit of dropping in at the Chattanooga plant to enjoy a free bottle of Coca-Cola. Mr. Thomas got to know him and was apparently impressed with him. Before the year was out, Mr. Thomas offered Mr. Adams the kind of deal he made with a number of men during his early efforts to spread plants across the land rapidly. If Mr. Adams would run the Philadelphia plant, he could own 55 per cent interest in it on credit, the debt to be paid off from proceeds of the plant.

In an account of all this in the fiftieth-anniversary issue of the *Bottler*, Mr. Adams wrote, "Being a natural-born gambler and having five orphaned brothers, I accepted the offer."

He moved his family to Philadelphia early in 1901 and they lived in the plant. His delivery fleet consisted of a horse and buggy.

About the tenth of March," Mr. Adams wrote, "I had the shop in running condition and we had bottled and labeled about ten cases. We loaded them on the delivery wagon and solicited everyone in sight. I sold one for cash and persuaded three other stores to let me leave a case with them to see if they could sell it. I never was paid for those three cases, but one storekeeper did continue as a customer."

Mr. Adams ended the account on the happy note of his eventual success, adding: "All of that happened fifty years ago. If any of you have another Thomas proposition to make me, here I am, ready to go."

In the same issue of the *Bottler* is Arthur W. Pratt's saga of "My Life with Coca-Cola." He and his brother started one of the earliest plants—in Huntsville, Alabama, in 1900. By 1902 it was thriving (and continued to make the brothers happy with its success for some years to come before they finally sold it). Mr. Pratt aspired to something much bigger—the New York City territory, no less —and went to Chattanooga to talk with Mr. Thomas about that. "Mr. Thomas operated from a small office on a side street . . . the appearance of which did not coincide with the build-up we had imagined for this new drink."

Mr. Thomas told Mr. Pratt he was saving the New York territory to see who among his growing bottling family might prove himself capable of such a huge assignment. Mr. Thomas offered Newark instead, and they agreed on a fifty-fifty partnership.

Mr. Pratt hied off immediately to Newark, rented a store building, and installed a sloping platform in it for the foot-power machine, carbonator, and bottle-washing machine. At the end of the platform, he built a syrup room high enough to gravity-feed the bottle machine.

By "continuous pressure day by day," he gradually built a clientele in Newark. There was not yet a great demand, he wrote, but he was confident it would come with time. A great difficulty was the long hard wintertimes when only saloons would give him orders. Earley Adams, the Philadelphia bottler, came over during one of these bleak seasons with a burlap bag to borrow a supply of crowns. The Crown Cork and Seal Company would not ship him any more because he was so far in arrears on his bills.

Mr. Pratt still had his eye on New York City. So, he made friends with a cigar-store owner there at 120 Broadway, and they worked out an agreement whereby Mr. Pratt would supply him with two dozen bottles a week. Mr. Pratt would pack the two dozen bottles in a suitcase and carry them by train, then ferry, and finally trolley to the cigar store.

After this arrangement had been established, Mr. Pratt approached "Uncle Ben" Thomas again about a contract for the big city. Mr. Thomas allowed him to present his case to the parent company's board of directors, and Mr. Pratt told the board members he was already serving New York City "temporarily," not mentioning that he had only one customer. He was given the contract for New York City and its population of eleven million at the time—1904. Again, it was a fifty-fifty partnership with Mr. Thomas.

His first plant in Manhattan was at 335 East Forty-sixth Street in the slaughterhouse district. As before, he equipped it himself, including laying a cement floor. He told the amusing story of a visitor who came in, wanting to discuss a business matter with the plant owner while Mr. Pratt was at work in the cement. The bottler took off the overalls he was wearing over his business suit and announced that he was the proprietor. It turned out the man had one share in Mr. Thomas' company, and, upon seeing this humble start of a bottling plant, promptly sold it.

Here again, it was a long, slow effort to build the trade. Mr. Pratt would begin his sales talk to a potential customer, and his driver would bring in a case before the person had time to say no. Mr. Pratt would then tell the storekeeper the case was his as a gift to pass out free bottles among customers to see how much they would like bottled Coca-Cola. Then he would return in a week seeking a reorder, and got it from 75 per cent of merchants so approached.

He did a good business in the Italian districts and later learned that frequenters of card rooms in those areas would mix Coca-Cola with Chianti in order to be able to drink and play all night long. The "foreign element" in New York generally provided his most numerous customers back then.

The happy day came when Mr. Pratt could sell two teams of horses, which had been hauling his crates, and buy one Packard truck with which he could cover much more than the same amount of territory. Out of sentiment, he kept the old horse which had been with him since Newark. But he needed an excuse for this extravagance to present to his business-minded partner. He planned to tell "Uncle Ben" that he needed the horse to haul manure from the stable to a suitable place of disposal until he realized the circular reasoning of that. Mr. Pratt wrote how he told this story to associates and they elected him, on the spot, president of The New York Horse Manure Association.

By 1918, Mr. Pratt decided to sell both the New Jersey and New York plants because "the territory was so thickly populated that it would take a lifetime to advance it to a point where the owner could enjoy the fruits of his hard work. It seemed as though every year we made a profit, twice as much capital was needed the next year to take care of the expanding business; it seemed to me the more we made, the more we got into debt." A sale of the New York plant was consummated with Charlie Culpepper for $160,000. The year before, 1917, the plant had produced 124,067 cases.

Fifteen years later, Mr. Pratt wrote, the estate of Charlie Culpepper was found to total $4.5 million from proceeds of the plant. Someone suggested to Mr. Pratt he had been foolish to sell it. "My answer was that I did not think I was foolish since I was alive with $160,000 and Charlie Culpepper was dead with $4,500,000."

Early Bottling in the Atlanta Area

While Mr. Thomas was establishing his bottling beachheads in the cold Northeast, Mr. Whitehead was building his base for expansion across the initially more receptive South. We have noted that one of his associates in establishing the Atlanta plant was Charles Veazey Rainwater, who took over the company after Mr. Whitehead's death. Mr. Rainwater divulged in the fiftieth-anniversary issue of the *Bottler* that he had worked previously for Charles T. Nunnally, the Atlanta confectioner who was among the early vendors of soda-fountain Coca-Cola. Mr. Nunnally told his young employee that there was a great future for bottled Coca-Cola and urged him to get in on the ground floor. It was advice he would always be grateful for.

Another perspicacious young man was soon to cast his lot with the plant after figuring out for himself the same thing Mr. Nunnally had said. Arthur Montgomery worked as a shipping agent in Atlanta for the Southern Express Company in 1900. During the happy spring, that year of the first deliveries of the bottled drink in the area, a mule and wagon would be dispatched to deliver thirty-five cases to Roswell, some twenty miles distant. The round trip required two days. But, soon thereafter, much of the transportation from Atlanta of those crates to outlying points was by fast freight rather than plodding mules.

Arthur Montgomery bemusedly watched the number of crates being shipped steadily increase over a period of three years. Knowing a good thing when he saw it, he sought out Mr. Whitehead and Mr. Lupton and secured a job as Atlanta bottling-plant manager. This was in 1903. Later that year, the company was reorganized, and Mr. Montgomery bought his one-third interest.

When Mr. Montgomery became one-third owner, the territory in which the Atlanta Coca-Cola Bottling Company enjoyed exclusive sales comprised thirty-five counties stretching to the Tennessee line. The early plants were built by necessity where the railroad tracks were. First to decentralize, the Atlanta company set up subplants handy to rail lines in Gainesville, Conyers, Griffin, Marietta, Newnan, Lawrenceville, and Ballground, Georgia.

The great-nephew of Arthur Montgomery, who is named after him and owns the Atlanta franchise today, recalled some of the lore about the early contracts with their setting out of exclusive territories. Often, areas were defined by citing a line from "Farmer So-and-So's barn to Farmer So-and-So's well." Territory disputes would arise when some place that had not been populated would get a manufacturing plant or a lake developed on it, or when a river designated as a boundary line changed its course. Colonel Bob Jones, legal counsel and fa-

COURTESY OF THE ATLANTA HISTORICAL SOCIETY

Atlanta's "grand-slam" golfer in the 1920s, Bobby Jones, son of Coca-Cola legal counsel, Colonel Bob Jones.

ther of Bobby Jones, Atlanta's grand-slam golf champion of the 1930s, would mediate these contretempts between bottlers.

Though success came faster in Atlanta and the rest of the South than in the North, it was still a matter of slow and steady, rather than spectacular growth. L. F. Montgomery, Arthur Montgomery's nephew and father of the present owner, recalled, in *The Coca-Cola Bottler* of January 1951 (fiftieth anniversary of the Atlanta plant), the day in the early 1900s that a new high of five hundred cases was sold. Arthur Montgomery was exultant and said to his nephew that he could not see how sales could possibly increase more. Surely they had reached the saturation point!

But of course sales did increase more, as did production capacity—from a single foot-power filler in 1900 to eleven of them in 1913 to two 32-spout fillers in 1916. L. F. Montgomery said of that day his uncle thought couldn't be bettered: "From then on it was just a matter of increased business and hard work."

By 1920, in Atlanta as elsewhere, the foundations had been laid for ever-accelerating growth. As though to round out the story of those first struggling twenty years, there was the report in the Atlanta *Journal* of September 8, 1920, of the death of Henry Gerwin, "faithful old Negro employee of the Atlanta Coca-Cola Bottling Company. He washed and bottled the first bottle sold in Atlanta." The story pointed out that though he was unable to work for several months, his salary had been paid until the end.

Today, the Atlanta Bottling Company's territory has increased from thirty-five to forty of Georgia's abundant 159 counties, and serves about one third of the state's population. Its plants have diminished to three, in Atlanta, Marietta, and Gainesville. They produce and sell, in all the variety of sizes, the equivalent of forty million cases of six-and-one-half-ounce bottles a year. The three plants and a series of storage and sales centers employ fourteen hundred persons and use a fleet of eight hundred vehicles. The operation has through the years been an innovative one, most recently noted for introducing some of the first metric-measure bottles.

The main office is on Atlanta's Spring Street near downtown, a wide two-story brick building with pleasant, shaded grounds, built in 1940. Its main lobby is a monument to the early struggles of Arthur Montgomery and his nephew, L. F. Montgomery. Portraits of both, with the years of their lives on brass plates (1854 to 1940 for the one, 1889 to 1964 for the other), hang on the marble walls. On the marble floor is inlaid a geometrical design of stars around a large depiction of the bottle. A round, 1930s modern chandelier of frosted glass and brass has the bottle embossed on four sides. In here, the sound comes faintly of bottles clanking and rattling on the filling lines.

Arthur L. Montgomery, a dapper middle-aged man, a third-generation bottler, part owner, and board chairman of the company, great-nephew of the original Arthur L. Montgomery, son of L. F. Montgomery, presides over the plant from a spacious second-floor office. He is courteous and genial in a no-nonsense sort of way. To play the tape of an interview with him is to hear, time after time, at frequent intervals, his hearty, genuine, infectious laugh ring out.

He tells about when the present plant was being built. His father kept it a secret from his great-uncle. The old gentleman had ever been conservative and frugal and set in his ways. He would not have approved the expense of building anew. L. F. Montgomery mercifully let him go to his grave without knowing about the extravagance and grandeur of the new plant.

Arthur Montgomery laughs when recalling his great-uncle's frugality. He tells about the time in the late 1920s when W. C. (Bill) D'Arcy, the advertising genius who was to follow in Frank Robinson's footsteps, was addressing a bottlers' convention and to make some point, which Mr. Montgomery cannot now recall, Mr. D'Arcy dramatically held up a five-dollar bill and set it on fire.

This infuriated the elder Arthur Montgomery. He got up and stormed out of the room and refused to attend any more of the meeting. "He said anybody who'd burn up money is a damned fool," Mr. Montgomery says, with again the hearty ring of his laugh.

When the present plant was built, he says, it was equipped with the most up-to-date machinery available. Now, it is obsolete. It was set up when there was just the one-sized bottle. Its machinery is slow compared with today's models and its production method, organized on three floors (including a basement loading room), is less efficient than today's one-floor operations. One can see the difference. Here, the little bottles, having been washed and sterilized automatically, delicately dance and clatter around several circular lines to receive their injection of syrup and carbonated water, and to be shaked up to mix the syrup and water, and then to be capped and carried off in crates or cartons. At the Marietta plant, the big bottles sway at a much faster clip in straight lines to have the same things done to them—that process which has been going on since the foot-pedaling days.

(Workers in bottling plants are on constant intimate terms with broken glass. Bottles explode with a startling, loud pop on the lines, and the automatic machinery must be stopped until the broken glass is thoroughly hosed out. Crates and cartons of empties get knocked over and broken in the loading areas and the broken glass must be swept up.)

Small plants just can't handle the diversity of bottle sizes, Mr. Montgomery says. The one on Spring Street is to be torn down soon to make way for one like that in Marietta. We may be permitted the hope that the splendid reception room will somehow be spared. The plant in Marietta has all the grace and soundness of construction of any other utilitarian building thrown up at today's costs and debased craft standards. The Spring Street plant was built beautifully in 1940 at a cost of only $3.50 a foot.

Mr. Montgomery says that from his great-uncle's day on, the Atlanta operation has prided itself on its cleanliness and will continue to do so, no matter how much rebuilding goes on. "It's a very clean operation here. We're very proud of that. We've had people say you can eat off the floor. And you can. It's that clean." His great-uncle and father preached quality, and Mr. Montgomery carries that tradition on, too.

There is yet another tradition of good employee relations. The operation is not unionized. When attempts were made to organize the workers, they voted it down, Mr. Montgomery says. "We think the reason is that we stay ahead of the other people in our industry on salaries, pensions, and fringe benefits."

He goes on: "We just never felt we needed a union. Of course management always says that." He laughs. "But I think we've proved we don't need one. If we did, we'd have one."

Asked if it was the bottlers who, back in the 1930s, provided the little yellow-painted, sign-bedecked Coca-Cola stands for youngsters to sell ice-cold Coca-Cola all over a town, Mr. Montgomery says, Oh yes. He had one when he was a boy. Back then, there were three truck routes for the stands. Mr. Montgomery later worked one of them. "You'd find Johnny, and Johnny wouldn't have his money. He'd try to find Mama to get the money from her. Or Johnny had got tired of working and had gone off somewhere to play. Then Johnny or his mama would call up irate. 'Where's my Coca-Cola?'"

The stands carried other lines of drinks, too. Mr. Montgomery recalls the time his father got furious to see him drinking a competitor's orange drink, not because of any disloyalty involved but because his father knew the competitor ran a filthy plant. "He took me over there and showed me, and I didn't drink any more of it."

Mr. Montgomery says the thing they liked about the stands, besides their contribution to depression-era profits, was that they were educational. "They taught a kid how a business operates. It was a good beginning for a business education."

Does the plant still distribute Coca-Cola inscribed rulers, pencils, and tablets to schoolchildren (a bottler promotion begun in 1909)? Oh yes, Mr. Montgomery says. Do the rulers still have on them—harking back to Asa Candler's blend of pious morality and go-getting promotion, along with the trademark—the admonition to "Do unto others as you would have them do unto you"? "A good rule." Mr. Montgomery answers. "As far as I know they do. As far as I know. I sure hope they do. The golden rule."

The company also still has schoolchildren in to tour the plant, with special buses to transport them. If they come from a rural area, the bus takes them by such points of interest as the splendid new Governor's Mansion on West Paces Ferry Road, on the assumption that at an early age the passengers might not have been to Atlanta before. Mr. Montgomery says that people in their forties tell him their memories of touring the plant when they were in school. "It's good. It makes a good impression."

In other ways, he says, the company tries to be of service. "It's always been our philosophy (and most bottlers feel this way) to be good citizens. We feel this community has been mighty good to us and we ought to try to put something back into it." He describes some of his own work on boards and committees of civic and charitable enterprises and hands over a two-page single-spaced list of all of them. "All our people," Mr. Montgomery says, "are so involved. They start out in small things when they first come to work and build to bigger ones."

The talk turns to the varying bottle sizes again, and such a new development as a plastic bottle, cheaper and lighter than glass, but with one disadvantage: When the drink is ice-cold, the bottle doesn't feel cold on the outside.

Mr. Montgomery's voice becomes suddenly enthusiastic, as he compares this with the old bottle. "One of the great things about that package—put your hand around that—that old six-and-one-half-ounce bottle. You know what you've got in your hand. You get the aroma. There's nothing like it. People tell me it just doesn't taste the same in another size bottle. It's psychological, of course. Because it's the same product, of course." Arthur Montgomery laughs again.

The Development of the Distinctively Designed Coca-Cola Bottle

The design of that bottle Mr. Montgomery exclaimed over grew out of the fight against the old problem of imitators. Once again, a logic of necessity suddenly sparked Coca-Cola magic.

The bottlers from the beginning, it is obvious from early copies of the *Bottler*, were just as furiously preoccupied with fighting imitators as were Asa Candler and his crew. The gentlemen of the parent bottling companies were equally concerned, and they saw as one important aspect of the problem the generic straight bottles that they used. Coca-Cola looked little different to the consumer from its imitators. It didn't help that the imitators often glued to their bottles diamond-shaped labels with a trademark that looked (and sounded) like Coca-Cola and was written in Spencerian script.

Part of the amicable disagreement which caused Mr. Thomas and Mr. Whitehead to part company was over what color bottle to use. Mr. Whitehead used a clear bottle. Mr. Thomas preferred amber because he thought it made the package more distinctive. He kept harping on the subject through the early 1910s, saying things like: "We need a new bottle—a distinctive package that will help us fight substitution." Those Coca-Cola glasses with the name inscribed on them that Asa Candler's crews were selling had the same purpose—to single out Coca-Cola as something special. Before his death, Mr. Whitehead, as well as Mr. Rainwater and Mr. Lupton, had come to full accord with Mr. Thomas on the need for a distinctive bottle.

In one of those utterances on the subject, Mr. Thomas set out in a remarkable way the specifications that were to result in the masterpiece of a bottle Coca-Cola finally got. "George," he is quoted as having said to his nephew, Mr. Hunter, "we need a bottle which a person will recognize as a Coca-Cola bottle even when he feels it in the dark. The Coca-Cola bottle should be so shaped that, even if broken, a person could tell at a glance what it was."

Another Coca-Cola person who was concerned about substitutes and saw the need for a distinctive bottle in the battle against them was Harold Hirsch, who as general counsel for the company had begun his lifelong, brilliant career of protecting Coca-Cola's trademark and other legal rights in the courts. In July 1913, he wrote to all the parent companies, urging their officers to adopt a uniform and distinctive bottle. They, in turn, began sounding out bottle manufacturers about designing one.

Among these was the Root Glass Company in Terre Haute. C. J. Root, the owner, speaking of approaches from such as Mr. Thomas, Mr. Rainwater, and Mr. Hunter, was later to say that he "could not escape the great enthusiasm of these men."

It was so hot in Terre Haute in the summer of 1913 that Mr. Root closed his plant down. This gave him time and the inclination to concentrate attention on Coca-Cola's need. He marshaled his men and told them to get to it. As recorded in company history, Alex Samuelson, his plant superintendent, instructed a company accountant, T. Clyde Edwards, to "get all the information you can on the coca bean and the cola nut."

One often repeated version of what happened next has it that Mr. Edwards hied himself off to the Terre Haute Public Library and looked up the coca bean and cola nut in the Encyclopaedia Britannica. And here the kind of magic that the two exotic ingredients inspired in Mr. Robinson when he named Coca-Cola was manifest again, so this story goes. The Britannica, of whatever edition it was, contained a line drawing of the coca bean. Mr. Samuelson brought in a machinist who carefully copied the drawing. And it was on the basis of that drawing that Mr. Samuelson came up with the famous design of a bottle with bulged sides and parallel longitudinal ridges with tapered ends—*shaped and marked like the coca bean!*

As wonderful as that story is, what actually happened was magic of another sort. "Serendipity," Wilbur Kurtz exclaims when setting the record straight. "It was pure serendipity." For the only thing wrong with the story, he points out, is that the coca bean by no stretch of the imagination looks anything like the

Two of the men responsible for Coca-Cola's traditional, hobble-skirt bottle design. Seated at right is Alex Samuelson, instrumental in the design. Next to him is C. J. Root, the founder of both the Root Glass Company and the Associated Coca-Cola Bottling Co., Inc.

shape of the Coca-Cola bottle. It looks, instead, like a buckeye. Nor does the cola nut bear any resemblance to the bottle, though some versions of the story have it as the model.

Mr. Kurtz grins with delight to explain what must really have happened in Terre Haute. What Mr. Edwards found in the Britannica was a drawing not of the coca bean but of the source of chocolate, the *cacao* bean—which does have the bulged sides and ridges. Not noting the crucial difference in spelling, he had the machinist copy it, and by that happy accident the bottle was born. So it was Coca-Cola luck, serendipity indeed, that sparked the magic of the exotic ingredients, this time to form the best-known and most-appealing package in the world.

The people at Root made models, first in wood and then in glass, modified the size to make it fit bottling machinery, and the Root company was ready with its entry into competition with those of other bottle manufacturers. Mr. Rainwater convened a committee of seven bottlers to make the crucial choice in Atlanta early in 1916. The committee members quickly eliminated eight of the ten entries, and after several days decided it was hands down between the other two for the Root design.

It was patented in November, 1915, in Mr. Samuelson's name. But as the company's *Profile* publication points out, the man who actually created the design was one Earl Dean, Root's mold shop supervisor at the time.

We are privileged to glimpse as a footnote to the story of the bottle's design one small scene of gentlemanly behavior in a business transaction back in the 1910s. It was described in an interview conducted at the archives some time ago with T. Clyde Edwards, the man who did the encyclopedia research. Mr. Edwards said that the Root Glass Company charged The Coca-Cola Company nothing for developing the design. Harold Hirsch subsequently wanted bottlers to pay the Root firm a royalty of twenty-five cents on every gross of bottles they got from it. C. J. Root demurred. The new bottles shouldn't cost the bottlers any more than they had been paying for the straight-sided ones, he said. They finally settled on a royalty of five cents per gross. This was, of course, adequate to greatly enrich the Root firm. Chapman Root, grandson of Mr. Root, inherited the family fortune while serving in World War II. He is said to have been the richest private in the United States Army at the time. (Other bottle producers were also enriched by contracts to manufacture the bottle.)

The new bottle went into production in 1916; Mr. Thomas did not live to see the distinctive package he had so aptly called for. But clearly the Root design fulfilled his dream of a bottle you know by its feel in the dark and recognize even when one is broken to smithereens. Called by Designer Raymond Loewy "the most perfectly designed package in use," the bottle itself was to be recognized as a trademark by the U. S. Patent Office in 1960, a distinction among bottles shared then only by the pinch model of Haig & Haig scotch whisky.

The happy discovery of the near-perfect package was another token of success to members of the bottling family; and the distinctive bottle, though proliferation of sizes might come, remains the highest symbol of Coca-Cola's rich meaning.

"Put your hand around that—that old six-and-one-half-ounce bottle. You know what you've got in your hand. You get that aroma. There's nothing like it. . . ."

IV

Success–and Then a Souring

All the while that the bottlers were happily establishing their dynasties during the first two decades of the twentieth century, The Coca-Cola Company, under Asa Candler and his small staff, was consolidating and building upon the solid start that had been made in the 1890s. In Samuel Candler Dobbs's phrase, Coca-Cola during the first two decades of the twentieth century was to progress "in ever-widening circles." The virtue of all that hard work of the previous ten years and all that personal stinting in order to reinvest all that profit into promoting and selling syrup was to be rewarded. And Americans were to see not only the most splendid and extravagant promotional effort yet in behalf of the drink, but also, by a curious, skilled use of imagery, they were to see themselves and the best of their lives reflected in the advertising, the beginning of Coca-Cola's effort to make the drink a symbol of the nation itself.

But for Asa Candler, the advancement during those years was not to prove happy, like that of the bottlers during the same period. Ironically, important happenings of the times, to which the boast of imperviousness had so often been made, were to intrude on Coca-Cola's life and, in Mr. Candler's mind anyhow, to threaten the company's steady, ever-increasing progress, even its very existence. It was as though Asa Candler had mixed up the biggest Coca-Cola syrup batch imaginable, and then to his dismay and helpless anger watched the goods go sour on him.

INTERNATIONAL EVENTS DURING COCA-COLA'S EARLY YEARS

The nation and the world were changing. Modernism increased apace in that future shock multiplicity of important developments and events. Somewhere in there, Mr. Candler lost within himself the ability to adjust to modernism. We have glimpsed in the previous chapter a few of the events that hammered away during the first twenty years of this century. Consider these others:

The 1900s started with missionaries murdered and diplomats besieged in China by that pioneer secret terrorist society called the Boxers, and it took the intervention of several nations, including the United States, to put the so-called rebellion down. Also in 1900, a tropical hurricane and ensuing flood left six thousand dead in Galveston, Texas, with $15 million in property damage.

The year 1901 was marked by an economic panic and the assassination of President William McKinley by Leon Czolgosz, an anarchist.

But progress was not to be stopped. Labor was on the move in the early 1900s, securing an eight-hour workday for government employees and a ten-hour one for street railway drivers, first of a long list of improvements in the lot of the working man (giving him more time to pause at a soda fountain) secured by the American Federation of Labor under Samuel Gompers. These achievements were not enough, though, for the organizers in 1905 of the Industrial Workers of the World (IWW), whose members called themselves Wobblies and were devoted to direct action and good inspirational songs.

Congress continued reform-minded, trying to harness some the unbridled power of big business (looked upon with apprehension by the average man as well as such as the IWW Wobblies). In 1906 was passed the Hepburn Act, giving the Interstate Commerce Commission theoretical power to put a stop to railroad rebates and discriminatory rates. Also passed that year was the Pure Food and Drug Act, aimed at putting a stop to widespread adulteration, formulating with harmful ingredients (like narcotics), and untruthful labeling of the nation's food and medicine. Coca-Cola's fate was to be strongly affected by this legislation, as well as by the constitutional amendment of 1913 imposing the income tax.

Meanwhile in 1906, General John J. (Blackjack) Pershing was leading his men, with horses rearing and rifles hoisted, in a bootless chase of the bandit Pancho Villa and his followers down in Mexico. In 1907, another panic ensued, even as a record high of 1,300,000 aliens were recorded as coming that year to these shores to seek economic well-being.

Woodrow Wilson was elected President in 1912 and, as we know, the Great War which was to lend fame to his name broke out in 1914 in Europe. In a curious episode of that war before America got into it, Henry Ford, in some ways a kindred spirit to Asa Candler, set off in his vessel, *The Oscar II*, to try personally to persuade the European powers to call off hostilities.

"He kept us out of war," was a slogan on which President Wilson won re-election in 1916, only to find the following year such a stance no longer possible.

"To make the world safe for democracy" then became the slogan, as men signed up for the draft, people bought Liberty Bonds, and General Pershing ("Lafayette, we are here") led his men, two million strong, through Cantigny, Château Thierry, Belleau Wood, Soissons . . . to, perhaps, a more noble end, with the Armistice of 1918, than that of the adventure in Mexico.

President Wilson began his hopeful effort to find peace for the world through the League of Nations and, though stricken with paralysis in 1919, was to prevail in the effort, if not in his dream.

The era ended on another hopeful note. Women citizens of the nation, following upon black males, at least theoretically, were enfranchised to vote in the democracy's elections. Great were the predictions of benefices to come and, again, far from the hope was the reality that ensued.

Even though the largest and most savage war in history up to that time did rage, and large events were to impinge on Mr. Candler's sense of well-being, The Coca-Cola Company through the two decades was able to record its own history of mighty accomplishment. Once again, let us see it in fast takes:

Coca-Cola Story Highlights: 1901–18

January 1, 1901: The year's budget for advertising expenditures is $100,000, a new high.

December 31, 1904: The year's sales are a little more than one million gallons—again a first.

August 23, 1906: The D'Arcy Advertising Agency takes over the full Coca-Cola account, to begin the writing of fifty years of advertising and promotional history.

October 21, 1909: Agents of the Food and Drug Department of the United States Government, acting under the authority of the recently passed Pure Food and Drug Act, seize forty barrels and twenty kegs of Coca-Cola syrup and begin an action against the company, charging adulteration, that is to drag on, with its threat to the good name and the trademark of Coca-Cola, for ten years.

January 1, 1911: This year the amount allocated in the company budget for advertising is a cool one million dollars.

An ominous day in December 1914: Frank M. Robinson retires from the company.

A day in December 1914: Asa Candler in his official report includes these portentous words: "Taxes that are needed to support government that is essential for protection of honest, industrious citizens, grow as Hagar's gourd vine and are to us, who must pay them, as offensive as gourd vines in wheat fields." Then he gets down to specifics: The new federal tax legislation contains provisions against accumulation of surplus capital by a business, and the Coca-Cola Company must distribute among stockholders a tremendous total of $5 million of this capital plus a dividend of $3,000 per share.

Christmas Day, 1916: As a gift to his wife and five children, Asa G. Candler divides among them all, but seven, of the majority of shares that he has held in the Coca-Cola Company—that personal cause, amounting almost to a religion, to which he had been so devoted and given so much of the energy and ingenuity of his soul.

The fateful month of April 1917: Coca-Cola feels the impact of war. Sugar, its main ingredient, is rationed. Sales are severely curtailed, because of the American war effort. Advertising proclaims a refusal to curtail quality, and to urge against acceptance of substitutes.

September 12, 1919: A consortium of businessmen and banks, led by Ernest Woodruff of Atlanta, buys The Coca-Cola Company from those to whom Mr. Candler had given the majority of the stock, and other shareholders, for a whopping $25 million—$15 million in cash, $10 million in preferred stock. *It is the largest single transaction in the history of the South to date.* The business is reincorporated as a Delaware corporation with Samuel Candler Dobbs, president, and Charles Howard Candler, chairman of the board. Common stock is put on public sale at $40 per share for those of foresight and good fortune enough to purchase it. An era is ended.

December 31, 1919: Total sales for the year augur well for the new era to come. The end of sugar rationing has meant an increase of more than eight million gallons of syrup over those sold in 1918.

The Rising Soda-Fountain Business

In 1901, Charles Howard Candler, of course, had no way of anticipating all that was to happen to the company his father had founded so soundly and to which the dutiful son had determined to dedicate his life. On a happy day in the fall of that year, in pursuit of his duties as a salesman, he personally installed the first window display in company history at a drugstore in Augusta, Georgia. It reflected his fascination with the concocting of Coca-Cola syrup, being an exhibit of the articles which went into it. The display, he declared, "made a favorable impression on the public."

His further account in the *Thirty-three Years* manuscript of his career in the early 1900s imparts a sense of the reality of those times for the company. Later in 1901, he joined the New York office under H. T. Applewhite, "a perfect Chesterfield of a gentleman," but old and hard of hearing and, hence, soon to be released. There was one other salesman.

"The work was hard and to some extent discouraging," Charles Howard Candler wrote and, speaking with a certain scorn out of his southern upbringing, continued: "The supercilious attitude of the ordinary run of New York small-caliber soda-fountain owners with whom we had to deal made progress difficult."

A New York City syrup salesman and his spiffy vehicle.

The three-man force was trying to cover all of New York City, an impossible task and this on foot and by trolley. To make things a little less difficult, they bought a two-passenger, wire-wheel automobile, which they "soon found to have already done its best," and traded it in on a brand-new Locomobile Steamer at a net cost of $950. Equipped with "all the latest improvements," the steamer was "in every respect a very nifty little vehicle," especially after they affixed a waterproof box onto the flat deck at the back in which to carry advertising signs, and then decked the box with some of them. These were the first pieces of automotive equipment for the company. The other salesman, appropriately named C. C. Ryder, learned to operate the steamer safely, becoming the first motorized salesman.

To round out the story, Charles Howard Candler told later in the same manuscript how a Knox automotive truck, used as a bus during the Atlanta AAA Automobile Show in 1909, was afterward bought by The Coca-Cola Company and converted so as to be capable of carrying a load of six barrels of syrup. It was the first automotive equipment for the Atlanta headquarters. Jim Keith, a black man, abandoned his two-mule team and learned to drive the thing, becoming the first Atlanta company driver.

Those were heady times—Coca-Cola becoming motorized. They were fine times, also, for the company's sales department. The famous first million-gallon year of 1904 marked the gains that had been made since 1900's mere 370,877 gallons. By 1910, gallonage sold to bottlers alone was more than a million (1,325,176) and that to soda fountains, nearly three million (2,864,973).

Those were the great days of the soda fountain which were to continue on through the 1930s. The men in their cutaways and the women in their long dresses would gather there to gossip and to sip from Coca-Cola inscribed glasses, which now had a flared lip. (The flared-lip glass had an unfortunate balance problem, tending to tip over and, often, break. To rectify this, the bell-shaped Coca-Cola glass replaced it in 1922, and an improved bell-shaped model replaced it in 1929, surviving to today.)

The first fountains in the 1830s consisted of crude wooden covers placed atop the heavy iron tanks used in carbonating water for the soda drinks, according to a company pamphlet, *The Development of the Soda Fountain*, by Franklin M. Garrett. By the 1850s, business was good enough at many fountains to afford the tanks marble tops. By the early 1900s, most drugstores had not only the beautiful marble fountains but also elegant urns and containers and elaborate rococo dispensers with names like Cathedral and Château. A Coca-Cola premium that came into being in the early 1900s added to the elegance of many fountains—a multicolored Tiffany-style stained-glass chandelier.

An advertisement in the Atlanta *Journal* of May 14, 1905, announced the opening of what must have been one of the finest fountains in the country. Called the New Terminal Station Independent Cigar Company, it was the latest addition to a chain of four other fountains owned by the Atlanta Soda Company, Frank M. Pearson, manager, "largest dispensers of Coca-Cola in the world, 3,930 gallons sold last year."

The ad went on: "We handle Nunnally's candies. We sell only genuine

Mrs. Asa (Lizzie) Candler (seated, third from left) and friends from Atlanta, on her first visit to son Charles Howard Candler's New York City office at 63 South Washington Square.

Coca-Cola. No trust cigars handled. The above handsome soda apparatus was placed in the new Terminal Station by Puffer Manufacturing Company."

Handsome is the word. Atlanta was still, of course, a big railroad town and for the New Terminal Station, Atlanta Soda Company and the Puffer establishment had gone all out. The photograph in the ad showed a long marble fountain, two lovely dispensing bowls, a most ornately decorated backboard, with cases for bottles and glasses at right angles to the fountains. And the marble floor had inlaid in it, and writ large, the script trademark, Coca-Cola, with Delicious and Refreshing in fine, fancy lettering.

The Puffer establishment mentioned in the ad was actually named A. D.

Puffer and Son. Among the elaborately decorated dispensers it offered for soda fountains were the Astor, the Tower, the Crown, the Capitol, the Necessity, the Druggist's Pride, the Economist, the Halcyon, Jr., the Superior, the Transcendent, and the Nonpareil.

Mr. Robinson continued to direct both the high-powered advertising program and the go-getting sales force servicing the fountains until 1906. By then, they had become too high-powered and go-getting for one man to handle, and Mr. Candler set up a separate sales department and put Mr. Dobbs in charge of it. (Mr. Robinson remained in charge of advertising, or nominally so, anyhow, as we shall see. He was also still secretary of the firm. Brother John S. Candler had been serving as vice-president, but resigned in 1906 to accept appointment to the Georgia Supreme Court. Charles Howard Candler was named to replace him.)

Cecil R. Stockard said that his grandfather, Mr. Robinson, and Mr. Dobbs disagreed over the ever-increasing advertising budget. Mr. Dobbs was the more conservative of the two on the matter. Mr. Candler would let each have his say before the stockholders each year. Then, Mr. Stockard said, Mr. Candler would decide how much to spend.

During those heady days of steadily rising sales, Mr. Candler always saw to it that there was adequate stock to meet the demand, even if it meant working nights. This occurred often, Charles Howard Candler noted in the biography, because the plants were never sufficient to the demand. He recalled having, himself, to work nearly every night during the summers of 1907, 1908, and 1909, when his children were babies. "Fortunately," he said, recalling the spirit of those times, "our people were not a lot of clock watchers. Everyone was personally concerned for success of the enterprise; none ever expected or received premium pay for overtime, although it was Father's custom to give each employee a gold piece every Christmas."

Oh yes. Oh yes. But there is a thin note of greater disillusionment to come in the opening part of Asa Candler's address to stockholders on the great progress made during 1908. He started out: "When I wrote my first annual report in 1892, I thought all presidents of industrial corporations made reports in full detail to stockholders. Since then I have learned much. I now know that such reports are not often given to stockholders. I believe they are entitled to know . . . how well or bad their investments are being managed, and so we will have this full report. . . ."

But then, when he got into the full report, his words become vibrant and excited: "We have paid more for everything needed to do business on during the year than any previous year. Still we have done well. The secretary gives you in detail a report on advertising expenses and says: 'This is conclusive evidence that our methods and mediums of advertising have produced good results.' The traffic manager shows how great we have grown as distributors of one single article, 'Coca-Cola.' The sales manager comprehensively exhibits how carefully and well he deploys his corps of salesmen throughout the length and breadth of this great country. They sell 'Coca-Cola' everywhere that commerce profitably keeps busy the traders of America."

Advertising themes focused on women shopping and beautiful people playing games— two themes which remained in company promotion for decades.

History-making Coca-Cola Advertising and Promotion Campaign

The means of advertising had now, of course, to accommodate the bottled, as well as the soda-fountain, drink. Some ads urged bottled Coca-Cola alone. Some recommended either—"from a bottle, through a straw," with pictures of the bottle and the soda-fountain glass, or "at soda fountains, carbonated in bottles." The time came, too, in 1916, to proudly present in many photographs and drawings the distinctive new bottle. All the while, the bottlers were carrying out their own local promotions and advertising in towns and cities across the land. Under the contract with Mr. Thomas and Mr. Whitehead, the company subsidized bottler advertising at a rate based on the number of gallons each bottler used.

The advertising took a couple of new directions during the 1900s. The schizophrenic presentation, sometimes a remedy, sometimes a refreshment, ended at about the turn of the century. Mr. Dietz, in *Soda Pop*, speculated that it dawned on Mr. Candler there were far more healthy persons than ones ailing, causing him to concentrate his advertising on the more numerous class. There is another possibility: Mr. Candler is known to have suffered from sick headaches and dyspepsia (he was too busy to eat regularly or slowly) and was among the first regular customers of Dr. Pemberton's concoction. It might well be that after more than ten years of trying it and getting no relief for head or stomach, the good Mr. Candler abandoned the medicinal message in the interest of a credo strongly espoused by Mr. Dobbs—truth in advertising.

The other new direction was one of tone. The Massengale Advertising Agency of Atlanta handled all the vast and varied advertising the company did during most of the 1890s through 1904 when part of the account was transferred to the W. C. D'Arcy Agency. W. C. D'Arcy had sold the company streetcar card space previously (Coca-Cola started with $45 worth for three months in 1896 and by 1910 had them on "almost every streetcar in the United States, Cuba, and Canada," in Mr. Dobbs's words). Mr. Candler and Mr. Dobbs liked Bill D'Arcy's style and persuaded him to set up the agency in 1904. When it was two years old, they turned over nearly the full account to it. (Massengale continued, at Mr. Candler's behest, to place ads in religious publications and a few others until 1913.) Thus began an association of more than fifty years between the company and the D'Arcy agency which would see two different eras of ongoing, inspired promotion of Coca-Cola.

The Massengale ads were heavy on elegant men and women in splendid surroundings; the lithographic posters and calendars with these were works of high art. They were fine for the 1890s, but looked somehow dated in the modern 1900s. And what was to be made of the offering of the Coca-Cola sheet music (for ten cents in stamps), including the favorite hymn of President McKinley (just before his slaying), "Lead Kindly Light." Also available were "Ben Bolt," "Juanita," "The Palms," "Old Folks at Home," "My Old Kentucky Home," "Rock Me to Sleep," and the hymn that was to be sung on the decks when the *Titanic* went down, "Nearer My God to Thee"? Each was graced with a "very handsome lithographic title page in colors." The one for "Lead Kindly Light" had an elegant young woman daintily lifting the glass to her lips and said, "At fountains, in bottles."

The D'Arcy touch expressed itself in such things as much increased use of testimonials from sports figures ("Ty Cobb is at the bat—"; Jack Prince, "strongest bicycle rider who ever lived"). The pretty girls were still elegant in their long dresses, but appeared in more relaxed surroundings, as in a horse and buggy, a rowboat, playing tennis, at the beach. And the focus is on such figures as the "modern businessman" being refreshed ("lightens the day's worries") and the mother and daughter out shopping together.

We find, too, a vigorous tone, almost bordering on hard sell, in the early D'Arcy advertising copy that was not there before. A 1909 example: "Shopper and businessmen/the headline/tired people and thirsty people—nerve-worn and brain-weary people—people who just like to tickle the palate occasionally with

W. C. D'Arcy.

a delicious beverage—all classes, ages, sexes Drink Coca-Cola/The Satisfactory Beverage/Has more to it than wetness or sweetness. It relieves fatigue of brain, body and nerves; quenches the thirst as nothing else will; refreshes and pleases. GET THE GENUINE. Delicious—Wholesome—Thirst-Quenching Coca-Cola." (This copy is interesting too in being as close as the company was ever again to come to the old medicinal theme.)

During this period, Mr. D'Arcy often employed arrows in the ads, straight ones pointing to the trademark, curved ones that encircled the copy to point at the trademark. He almost appeared to be seeking to identify the rather blatantly phallic symbol with Coca-Cola, though it might very well be he was unconscious of the symbolic overtone.

The D'Arcy agency presided over Coca-Cola's first appearance in national magazines in 1904, and the presentation in 1912 of the first in a long, fetching line of bathing beauties in ads and on trays and calendars, the first one in a skirted suit with black stockings and beach shoes hiding her lower extremities.

Mr. Dobbs, in his 1908 magazine article, reviewed the printed media use following that first magazine ad in 1904. There were a few other magazine ads in 1904. In 1905, the company bought space in some Midwestern newspapers, with "very satisfactory results," and in a still small number of magazines. But in 1906, it was "a large user" of magazines. There was no way to measure results. But there was increased business over the country that year, so they would continue to be used. In 1908, the same copy was being used in newspaper and magazine ads, on the notion they would re-enforce one another.

Mr. Dobbs also pointed out that, by 1908, the company had splashed Coca-Cola painted signs on 2.5 million square feet of the walls of American buildings, and another ten thousand in Cuba and Canada—in every city in the three countries.

The incredible list of mediums (multimedia with a vengeance) employed in the 1890s grew even more in the 1900s, including eight-day clocks, celluloid novelties, paper napkins, matches, thermometers, door plates, pocketknives, decalcomanias, watch fobs, blotters, pencils, mirrors, and wagon umbrellas. By 1909, the last of the old oilcloth awning signs had come down, replaced by the much easier posted red-and-white or red-and-green metal signs. In 1910 alone, $10,000 worth of these became a familiar element of the land and cityscape over the nation. By 1914, the nation was posted with four hundred tons of them.

In that year, also, there appeared the first pictorial metal sign, showing "Betty," the calendar girl for that year and symbol, in the perfection of her look of wholesome, modest beauty, of the company's ideal for its pretty Coca-Cola girls.

In 1907, an inspired Coca-Cola employee, whose name has not been recorded, invented the festoon for the backboards of soda fountains, and these have followed changing styles of the years ever since. In addition to Charles Howard Candler's first window display early in the century, the first window sign with a space for a "privilege" message by the store's proprieter was painted in 1908. In the early 1920s, metal privilege panel signs were to appear.

Mr. Dobbs noted that there were ten thousand window displays in 1908, saying they not only appealed to consumers but also helped "cultivate the good will of dispensers." Another innovation was the cardboard cut-out for these displays; a most famous one was "the man on the grass," in 1909, sitting cross-legged, with a Coca-Cola glass to his lips and a Coca-Cola straw fan in his other hand. The next year a woman in the grass was added. The May 1909 *Coca-Cola Bottler* extolled the Man on the Grass: "When placed in a window, it is like going outside and grabbing customers by the collars and making them drink Coca-Cola. It costs less than 30 cents, looks like a dollar and a half." (Today, to collectors, it looks like and will bring at least $300.)

In 1908, the earliest of many animated billboards was erected alongside the Pennsylvania Railroad between Philadelphia and New York City. A D'Arcy creation, it depicted a young man (wearing the familiar white cap) drawing Coca-Cola from a crockery urn. Real water was used, flowing from a two-inch pipe running four hundred feet from a city main. Travelers by the many thousands saw this marvel out their train windows.

In 1909, a dirigible floated over Washington, D.C., with large Coca-Cola signs on its sides; and a lighter-than-air balloon giving free trips on the local bottler's behalf displayed the signs as it floated over Charleston, South Carolina.

For all of this, Mr. Dobbs, in his 1908 article, rated outdoor painted displays and streetcar cards more effective than any other media, including newspapers and magazines. "After all," he wrote, "advertising in its last analysis is getting your sign where the people can see it, as close as possible to the place where your goods are on sale."

The company was spending half a million dollars for advertising in 1908, more than the gross proceeds in 1900, Mr. Dobbs noted. And all of that advertising for a product that cost a nickel by a company that counted its profits "in fractions of a penny!" It was all made possible, Mr. Dobbs concluded with conviction, by keeping faith with the consumer, "claiming nothing for Coca-Cola that it did not do, no virtue that it did not have."

It is small wonder, considering the full panorama of Coca-Cola promotion in this era, that the drink was termed "the best advertised article in America" in 1909, and Mr. Dobbs was elected president of the Associated Advertising Clubs of America.

Advertising's Relationship to Sales

Why it was Mr. Dobbs, who was sales manager, and not Mr. Robinson, the advertising manager, is perhaps explained in a speech Mr. Dobbs made before the Kansas City Advertising Club in March 1909, setting out his philosophy of the relationship between sales and advertising. As quoted in the first issue of *The Coca-Cola Bottler*, Mr. Dobbs declared:

". . . No man who isn't at heart a salesman has any right to direct the advertising policy of any concern. As sales manager of the Coca-Cola Company, I travel approximately thirty thousand miles a year feeling the pulse of the country, carefully studying conditions, meeting the trade with our salesmen, seeing and studying their problems, and endeavoring to meet and know the difficulties they are up against. Once each year, the entire sales force is brought to the home office in Atlanta, and then we discuss the needs of our business, and the sales force make their requisitions on the department of advertising for what they think is best suited to the needs of their particular territory."

That sort of practical tying together of the closely related sales and advertising functions has not endured to this day of superspecialization on Madison Avenue, but it goes a long way toward explaining the excellence of the ads and strong sales growth while it lasted. It also suggests that more than a difference of opinion about the advertising budget existed between the bright young Mr. Dobbs and the older Mr. Robinson. He was not, except in a nominal way while associated with Dr. Pemberton, a salesman.

By 1913, salesmen did not make sales directly to retailers. As is done today, they called on the trade to encourage them to place orders with jobbers, mostly wholesale druggists. They also made themselves available to improve the soda fountain if needed, placed the point of sale signs, and found wall-sign locations. The customers looked forward toward the end of each year to seeing what the pretty girl on the new calendar would look like, one salesman, Ross Treseder, recalled, also noting that there were never enough Coca-Cola trays to keep up with the customers' need of them.*

The routes still followed the rail lines, and Mr. Treseder, with his trunkful of advertising and his report sheets in his handbag, plied the lines, staying often at night at a luxurious Harvey House for $3.50 or $4.00 American plan. His territory included gold towns in Colorado and copper towns in Arizona. Such places were thriving; "everybody seemed happy."

In his hometown of Denver, Mr. Treseder often saw Colonel William F. Cody, the famed Buffalo Bill, at the soda fountain of the popular A. G. Clarke Drug Company in the Albany Hotel. "He came in frequently and bought quinine and washed it down with Coca-Cola. He was my hero. Still is! A beautiful man! Long flowing white hair, and beard topped by a black sombrero hat, black cutaway coat, and black trousers tucked into the tops of highly polished black boots. He was really something." They were good days, traveling for the company. The sales staff was still small enough so that everyone knew everyone else. "There was a great feeling amongst the men and the ownership from Asa Candler down through the entire organization."

The Eighth "Home" of Coca-Cola

Meantime, back at headquarters business was so good that the seventh home built for all time had been outgrown after only eleven years, and a move was made in 1909 to the eighth—a blocky, three-story and basement building on Magnolia Street, a half block west of Marietta Street where it all started. It ac-

* Mr. Treseder's recollections of his years as a salesman and later advertising man are contained in an unpublished, bound document, entitled "As I Remember," in the Coca-Cola archives. It was written by Mr. Treseder at Wilbur Kurtz's request in 1972.

commodated another enlargement of the syrup-manufacturing equipment. There was plenty of room in the production area, Charles Howard Candler wrote in the *Thirty-three Years* manuscript, because as fast as barrels were filled, they were shipped. The company in 1912 bought out a bankrupt cooperage for $750 and manufactured its own barrels to augment the supply of secondhand whiskey barrels which could not keep up with the demand for Coca-Cola.

Atlanta's Candler Building

In only a few years, the Magnolia Street home was overcrowded. One of the other grand things Asa Candler had done back there in his heyday provided a temporary solution to the problem. This other grand thing had been the erection from 1904 to 1906 of the $2 million Candler Building in downtown Atlanta at the corner of Peachtree and Houston streets, a block north of the first Candler home of the company, 47 Peachtree. Atlanta, though it was beginning a development of downtown that has not ceased yet, had not seen the likes of the eighteen-story skyscraper. "As tall as the Candler Building" became a standard local comparison.

The faded grandeur of the Candler Building can be viewed today; it is one of the few buildings of the past to have escaped frenzied demolition for new construction in the continuing development of downtown Atlanta. The first three stories of the Candler Building are made of pretty, white Georgia marble, the remainder of terra cotta. Between the first and second floors on the front and side exteriors are elaborate carved panels representing the arts and sciences and early pioneer life in Georgia.

On the day of its opening, the local press told how great crowds of "elegantly gowned ladies" and "men whose attire showed their business standing" flocked in to see the marvels inside. These included in the central lobby busts of Mr. Candler's parents and of various famous Georgians. Brass, marble, and bronze details were everywhere about, with the Candler crest on all the interior hardware. The grand staircase had dolphins as a decorative motif. There were even a barbershop and baths, featuring a marble "plunge pool" six feet deep.

Among the early tenants of the Candler Building was the Merchants and Manufacturers Club which occupied the entire seventeenth floor. Charles Howard Candler in the *Thirty-three Years* manuscript wrote that the club was one of a number started in the city after Georgia passed a prohibition law in 1907, their main purpose "to keep those who wanted it supplied with spirituous liquors." Naturally, his father was "never very well pleased" to have such a tenant. When in 1913 the club, for whatever reason, ceased to exist, the offices of The Coca-Cola Company were moved from the cramped Magnolia Street quarters into the seventeenth floor of the Candler Building where they remained until the next new home was built at the site of today's headquarters on North Avenue.

Atlanta's Candler Building on the corner of Peachtree and Houston streets.

The Souring

The Candler Building, the development of Druid Hills, and the beginning in the 1900s by Mr. Candler of the many beneficences he was to bestow on Atlanta institutions were the grand things that his strong stewardship of the company had enabled him to do. But the souring had begun.

Charles Howard Candler sounded the sour note in one of those flourishes at the end of a speech at a company gathering: "Through wars and unfair competition, through depression and inflation, through regimentation and ruinous taxation, this extraordinary business, with ability and perseverance has conducted its honest industry with wisdom and for the betterment of the enterprise."

Coca-Cola Imitators and Legal Battles

One by one, the company did experience each of those vicissitudes he listed. No longer was it impervious to large events. First, the unfair competition. Through the 1900s and worse in the 1910s, the *imitations* proliferated. In 1916, there were 153 of them to be fought down in the courts, including Koca-Nola, Fig Cola, Candy Cola, Cold Cola, Gay Ola and Coca and Cola. The names down the years are a study in unethical ingenuity: Caro-Cola, Coca Kola, Kora-Nola, Kola-Nola, KoKola, Co Kola, King-Cola, Coke Ola, Kos-Kola, Toca-Cola, Sola Cola, Kel Kola (It Has the Kick), Kaw-Kola (Has the Kick) Dope, Ko-Co-Lema, to mention but the closest to the original. Sadly, Ed Venable, son of Willis, who once had part ownership of two thirds of the stock of the original item, turned up in 1907 as one of the incorporators of a Coca-Kola Company.

The similar problem of soda-fountain dispensers' palming off substitutes when people ordered Coca-Cola also increased. And there were various slanders. People continued to call it dope. A doctor in Virginia, in 1902, claimed one of his patients had been driven to suicide by Coca-Cola and tried to get the legislature to ban it. A man in North Carolina was reported to have swigged down a glassful and keeled over dead with acute indigestion. About this canard, *The Coca-Cola Bottler* commented: "This story reminds us of the druggist in West Philadelphia who for a number of years drank his Coca-Cola one-fourth Coca-Cola and three-fourths rye liquor, varying it with gin, rum, and other exhilarating beverages, according to the stock of his 'medicine case.' Whenever his wife would take him to task, he would tell her that he had been drinking Coca-Cola and she firmly believed that he died of the effect of too much Coca-Cola, when in reality, he died of the 'jimmies.'"

Such ongoing tribulations could be resolved, largely through the courts. But the biggest problem, that of the government seizure of the forty barrels and twenty kegs, was a source of much anxiety for the company's people, Asa Candler particularly, because, unlike most of the company's litigation, the outcome of this case was by no means certain, and on the outcome might hinge the very life of Coca-Cola as a product.

It was Charles Howard Candler, according to his own accounts, whom "one J. L. Lynch," secret agent for the Pure Food Department, approached on that gloomy day in October 1909, at the factory on Magnolia Street. Mr. Candler courteously showed this Mr. Lynch through the plant and explained the processes of the manufacture. Mr. Lynch took notes and was given several samples of finished Coca-Cola as well as a sample of caffeine. However, he was refused a sample of one of the ingredients, possibly 7X.

On the bases of Mr. Lynch's visit, the government seized the barrels and kegs and entered against the company a libel action which Charles Howard Candler flatly named "persecution at the hands of one Dr. Harvey W. Wiley," who was the director of the Pure Food Department. Charles Howard Candler in the biography also called him "overzealous" and "notoriety-seeking," adding that his father and associates were outraged over their government's "persecution" of the company. The Atlanta *Journal* thundered in an editorial about the case: "There is strong ground for suspecting that this entire agitation was incited by a muckracker, envious of honest men's success."

Interestingly enough, Dr. Orville May, the retired company chemist, was an employee of the food and drug regulation agency for a number of years before he joined Coca-Cola. He worked under Dr. Wiley and knew him well and put in a good word for this man whose name yet lives in infamy among Coca-Cola people. He said that Dr. Wiley was a man of utmost integrity who, in undertaking any action like that against Coca-Cola, operated on the conviction that something harmful was being offered the public rather than out of any personal or political motivation. He was an ardent foe of caffeine, and pushed the case against Coca-Cola diligently.

Dr. May tells an interesting tale about Dr. Wiley. Among the ingredients, other than caffeine, he was dead-set against Americans swallowing was saccharin (which would in our own time come to cause trouble for the company with the government). Dr. Wiley was a confidant of President Theodore Roosevelt and, as Dr. May's story has it, the President seemed in a mellow mood during one discussion, so Dr. Wiley thought it an opportune time to suggest an all-out drive to rid the food industry of saccharin. Teddy Roosevelt's head jerked and eyes flashed. "What say?" he demanded. "Saccharin?"

"Yes," Dr. Wiley replied. "It's very dangerous."

"Don't say that, Wiley. Don't say that," Teddy Roosevelt sputtered. "I don't want to hear you mention that again. Saccharin is a wonderful thing, a fine thing. I've been using it eight years." And that was the end of that.

The brunt of the government's case against Coca-Cola was the caffeine content, with the charge that it was both an added ingredient, forbidden by the pure food law, and, worse, harmful to the public. The company of course contended that caffeine was an integral part of the distinctive taste and argued that there was less of it in Coca-Cola than in your regular cup of coffee or tea. Some have suggested that Dr. Wiley's persistent but unsuccessful efforts in the case to learn the secret formula, the ingredients of Merchandise 7X, were based on a suspicion that something worse than caffeine—the old cocaine specter—was in there too.

Archivist Kurtz points out that, regardless of what might have been Dr. Wiley's motivation, a victory against such a big boy on the commercial block as Coca-Cola would have set his new agency off to an excellent start in the public eye.

The case of *The United States* v. *40 Barrels and 20 Kegs of Coca-Cola* went on trial in Chattanooga on March 13, 1911. The company won that round but had to pay court costs. (In all, the case was to cost the company $85,157.62, according to the biography.) Appeals dragged on through the courts until 1916 when the U. S. Supreme Court ordered the case back to the original lower court for proceedings to start all over again. By this time, Dr. Wiley had departed the regulatory department, and the government had lost interest in the case. A settlement was reached in 1918.

That sword hanging overhead was, for more than ten years, "an annoyance and mental disturbance" to Asa Candler and his associates, Charles Howard Candler wrote in the *Thirty-three Years* manuscript, "very trying" for all. At one point, in 1916, a plan was drawn up to completely reorganize the company on the expectation that the suit would be lost. The plan though was never accepted by the directors.

The Causes Behind Asa Candler's Abandonment of Coca-Cola

Certainly the case was one of the reasons that Asa Candler came to his sad decision to quit the company he had loved. The decision had to have been difficult and heart-rending for him. As early as 1908, he had spoken of ending the burden of business, and letting son Charles Howard take it on, the biography tells us. Such talk was in sad contrast to the good, grand spirit of Asa Candler in 1900 when, on bidding farewell to Charles Howard embarking on a pleasure trip to Europe, he told his son to keep his eye peeled for possible markets, and gave the same instructions to Asa, Jr., when he set off for the Orient. ". . . Together, we may map out for great conquests," the father exulted to his sons.

The biography tells us another reason for the gloom that came upon Asa Candler and his eventual decision to abandon the company. Noting Frank M. Robinson's retirement in 1914 (the loss of his magic touch), Charles Howard Candler wrote: "There is no doubt in my mind that the dissolution of the long-time and affectionate partnership between Mr. Robinson and my father had a definite part in Father's determination to discontinue his active official relationship with the company only two years later. . . ."

Charles Howard Candler went into great detail in the biography on the one further reason for his father's decision. "Father," he began sadly, "severed his official identification with the company at the 1916 meeting, after twenty-four years' service at its helm, directing its affairs and identifying its phenomenal progress with his own dominant personality. His announced reason for discontinuing as an officer was to enable him to give all his time to the mayoralty of Atlanta. While this undoubtedly had a bearing upon his decision, it is also true that he was discouraged and concerned for the future prosperity and growth of the company. He felt that he could no longer conduct his business in the way he believed it should be conducted to assure its best progress and to realize its potential greatness."

Specifically, what was so bothering Asa Candler was "federal legislation adverse to the accumulation of surplus in excess of the amount necessary for

Asa Griggs Candler, owner and president of Coca-Cola from 1892 to 1916.

profitable and safe conduct of our particular business." The old practice of plowing the profits back into the company was no longer possible. During the time of increasing prosperity through the 1900s and into the 1910s, Mr. Candler had been investing heavily in real estate with company funds and money of his own. In addition to the Candler Building, he built another with the same name in New York City, and had others erected in a dozen other cities, most of them

Coca-Cola syrup plants and offices, but with other space in them to lease. There were considerable landholdings in Atlanta and elsewhere. Mr. Candler was to continue to make some real estate investments after his retirement.

In 1915, though, the profits couldn't be plowed back any more, and the $5 million surplus had to be distributed among stockholders that year. Wrote Charles Howard Candler in the biography: "When this forced liquidation of the bulk of the assets which he had wisely and carefully accumulated against possible hard times (he had predicted an early war upon his return from Europe in the summer of 1913) was accomplished, he was ready to quit trying to make money. . . ."

He would, Charles Howard Candler went on, sadness giving way to some of the bitterness that stirred his father's soul, relinquish direction of the business to others, hoping they would further succeed "despite what he considered to be bureaucratic federal restrictions upon a concern which, managed by capable executives, was trying to market a good and popular product."

Mr. Candler believed very strongly that the only way an expanding economy could flourish was by the constant reinvestment of accumulated profits, and he deplored a "share the wealth" philosophy that prevented this and hamstrung business development. "To those who argued that new capital should be borrowed from the public to provide for expansion of business, Father replied that to borrow against potential profits . . . is speculation. Permission by bureaucracy to use profits in retiring debt, he felt, was an obviously roundabout and expensive method of making profitable use of earnings. . . ."

Asa Candler had somehow found an analogy in the Scriptures and often remarked, his son wrote, "that Moses, against his better judgment, had tried such a system in Biblical times and saw it fail to accomplish what the Israelites sought." The argument against the new tax system was an abstruse one and, more than anything else, shows an inflexible inability to change with the times. But Asa Candler, in his concern about federal bureaucracy, proved himself once more ahead of his time, raising back then an issue that was to have burning relevance in our own time.

Curtailment of Company Growth by World War I

And—despite his retirement—Mr. Candler's spirit, his instinct from the past for the gentlemanly thing to do, expressed itself in the company's immediate response to the sugar shortage caused by World War I. W. C. Hughes, Federal Food Administrator, is quoted in the biography: "As soon as Mr. [Herbert] Hoover's ruling [on sugar] went into effect, the Coca-Cola people went to Washington and saw the food officials and found out definitely what Mr. Hoover wanted them to do, and then they went and did exactly as requested. Their attitude was so sincere and their endeavors so patriotic that the food administration pointed to them as an ideally patriotic firm."

What Mr. Hoover wanted them to do was get along on half the sugar they had used the year before. They resolved not to dilute quality, but did experiment with corn syrup, glucose, and invert sugar to make syrup "without to a noticeable extent . . . affecting the flavor," Charles Howard Candler wrote in the *Thirty-three Years* manuscript. Nonetheless, the company couldn't keep up with the increasing demand for Coca-Cola and had to ration syrup to its customers.

Advertising was curtailed too, only seven ads appearing in magazines during 1918; two had to do with the sugar shortage. One set out Mr. Hoover's dictum and asked in the name of "common justice" that readers insist on genuine Coca-Cola. Another told how Coca-Cola was doing its bit toward "Making a Soldier of Sugar."

Another wartime shortage brought forth from Charles Howard Candler a touch of magic akin to Mr. Robinson's, an invention born of necessity, like unto the fortuitous evolvement of the franchise system for bottlers. The company was notified in 1918 by the government that since its product was nonessential to the war effort, it could no longer use coal. This was a more serious hindrance than the sugar shortage, since coal was what had always been used since Dr. Pemberton's kettle to heat the sugar-and-water base of the syrup.

In the *Thirty-three Years* manuscript, Charles Howard Candler tells how he worried and pondered over the problem and, somehow, his mind went to the way that one would stir sugar in the many beaded glasses of iced tea consumed during Atlanta's hot summers. If water and sugar could be satisfactorily blended when ice cold, why not . . . ?

An advertisement in the Atlanta *Constitution* provided the further inspiration he needed. It was for the hand-cranked Dazey glass butter churn, on sale at King Hardware Company. Charles Howard Candler went to that store, operated by one of his father's oldest friends, George E. King, and bought one of those Dazey churns and took it home to try it out. He put in the sugar and water and watched the four blades stir with "extremely vigorous agitation, throwing the liquid outward and upward against the sides and top of the churn." Eureka! Without benefit of heat, the sugar and water coagulated. Charles Howard Candler was "really amazed" at how quickly it was done. He rigged up the company kettles with a device to allow compressed air to provide the extremely vigorous agitation needed to mix cold water and sugar, and the production of syrup went on uninterrupted.

Later, enameled steel tanks, engineered to do the stirring more efficiently with propellers, were installed in the factory. The effect was like that when two men with paddles, at either end of the tank, would push the mixture toward one another in the olden days at Ivy and Wheat streets.

The process saved on fuel cost, eliminated the need for operation and upkeep of the boiler, and saved considerable time since it eliminated the twenty-four- to thirty-six-hour cooling period required by the old method.

It was Charles Howard Candler's shining hour in the waning days of the Candler era of Coca-Cola. The process, as he dreamed it up and designed it, is still in use today.

Ernest W. Woodruff, organizer of the purchase of The Coca-Cola Company from Asa Candler's heirs in 1919 for $25 million and father of the company's major figure, Robert W. Woodruff.

The Ernest Woodruff Consortium Buys Coca-Cola from the Candler Heirs

"Victory's Reward Means Volume Restored," The Coca-Cola Company triumphantly announced in its 1919 advertising. Sugar rationing was over, and production immediately zoomed back to its old, constantly increasing pace. In 1920, gross sales amounted to $32 million.

That was, of course, after the biggest single change had occurred in the life of Coca-Cola since Dr. Pemberton relinquished his ownership—the sale of the company to Ernest Woodruff's consortium.

The Trust Company of Georgia (from then on to be known as the Coca-Cola bank), the Chase National Bank, and the Guaranty Trust Company, both of New York City, were main members of the consortium. Those from whom it bought numbered Charles Howard Candler, Asa Candler, Jr., Walter T. Candler, William Candler, and Mrs. Henry C. Heinz, the Candler children, Judge John S. Candler, the brother, and Mr. Dobbs, Mr. Robinson, and Samuel L. Willard of the company.

George Woodruff recalls that his father, Ernest, kept his role in the purchase a secret from Mr. Candler until the sale was consummated. Mr. Woodruff wasn't sure why. Maybe it was out of deference to Mr. Candler's feelings. The two men had been neighbors and friends for years.

None of those who agreed to the sale told Mr. Candler about it in advance. He was not consulted about this most important moment in the history of the company he had founded and built. Charles Howard Candler does not tell us in any of his writings why this was so. Perhaps, though it was, again, out of deference to Mr. Candler's feelings. His beloved wife, Lizzie, had died in February before the company was sold in September. Asa Candler was overcome with grief all that year, indeed mourned after her the remaining years of his life.

Charles Howard Candler merely commented in the biography that his father was "shocked" and "chagrined" that his old associates and the kin to whom he had given the company did not consult him. Asa Candler's only comment about the whole thing, given to a reporter out west where he was traveling, was: "When I gave them . . . the business, it was theirs. They sold out a big share for a fancy price. I wouldn't have done that, but they did, and from a sales standpoint, they drove a pretty keen bargain."

Coca-Cola's magic life, under new ownership and soon a new, strong leader as remarkable in his way as Asa Candler had been in his, was to continue to be one of unprecedented success, one of victory after victory for those of the South's heritage of defeat who were associated with it. But Asa Candler's remaining years were in the southern tradition of defeat. His wife taken from him, his beloved company in the hands of others, he wandered the earth lonely and grieved, writing plaintive, sometimes peevish, letters from Europe or New York or California to his sons. The syrup of life by now had, for him, entirely soured.

V

Why Did Asa Candler Give Away His Coca-Cola Empire?

Asa Candler died on March 12, 1929, at the age of seventy-eight. He had been confined for several months at Wesley Memorial Hospital, an institution he had heavily endowed. From the window of his hospital room before death took him, he could look out on the Emory University campus which would not have existed at all had it not been for his beneficences. Perhaps that gave him comfort, knowing as he probably did that he was near the end of the long drama of his life.

He had moved Coca-Cola during three decades—the years of his prime—to the zenith of success before the souring set in. Charles Howard Candler told us the external causes—the retirement of Mr. Robinson, the Food and Drug case, the new tax laws. But these external things do not explain why Mr. Candler should have become so bitter or disillusioned or maybe even fearful as to give away the company he had founded and end the work that he had loved, the fulfillment he once found sitting on those crates and barrels across the land, talking Coca-Cola. What were the forces within that caused Mr. Candler to lose the grip he had held on the past and the present which had enabled his success? Maybe some of the answer might be found in looking more closely at his formative years back there when the South's past was confronted with the clamor and bustle of late nineteenth-century modernism.

The Candler Family Background

Asa Griggs Candler was born on December 30, 1851, on a farm near Villa Rica, Georgia, to Samuel and Martha Beall Candler. There were seven other children in the farm family, three of them girls.

Candlers had been in Georgia since the 1700s, according to the biography, and they were substantial citizens, landholders, slaveholders. For all of that, Asa's father, Samuel Candler, seems to have been something of an adventurer. He served for some time as a sheriff, was a member of the Georgia legislature, and prospected for gold (unsuccessfully) in west Georgia before settling down in Villa Rica as a farmer and merchant. The farm was small by the day's standards; it worked only a few slaves.

Samuel Candler, according to the biography, "passed on to his children a strong sense of honor and a strong predilection for standing upon their own convictions, whether they happened to be popular or not." As a delegate from Georgia to the 1860 National Democratic Convention in Charleston, South Carolina, he was one of a minority of ten (against twenty-six) who voted no to the delegation's seceding from the party. He had no formal education beyond the elementary grades, but culture was present in his home, and until the Civil War wiped him out financially, he offered his children most advantages.

A friend of the Candler family in Villa Rica is quoted in the biography as saying, "There was never a man with better knowledge of how to raise children than Sam Candler, who raised a houseful and kept them all at work. . . . They had time to learn and they could find play in work. Even on Saturdays, when other boys would be idle, the Candler boys were doing something."

From all accounts, Martha Beall Candler fit Stephen Vincent Benét's ideal of southern womanhood for her time, " slightly made and as hard to break as a rapier blade." She was both deeply religious and culturally inclined and imparted these gentling influences to her children. Asa Candler worshiped her to the day she died. She was also capable of facing Union soldiers down when they approached her farm home and threatened to shoot her head off.

There were morning and evening prayers in the farm home from the English Book of Prayer. The Candler daughters would take turns playing the piano while all the family sang hymns. Martha Beall Candler took her children to Sunday school at the Primitive Baptist Church until Samuel Candler, late in life for such an act, joined the Methodist Church to which the rest of the family followed him.

If all of this—the strongly masculine, hard taskmaster, farmer-merchant father; the gentle, yet strong-spirited mother who instilled religion deeply in her young—has a more than slight resemblance to another Georgia farm family a century later near the town of Plains, there are further parallels.

Just as the 1930s Depression meant hard times for the previously well-off

Carter family, the aftermath of the Civil War saw the Candler family in virtual poverty. Because of this and out of principle, Sam Candler impressed strongly on his young the value of money and the virtue of hard, honest labor. The only spending money his children had, they earned. Jimmy Carter, we are told, sold peanuts as a small boy to get his spending money. Asa Candler sold pins which he bought cheap in Atlanta and sold dear in the country. One day, a mink intruded on the Candler household and young Asa caught it, killed it and skinned it, and then took the pelt to Atlanta where it brought one dollar. Thereafter, he became a trapper and encouraged other youngsters to set lines while he served as commissioned middleman in the sales.

From an early age, Asa Candler wanted to be a physician. As a boy, he would concoct imaginary potents, and then try to treat sick birds and animals. He got through the fourth grade in a private school (there being no public ones) before the Civil War started. The school was closed during the war years, and Martha Beall Candler instructed her children as best as she could at home, continuing to do so in the impoverished years afterward. Finally when young Asa was fifteen, he had accumulated one hundred dollars from his enterprises and was enabled to attend high school for a year in Huntsville, Alabama, where he lived with a married sister.

After that, with still the dream of medicine in his mind, Asa Candler apprenticed himself to two physicians who owned a drugstore in Cartersville, Georgia. He was man of all work in the store. Nights, he taught himself Latin and Greek and pored over medical books. He was self-taught in chemistry, too, and applied what he learned to compounding prescriptions, in the process learning pharmacy in the drugstore.

Shortly before he was twenty-one (in 1872), the dream of medicine had died. He wrote to the man after whom he was named and who had been for a short time his childhood tutor—Dr. Asa Griggs—asking assistance in getting a job as a pharmacist in some place larger than Cartersville. Not merely the reality of his financial and educational limitations prompted his decision. He wrote in the letter: "I went in at first . . . with a view of becoming a physician but have now almost given out the idea. The country has enough without they were better. Besides I think there is more money to be made as a druggist than as a physician and I know it can be done with a great deal less trouble of soul and body." Evidently Dr. Griggs was no help to him, and it was not until the next year that Asa Candler marched into Atlanta in his home-made suit to begin his Horatio Alger career there.

By the time he had reached manhood, Asa Candler had thus been thoroughly familiarized with the South's legacy of defeat—in the war, in the deprivation after the war, and, maybe most of all, in the personal loss of the profession he had chosen. He had come close, once, as a youngster on the farm, to the ultimate defeat of death. He was riding on a hay wagon and, boylike, got himself up on top of the high load—and fell off. He landed under the wagon. One of its wheels ran over his head—fortunately not crushing it, but leaving him deaf in one ear. It was an early-in-life lesson against hubris.

His father's intimacy with defeat continued; he was never able to recoup his fortunes. Young Asa had to interrupt his promising career (he was already chief clerk in Mr. Howard's drugstore) in its first year to return to Villa Rica and get the family farm fit to be sold after his father's death. It took him a year.

But Asa Candler was also, starting out, well grounded in the nobler traditions of the South. He got from his older brothers and other kinsmen the gallantry, the mistaken idealism, and the belief of a Confederate soldier. Of those, the capacity to believe in a cause was the strongest in him. The whole story of what he did with a mixture of mainly sugar and water is that of his unshakable belief in the product, pouring his money and his being into its promotion. "Many instances have demonstrated that he was completely sold on Coca-Cola," Charles Howard Candler wrote in the biography. "He believed in it with an almost mystical faith."

From his mother, Asa Candler had got the South's deep religious fervor and also its notions of gentility and culture. Such were the things out of the past that he blended in his soul with the capacity for hard work he had got from his father, and the streak of acquisitiveness he had showed early in his boyhood. These attributes he took with him to hustling, bustling, modernizing Atlanta, and we know the drama of unbounded, uncharacteristic southern success that followed.

The same combination of heritage and genes possessed by other of Sam Candler's progeny produced similar, if less spectacular, successes. Of the brothers, there was Warren, the bishop and president of Emory University; Milton who was elected to Congress from Georgia; Ezekiel who earned the same honor in Mississippi, and John, the state Supreme Court justice. A cousin of theirs, Allen Candler, was a distinguished historian who won election as governor of Georgia.

How Business Associates Viewed Asa Candler

We get insights into how Asa Candler built his particular success from views of him at the helm of the company, as the boss. An early Coca-Cola salesman, later a successful businessman elsewhere, had this to say in a letter to Charles Howard Candler quoted in the biography: "The Coca-Cola Company did not pay any large salaries in those early days, but your father made us feel that each one was an important cog in the business and we worked in friendly rivalry like a large, happy family to keep the sales of Coca-Cola growing." As a person, Mr. Candler was readily approachable, very human, with a fine sense of humor. He "accepted his success in humility."

And he instilled in his salesmen this psychologically sound credo: "Sell the enterprise to yourself; sell yourself to your employer; sell the enterprise to the public. You must be convinced that you have something valuable to sell which the public needs and wants. Convince others of this and you have not only made a sale, but created a continuing source of business." Another dictum to his salesmen: "To sell is good, but to collect is better."

The tradition of low pay in the early days continued through all the Candler era. Archivist Kurtz said he had always heard that Mr. Candler thought no man was worth more than $5,000 a year, which was not much even in his day. Mr. Kurtz chuckled, too, over the story that Mr. Candler always began sales or business meetings with a prayer which added to the anguish of those on the force suffering on a particular morning with a hangover.

There was a tradition, too, not entirely gone from the company, even in today's hardnosed world of business, of kindness to employees, respect for their humanity. The biography tells of a young salesman who was having a bad year due, he would report to the home office, to frequent onsets of illness. Mr. Candler grew suspicious and undertook a discreet investigation through letters to acquaintances of the salesman. Then he sat down and wrote to the young man telling of answers he got to letters of inquiry: ". . . I am sure from the letters that you have been on *sprees* to the detriment of the Coca-Cola Company's good name. I am sure that you know such conduct was unbecoming." Reminding his errant reader that he knew the personal habits and moral conduct expected of him, Mr. Candler continued: "Now, I don't want you to discontinue with this company, but I do insist that you discontinue a habit that will *ruin you*. Write me as you would *your* best friend. . . ."

It was a terrible letter to receive and most certainly the epitome of old-time paternalism in commerce. But Mr. Candler was true to his word. He suspended the fellow, but did not fire him. And eight years later, Charles Howard Candler assures us, the man told him the incident had "inspired him to live a proper life." He was by then in a position of trust at a bank.

The unsigned masterpiece of an article in *Fortune*, in July 1931, gives yet another view of Mr. Candler at the helm, this toward the souring time at the end: "At executive conferences old Asa Candler, able but conservative, would listen to some proposed change, some suggested expansion, and then, with his eyes gleaming behind steel-rimmed spectacles, and his thin, narrow mouth thinner and narrower than ever,* remark: 'I vote 479 shares [out of 500 shares outstanding] against that. . . .' His remark concluded all discussion." The biography tells how through his career, Mr. Candler would get angry at letters addressed to him as Asa *Chandler*, sometimes throwing them away without opening them.

Asa Candler at Home

In his home life, Asa Candler revealed other aspects of his character. We see him in impotent rage at a pony he owned named Frank who would allow only women to touch or work him. We see, too, his tender devotion to his good

---

* No masterpiece is without its flaw. Mr. Candler, as his portraits show, had a quite broad, turned-down mouth.

wife, Lizzie, who combined much the same traits of gentleness and strength that his mother had. He would come home of an evening to Inman Park weary and sick with one of his headaches, and she would have him lean back in an easy chair and soothe his head with wet towels.

There were prayer and the reading of the Scripture every morning at breakfast. When once, one of the boys accused another of not closing his eyes during the prayer, Father Asa demanded: "How do you know?"

Asa Candler loved for his family to gather around the piano to sing hymns and songs of the olden days. In his last and most splendid home on Ponce de Leon, called Callan Castle after a supposed ancestor's estate in Scotland, they had a pipe organ equipped to play rolled music. He and Lizzie preferred listening to it over going to fancy concerts. For reading, Asa Candler loved the Bible, which he accepted literally, Shakespeare, and biographies, particularly of Georgians and Southerners.

He was a splendid Victorian father. When two of his boys each expressed a hope for a set of tools one Christmas, Asa Candler bought one set for them to share, and then wouldn't let them touch the tools on Christmas Day because it had fallen on the Sabbath, when all work was forbidden. When Charles Howard Candler was off at college, he had to turn in expense accounts of his spendings. The relationship was as "impersonal" as between employer and employee. This was not frugality, Charles Howard Candler wrote, so much as an effort to pass on his own father's lessons of the value of a dollar. Charles Howard Candler had to execute a promissory note to receive fifteen hundred dollars for medical

The Asa Candler family in 1895. Left to right, bottom row, William, Asa, Walter, Lucy, and Lizzie, Asa's wife. Top row, Charles Howard and Asa Griggs, Jr.

COURTESY OF THE
ATLANTA HISTORICAL
SOCIETY

COURTESY OF THE ATLANTA HISTORICAL SOCIETY

Atlanta, 1895. Asa Candler's neighborhood on Edgewood Avenue in Inman Park.

school. He retired it some time after his marriage. In a letter to one of his sons, Asa Candler urged on him the virtues of honesty and integrity, reminding him that "God, who loves us all, sees you every minute, everywhere."

In attitudes he expressed about his sons' lifework, Asa Candler revealed a certain ambiguity of attitude about his own. He often said, with pride, that his sons would never have to beg for a job the way he did when he came to Atlanta. When Coca-Cola was ready to begin taking off in 1889, he wrote to Asa: "I do not care for either you or your brother to permanently engage with the Coca-Cola Company." The same year, he told Charles Howard not to limit his usefulness "to the narrow compass of a five-cent soda fountain beverage." When Charles Howard was pursuing medicine, Mr. Candler wrote him: "I have thought it wise not to involve your life in a mere money-getting machine."

Later, of course, Asa Candler would hold the company entirely worthy of his sons' dedicating their lives to it. But, Charles Howard Candler tells us in the biography, "he saw in his children the great hope for realization of his own dreams of helping to build a better world. . . . His ambition for us far outreached the mere accumulation of wealth—in fact there is reason to believe that *he felt wealth was a dangerous thing.*† Certainly he knew that it was a grave responsibility."

Perhaps the ambivalence of attitude toward his work was no more than an expression of an Old-South notion that engaging in business was dishonorable and ungentlemanly. On one occasion Asa Candler said, almost defensively, ". . . Commerce is not the selfish and groveling thing which many esteem it."

† Italics added.

The Philanthropist

During the years of grand, unsoured success, Mr. Candler started divesting himself of some of the grave responsibility of his wealth. He began by buying for $1 million the land on which to locate Emory University and, in all, gave some $8 million to the school and its hospital.

The biography suggests that these gifts to an educational institution were prompted by Mr. Candler's own missed opportunities for schooling. But the immediate cause for Emory's creation in 1914 was a clash between one of those lingering traditions of the South's past, its old-time religion, and a phenomenon of modernism, the privately financed foundation. Vanderbilt University in Nashville, Tenneessee, long supported by the Methodist Church South and its main theology school, had fallen into the hands of the Carnegie Foundation and had broken off its ties to Methodism. Emory was created to take its place.

Mr. Candler stood clearly on the side of the Old South's religion, writing to brother Bishop Candler, in 1914, words that are not without relevancy for much world history that has since transpired: "In my opinion the education which sharpens and strengthens the mental faculties without at the same time invigorating the moral powers and inspiring the religious life is a curse rather than a blessing to men; creating dangerous ambitions and arousing selfish passions faster than it supplies restraints upon these lawless tendencies in human nature; stimulating into activity more of the things by which men are tempted to wrong than it quickens the powers by which temptation is resisted with success."

Mr. Candler on several instances tried to use his wealth to prevent economic disasters befalling his fellow citizens. In 1907, when a real estate panic threatened Atlanta, he averted it by buying a million dollars' worth of homes at prepanic prices. Then he sold the homes to people of moderate income for 10 per cent down and one hundred payments at quite low interest—a model of what the Federal Housing Authority would start doing twenty years later.

When World War I sent cotton prices tumbling in 1914 and bales were piled up unsold over the South, Mr. Candler, through his Central Bank and Trust Corporation, offered to lend money for low interest on cotton at the rate of six cents a pound. He would provide warehouse space to store the cotton until the prices rose. He built a warehouse covering forty acres to put the plan into operation. Though, as George B. Tindall notes in *The Emergence of the New South, 1913–1945*, the plan wasn't quite the panacea that Atlanta boosters back then claimed, it did alleviate the situation some.

The wealth created by Coca-Cola and the bottling plants was a healthy influence on an unhealthy economy. That tradition, of course, continues today (the South is yet the nation's poorest region), as does the one Mr. Candler established of generous acts of philanthropy, carried to the ultimate by Robert W. Woodruff.

Asa Candler with Chamber of Commerce officials meeting the first train of the Atlanta, Birmingham, and Atlantic Railroad, June 19, 1908.

Asa Candler started one other tradition that continues today—an active role by The Coca-Cola Company, and its top officials, in Atlanta's civic and governmental affairs.

One instance of this was when he served as president of the Atlanta Chamber of Commerce in 1908, building its treasury for boosterism high. In this capacity, he personally greeted President William H. Taft, when that dignitary visited Atlanta, and served as toastmaster at the elaborate banquet given in his honor.

The following year, Mr. Candler organized the Atlanta Automobile Association, drawing for membership on the owners of the nine thousand cars then being operated in the city. Next, he set up, under sponsorship of the AAA, an Atlanta Automobile Show that was hailed as one of the best ever anywhere. For the show, he bought three hundred acres of land near Hapeville (which was later to be used for another mode of transportation as the Atlanta-owned airport, Candler Field, and is now a part of the Atlanta-Hartsfield International Air Terminal).

On display at the auto show were cars from Cadillac, Oldsmobile, Stoddard-Dayton, Maxwell, Pierce-Arrow, Franklin, Peerless, Brush, Austin, Reo, Locomobile, White Star, Mora, F. A. L. Waverley, Black, and Rapid. Arthur Chevrolet, Louis Strong, and Barney Oldfield were among participants in daily races which set new speed records.

The show Mr. Candler put on demonstrated to "the most skeptical citizens that the automobile was here to stay," wrote Herbert T. Jenkins, retired police chief of Atlanta, in his book, *Atlanta and the Automobile* (Emory University, 1977). And Mr. Candler showed himself thoroughly modern and go-getting in his attitude toward the automobile. Those were the fine old times before the souring, during which he and Lizzie made the grand tour of Europe, Mr. Candler writing his sons glowing letters about the marvels he was seeing.

Mayor of Atlanta

Asa Candler's greatest performance of civic duty was when he offered himself for the office of mayor of Atlanta in 1916. He was a reform candidate at a time when the city was near bankruptcy and its police were considered corrupt. Here was a millionaire making stump speeches by torchlight every night for a $4,000-a-year job. He was to carry every ward in yet one more overwhelming success—but by then the souring had set in. Taking a brief rest from the campaign at Mount Clemens, Michigan, he wrote to Charles Howard on August 2, 1916: "It was nothing less than calamity that befell me when Atlanta men forced the mayoralty candidacy on me but I'll go through with it if they keep up their efforts. I'll be mayor with my city financially and moraly [sic.] bankrupt."

Go through with it, he did, stressing fiscal responsibility and morality in government, in another parallel to Jimmy Carter. He tried unsuccessfully to get the aldermen to cut his salary as mayor down to $2,500, but was able to cut the pay of city employees considerably. During his term, a holocaust cut a swath down the Atlanta street known as Boulevard and threatened to take the whole northeast section. In the aftermath, Mayor Candler motorized the fire department and augmented the water system with $265,000 worth of pumps out of his own pocket in order to have more water to fight fire.

The Atlanta *Journal* described a sort of shabby grand moment of his mayoralty, when on December 6, 1917, he was so inspired by the preaching of Billy Sunday that he got up and led a large group of city employees down the sawdust trail to shake the evangelist's hand.

While he was mayor, too, in 1917, the Candler family paid $67,000 in city taxes, *12 per cent of the total digest.*

Through those years of the souring, Asa Candler was to make pronouncements that gave no hint of the anguish in his soul.

Pleading for money for Methodist missions, he espoused a form of internationalism in 1915: "The wealth of America must, by its very nature, curse our own land or bless all other nations. . . . Either good or bad—with it we must save the world or destroy ourselves."

Speaking to Atlanta realtors in 1913, he called for national unity: "If, while we grow wealthy, we do also grow wise and noble, under these bright southern skies will be wrought out a civilization unprecedented in the annals of his-

tory. . . ." In another address, he declared: "Our section has a part in the
united life and government of this great nation. For many years we have been
far too disposed to count ourselves out of its history and its mission. . . . We
may justly claim our place in the Union, not as a matter of sufferance, but as a
matter of right, and we should cultivate a profound sense of responsibility for
its welfare."

And in 1917, he cast his lot with the common man: "The 'Common
Wealth' is the 'Common People.'"

They were fine words and noble sentiments, reflecting the maturity of
judgment Asa Candler had come to even as he rose to business success. But the
success soured within him and we are not yet at an understanding of why. In
1907, he had $30 million to put behind the cotton-loan scheme. Even consider-
ing all the new taxation that came, he and his company still had enormous resources to battle the vicissitudes besetting them. Why did he abandon the fight?

Little in the remainder of his history sheds much light. The July 1931 *Fortune* article made this brief comment on the last years: "Mr. Candler then withdrew himself from Coca-Cola, devoting himself to charitable and personal enterprises which, however interesting, have little place in the present discussion."
Would that the personal ones did not in this one. During one of those years
spent lost and wandering, grieving for his Lizzie and the company he had
thrown away, Asa Candler was to know the humiliation of a widely publicized
breach of promise suit. There were lesser missteps. Of those last years, Charles
Howard Candler had only a few words in the biography.

"The decade after my mother died was a period of tragic errors piled on
tragic mistakes—mistakes which should not have been made and against which
Father knew how to guard, temptation to which he should not have yielded but
which seemed to offer, perhaps, some solace in the gulf of loneliness and lassi-
tude into which he felt himself plunged.

"That he was sick in mind, soul, and body is a charitable justification for
the weakness which caused him to suffer so much mental, spiritual, and physical
anguish during those last years. Certainly they were years from the life of a
different man, completely out of character with the buoyant courage and the
clear faith of the fruitful days that had gone before."

Daddy Asa's Death

Asa Candler did find a second wife six years before his death. He was wed
in 1923 to Mrs. May Little Ragin, a widow whom he had known when she
worked as a stenographer in the Candler Building. We may hope he found
peace, happiness in this marriage. In that same year, grateful Atlanta citizens
held a gala dinner at the Piedmont Driving Club at which he was the guest of
honor as "First Citizen of Atlanta." May that, too, have comforted him.

When death came, the city of Atlanta declared a day of official mourning.
The best citizens attended the funeral whose time and place Asa Candler had set

out in his will. The local newspapers eulogized him. (Not so the Hamilton [Kansas] *World* which commented: "In dying Daddy Asa is at least free from women who chased him for his money. They can't follow him across the big ditch.") In Atlanta, to this day, with a street and park called after him, Asa Candler's name is honored. He is remembered for the grandness of his success, not the sour end to his days.

What happened? Asa Candler put together from the best parts of his southern tradition and the more honorable motives of modernist big business the beginnings of one of the most successful companies in the history of the world. But his own life soured. Maybe the answer simply lies in the other part of his southern heritage—the long, sad, tradition of defeat. From the evidence of what we know of his life and character, we might well conclude that Asa Candler just couldn't stand success.

VI

A Real Winner

The company which Asa Candler had made such a winner was close to becoming a loser; the Southerners who had found Coca-Cola such a sure-thing were now experiencing the familiar, sinking feeling of defeat. But then, to the magic life of Coca-Cola, came Robert Winship Woodruff to snatch new and unparalleled victory out of the bottle's neck of near defeat. If the fate and background that Asa Candler knew did not prepare him for the heady world of success, Robert W. Woodruff's upbringing seems to have been designed for nothing else.

"Robert Woodruff was born with style," his 1970s successor, J. Paul Austin, once said. Both grandfathers of Mr. Woodruff were pre-Civil War prosperous and, interestingly, not in the usual southern way of slave-holding agriculture, but as businessmen. His mother's father, Joseph Winship, had a cotton-gin manufacturing machine shop in Atlanta which, when war did come, turned out guns for the Confederate Army. The other grandfather, George Waldo Woodruff, had a flourishing flour mill in Columbus, Georgia. Both businesses were destroyed in the war, and the offspring of both men knew the kind of hard times growing up that Asa Candler did. This left its mark on Ernest Woodruff, Robert's father, who was legendarily frugal with the great wealth he won as a banker, a putter-together of trusts, and from ownership of the Atlantic Steel Company, the Atlantic Ice & Coal Company, and the Atlanta Consolidated Street Railways.

Robert W. Woodruff got from his parents a blend of the old and new, but not of the same ingredients as Asa Candler had. His mother, Emily Winship Woodruff, was a sweet and gentle woman in the southern tradition, deeply religious and possessed of a regal charm. Her son worshiped her and got from her, most of all, her quiet gentleness. In moments during his long career when he felt he had let his heart overcome his business judgment, Robert Woodruff would say that it was his mother in him. The business judgment that he used was formidable, and for it he had father Ernest to thank. And Ernest Woodruff's tough-minded and thoroughly modern acumen in commerce came out of the New England trader tradition, his father having spent his formative years in Connecticut.

Of the many, many anecdotes about Ernest Woodruff's frugality, the two best are clues to his character and influence on his son. E. J. Kahn tells one of them in a biography, *Robert Winship Woodruff*, published privately by the company in 1969. Mr. Ernest was standing in one of Atlanta's train stations and searched about in his pockets, saying, "I have a quarter here somewhere," to the patiently waiting porter who had handled his bags. "Well, Mr. Woodruff," the porter replied, "if you ever had one, you still got it."

Mr. Kahn tells the other in his book, *The Big Drink* (Random House, 1960). Ernest needed to ship a million dollars worth of negotiable bonds from New York to Atlanta. Rather than pay a small amount for express and insurance on them, he and a business associate strapped the papers to their bodies under their clothing and transported them by train. The two men crackled with every move that they made.

Like Asa's sons, Robert Woodruff had to work as a boy (selling ice coupons) during summers for his spending money. But part of that went to purchase feed for the pony he owned and galloped about on in Inman Park. And he knew such rich boy privileges as riding out west in the private Pullman car of one of his father's associates, and once to Montgomery, Alabama, for the great thrill of meeting Buffalo Bill performing there.

After two years at the public Boys High School, he transferred to a private one, Georgia Military Academy (now Woodward Academy). He was dark, tall, ramrod-erect in posture, a student leader there but not—as was subsequently to prove true at Emory-at-Oxford—much of a student. He dropped out of the small college after a year, much to his father's displeasure. "Damn it, Bob," Ernest Woodruff is supposed to have said, "it's three generations from shirtsleeves to shirtsleeves. Learn something."

"I'll take the shirtsleeves young," the son is said to have replied. Ernest Woodruff then decreed that the shirtsleeving would have to pay college debts, and his son set to it, starting out as a sixty-cent-a-day apprentice at a pipe foundry company on Highland Avenue in Atlanta. He then sold fire extinguishers until his father was satisfied enough with his progress to take him on as purchasing agent for Atlantic Ice and Coal.

Robert Woodruff's first purchase in that job was a fleet of White trucks to replace horse and wagons (in use by frugal Ernest as late as 1912), and, as might be expected, his father was aghast. Walter White, with whom Robert Woodruff truck-traded, was not aghast, but something close to it. He was so impressed with the skill at which he had been out-traded that he offered young Robert a job. And young Robert, with plans to marry Miss Nell Hodgson of Athens in October, took the job because his father now refused to come forth with a promised raise in pay. Young Robert was made Atlanta branch manager for White the following year. After service in the Motor Corps during World War I, he became a vice-president of the motor company in 1922. By then he was also on the board of directors of the Trust Company of Georgia. When on April 28, 1923, at the age of thirty-three, he came home to be president of The Coca-Cola Company, it was to leave an $85,000-a-year job in Cleveland.

The company—*though wars might rage*—had itself another winner, this time a real one. William C. Bradley, the Columbus industrialist and Coca-Cola board member, himself a multimillionaire, was to say of him later, as quoted in *Fortune* ("Bob Woodruff of Coca-Cola," September 1945): "Bob's grandfather made a lot of money and kept it. Bob's father made a lot more money and kept it. Bob has made a lot more than either of them and kept it. A *wonderful* family!"

Bob's father, in making his, was able to ride with the times, to master and manipulate the new laws and tax structures which so demoralized Asa Candler. And Robert W. Woodruff himself would show a similar ability to adapt and take advantage of the many changes in American life that were to occur during his career.

INTERNATIONAL EVENTS DURING COCA-COLA'S EARLY YEARS

Let's look at history during the first two decades (1920 to 1940) that he was in charge of Coca-Cola—the time during which he saved the company—and note just how fast the changes came, the rate constantly accelerating.

This is a history that includes the evolution from the hazardous one- or two-passenger aircraft of the early 1920s to the sleek (but tiny by today's standards) airlines of the late 1930s, and, unfortunately, the big propeller-driven bombers of World War II. These were the years when radio moved from amateurish local stations broadcasting for crystal sets to the networks sending Jack Benny, Fred Allen, and all the others (including "Gang-Busters") over national broadcasts to the cabinet or console model in nearly every living room in the country. The rattly Model-T Ford and the chugging Model-A were to be during the twenty years supplanted by the smooth-running, fast Ford V-8. And finally, tragically, there was the transition from the cavalry charges of World War I to the mechanized slaughter of World War II, ending with the earth-periling advent of nuclear weaponry.

The milestone events of the epoch ticked off with a similar march: from the now quaint-seeming Teapot Dome scandal of big business bribes for political favors through the era of gangsters during Prohibition, and the heyday of sports figures—Jack Dempsey, Babe Ruth, Bobby Jones—to far more serious happenings. Came the calamity of the 1929 stock-market collapse, with attendant bank failures, unemployment (fourteen million jobless in March 1933), and resulting governmental instability. Then, as we know, Franklin Delano Roosevelt salvaged the government and saved the free-enterprise economy with his

Atlanta—rising in national prominence—1932, as President and Mrs. Franklin Delano Roosevelt visit.

New Deal (all those alphabetical answers to the problems: NRA, PWA, WPA, CCC, AAA).

Concurrent with the New Deal recovery, labor unions moved in a friendly federal government climate to strengthen their position, and to seek safeguards for workers from a repetition of what had happened to them during the worst of the Depression. The old AFL was abetted by the upstart Congress of Industrial Organizations. The CIO organized vast numbers of workers not in the traditional skilled crafts at a rapid clip (but not many, as we have noted, connected with Coca-Cola enterprises), making itself a second powerful and influential force for labor in the national life. Another bright note: At the low point of the Depression, 1933, came the high old day of Prohibition's repeal. Happy days are here again. . . .

But out of the same economic and political instability from which Roosevelt's leadership emerged, the unspeakable Adolph Hitler clawed his way to threaten civilization and, of course, set off the worst war in mankind's long history of war.

The era started as the *jazz age* and old-timers in Atlanta remember when Bessie Smith would cry her inimitable wail of the blues at the old Bailey's 81 Theater on Decatur Street, "I've got those old gin-house blues." When the spirit, and spirits, would get too much for her, a Coca-Cola crate would be hauled out on the stage for her to sit her considerable self on and keep on wailing. Came the days of bootleg whiskey and bathtub gin (mixed with Coca-Cola for a gin rickey), and then in more sophisticated times, Xavier Cugat was to lead his Latin orchestra in renditions of "Drinking Rum and Coca-Cola." It is well that Asa Candler had passed from the scene.

Even in the small matter of the way people looked, change was great and continuing during those twenty years. From the long dresses of yore, empha-

sizing large busts and hips, the flappers of the 1920s changed to styles and standards favoring small busts and hips, but, to make it complete, no longer favoring
small waists. The waistline, therefore, dropped and, lo, for the first time in the
history of civilization, skirts rose above the ankles all the way up to mid-calf
level. Not only did those bold ladies display their legs, but displayed them
sheathed in silk stockings, shimmeringly flesh-tinted. *Gads!* And they painted
their faces and smoked cigarettes (and sipped Coca-Cola at the corner drugstore, perched on bent-cane chairs at round tables)—all of it the quaint beginnings of liberation. The frock-coat suit for gentlemen was gone, replaced by
lounge suits and even sports jackets and flannel trousers. And for golf and other
outdoor activity, the sports wore the plus-four baggy knickers and knee socks.
Twenty-three skidoo! Along with the first backless bathing suit for women, the
1930s saw both sexes dressing pretty much as they do today, give or take the
delight of the miniskirt and the abomination of double-knit polyester.

ATLANTA

*One can picture Robert W. Woodruff striding his tall, big frame in his lounge
suit along crowded Peachtree Street (Atlanta's population totaling more than
200,000) on the day of April 28, 1923, when he took control of the destiny of
The Coca-Cola Company.*

A small story in that day's Atlanta Journal *recorded the fateful moment in
company history, noting that Charles Howard Candler had resigned the presidency to be a member of the company's Advisory Committee.*

*More prominent news in the paper that day was the closing of the thir-
teenth "and most brilliant" annual week of the New York Metropolitan Opera
Company, with a grand performance of Rossini's* William Tell. *The once
rough-and-tumble little town was putting on citified airs, including a round of
opera parties all week where society leaders, even as they do during Opera
Week to this day, entertained and fawned over the opera stars in big homes and
at the country clubs.*

*A ten-year-old boy was playing with his top on a sidewalk and a car
jumped the curb and ran over him, doing serious injury. The driver was
charged with drunken driving.*

*A toothless, one-eyed mule which sustained itself on cornflakes was among
stray animals to be auctioned by city police.*

*The annual burial service of the O'Hara band of Irish horsetraders had been
conducted at the Church of the Immaculate Conception, seven O'Haras having
been interred.*

*A full page was devoted to news of the fine new thing of radio. WSB had
presented a list of speakers on universal progress and invited listeners to write a
twenty-five-word essay on who was best—first prize a $200 long-range radio re-*

ceiving set manufactured by the Colin B. Kennedy Company of St. Louis, Missouri. Fiddlin' John Carson from Fannin County, Georgia, with his big squad of champion pickers and fiddlers, also rated a big hit on WSB, played such numbers as "Log Cabin," "Casey Jones," "The Old Hen Cackled," and "Ole Sally Goodlin."

A prominent physician was on trial charged with 118 counts of violating the narcotics law. His defense: The relief of human suffering.

One George Baker was executed in LaFayette, Georgia, for murder of a deputy sheriff, thus becoming the first white man hanged in that locale since 1856. To his family among a crowd of several hundred, he said these last words before marching manfully to the gallows: "I've got to go now and I want to tell you all good-by. I'm not guilty of murder. I want you all to keep out of trouble. Good-by, boys. Good-by, Buck. Good-by, son. I'm going to leave you now."

Hightower Hardware featured an ad for the New Perfection Oil Range with the new Superflex Burner.

A full-page ad proclaimed the economy of Bull Durham roll-your-own tobacco for cigarettes. Ten cents worth would make fifty cigarettes. You could save $52 to $78 a year on government tax alone (which was fifteen cents for fifty of the manufactured variety).

Four automobiles had been stolen on the previous evening.

"Near East Relief" would be the topic of many sermons on the morrow, a Sabbath.

Georgia Tech had beat the Mercer University (of Macon, Georgia) Bears 9 to 3 in baseball. Mercer's performance was "absolutely disgusting," the Journal *editorialized in the sports story.*

D. W. Griffith's sensational new film, One Exciting Night, *was playing at the Atlanta Theater.*

A reading from James Whitcomb Riley was on the program at a meeting of the Agnes Lee Chapter, United Daughters of the Confederacy.

And the Forsyth Theatre Players were presenting, Nice People, *a "dramatic exposé of the Jazz-Life of today."*

Coca-Cola Story Highlights: 1919–40

What might have been Robert W. Woodruff's thoughts on that day when he embarked on his odyssey of success with Coca-Cola? We know that he had bought a considerable amount of Coca-Cola stock in 1919 at $40 a share, and it had since declined in value to $18 a share. He told his friend Walter White, "If I ever get even, I'm going to get out."

But of course he did not. By the time he got even (which was not to be long), he was as completely caught up in Coca-Cola as Asa Candler had been and, in his own style, building it with the same sure hand. We may see the Woodruff touch and his building apace during those first two decades of saving the company, prefacing this with important company events that transpired just prior to his taking over:

Archie Laney Lee, the D'Arcy advertising man who became a partner with Robert Woodruff in the management of Coca-Cola's national advertising.

A fortunate day in 1919: Archie Laney Lee, formerly a reporter on the Atlanta *Georgian,* joins the D'Arcy advertising agency. Bringing yet another magic touch to the merchandising of Coca-Cola, he is to guide, in close association with Robert W. Woodruff, the drink through a golden age of advertising and promotion.

A day in August, 1920: The Coca-Cola Company moves into its ninth and longest-lasting home, a building of its own construction at North Avenue and Plum Street which, with additions over the years—including 1977 construction—remains its home.

December 6, 1920: Justice Oliver Wendell Holmes of the United States Supreme Court renders, in one of those many cases against imitators, the Koke Company of America, an opinion which not only holds that the nickname "Coke" could only mean Coca-Cola, but also, more importantly, forever seals the right of the company to the trademark, *Coca-Cola.* "It means a single thing coming from a single source, and well known to the community," Justice Holmes rules, in words joyously inscribed today on more than one Coca-Cola bottling plant. The opinion continued: "It hardly would be too much to say that the drink characterizes the name as much as the name the drink. In other words, Coca-Cola probably means to most persons the plaintiff's familiar product to be had everywhere, rather than a compound of particular substances."

October 5, 1921: Strife, which had risen between the new owners of Coca-Cola and the vast family of bottlers, temporarily unhappy, is settled by consent decree in a United States District Court in Delaware. The new owners had questioned the precious perpetuity of the bottling contracts, and the bottlers went to court. By mutual consent both parties, at the end of the litigation, agreed that perpetuity was guaranteed under certain conditions.

April 28, 1923: Robert Winship Woodruff is elected president of The Coca-Cola Company. Once more, ownership and management are combined in the running of the company and will continue to be so, a remarkable and significant record of continuity in an American business.

A day in 1926: Fountain-drink salesmen of the company are assembled for their first training school, part of a "Quality Drink" campaign of Mr. Woodruff's.

An anxious day (and night) in 1927: The fountain salesmen are assembled in Atlanta and told by Mr. Woodruff that the Fountain Sales Department is no more and their jobs have been abolished. On the next day, they are reassembled, and this time Mr. Woodruff tells them of a new service department to tend the needs of the soda fountains, and offers each a job in it. It is his way of impressing on them his goal of perfect service of Coca-Cola to the public.

The annual meeting day, 1928: Mr. Woodruff sums up for the stockholders the actions he has taken to improve the company: "There are certain general developments of the last five years which bear rather vitally upon our future operations. It has been possible to establish a very reliable production control. . . . Likewise, the distribution system has been further perfected, resulting in substantial savings. . . . More important has been the creation of a sound basis on which to build an effective selling organization and the formulation of a definite advertising policy."

A happy day, 1928: The year ends with, for the first time, more total gallons of Coca-Cola sold in bottles than over the fountain.

The Saturday Evening Post, July 27, 1929, issue, introduces the first use of Coca-Cola's now legendary slogan.

COURTESY OF THE ARCHIVES, THE COCA-COLA COMPANY

1929: An open-top cooler, especially designed by John C. Staton of the engineering department for maximum display of the product and advertising, is offered at a remarkably low price to storekeepers and filling station operators across the land.

The end of 1930: Despite the onset of the Depression, as it had happened each year since Mr. Woodruff took over, a new record of sales and profits had been set. Sales totaled $34,580,493, and the net profit, $13,088,616. Increases are to continue.

A day in 1935: The first coin-vending machines for Coca-Cola are set up in factories, offices, and other places of business—a lure to the "at work" market.

A day in 1937: A company-developed automatic fountain dispenser is introduced. Soda jerks across the land need now only to pull a lever and out pours a uniform, properly refrigerated Coca-Cola. The machine assures the perfection that human hands could never be counted on always to produce.

An inspired day in 1940: The advertising department launches the most successful consumer public relations campaign in company history, the first of three free colorful booklets entitled *Flower Arranging in the Home.*

Problems During the Early Years of Woodruff's Ownership

The outcome of the Koke case was fortunate for the company amid much that was bad in the early 1920s. The ruling was the foundation on which Attorney Harold Hirsch would rest his diligent and successful cases in the coming years to fend off imitator after imitator (including an Afrikola in 1928 possibly named to appeal to the black trade).

Otherwise, the souring that had set in during Asa Candler's last days with the company continued under the new ownership, with Mr. Candler's once red-hot team of Mr. Dobbs and Charles Howard Candler in charge. Mr. Dobbs, as president, made a most unfortunate purchase of sugar in 1920 when it was selling for twenty-eight cents a pound, up from seven cents a pound at the outbreak of World War I. But soon after the purchase, the price plummeted almost as low again. Archivist Kurtz chuckles to tell that Asa Candler's practice of starting each company day with prayer was resumed during this crisis. The company's people would get on their knees and pray each morning that the ship carrying the unfortunate cargo of sugar would sink. That failing, the company had to borrow $22 million to continue operations.

That high-priced sugar was part of the contretemps between the company and the bottlers. Some have suggested that another part of it had to do with Ernest Woodruff's characteristic way of doing big business—which was to buy up or merge a corporation, quickly increase its productivity and profits, and then sell it off at a handsome take. Author Campbell in his fictional version of the situation uses the harsh term, "shakedown," in describing the company's attempt on the bottlers. But one can see the company's point, caught as it was with a syrup price that was fixed and a price for the main ingredient of the syrup that fluctuated wildly.

Whatever the case, company spokesmen approached bottler kingpins and suggested that the time had come to increase the price of syrup to them. The bottlers said wait a minute. The price is fixed by the precious contract between Mr. Candler and Messrs. Thomas and Whitehead. Well then, the pressed company spokesmen said, we'll have to see about ending the contracts between bottlers and the parent companies. No, no, rejoined the bottlers. They are signed and sealed in perpetuity, and thus the issue was joined in court in 1921.

The federal magistrate presiding over the lengthy hearings is said to have finally called the contending sides together and pointed out to them that they were so mutually dependent on each other that the only reasonable course was to find a compromise, lest both symbiotic sides perish from a victory by one or the other. Such reasoning prevailed, and the compromise settled upon in October 1921 was that the perpetuity of contracts and the fixed price of syrup were guaranteed by the company, while the bottlers conceded that the fixed price would be adjusted on a sliding scale based on the current price of sugar. (So things stand today.)

It was an acrimonious encounter. Charles Howard Candler, whose ascension to the presidency had come after that errant judgment by Mr. Dobbs on sugar, felt compelled to write a letter to stockholders denying charges by the bottlers of fraud by the company and lack of good faith. The company convened the first bottlers' convention soon after the compromise was reached as an occasion for healing the wounds.

Harrison Jones

And here emerged one of a number of strong men who would function under Mr. Woodruff to pull the company back together. Harrison Jones, at that time vice-president in charge of sales, organized the convention and then used his considerable eloquence to move the still unhappy bottlers to reconciliation with the company.

The words he spoke were not recorded, but we can assume from various testimonials to Mr. Jones, that they were well chosen and strongly delivered. Pointing out that Mr. Jones had handled the 1919 sale of the company so well for the Trust Company of Georgia that he was persuaded to join Coca-Cola as a vice-president, the unsigned 1931 *Fortune* article said of him: "He masks a kindly and patient disposition with a slightly ferocious exterior and a vocabulary more graphic than recordable."

At the convention, Mr. Jones began the active involvement of the company in the selling and advertising endeavors of the bottlers, a relationship that would

Harrison Jones.

continue to benefit both. Through his years with the company, he was a close friend of the bottling family.

Harold Hirsch

Another strong man whose efforts Mr. Woodward encouraged, Harold Hirsch, was also close to the bottling family. Mrs. J. B. Weil, who with her husband, Julius, owned The Coca-Cola Bottling Works of Nashville, Tennessee, wrote in the fiftieth-anniversary issue of *The Coca-Cola Bottler* of Mr. Hirsch's handling of the Koke case: ". . . Those of us then in the bottling business could see all that we had worked for and built up flying out the window." But Mr. Hirsch "never wavered in his confidence," and won for them.

COURTESY OF THE COCA-COLA COMPANY

Pope T. Brock.

Mr. Pope Brock had good words also to say of Mr. Hirsch. He was not only invaluable as an attorney, but was "a thorough master" of the company's business problems, including those with the bottlers. "Mr. Woodruff told me more than once," Mr. Brock said, "that when he came here in 1923, new to the Coca-Cola business, he couldn't have gotten by except for Mr. Hirsch's invaluable assistance."

Mr. Woodruff was, of course, still in Cleveland working for Mr. White when both of the important court cases were decided. How much firsthand information he might have had of the battle with the bottlers we do not know. But, in later years, he was to express the truism arrived at by the judge in the case in a more positive way. According to J. Lucian Smith, president of the company in the 1970s, Mr. Woodruff held "that there could not be a conflict of interest between the bottlers and The Coca-Cola Company. If there appeared to be one, somebody had made a wrong decision. The company and the bottlers succeeded or failed mutually."

As a substantial Coca-Cola stockholder, Mr. Woodruff had been elected to the company's board of directors and its executive committee a short while before he was offered the presidency. It is legend that Ernest Woodruff opposed the placing of his son in the job of president.

Also often told is the fact that Robert Woodruff asked his future employers for an agreement that he be paid 5 per cent of any increases in profit that might accrue under his leadership—which would have made him a far

richer man than the very rich one he became—but his father vetoed that proposition. When Robert Woodruff first went to work, he would return from a trip
and learn that Ernest Woodruff had countermanded various of his orders. He
soon put a stop to this by informing company officers that he would fire any
who chose to take orders from his father rather than himself. Ross Treseder, in
his recollections of Ernest Woodruff some years after the time of such mischief-
making, presents a more mellow figure, characterizing him as the "elder states-
man" of the company. "He came to the office frequently and was a rugged but
very friendly man with a winning smile and a twinkle in his eye. He was keenly
interested in the Company activities. . . . His presence . . . gave everybody a
feeling of confidence and trust."

Coca-Cola's "Triple Crisis"

The company that Mr. Woodruff took over had, from the time of the souring, another formidable problem beyond that of costly sugar and the attendant
battle with the bottlers. This further problem can be summed up in the annual
sales figures, always so happily quoted before. In 1918, last year of the war, the
total gallonage sold was just over ten million. In 1919, true to past form, the
figure jumped to almost nineteen million. But in 1920, first full year of the new
ownership, it dipped slightly. And in 1921, it sank to a dismal 15,837,499. In
1922, the year before Mr. Woodruff took over, the figure held at 15,437,612.

Pointing out that had not Mr. Hirsch saved the day in the Koke case and
Harrison Jones in the bottler battle, the triple crisis of those two events, plus the
loss in sales, might well have done the new ownership in. Mr. Dietz, in *Soda
Pop*, attributes the sales losses to demoralization among the bottlers during the
battle. Another possible cause is cited in the 1931 *Fortune* article. Discussing the
last years of the souring, it explains: "The company . . . lacked a sales organization in the modern sense of the word. Between Mr. Dobbs and a salesman in,
for instance, Seattle, there was hardly anything except large stretches of geography. If the Seattle man concentrated on decorating hotel lobbies, it took a long
while for his dereliction to show in sales, and for his replacement with another
man who might easily repeat the same process." The Candler-era sales effort had
been hot stuff in its day, but—like Mr. Candler—didn't keep up with the times.

New Directions under Robert W. Woodruff

Robert W. Woodruff, as we have seen, was to turn the sale figures around
in short order. Part of how he did it was, as one would expect, reorganizing and
beefing up the sales department. But this was only one facet of a large, co-ordinated effort throughout the organization whose ultimate purpose was to in-

COURTESY OF THE ARCHIVES, THE COCA-COLA COMPANY

Coca-Cola officials in the 1920s, including Ross Treseder (fourth from left), Robert W. Woodruff (fifth), William C. Bradley (eighth), Samuel Willard (ninth), Harold Hirsch (tenth), Eugene Kelley (twelfth), and Harrison Jones fourteenth).

crease sales. The effort included strenuous improvement of syrup and bottling productions' "quality control," harking back to Asa Candler's first instinct to concentrate on the taste of the drink as a means of selling more of it. It included, too, a continuation of the company's old practice of extensive promotion and advertising, the already large budget allocations for this increasing each year, reaching to ten million dollars at the end of the two decades. Under the guidance of Mr. Woodruff and Archie Lee, the promotion was to take on a more cohesive, more purposeful character, with definite campaign objectives. The two also contrived an ever more subtle and successful promotion of *Coca-Cola as a symbol of America itself*, the way of life that, at the end of the two decades, the nation would go to war to defend. Beyond all of this, Mr. Woodruff worked even stronger than during the Candler era on the profit motive of Coca-Cola's many customers, doing this by improving service in every possible way to them—including providing them with a series of technological developments, beginning with the company-developed cooler, which made it easier to sell Coca-Cola at established points of sale and possible to sell it at points where it had not been sold before. In all facets of this effort, adequate training of personnel was a dictum, with more improved techniques for its accomplishment. At an early point, Mr. Woodruff is said to have concluded that the bottled drink had the higher sales potential, and this was a part of the planning of the co-ordinated sales effort.

That effort was largely a consolidation and extension of the beginnings made during the Candler era. By the end of the two decades, Mr. Woodruff and his staff had in motion a streamlined marketing machine that would continue ever more proficiently to push Coca-Cola sales in the United States, an improvement over the Candler era marketing as marked as that of the Ford V-8 over the Model-T.

To back up the sales effort, the new president set up a "research" department that soon developed into a pioneering, highly sophisticated market research agency which today is one of the most extensive in the world.

Mr. Woodruff went beyond the thinking of the Candler era in another coordinated effort going on simultaneous with the sales campaign.

His thinking here grew out of the basic problem in the bottler battle—the price structure. He was determined not to increase the nickel price of the drink. This would in all likelihood have adversely affected volume, to the company's disadvantage. But the main point is that it would bring in no more money to the company anyhow, locked as it was in the fixed price of syrup to bottlers and, for purposes of good will, to the fountains as well. The price compromise with the bottlers ended any chance for whatever plans Ernest Woodruff may have had for a quick build-up and sale of the company. So what his son, Robert, did was to bow his head and manfully struggle to increase not the price, but the percentage of profit deriving from every sale of Coca-Cola syrup. And this he did by improving on the efficiency of every phase of the business, continuously whittling down costs in every kind of ingenious manner, a process still underway today.

Overlying these simultaneous efforts were stated philosophical principles Mr. Woodruff set out for the company. One of these was the determination that *everyone who had anything to do with the production and marketing of Coca-Cola, down to the last supplier and subcontractor, should profit handsomely from the association.* Another was that *the company would do business honorably with honorable people,* a touch once more out of the Old-South tradition.

The Woodruff Style

Mr. Woodruff has always been a prodigious worker, and, by all accounts, those first two decades of putting the company back together were strenuous ones even for him. Mr. Kahn in the biography noted that Mr. Woodruff read every single piece of mail coming to him. He went to Europe in 1925 to study (that early) the possibility of establishing bottling plants there and spent sixty days at it. He worked hard, but was not hard-driving or high-pressured. It was like the advertising, a relaxed, low-key kind of hard working. J. W. (Joe) Jones, a company vice-president who has for many years been Mr. Woodruff's assistant and close associate, related during an interview how his boss operated on such a trip.

Mr. Woodruff would not write for an appointment, but would telephone the person in advance and say he planned to be in the locale the next week and that he hoped they might get together. Then upon arrival, he would phone and arrange to have dinner or cocktails with the person in a relaxed way to allow "personal association." Sometimes he might spend two or three days before the mission was accomplished, busying himself all the while with the everyday work of running the business.

Commented Mr. Jones: "People now who use airplanes take great pride in the fact they can be in three places in one day. Maybe they accomplish their business that way. I don't know. But I like Mr. Woodruff's style of doing business much better."

Mr. Woodruff's style of dealing with associates in the running of the company from those early days on has been much commented upon. He did not talk much. He listened a lot, though sometimes with eyelids closed so that he appeared to be asleep. And he thought a lot. A description of Mr. Woodruff over and over is of him with, first, a pipe in hand, later a cigar, staring off, deep in thought.

We are indebted to Mr. Kahn, again in the biography, for a revealing anecdote about Mr. Woodruff's personal manner and an expression of that soft side of him during those hard-working early days. One of his first acts as president of the company was to put a Mr. Jim Key on the company payroll for life. When Robert Woodruff had that pony as a boy in Inman Park and was expected to pay for its feed out of his summer earnings or the allowance he got during the school year, Mr. Key was a company stablehand for Asa Candler and, through some pact forged between the man and the boy, would feed the pony on the sly. Whenever anyone would ask president Woodruff what Jim Key did (which was not much) to warrant his being on the payroll, Mr. Woodruff would, according to Mr. Kahn, "mumble, 'staff vice-president' and change the subject."

An extraordinary part of the Woodruff legend is that during those years of hard work, he also served for one and a half years as president of the White Motor Company, working doubly hard at the helm of two companies simultaneously. His friend Walter White was killed in an automobile accident on the Friday before the blue Monday of the stock-market crash in 1929, and Mr. Woodruff agreed to run the company until a successor for Mr. White could be found. He accomplished this by commuting by train between Atlanta and Cleveland.

In the process, he formed a long-held habit of doing much of his work on trains, refusing to fly until late in life. Joe Jones, who accompanied Mr. Woodruff on his travels, said that his boss could utilize his time on trains uninterrupted, reading and sorting his mail. He liked the isolation, though invariably he would run into some friend on the train, often a top executive of some other company, and there would be a festive dinner in the dining car or a session of gin rummy.

In one of his rare statements to the press, Mr. Woodruff was quoted in the 1931 *Fortune* article as commenting about the time of the two presidencies: "It wasn't so different. It was mostly a matter of working all the time. I mean the time you would take for a vacation you just didn't take. You kept on working, you see. That was all there was to it, really." (Mr. Jones pointed out in an interview that Mr. Woodruff never has during his career taken a vacation in the sense of leaving his work behind at the office.)

WCTU Attacks Coca-Cola

As things hummed along during the 1920s, there were gadfly attacks on the drink as somehow sinful, some of these raised by various chapters of the Women's Christian Temperance Union. They had rid the land of demon rum and now were out to exorcise the curse of Coca-Cola. We may be certain that the ever-alert and image-conscious company officials took note of these attacks, probably Mr. Woodruff included, and certainly it must have come as sweet comfort to them when the famous Emporia, Kansas, newspaper editor William Allen White wrote about the matter in his *Gazette:* "*At the spectacle of men returning home sodden with Coca-Cola to beat their wives, at the sight of little children tugging at their father as they stand at the Coca-Cola bars long after midnight to get them to come home to Mama, we remain unmoved.*

"*Workmen, victims in the grip of the Coca-Cola habit, may squander their money across the marble soda-fountain counters instead of saving it to pay installments on the home, and we harden our hearts against the sight.*

"*Innocent girls, with passions which they themselves only half understand released by the pernicious drug, gaze at us bleary-eyed, but we still remain indifferent to the anti-Coca-Cola crusade of the good ladies of Arkansas City (Kansas).*

"*If they succeed in saving the world from the grip of Coca-Cola, to them is all the credit. The trumpet and banners of reformers sweep by, and we stand ready to heave the first stone.*"

When Prohibition was finally ended on that happy day in 1933, some saw that as a problem for the "temperance beverage." Major John S. Cohen, then editor of the Atlanta *Journal*, was among these, according to Hunter Bell. Major Cohen wrote to Mr. Woodruff, asking if he wanted to make a public utterance about Repeal that might help prevent stockholders from bolting the company. Mr. Woodruff said, Why certainly. Repeal could do Coca-Cola nothing but good. The drink had been selling well, every year with increases, in wet Canada during Prohibition. Repeal would only open more outlets for Coca-Cola. Whether due to this statement or not, stockholders, to their good fortune, did not bolt.

Interestingly, that little attack on the WCTU was but the first of three different times, as we shall see, that Mr. White, whose editorials spoke for the decent aspirations of plain Americans, was to come down on the side of the drink, which was insinuating itself as a symbol of that same streak of decency in the American consciousness. Mr. White's WCTU words were written in March 1929. Soon, serious problems would occupy him, the challenge to guide his plain American readers through the tragedy and terror of the Depression.

Coca-Cola's Southern *"Pause that Refreshes"* During the Depression Years

The Coca-Cola Company weathered the large event of the stock-market crash and subsequent worldwide depression, largely by continuing and perhaps intensifying Mr. Woodruff's basic policy of cost-cutting by efficiency. There were no large layoffs of company or bottler employees.

Perhaps because of the company's success during hard times, we find Mr. Woodruff making a rare error in judgment about economic matters. The Atlanta *Journal* of July 28, 1930, quotes him as declaring: "General business conditions are not far from normal and the main thing retarding the upward movement is the psychology of the public in comparing present conditions with the abnormal conditions of 1929. . . . The sooner we realize business is what we make it, the better off we'll be." He went on to report what Coca-Cola had made of business during the first six months of 1930, a net profit of $7,818,812.80, up $698,848.09 over the same period (which was before the crash) in 1929.

People could always find a nickel during the depression years: They needed those little lifts from anxiety that an ice-cold Coca-Cola would give. And there were all those reminders about *the pause that refreshes*, as though Archie Lee had the impending depression in mind when in 1929 he introduced the inspired slogan. Through the depression years and into the postwar period, the company owned the Atlanta Crackers baseball team and offered Atlantans the respite from money worries of far better minor league ballplaying than has ever been achieved by the city's current big-league team. "Ko-Ko-laaaaa, git yo' i-i-i-ice co-o-o-old Ko-Ko-laaaaaaaaa," resounded through the old Ponce de Leon Ballpark, a song, like the cry of shrimp vendors in Charleston, South Carolina. Admission cost little, but the baseball enterprise made money which in turn was plowed back into things like an improved scoreboard and rest rooms for lady fans, of whom there were many. One, Mrs. Grace Toole, who moved into a house overlooking the ballpark so she could walk to every game, still lives in that house, but now it overlooks a state office complex, and the virulent vine, kudzu, covers over what used to be the outfield.

The 1931 *Fortune* article recorded how well Mr. Woodruff and his men were doing with the larger enterprise of Coca-Cola, with their policy of cost-cutting. Profits had increased as we know, by 5 per cent in 1930, and the ratio of profit to gross income had been "an astounding" 38 per cent, and that with an advertising bill of $5 million. The article went on to describe Coca-Cola's "virtually unique position in the manufacturing world," again describing advantages of the manufacturing method handed down from Dr. Pemberton.

There were, the anonymous author wrote, no labor problems because there were so few laborers, only seventy-five in the Atlanta plant which produced one fourth of the thirty million gallons sold the previous year, and the most of these workers were devoted to the manufacture not of syrup but barrels in which to contain the syrup. A few chemists comprised the only skilled labor involved.

There was, the recital continued, no major investment in machinery to consume power and to depreciate. The sugar arrived in sacks and was dumped into 2,500-gallon tanks of water. When the sugar was dissolved, the vital ingredients were added, and the resulting syrup was poured into barrels and loaded on freight cars. And that was it.

"It has no noise," the unnamed writer rhapsodized. "It has no dirt. It sweats not, neither does it roar. Waiting for the sugar to go into solution is the major operation in the Coca-Cola plant." The article goes on to sing the praises of the simplicity of the distribution system, including the bottling operations, and the high profit made by retailers selling Coca-Cola.

It also gives us a nice vignette of a typical Southerner of the time, walking down the street. "He meets a friend. He knocks his friend's hat over his friend's eye—Southerners are continuously punching each other—and arm in arm they turn to the nearest fountain (which is never distant) and make a small contribution to Coca-Cola's income account." There is also a description of half a dozen 1930s southern gentlemen, sitting at a table in one of the many Nunnally candy stores in Atlanta, discussing cotton and drinking Coca-Cola. "The Southerner," concludes the writer, "exhibits an inexhaustible capacity for pausing and an inexhaustible capacity for being refreshed. To both these basic needs, Coca-Cola lovingly ministers."

But the main point for *Fortune* readers was the success the southern-born company was having while other businesses floundered in the beginnings of the nation's worst depression in history. The company would continue to flourish through the 1930s, continue to whittle at costs and to increase sales.

Coca-Cola Sales Strategies During the Depression

We can learn, as was not possible for the Candler era, some of the strategies behind the depression-era prosperity of Coca-Cola from men who still live with memories of those days. As each tells what he did, and how he did it, an extraordinary, earnestly genuine love for the company and its product is expressed again and again. This does not have to do with how the company enriched them, though they are comfortable in retirement. Pay was never all that good, they say, though the company did pioneer such fringe benefits as group life insurance in 1926, group accident and health policies in 1939, and finally a retirement program in 1948. No, it wasn't the pay and benefits. It was the spirit of the company, the feeling of being among good companions doing something worth the doing, and doing it right. Invariably, these men say that that spirit emanated and moved down through the ranks from the personage of Robert Winship Woodruff.

Ezekiel S. Candler, who related how his father opened up the Texas territory under Great-uncle Asa, is one whose memory goes far back. He started working for his father in Dallas, in 1924, after graduating from the University of Virginia. Soon after, Ross Treseder came down from Chicago to fill in temporarily while Daniel Candler was on some mission in South America. Mr. Treseder politely suggested to Zeke Candler he would never get anywhere working for his own father and offered him a job as a fountain salesman in Chicago. Mr. Candler thought the suggestion a wise one, and accepted.

He said he received "hit and miss" training by some of the old hands in Chicago before setting out on his rounds. At that time, five to ten salesmen worked under a district manager covering a territory of a size that allowed no more than three or four visits a year to each customer. Mr. Candler was working Lincoln, Nebraska, two thirds of the rest of the state, and a part of Iowa. He still recalls winters in that area with a shiver.

When he entered a drugstore on his rounds, Mr. Candler (as did all salesmen), without revealing his identity, would order a Coca-Cola from the fountain and check out, first, its temperature, then its taste. If either was not up to standard, it was his duty in a diplomatic way to urge and assist the store owner to correct the situation.

"We did everything—and I mean everything—we could to help the person serve a better drink," Mr. Candler said. Everything included diagnosing that the customer was stocking too much syrup at a time, causing it to weaken. The carbonator was always suspect and, when at fault, had to be fixed so as to eject properly cooled (40°) carbonated water. "We did a hell of a lot of plumbing work to help the guy get the best drink he could with the equipment he had."

Before mechanical refrigeration, the plumbing work often included cleaning out cooling boxes in which ice was placed around coils of the carbonator. These could get quite filthy and have an unpleasant odor. Sticking your hands in there to clean it up was not pleasant. Of course Mr. Candler's duties in the store also included putting up or replacing Coca-Cola signs in the lithograph festoons. He and his fellow salesmen drove about their territories in bright red Coca-Cola cars back then, usually a coupé with room in the big trunk for the advertising material. The company furnished the cars and affixed the trademark on their bright red doors, their trunks, and even their tops. "What the hell that was for I don't know," Mr. Candler grunted about the trademark on top. He didn't like those conspicuous cars and finally persuaded company officials to get "civilized" ones.

Mr. Candler was one of those salesmen who had their jobs abolished and were then offered a new one as serviceman. But he doesn't remember it the way legend has it. When it happened to him, he said, it was not Mr. Woodruff but a regional manager who made the announcement. And this emissary did not keep the men in suspense overnight, but told the good news after only a pause following the bad.

"That story is exaggerated," Mr. Candler said. But the thing did have a psychological effect. It impressed on the salesmen the new emphasis on quality and service. Mr. Candler's version of the story is more in line with all we know about Mr. Woodruff's character, his kindness. But maybe some heard the news one way, some the other. The main thing is they got the message. Promotion had the effect of constantly increasing demand. The need now was not to sell to customers so much as help them meet the demand satisfactorily.

Later, Mr. Candler was in charge of the special training schools instituted by Mr. Woodruff to instruct new servicemen. The sessions were held at leading hotels, often at resorts. Instruction was given on the mechanical operation of soda fountains and on advertising. Heads of other departments explained their operations. Professional writers wrote plays to dramatize various messages, and professional performers enacted them.

Another kind of company gathering, in incomparable style, hosted a fiftieth birthday dinner for Harrison Jones (on May 25, 1937). The banquet was held at the Brookhaven Country Club, and there was a theatrical performance, singing of spirituals by a black choir, and the playing of modern music by Perry Bechtel's orchestra. Tables were arranged around a pond and garden created for the occasion on the ballroom floor. Real ducks glided on the pond, and when the cake was cut, a flock of twittering zebra finches flew out. (A club employee with a butterfly net gathered the zebra finches up and took them elsewhere before any, following their dramatic appearance, might do anything to spoil the cake or dress of any of the guests.) At the end, each of the hundred guests was presented with a red, leather-bound book of twenty-one photographs of the very occasion they had just enjoyed. Walton Reeves of the Reeves Studio in Atlanta made the pictures at the start of the evening, and rushed to his darkroom to perform this prodigy of photography. DeSales Harrison, creator of the banquet, had drawn up minute instructions on how each phase of it should go, including a list to the orchestra leader of some favorite songs not of Mr. Jones, the guest of honor, but of Robert Winship Woodruff. These included "Moon Over Miami," "Serenade in the Night," "Beautiful Lady in Blue," "The Night Is Young," "Lights Out," "The Way You Look Tonight."

But out in the field reality could be grim. Ross Treseder recalled how salesmen in the 1920s were still contracting to have wall signs painted. If one got a union job done, the sign painter was better paid than the salesman. And in some locales, if one didn't hire a union man, he would find the next day that his scab sign had been smeared over with union-made paint.

His recollections also include one about the dark days when President Roosevelt ordered all banks closed to stop withdrawal stampedes. Coca-Cola servicemen were unable to cash expense checks. "Fortunately, somebody in Atlanta could put his hands on great quantities of one-dollar bills. We used only post office money orders. . . . After a few days the money crisis was over, but the depression was still on."

And Coca-Cola servicemen counted themselves lucky to have work, even if at low pay. Delony Sledge, the retired advertising man, recalled how the servicemen would work through Saturday night, and then spend Sunday afternoon washing and polishing their bright red cars so as to make a good impression when they headed out for another six days the next morning.

Such a serviceman was J. H. (Red) Hall. Mr. Hall finished Mercer College in Macon, Georgia, in the depression year of 1930, and immediately went to Mr. Woodruff's office in Atlanta to ask for a job. He had dreamed of working for Coca-Cola for two years. He did not know Mr. Woodruff, but Mr. Hall's family owned land in Baker County, Georgia, where Mr. Woodruff had bought a plantation to use mainly as a hunting preserve (and called it Ichauway after the name Indians gave a creek on the land). Mr. Hall thought Mr. Woodruff would recognize his name and maybe think he wanted to sell him some more land and so consent to talk with him. After three days, Mr. Woodruff did. Mr. Hall told how he wanted to start at the bottom at beginners' wage and pressed on with salesman verve, saying: "Mr. Woodruff, it don't matter where a fellow starts or where he ends up. It's what he does on the way that matters." Soon Red Hall was attending the servicemen's training school.

And soon thereafter, he was making his rounds in the cold New England territory. It bothered him to find a casual attitude up there about reordering Coca-Cola syrup. Too often, soda-fountain operators would report they were out of the drink. Mr. Hall went in one store, which was run by a Syrian, and got off to a good start with the proprieter by doing what other salesmen ahead of him did not do, shaking the man's hand and calling him by name.

The man was intrigued with Mr. Hall's southern accent and asked him to sit down and talk some more. Mr. Hall said he'd be delighted and offered to buy his new friend a Coca-Cola. Sadly, his new friend replied that he had run out the week before. Red Hall was indignant. "I said, 'Man, you want me to talk for you and you haven't got any Coca-Cola? How do you buy it?" The man said by the gallon. He was persuaded to buy a five-gallon keg. Then Mr. Hall checked out the fountain and urged upon the proprietor a Coca-Cola festoon for his bare, mahogany backboard. The man said no, it was too pretty to drive nails into, and of course Red Hall showed him how a thumbtack did the job for the cardboard display.

All the folks up there loved to hear Red Hall talk. Both a sale of glasses (the proper package) and friend were made by singing upon request, a southern song: "I come from Alabammy with my banjo on my knee," at the top of his lungs in the crowded drugstore. The proprietor was delighted and said, "Any kid that's got that much guts, you just go put up all the advertising you want, and send me a half a gross of those glasses."

That was selling himself, Red Hall said. "I never have lost my accent in all my moving around. I wouldn't take anything in the world for it. Because it gets people's attention."

He was to go on to many other successes. One was a personal score with a bottler in Hot Springs, Arkansas. Mr. Hall believed in cultivating bottlers and called on this one as soon as he got the territory. On that occasion and two others within a week, the bottler on wanting to introduce Mr. Hall to someone, said to him: "Fountain boy, what's your name?" The fourth time that happened, Red Hall was ready. He pulled out one of his cards and a hammer and tack he had brought for the purpose and, blam, blam, tacked the card to the beautiful mahogany wall of the bottler's office. The bottler thenceforth remembered Red Hall's name.

"I saw him in the 1950s," Mr. Hall said, chuckling, "and he put his arm around me and he said, 'I want you to know we've had the office remodeled several times. But your card is still on the wall.' "

Another time, Mr. Hall was dispatched to a Louisiana town where Mr. Ollie Biedenharn had been displeased to find Dr. Pepper signs all over drugstores where Coca-Cola ones should have been. Without letting Mr. Biedenharn know he was in town, Mr. Hall spent a week reminding each drugstore owner how much Coca-Cola he sold and how much profit was thus derived and then, pointing at the offensive Dr. Pepper signs without mentioning the product by name, asked: "How much of *that* do you sell?" Then he was able proudly to conduct Mr. Biedenharn on a tour of all the stores in town to show them properly and permanently blanketed exclusively with Coca-Cola signs.

The Dr. Pepper man, a Mr. Duggan, came to Red Hall with a proposition to take turns, each to have signs in a store "every other time." What did Mr. Hall think of that? "I said, not much. I don't get my check every other time. It was nice to see you, Mr. Duggan."

Mr. Hall was later instrumental in helping a theater owner in a southern Illinois town get a custom-made rig to sell Coca-Cola to his audiences. This was in 1948, and was one of the first entries of the drink into that market. In the 1950s, by then a fountain serviceman in Atlanta, Mr. Hall helped with the big push into theaters that occurred then.

Red Hall told of the credo by which he did what was required during his years of helping in the drive to improve quality and service and thus increase sales: "Sell yourself. Know your product. Tell your story with conviction and with enthusiasm." Though retired, he still represents the company at state pharmaceutical and theater owners' conventions each year. "I still work for the company," he said. "Hell, ain't no way I wouldn't. Mr. Woodruff told me one time there ain't no way to separate Red Hall from Coca-Cola—you needn't try. I wouldn't want to be separated from it. I love it."

Company Technological Advances Including the First Coca-Cola Cooler

Abetting the sales effort were those technological developments by the company. The practice on all was to work with established manufacturers, who would reap the profits, and to provide the equipment to retailers at cost.

John C. Staton's work on the first cooler is typical. A reticent gentleman who has shunned the spotlight since his days as a Georgia Tech football star (and in his retirement years still a husky and vigorous man), Mr. Staton doesn't like to talk much about his achievement. But from others we may glean the story.

Turner Jones, vice-president in charge of advertising in 1928, had the vision of the cooler. He felt it was time to get Coca-Cola out of back rooms and dark corners of stores. Some bottlers and merchants had improvised coolers by sawing

The first, and subsequently famous, company-produced cooler, designed by John C. Staton, providing efficient refrigeration at low cost with maximum display of signs and product.

the bright red Coca-Cola kegs in two and putting legs on them. And there were a few commercial models, including an Icy-O, but none was very satisfactory. Mr. Jones assigned Mr. Staton, an engineering graduate, then only twenty-five. the job of designing a satisfactory cooler for the company and gave him a year in which to accomplish the task.

Mr. Staton gathered in a room at the company headquarters all the kinds of coolers then available and took them apart to study them, noting the flaws in their insulation and other features. Then he drew up specifications to eliminate the flaws, attending to every detail such as having nuts and bolts plated so they would last longer and not rust. The cooler box itself was galvanized so as not to rust and very effectively insulated. In six months' time, Mr. Staton was ready to take a model and specifications of a satisfactory cooler to Glasscock Brothers Manufacturing Company in Muncie, Indiana.

There ensued negotiations over method of manufacture and over price, particularly the latter, with the plant manager, a Mr. Frick. Mr. Frick said the price would have to be $20. Mr. Staton, representing the company's firm position, said no, $12.50. He finally got Mr. Frick down to $15, based on Mr. Frick's prediction that five thousand would be sold the first year. Mr. Staton assured him fifteen thousand merchants would buy them, and Mr. Frick finally agreed to take a chance on $12.50, based on that projection.

The manufactured cooler, on display and highly touted at the bottlers convention in January 1929, was shiny red with green trim, and was adorned with standard-size Coca-Cola signs on all four sides along with four familiar yellow crates of Coca-Cola bottles displayed on a shelf under the cooler. One lifted the top and saw inviting beaded bottles encased in ice. It was both an inexpensive, efficient marketing device and a spectacular point-of-sale advertisement. Sales of the coolers the first year were more than double the estimated fifteen thousand. The at-cost price of $12.50 to retailers compared with a $90 price tag on the Icy-O, soon to be manufactured no more. His cooler a success, Mr. Staton went on to become a top salesman, and then established bottling plants overseas.

A mechanically refrigerated cooler came out the following year, 1930. The coin-vending machines appeared at places of work and other locations in 1932.

That quality-assuring automatic dispenser was installed at soda fountains around the country in 1932. Its guarantee of a uniform glass of Coca-Cola everywhere was achieved for the bottled drink also by a Syn-Cro-Mix machine (not developed by the company) which came out in the late 1930s.

Meanwhile, Harrison Jones, back in 1922, had had the vision of the six-bottle (for 25 cents) carton as a major means of getting Coca-Cola into more homes. (Taking them home by the case was cumbersome.) The carton was introduced in 1924, was slow at first to catch on, but by 1939 the "handle of invitation" was picked up by seventy million Americans.

Other parts of the effort to improve and standardize quality included intensive work to assure use of pure water in bottling plants and removal of alkalinity and other matter that might flatten or change the desired taste for the drink. To aid the bottlers in these and other quality-control matters, Dr. W. P. Heath set up a fleet of ten traveling laboratories which were staffed by chemists and engineers. By the end of the 1930s the company was close to its goal of a drink that had the exact same good taste in every locale.

Mr. Woodruff had hired Dr. Heath in 1923. One story has it that he had to buy the Pratt Laboratory before its owner, Dr. N. P. Pratt, would consent to let his loyal employee leave. Dr. Heath retired in 1949. (He was the great-grandson of Roswell King, founder of the town of Roswell where stand some of the few remaining antebellum plantation houses anywhere near Atlanta.) He was succeeded by Dr. Orville May, who had been lured from the Food and Drug Administration, and trained under Dr. Pratt to take over the job. He inherited the traveling laboratories and had twenty-one of them zipping about the country in the continuing quest for Coca-Cola purity. A scientist to his toenails and a man of considerable worldly experience, Dr. May spoke with dispassion about his association with the company. Scientific colleagues, he said, sort of looked down their noses at his going to work for a soft-drink company. "But I've said very often that I've never encountered such a fine, able group of men as the company has at the top level. The whole organization, I found very compatible."

So there were all those simultaneous efforts by servicemen, engineers, and scientists to do everything possible for the trade toward the end of selling more and more Coca-Colas at, by cost-cutting, a better and better profit margin.

The Leadership Team of Robert W. Woodruff and Archie Lee

And to top it off there was the build-up of the already huge Coca-Cola advertising and promotion machine, guided in new directions and increased effectiveness by Mr. Woodruff and Archie Lee. They were a team in the endeavor, from all accounts, the one sparking the other's creativity and shrewdness. They had been friends before either joined the company, and the friendship deepened. Mr. Lee, another Southerner, hailing from Monroe, North Carolina, was always described as low-key and dignified. He enjoyed the hunting and horseback riding outdoors life that Mr. Woodruff loved so, and much of their work, when Mr. Lee would journey frequently down from D'Arcy headquarters in Philadelphia, was accomplished at Ichauway. Mr. Lee was a reader, a scholarly soul. Mr. Woodruff was neither. They complemented each other. Mr. Lee was slow talking and easygoing, "not one of these tensed-up ad men," as Hunter Bell put it. After Mr. Lee's death in 1950, no one was ever found to take his place on the team with Mr. Woodruff, perhaps because Madison Avenue by then did not attract exactly the robust outdoorsman type required for the job, but the tensed-up type instead.

The two agreed about the potential of the bottled drink, Mr. Lee spelling it out: The bottle could go with people; it didn't have to wait like the fountain drink for someone to come in for it. Mr. Woodruff knew what he wanted in the advertisements. They must not claim any virtue for Coca-Cola that it did not possess. And they had to do more than make claims. They would be distinctive, with a quality all their own, implying, as well as proclaiming, the quality of Coca-Cola and making the product an inherent part of people's lives, "central to the American experience," in Mr. Dietz's words in *Soda Pop*. Mr. Lee knew how, in many soft-sell ways, to do what Mr. Woodruff wanted. Not the least of his methods was to refine and sharpen the focus of the tradition started in the Candler era of showing people drinking Coca-Cola in nice, high-class surroundings. His pleasant and fresh and wholesome people were younger than the Candler era ones and, if possible, fresher and more wholesome.

Woodruff-Era Advertising Campaigns

Delony Sledge, during his years in the advertising department in Atlanta, including the directorship, had many opportunities to observe the team of Woodruff and Lee in action. Mr. Lee presided over and served as catalyst to a talented staff of "wild Indians" in the agency, and he would bring to Atlanta the best of the ideas, sketches, and copy he and they collaborated to produce. He would present these to Mr. Woodruff, knowing they were in the range of what he wanted, but not knowing whether Mr. Woodruff would find them on target. Mr. Woodruff's response was always mainly instinctive. Mr. Lee was patient, exquisitely considerate of Mr. Woodruff, never showing overenthusiasm lest he get the boss in a corner. He never argued with Mr. Woodruff, but always allowed him time for a particular concept to sink in and perhaps find acceptance. But one knew Mr. Woodruff's initial reaction by his facial expression. "If he walked out, you knew damn well he didn't like it," Mr. Sledge said with a laugh. These were conferences over individual pieces of a campaign. So close were Archie Lee and Robert Woodruff in their thinking that Mr. Lee never presented Mr. Woodruff with a campaign that he didn't accept, according to Mr. Sledge.

The conferences could get down to minute details. Mr. Sledge recalled a painting of a little girl, her back to the viewer, bending over to look at a rose, the ruffles of her drawers showing. There was some question of whether the painting was in good taste. How much of the little girl's drawers should show? There were several repaintings before the drawer ruffles were deemed in good taste.

Ross Treseder, who served as vice-president and advertising manager from 1922 to 1925, described how things could go wrong before the Lee-Woodruff team took over. One year one of the best of the creative lithographers (a subspecies of advertising agency since extinct) submitted a painting of an extraordinarily pretty girl for the calendar. "Somebody's wife did not like it, or a director preferred brunettes to blondes and God only knows why," but the

An example of expanded exterior advertising under Coca-Cola's massive 1930s campaigns.

painting was rejected; the one ultimately selected was a "dog." Mr. Treseder said he learned to "float through" such crises.

But even in those disorganized days during the transition to the Woodruff era, there was a final flourish, akin to Charles Howard Candler's inspiration to stir the syrup cold, and a monument to Asa Candler's determined drive to make Coca-Cola a year-round drink. Someone in the D'Arcy agency came up in 1922 with a slogan as direct and purposeful as any of the masterpieces Archie Lee would produce. "Thirst Knows No Season," it proclaimed in a four-color magazine ad showing a snow scene with a pretty girl on skis.

In the transition years, too, in 1920 and 1921 there was a series of ads depicting comic-strip-style drawings of fine detail, small town scenes—town squares, a baseball game, a train station ("When Number 2 from the South Pulls in"), the corner drugstore, culminating in "The Little Town That Grows Big Men," showing the town and heralding it: "There's where good old human nature shapes the destiny of the nation." Mr. Dietz in *Soda Pop* says that another error of judgment on Mr. Dobbs's part was a conviction that the real market for Coca-Cola was actually the dwindling number of farmers in the nation, and perhaps these ads reflect that mistaken notion. But they were, in their way, a foreshadowing of the Woodruff era's equating Coca-Cola with the American way of life.

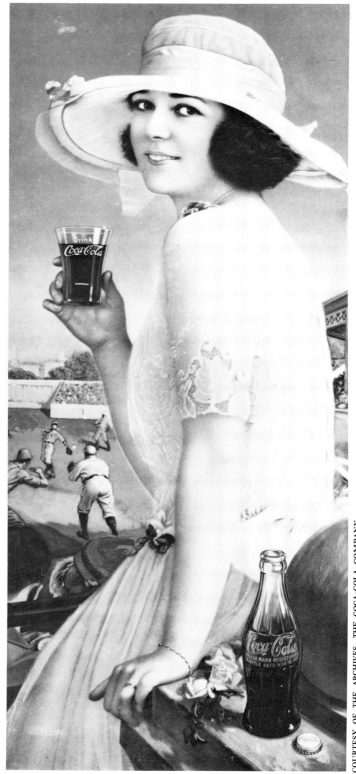

A classical "pretty girl" calendar from 1922.

The Candler era's use of trays, calendars, premiums, and all the rest of the multimedia playing upon the American consciousness was continued under the Woodruff-Lee guidance of the promotion. And there were the inspired flower-arrangement booklets, replete with subtle shots of Coca-Cola in some of the photographs.

Slogan Advertising

When the Woodruff era begins in 1923, we soon see an improvement in the graphics of the four-color magazine ads, and a lessening of copy. "Enjoy Thirst" is the imperative over many 1923 pictures, including one of a young woman in bloomer-style bathing gear water-skiing that early in the country's history. And that same year, like the sounding of a symphonic theme that is to become major, we have "Pause and Refresh Yourself" in an ad about America being the busiest nation on earth, and then, "special little pauses for moments of ease."

Then the slogans, from the inspiration of the Lee-Woodruff team, begin to proliferate: "Refreshment Time," "Around the Corner from Anywhere," "Continuous Quality," "With a drink so good, 'tis folly to be thirsty," "Stop at the Red Sign," "A Hot Day Made Cool," building to the breakthrough in 1926, "It Had to Be Good to Get Where It Is," tapering off to "7 Million a Day," "Pause and Refresh Yourself" repeating itself, and then, "The Shortest Distance Between Thirst and Refreshment," and "The Best-Served Drink in the World," and then, shimmering, first on July 27, 1929, and afterward in ad and sign and billboard over and over again all that year and to this day, "The Pause that Refreshes." One of the first ads showed women in fur coats in a drugstore and the full headline said: "All think alike about The Pause that Refreshes."

The Santa in Coca-Cola Ads

That was the slogan zenith, but other wonders were to come, including a painting of a Santa Claus in a department store in 1930, to be followed the next year by the first of artist Haddon Sundblom's grand drawings each December for many years of Santa Claus in Coca-Cola ads. These not only changed the nation's perception of how Santa looks, from jolly dwarf to the way we envision him today (big, fat, kindly), but also managed to associate Coca-Cola with the most delicious memories of everybody's childhood. (Hunter Bell, the delver into company history, recalls the recent history of how, every year, Marshall Lane, now retired art director, would have to go up to Chicago "and get Sunny cranked up on Santa Claus.")

Wyeth Ads

Soon after, in 1935, came the first of artist N. C. Wyeth's summertime depictions of Coca-Cola as the epitome of what one longs for in the hottest weather, the bottle beadingly cold in a deliciously frigid-looking drift of snow. Sometimes it would be piles of ice rather than snow, but the bottle and glass pictured that way each summer set up an association in the mind entirely satisfying to Coca-Cola.

Billboard Advertising

The technological developments—first cooler, six-pack, and all—were included in, and buttressed by, the advertising and promotion. In the meantime, signs were still going up everywhere. The twenty-four-sheet billboard poster was first put into use in 1925, showing the "Ritz Boy," a Coca-Cola-bearing bellboy. The billboards would repeat all the themes and slogans of the magazine ads across the land in those innocent times when nobody had thought to scorn that medium as visual pollution. Neon and electrically illuminated signs were soon to follow, the first in 1929 at Times Square.

Billboard advertising, 1933.

COURTESY OF THE ARCHIVES, THE COCA-COLA COMPANY

Radio Advertising

Not until 1927 did Coca-Cola advertise on the new medium of radio, with what amounted to the forerunner of the soap opera—short dramas about the life and love of "Vivian, the Coca-Cola Girl," starring Jessica Dragonette. In 1930 began a series of programs featuring sports personalities Grantland Rice and Graham McNamee, and broadcasts of Len Joy's Orchestra. In 1931, it was Gustave Haenschen's Orchestra and in 1934, Frank Black's on "The Pause that Refreshes on the Air." Then came "Refreshment Time" with Ray Noble and his orchestra in 1935 and good old "Singing Sam" in 1937. As the Coca-Cola theme song became a familiar sound, Coca-Cola's approach to the airwaves continued to be one of pleasant, innocuous programs, sports and some comedy, but mostly music, "relaxed listening and wholesome enjoyment in keeping with the character of Coca-Cola itself," as one company publication put it.

The Victorious Coca-Cola Image—Woodruff Style

Anyone from another planet perusing the 1930s advertising would never guess that America was during those years going through the worst depression in its history. To such an alien, America as depicted in the ads was a pleasant place full of pleasant, wholesome people, mostly young, doing pleasant things. But to the people of that time who did know what was going on, there were subtle messages of hope in ad scenes of people gainfully employed (not standing in breadlines) in offices, shops, factories, and, in another ongoing ad tradition, of boys on bicycles delivering Western Union telegrams. But that was as close as the promotion got to reflecting harsh reality. The large exception to the rule of ignoring the unpleasant was to come in the next decade when Pearl Harbor plunged the nation into the worst war ever.

Though wars might rage . . . Robert W. Woodruff, at the helm of the company, had proven himself thoroughly to be a man of his own times, not dismayed or frustrated like Asa Candler by the onrushing developments of modernity, but shrewdly capable of using new realities, new technology, new moods of the American people to aid in selling more and more Coca-Cola at a higher and higher percentage of profit.

J. Lucian Smith, most recent of his successors as company president, says that whenever anybody tries to speak to Mr. Woodruff of what a many-splendored performance of achievement he made during the 1920s and 1930s, he will hear none of it. "If you ask him how he did it, as I do often these days, he says, 'I saved the company. When I came in, it was broke. All I did was save it.'"

Save it he had, by 1941, and in that fateful year he stood ready to move

Atlanta's Grand Ball at the City Auditorium for the December 15, 1939, premiere of *Gone With the Wind.*

with the perilous times to make Coca-Cola an integral part of America's World War II effort, even as the fighting men of the country, the GI Joes, proclaimed the ultimate success of five decades of company promotion by incorporating Coca-Cola into the Trinity of Home and Family and the Girl Next Door for which they endured the hell of foxholes and flame throwers, trench foot and bombing raids. And what Mr. Woodruff was to do with Coca-Cola during World War II was to lead to his next and greatest achievement of all—establishment of the world market.

The company had found a winner to save it, to guide its dedicated workers, including defeat-haunted Southerners, in all the ways of winning, and they would move on together to more and more of the sweet taste of Coca-Cola victory.

VII

Coca-Cola Confronts World Conflicts

There was one bothersome worry for Coca-Cola people during those first two decades of Woodruff-era success. Out of the memories of his childhood, an Atlanta man tells a story illustrative of what an annoyance it must have been. He said he and another boy had a partnership in the summers of 1937 and 1938 running one of those Coca-Cola stands Arthur Montgomery told about.

The man said, "You remember the stands? Bright yellow, with tin signs plastered all over them. A box on legs with a rectangular frame extended upward to accommodate the signs. The signs I liked best were in the shape of the bottle.

"We bought Coca-Cola for 80 cents a case, sold it at a nickel per bottle, retail to gross a dollar twenty, or forty cents profit per case. Some days we sold as much as two cases. But we drank up most of the profit. It was hard to resist those glistening bottles in the washtubful of ice down there in the box part of the stand.

"We weren't really loyal to Coke. We diversified our stock. All the stands did. You'd think the company would have insisted on Coke only, as long as they were providing the stand. Maybe though that would have been in restraint of trade. Anyhow, we sold twelve-ounce Pepsi-Cola and RC Cola, and each of them, unlike Coke, had a line of twelve-ounce, fruit-flavored drinks. Big oranges. Grape. Strawberry. We called them belly-wash. The twelve-ounce drinks sold better than the six-ounce Coke, and when we would uncap a bottle for ourselves, it would usually be one of the twelve-ounce colas. I seem to remember Pepsi tasting the sweetest and RC seeming to fizz more.

Guam, July 1944.

"During one of the summers, there was a WPA project about three blocks from our stand. A crew of fifteen or twenty men were moving dirt with picks and shovels and wheelbarrows into a landfill for a road. Hard labor out in the hot sun. Every day at noon, we would load our washtub into a red wagon and pull it to the worksite to sell our drinks to those thirsty men during their lunch hour. Blacks in the crew would sing work chants handed down from slavery days, and the whites sometimes tried to join in. That was one of the few times when as a boy I ever saw whites and blacks working side by side. It would be a long time after the WPA before I would ever see it again.

"During the lunch break, the workers would rest in the shade, eat from their lunch sacks, and wash their food down with our drinks. But it was usually the twelve-ouncers they clutched in their work-hardened hands, not Coke. *Twice as much for a nickel* is what they liked. And that principle is what did us in there at the worksite.

"For soon, from the other side of the fill, competitors came with their washtub on their red wagon, and they had somehow got hold of a brand of belly-wash called New Yorker which sold an eighteen-ounce bottle for a nickel. They took all our business away there. Quantity, not quality, was clearly preferred by those men who had been sweating all morning doing hard labor in the hot sun. Why we did not stock New Yorker and compete, I cannot recall."

Pepsi-Cola: The First Formidable Competition

"Twice as much for a nickel, too, Pepsi-Cola is the drink for you, nickel, nickel, nickel, trickle, trickle, trickle" had caused Coca-Cola people to look over their shoulders since 1933 when Pepsi was inspired to lower the price of the twelve-ounce drink from ten to five cents. (Interestingly, as Mr. Dietz tells in *Soda Pop*, Pepsi-Cola had a history parallel in time and place, if not in rapid rise, to Coca-Cola's. It was invented in the South, in New Bern, North Carolina, by a pharmacist, Caleb Bradham, in 1893. He named it in 1898 and went into business with it full-time in 1903. But his was the southern fate of defeat, and after bankruptcies and revivals, it was in the hands of sophisticated northern businessmen when the "twice as much" campaign began. According to Mr. Dietz, they reaped profits of $2 million from it in 1936, $3 million in 1937, and $4 million in 1938. Coca-Cola, of course, was making far more than twice as much profit for a nickel drink during those years, but the surge toward success by Pepsi was an ominous sign, a nagging worry to company people. It was the first real competition a cola drink had given the company, and of course Pepsi-Cola would continue to drink of Coca-Cola's market from then on, including the overseas one.

ATLANTA

The Atlanta of the late 1930s, where the young drink-stand merchant learned his lessons of business and the competitive system, was still a bustling place, though slowed down (and made perhaps more peaceful by the Depression). People in their pretty homes on tree-lined streets were startled to hear in September 1939, their neighborhood paper boys shouting from bicycles, "Extra, Extra, Germany invades Poland!" There were subsequent extras about subsequent conquests by Adolf Hitler's new military strategy, the mechanized and motorized *blitzkrieg*, as the city's three dailies, the *Journal*, the *Constitution* and William Randolph Hearst's Atlanta *Georgian*, turned a little depression-era extra profit from the disaster and tragedy occurring in far-off Europe.

Adults there remembered that other war, so this one didn't seem quite so far off. But mostly, Atlantans tried to forget it, preferring to flip by the terrible stories of concentration camps in *Life* magazine to get to "Life Goes to a Party," or the Picture of the Week.

And there were festivities going on later in 1939, right in Atlanta, worthy of *Life*'s going to and drawing Atlanta's attention away from war clouds in Europe. The world premiere of Metro-Goldwyn-Mayer's film version of *Gone With the Wind* was held on December 15 at the Loew's Grand Theater, the old DeGive's New Grand decked out with big white plantation-house columns, spotlights playing on them. Clark Gable, Vivian Leigh, and hosts of other Hollywood celebrities were right there in the flesh, waving from open cars during the grand parade, sitting in the theater watching themselves enact the Atlanta scenes of southern-lack-of-success that Atlanta writer Margaret Mitchell set down in her phenomenally successful novel, and, the night before, dancing and chatting until dawn with bedazzled, but charming, Atlanta socialites during the brilliant ball at the old Atlanta City Auditorium on Courtland Street, followed by a festive breakfast served flawlessly by black hands onto the Piedmont Driving Club's pristine white tablecloths.

Caught up in the spirit of the day, the Atlanta Gas Light Company had run a line to reactivate the last standing lamppost, which had been erected downtown in 1855—this one at the corner of Whitehall and Alabama streets, with a dent where a Union shell grazed it in 1865. Mrs. Thomas J. Ripley, president of the Atlanta Chapter, United Daughters of the Confederacy, touched a match to light "the eternal flame of the Confederacy," amid ceremonies carried out by members of the Atlanta Old Guard in their Confederate-style uniforms. The worst of southern defeats had been turned into victory, and we may be certain that the people of Coca-Cola were among the happiest and most charming of the celebrants. (The eternal flame no longer burns. Subway construction did what Sherman's shells could not to the lamppost. It is no more.)

Clark Gable and Vivien Leigh with Atlanta author Margaret Mitchell (center), during the premiere of the film based upon her book.

It was quite a year, 1939, for Atlanta. That summer, just before war came, the World Baptist Alliance was held in the city, and Atlantans saw among them, attending the sessions at the Ponce de Leon Ballpark, all of the earth's variety of people, soon to be at each other's throats. But then the sight merely foreshadowed the international city that Atlanta was to become in the 1970s, with Coca-Cola, of course, leading the way to that. A photograph of flags of participating nations draped over Peachtree Street appears in the book, *Yesterday's Atlanta* by the city's long-time historian in residence, Franklin M. Garrett,* and included is Germany's swastika hanging down—the sight of which is capable, to this day, of sending a chill through the viewer, idly leafing through the book and suddenly coming upon it.

Two years later, history repeating itself, America was no longer able to stay out of the war in Europe. When that fateful year of 1941 came, Ol' Gene Talmadge, in and out of the governor's office in the 1930s, was in it once more. A rip-roaring Populist *cum* racial demagogue, he was the great favorite of the state's then considerable number of farm folks who absolutely controlled state politics. It was said of his rural followers that if Ol' Gene prophesied it would rain buttermilk at a certain time and place, they would be there in great throngs with pails in which to catch some. Ol' Gene boasted that he had never carried a town big enough to have streetcars and never wanted to. (One of his Populist

* Published by E. A. Seemann Publishing, Inc., Miami. Mr. Garrett, after many years with The Coca-Cola Company, became historian of the Atlanta Historical Society and for the city of Atlanta.

tax measures had sent The Coca-Cola Company executive headquarters into exile in Delaware where the company was incorporated. But the bottling plant and offices remained in Atlanta. Georgia Senator Herman Talmadge, Ol' Gene's son, was, as we shall see, instrumental in changing the law, when he was governor, so that the headquarters could return to Atlanta.)

Atlanta, in 1941, still had its streetcars—their whine and rattling and small roar, soothing to the sleep. They were not to disappear until 1949 when, in the name of progress, trackless trolleys, more awkward and with no style, replaced them, only to be replaced themselves later by even more awkward buses to consume energy and help poison the air. (Currently, subways are being tunneled, the largest single construction project underway in the South.)

In 1941, Mayor William B. Hartsfield was at the start of his long and progressive rule of the city, regarding the municipality as his private possession and guiding it, with the advice, often, of his friend since childhood, Robert W. Woodruff, sanely and civilizedly through much growth, including the early rigors of the subsequent 1960s racial revolution, making it the pre-eminent leader among southern cities.

Atlantans by 1941 had escaped some of the depression's deprivations. They could afford an occasional night out at the Rainbow Roof of the Ansley Hotel or the Paradise Room of the Henry Grady Hotel, carrying their liquor there in brown bags. Or they could dine at one of a number of fairly good restaurants, including Camellia Gardens on Peachtree Road whose Japanese proprietors were soon to be taken off to an internment compound. Or, as the young folks liked to do, Atlantans could stop by the Varsity, "World's Largest Drive-in" on North Avenue near the Georgia Institute of Technology for an M-K dog (mustard-ketchup hotdog) and a PC (plain chocolate milk).

Atlantans enjoyed first-run movies at five downtown theaters and second-runs at countless neighborhood houses. Among the downtown theaters, they could sit in the Fox, whose architecture suggested Moorish opulence and, during dull moments of the movie, gaze up at the ceiling which was contrived to look like the heavens, with stars twinkling. By this time the enormous pipe organ which used to be played between features was no longer in use. Public-minded citizens of the 1970s were to fight to save the old Fox from the ravages of ongoing demolition for new downtown construction and, for the time anyhow, were successful.

People, too, still enjoyed an afternoon at the Grant Park zoo, or a picnic at Stone Mountain before it lost dignity by becoming a Disneyland-like state park. And in droves during the hot summers, with no home air conditioning, they went swimming. A favorite pool was on Briarcliff Road. Asa Candler, Jr., who had deserted Coca-Cola in the 1920s to raise poultry and fine horses, among other enterprises, owned the pool. He had gotten into a quarrel with the city about his water bill at his mansion there and had had a well dug. Its flow was so prodigious, he built a laundry on one part of the estate and had the large swimming pool built right on the vast rolling lawn in front of the mansion. For a time during the 1930s he had, adjoining the pool, a good-sized zoo, including two elephants named Coca and Cola and lions whose roars echoed in the night through Druid Hills and much of the rest of the middle-class Northeast section.

The site is now occupied by a state mental health center specializing in treatment of alcoholics.

We have, of course, been following the ordinary pursuits of middle-class Atlantans. The poor of both races in their considerable number were all the while living out lives mired in the old tradition of southern defeat.

The young of the middle class followed a tradition of pretentious elegance and courtly ways that began in the 1920s and harked wistfully back to the times of big barbecues and grand balls exaggeratedly described in *Gone With the Wind*. On weekend nights, high school fraternities and sororities would, two to a weekend, hold elaborate dances in the hotel ballrooms and country clubs of the city, with excellent local swing bands and sometimes a name band (Gene Krupa, Cab Calloway). The girls, who from their 1920s mamas had got a strange language of triple negatives ("He's not very cute, oh no," meaning he's cute), wore lovely net evening gowns, sometimes strapless, and the boys, tuxedos with boiled-front shirts and the vestigial descendant of those turn-of-the-century stiff collars.

They danced no-breaks and specials and the sorority or fraternity lead-out to "Night and Day," and "Stardust," and they jitterbugged to such Glenn Miller favorites as "String of Pearls," "In the Mood," and "Song of the Volga Boatmen." On Sunday afternoons, following the dances on Friday and Saturday nights, they held sorority and fraternity meetings in members' homes where Coca-Colas and party sandwiches were served. After these, the girls (called pinks) would sit home waiting hopefully while the boys (called jellies after jellybean, a derivative possibly of Coca-Cola cake eaters, *circa* 1920) in carloads would drive about, calling on pinks of their choosing, making seven or eight such visits of a late Sunday afternoon and evening, assured at each stop of banter and horseplay among their fellows and flirtatious attention from the hostess—who always had ready ice-cold bottles of Coca-Cola, bought by the caseloads by her parents for these occasions.

Coca-Cola Intermeshes Its History with International Events

In the world of this ritual there was a particularly splendid dance one Saturday night at the Brookhaven Country Club with a touring band of black musicians providing unusually spirited and sometimes downright raucous music, and the band leader, sweat beading his fat, quite black face, would intermittently shout out as the music blared, "Peace! Peace! There ain't nothing like a good peace," at which double entendre the boys would guffaw and the girls would grimace and say, "That's not vulgar, not very."

The roads were icy that night, adding daredevil delight to the ritual of going to the Varsity (a good ten miles) at intermission, and getting home after the dance ended at 2 A.M., pausing along the way perhaps to catch a little monk (pet). On the morrow, the fraternities and sororities held their regular meetings, but the mood on this Sunday was extraordinary. The news had come that morning concerning the bombing of Pearl Harbor. Boys sat or stood about in knots, serious and somber, talking of going off to war. The girls, similarly sobered, began to realize that their jellies would soon be marching away from them.

Atlanta, the United States, and the world would never again know the serenity of those simple days and years leading up to America's being precipitated overnight into the awful fray of World War II, with a jarring suddenness.

Wars might rage . . . the Coca-Cola history from 1941 to 1945 was to be totally involved in that one big important happening, no longer, and not wanting to be, apart and immune. The company's wartime history is brief, but most crucial:

January 1, 1941: The Coca-Cola Company starts the year with the first advertising budget exceeding $10 million.

December 10, 1941: Three days after Pearl Harbor and the nickname "Coke" is first used on bottles and subsequently in advertising and promotion interchangeably with the older trademark.

December 1941: Robert W. Woodruff announces The Coca-Cola Company's wartime policy: "We will see that every man in uniform gets a bottle of Coca-Cola for five cents wherever he is and whatever it costs."

The start of 1942: History repeating itself—Coca-Cola is beset by the wartime shortage of sugar. The company is rationed to half its prewar average consumption of the main ingredient of Coca-Cola.

June 29, 1943: General Dwight D. Eisenhower, from the Allied Headquarters in North Africa, near the beginning of the first of the offensives to get into Europe and retake it from the Nazis, sends a message to Quartermaster officials in the States: "On early convoy request shipment three million bottled Coca-Cola (filled) and complete equipment for bottling, washing, capping same quantity twice monthly." It is a call for Coca-Cola plants to be set up as near as possible to the fighting front of the war in the interest of maintaining the morale of America's GIs. The Coca-Cola Company, already fully following Mr. Woodruff's orders to get the drink to servicemen at home and behind the lines, responds with alacrity, beginning an adventure unparalleled in the annals of military and commercial history.

July 10, 1944: Though war might rage and sugar be rationed, one of the plants turns out the billionth gallon of Coca-Cola syrup since Dr. Pemberton stirred the first one.

The winter of 1945: The triumphant fighting Americans, men and women, are coming home from all the reaches of earth, and an eloquent public relations man can write of Coca-Cola without exaggeration: "What was once in far places a reminder of home is now again the happy symbol of a friendly way of life." Now The Coca-Cola Company could get back to the business, as usual, of increasing efficiency and selling more drinks. That year, it set up in Atlanta a production school for bottling personnel.

Coca-Cola Follows the American Troops Overseas

Robert W. Woodruff promulgated that famous *wherever-at-whatever-the-cost* order of his without consulting any committees or calling for a meeting of the board of directors to approve it, according to J. Lucian Smith, Coca-Cola president in the 1970s. "It came out of his head and his soul."

This is the
1 Billionth
Gallon *of*
Coca-Cola Syrup
MANUFACTURED BY
THE COCA-COLA COMPANY
July 12, 1944

Presented to MR. CHAS. HOWARD CANDLER.
Son of the founder of Coca-Cola and former
president of the Coca-Cola Company. Mr. Candler
is at present a director of the Coca-Cola Company
and of the Trust Company of Georgia.

By war's end, five billion bottles of Coca-Cola had found their way to all those places where our fighting men and women were. The sugar for these was allotted to the company above and beyond the half-share ration for civilian consumption. In our own cynical and disillusioned time, the immediate assumption about what was in Mr. Woodruff's head and soul when he issued the order would be that it was the obvious production and promotional value which the campaign would have for the company. But those years when Americans joined people of many lands to fight down the ugly totalitarianism of Nazism were not cynical ones. The war was history's ultimate melodrama of good against evil. The evil was all too genuine, and the best was brought out in those who fought it. The nation had reached a height of its idealism—perhaps *the* height. And when men like Mr. Woodruff at the head of large companies spoke of helping the war effort, of abetting the fighting forces, they can, in the context of the time, be credited with speaking as much out of patriotic as profit motivation.

The vast and, by then, sophisticated company and bottlers' distribution systems swung into action to carry out Mr. Woodruff's order. James M. Kahn, in an unpublished manuscript resting now in the company archives,† tells how—first with the bottlers in charge, but soon with the company taking over direction—the distribution system provided 212 million cases of Coca-Cola to military installations and vessels in this country during the war years.

Then he recounts the adventure of shipping it overseas. The idea of shipping plants about the world had been born even before America entered the war, when the company encountered difficulty getting seventeen thousand cases to peacetime draftees stationed in Iceland in October 1941. But it took a War Department Circular signed by General George C. Marshall, allowing theater and area commanders to order the plants (as well as General Eisenhower's dramatic message), to set the adventure in motion in 1943. General Eisenhower's message called for "ten separate machines for installation in different localities, each complete for bottling twenty thousand bottles per day." Shipments were not to displace military cargo.

"Data here very meager as to these installations and operations," the message said. "Request they be checked by fully qualified sources. . . ." The Coca-Cola Company, of course, had such sources, and a program was set up whereby company men were attached to the Army as "Technical Observers," with officer rank and pay but not commissions, to be in charge of the overseas bottling plants. There were 148 of these TOs in all, and they set up sixty-three full-size plants the world over. Two were killed in the line of duty, Mr. Kahn having recorded their names: Turk Beard and Jake Sutton.

Beginning in North Africa and moving up into Italy, the bottling plants followed the battle fronts; some of the plants picked up and relocated as the fighting moved on. In Mr. Kahn's words, they went into the "heat and mud and foul jungles of the Pacific, the foggy cold and snow of the Aleutians," to Africa, Italy, France, Germany, India and the Philippines, England and Australia

† He wrote it for the company as an employee of Steve Hannagan's public relations organization in 1946. An eloquent, factual account, it was finally rejected for publication on the simple reasoning that people were tired of hearing about the war, wanted to put it behind them. The manuscript would be set aside "until historians begin to resurrect it," a company letter on the matter stated.

—on every continent of earth. One was at Brussels six weeks after D-day in 1944, and the plants followed the Army from there on to victory in Berlin.

Five were in operation in Japan when V-J Day came after the fearsome bombing of Hiroshima and Nagasaki. Installations in the Pacific didn't begin until 1944 because the war out there shifted about so much. Before 1944, small portable bottling units, capable of being hauled behind a jeep, were used. Mr. Kahn also tells how portable dispensers of the fountain drink were used. This began early in the war in 1942 when the Japanese were threatening Australia, and young, inexperienced American airmen were trying to do battle in B-26 bombers with heavy casualties. Their commander appealed to a bottler in Australia for Coca-Cola to help boost morale. The bottler came up with a portable dispenser that had been used for demonstrations at drug conventions. Soon after, General Douglas MacArthur, through the agency of the Coca-Cola Export Corporation, had a more durable jungle dispenser designed, and it was used throughout the Pacific campaigns. (General MacArthur, like General Eisenhower, was a Coca-Cola fan. He showed up when the first Pacific war plant was opened in Manila and signed a tag attached to the first bottle. This is now among the company's treasures.)

Lynn LaGarde, a retired director of the engineering department, recalls his work designing the portable plants used in the Pacific. They were small, capable of producing seventy to seventy-five gallons of the drink in an hour, with two people operating one. The Liquid Carbonic Company of Chicago built the plants. They were designed to use cylinders of carbon dioxide. But when the first twenty models arrived in Australia, it was discovered that the cylinders over there had British threads which wouldn't fit the American threads on the machines. "They couldn't connect the damn things," Mr. LaGarde said with a Southerner's wry chuckle over defeat. "They had to get adapters. Things like that, you can lose a war."

Coca-Cola Goes to France

John Talley, who was with the company in various capacities, including president of the Export Corporation and now retired, has his own wry chuckling recollections of experiences as a TO. He was in the first group to head out for England in September 1944, shortly after the D-day invasion of the Normandy coast. From England, after a short wait, he went to France to install in Paris the $250,000 bottling equipment he had found with difficulty (spare plants were scarce) in New York.

The equipment had landed in Le Havre, and when Mr. Talley arrived to have it transported to Paris, he learned to his dismay that a sixty-spout filler had, during the unloading, met the fate that jeeps and trucks often did in such operations. It had broken the line of the crane and sunk in ninety feet of water.

The Battle of the Bastogne Bulge was mercilessly underway in the winter's snow. GIs wanted Coca-Cola, Mr. Talley said, but to fighting men at such a time, something like a sunken sixty-spout Coca-Cola filler was an insignificant matter. "And," Mr. Talley sort of wailed his memory of the time, "a pore little old fellow from Alabama was going to try to get somebody to stop doing what they were doing, with the war in a critical state, and go down and get a bottling unit."

But as might be expected, the pore little old fellow from Alabama worked diligently and intrepidly to find where the filler went down and then, with his charm, talked a second lieutenant into donning his diver's suit and mucking around in mud on the harbor floor to locate it. But when it was found and hauled to the surface, Mr. Talley saw, again to his dismay, that disaster had followed fast and followed faster. The crate in which the filler was packed had split asunder when it fell from the broken crane line onto the surface of the water. The piece of machinery was "just a pile of rust."

More diligence and charm were required to get a Navy Ordnance crew to take it apart, get rid of the rust, and put it back together "better than it had been before." Now Mr. Talley was ready to haul it triumphantly to Paris, only to discover yet another obstacle. The thing weighed thirty-five tons and no barge or small-gauge rail equipment in France could handle it. The icy slaughter of the Bulge was still going on, so Mr. Talley had the task of trying to talk an officer of Ordnance into letting him use a tank retriever. The officer said all tank retrievers were needed at the front. What did Mr. Talley need one for anyway? Mr. Talley replied that he was trying to get Coca-Cola into production for the troops. The officer said he hadn't seen a Coca-Cola in two years. Did Mr. Talley happen to have any? Mr. Talley said he thought he knew where a couple of cases might be found. The officer smiled. "He said, 'Get me a case of Coca-Cola and I'll get you a tank retriever.'"

Now, the triumphant entry to Paris was eminent—except that, when the tank retriever with its thirty-five-ton cargo approached the city, Mr. Talley and its crew discovered that the filler was too high to go under the many railroad underpasses on their route. They tried three other routes only to come up each time before an underpass three or four inches too short. Finally a sergeant in the crew solved the problem by deflating the tires on the retriever. At last, wobbling along on flats, the triumphant entry was made.

"That plant is still there today, supplying Coke to the French," Mr. Talley said. "And that's how it got there while the Bastogne Bulge was raising hell and Patton was running out of gas."

Such scrounging and improvisation were common in getting plants set up in all the theaters of war. When a plant got into operation, Mr. Talley said, word would get around among the troops, and drivers of six-by-six troop transports would come in from the forward areas and load up at no charge.

When Mr. Talley was running the plant in Brussels, he encountered an old friend from Alabama one day on the street. The friend was an Airborne colonel with battle scars and a chestful of medals. Mr. Talley, at the moment of encounter, was returning from the respite of a game of golf, and had his golf bag over his uniformed shoulder. His old friend, hands on hips, surveying him, said,

"John, this is a hell of a way for you to be fighting a war." Mr. Talley laughed. "I said, 'It sho' is, Hugh.'"

Then he explained his mission, and the Airborne colonel said, "You mean you have Coca-Cola just for somebody's coming to get and take it?" Mr. Talley allowed as how that was the way it was, and, in a few days, a convoy of twenty-six trucks, dispatched by the colonel, arrived at the plant where three hundred cases were loaded on each truck. When they arrived back at the Airborne base, the colonel was a hero to his division.

Coca-Cola in Brazil

H. Burke Nicholson, Jr., an overseas Coca-Cola man through his career, told of his experience as a TO in Brazil. He had a plant moved from a site at the mouth of the Amazon River (a hellhole, he said quietly) two thousand miles inland where it could service Navy personnel and the U. S. Armed Forces, South Atlantic. The big bombers refueled here, and there were many servicemen to provide with Coca-Cola. Mr. Nicholson got the plant running, organized the distribution, hired the labor, set the prices, and operated for two years until the war was over. Then he closed the military operation and sold the plant to a Brazilian subsidiary. In all that time, he was the only company representative in the vicinity. For all they knew at headquarters, Mr. Nicholson said with a smile, the profits he sent in might have been won at some gaming table.

An early Coca-Cola pushcart and poster in Brazil.

COURTESY OF THE COCA-COLA COMPANY

Coca-Cola Behind Enemy Lines

While the bottling plants were following the battlegrounds, another kind of wartime drama was going on in enemy countries or ones occupied by the enemy where Coca-Cola bottlers had to survive. From those Candler-era plants in Cuba and the Philippines, Coca-Cola had, haphazardly and in no great strength, been spreading into other countries, a number of them in Europe. In most instances, the bottlers were citizens of the country, and when America entered the war those in Germany or German-occupied territory found themselves in the touchy position of representing an American company.

Dr. May, the retired chief chemist who traveled extensively in Europe after the war, told the story he heard from Carl West, the Belgian bottler. When Mr. West heard on the radio that the Nazi *blitzkrieg* was aimed at his country, he gathered all his trucks and drivers in a desperate attempt to flee the country ahead of the enemy. When he saw they couldn't make it, so great was the speed of Hitler's mechanized forces, he turned his convoy around and sneaked it back into Brussels.

Max Keith

By far, the most extraordinary of those indigenous bottlers in enemy territory was Max Keith (pronounced Kite) who had been operating successfully in Germany since 1933. A tall, imposing figure, handsome, with dark hair and a small mustache, Herr Keith emerges as yet another strong man working under and encouraged by Mr. Woodruff. Hunter Bell tape-recorded Herr Keith's recollections of the war years in 1966, a short while before his death. The recollections were of a harrowing time throughout.

"After Hitler took over, they claimed we were an American-Jewish company, because to many of the Nazi people, Americans and Jews were just identical. Consequently, our salesmen had also quite a few battles in the taverns with party members. . . .

"One of our competitors went visiting the United States, made a tour of the New York Coca-Cola bottling plant and picked up some crown corks with a Kosher sign on them. After his return to this country, he reproduced pictures of these crowns with millions of copies and mailed them all over Germany to party members, officials, everywhere, saying that this was the proof that The Coca-Cola Company was Jewish. So we had a very difficult time to withstand this attack."

Another prewar problem was restrictions on imports. "They said they had to import more important things." To get clearance to keep getting syrup con-

COURTESY OF THE COCA-COLA COMPANY

Max Keith.

centrate, Herr Keith used the intermediary efforts of the European representative of an American bank who had "contacts" with Air Minister Hermann Göring's office.

Shortly before the war, H. B. Nicholson, Sr., then European manager for The Coca-Cola Company, asked Herr Keith to look after the other European operations if hostilities should break out. When they did, Herr Keith, through his company's lawyer in Berlin, succeeded in getting the Office of Enemy Propaganda to appoint him an official administrator of soft-drink properties in the occupied countries. He was not a member of the Nazi party (though Claus Halle, a company official who worked under Herr Keith after the war, said there were numerous attempts to force him to join, which he somehow "was able to resist"). The appointment was apparently by default and considered of not much importance.

But for Herr Keith, it "made it quite easy for me to travel all round and help these people to stay out of trouble." He went to Luxembourg, Belgium, and France throughout the war, and to Holland and Italy where there were company-owned plants, as well as Norway and Switzerland where there were field offices. At the start of the war, Herr Keith had too little syrup concentrate to supply the demand for Coca-Cola in Germany, so he divided it among the other countries where the demand was less, and the bottlers in them were able to produce the drink for several years.

In 1940, Herr Keith concocted a drink from available ingredients (and these would vary through the war years) which he named Fanta, from the concept of "fantastic," and bottled and sold it through the war years in Germany, sharing its formula with the other countries to keep their plants running.

One of those whom Herr Keith got out of trouble during the war was Mr. West, the bottler in Brussels. "One of his employees . . . went to the occupation authorities saying that West hoarded sugar which actually should be reported to the food office for distribution. Actually what Carl had was a kind of prefabricated raw material—a mixture of sugar and caramel. So he was in a bad spot and I had to go there and see that it was straightened out. Fortunately, I could do it. Then there were many other instances of that sort, because disloyalty among employees during the wartime was quite a regular occurrence—the same as in Germany."

Dr. May filled in details of that escapade. He said Mr. West told him he did have sugar, precious sugar, and when the calls kept coming to turn in sugar, he just couldn't bring himself to do it. "You don't act normally in such a situation," Dr. May commented. When severe penalties for not turning in sugar were announced, Mr. West and his chemist furtively and frantically mixed the sugar with caramel, making a thick, gooey, and entirely useless mess which they put in sugar bags. They hid the bags in the middle of a stack of hundreds of Coca-Cola cases. When a search party, armed with guns, came, Mr. West and his chemist stood back watching helplessly while the searchers started pulling the crates away one by one. The foolish contraband was back behind stacks of crates one hundred deep, and as Dr. May tells the story, the searchers reached the ninety-eighth stack before giving up in disgust.

Though war might rage all about him, Herr Keith was as single-minded as any loyal Coca-Cola man in America. "During the war," he said in his interview with Mr. Bell, "you should not make too high a profit, particularly not as an enemy company, and so we tried to have a reasonable level of sales volume that would give a fair profit and no more and keep a good stock of material on hand, which I always did. So you see we had a good business volume in spite of factories being blown up or getting on fire. . . ."

The way he was able to keep producing Fanta during the increasingly fierce air raids was to set up what he called "siding plants" on the outskirts of cities. He put small bottling machines, obtained from fifteen company plants and thirty-four independent bottlers, in old farmhouses, country dairies, and the like. When the big plant in a city would be bombed out, production would start up in the side plant until the big one could be repaired.

Of the side plants, Herr Keith told Mr. Bell, "We would have been pushed out of the business if we had not had them." But he had them from 1942 on through "the height of the war when we had air raids day and night. . . . We were in this way in a position to keep our sales on an almost even level, and that was not just because it happened that way, but it was a planned program. We did not want to sell out of ingredients, to sell out of bottles, to sell out of this and that. I wanted to keep the business on a level where we made a reasonably good profit. . . ."

Herr Keith said another problem was the water supply. "In the cities after an air raid, even if the plant was not hit, you had no water, no electricity; you had nothing. However, with the siding plants in the country, you see, we had everything. It was quite a program and it paid off. We made money every year in spite of the war.'"

Mr. Halle, a vice-president in charge of foreign sales, described the ingenious way Herr Keith was able to hang onto at least the more decrepit trucks of his fleet. Since he was using another bottle for Fanta, he had thousands of empty Coca-Cola bottles. By arrangement with the authorities, he filled these with carbonated water and stored them in each city to provide drinking water to the populace when air raids shut off the normal water supply. Thus was Max Keith allowed to keep his trucks and get some fuel for them. Also, Coca-Cola indirectly saved lives among a civilian population under the worst bombardment in warfare's history.

Dr. May in his postwar travels picked up two stories, suggestive of Divine intervention, about close calls Herr Keith had. Early in the war, a Nazi army colonel noted repeated draft deferments for the Coca-Cola man and ordered him to report to his office so that the colonel might personally induct him into the army. When Herr Keith reported on the appointed day, he was told that the colonel had been killed the night before. Drunk, he had refused to heed a sentry's challenge and was shot to death.

Toward the end of the war, the Nazis began to carry out threats to take over Herr Keith's business. He was to report to another office, a general's this time, to sign over the company he had given as much of himself to as Asa Candler had to his. He was also to discuss "other matters" with the general, meaning that he was to be sent to a concentration camp. Again, at the appointed hour, Herr Keith learned of a sudden fatality. The general, wearing spurs, had tripped on one of them at the head of a flight of marble stairs and fallen to his death—again just the night before. Herr Keith and his company survived to the end of the war a few months later. His first contact with Coca-Cola people at war's end came when a group of TOs, John Talley among them, drove up to his plant in a weapons carrier. The reunion must have been joyful.

Coca-Cola's Wartime Advertising and Promotion

The formidable Coca-Cola advertising and promotion machine swung solidly in line behind the war effort. On December 27, 1941, a hand thrust a Coke bottle from an Air Force-looking wing, and the ad copy read: "A time of crisis comes to America. The rising tempo of emergency is felt in factory and camp. It reaches into home and school. . . . Americans must be fit . . . avoid the tensions that lower efficiency." Many things contribute to fitness. "One of

Pause...
and shop refreshed

Going from shop to shop, counter to counter, you spend something you didn't bargain on ...energy. So when you're tired and thirsty, go straight to the soda fountain and enjoy *the pause that refreshes* with ice-cold Coca-Cola...a little minute that's long enough for a big rest.

Drink

Coca-Cola
TRADE MARK REG. U. S. PAT. OFF.

Delicious and Refreshing

5¢

THE PAUSE THAT REFRESHES

A continuation of the "women shoppers" theme, this time in an October 1940 issue of *The Saturday Evening Post*.

them is the pause that refreshes with ice-cold Coca-Cola. . . . On sea and land it follows the flag."

Early in 1942, an ad headline announced: "Again Sugar Enlists for Victory," and, with a copy of the World War I "Making a Soldier of Sugar" ad in the layout, this one went on to say: "Our volume had been reduced. But this we pledge: The character of Coca-Cola will be unimpaired."

The company began sponsoring Spotlight Bands on radio in November 1941. When war came the next month, it began sending the bands to military installations and defense plants, broadcasting such greats as Count Basie, Duke Ellington, Artie Shaw, and Harry James on the Victory Parade of Spotlight Bands. On Christmas Day, 1942, Coca-Cola presented eleven hours of fifteen-minute musical segments, each by a different Spotlight Band. The bands played on until 1946. Morton Downey began singing for Coke in 1943. All of it was, of course, a pleasant respite from news of the war.

"Work refreshed," rang out the slogan in 1942, showing defense workers hard at it. Every phase of the war effort and the people fighting it was depicted in the ads with the same encouragement of pride and self-respect that had characterized peacetime promotion. One masterpiece depicted, simply and starkly, a factory whistle with Coke bottle superimposed, and extrolled the role played by defense workers. Increasingly toward the end of the war, the ads told how people of other nations were enjoying Coca-Cola's pauses. And of course it was pointed out: "Despite the fact that many bottling plants are cut off in many occupied lands, Coca-Cola is still being bottled in over thirty-five allied and neutral nations. So our fighting men can still enjoy it many places overseas."

The Soldiers' Image of Coca-Cola

The fighting men overseas. Many were like those Atlanta jellies, fresh-faced and eager, having grown up in the pinch of the Depression and felt only in their teens the beginning lift to life that prosperity brings, only to be marched, eighteen years old, into a hell of mechanized mayhem and slaughter in war's unchanging setting of mud and filth; the fresh faces, soon to have the weary and sad lines of the faces of Bill Mauldin's Willie and Joe. But like those two, they held to their humor and good sense in an insane situation and kept, most of them, their decency. More than one German who was a child when the GIs came marching in has told how one of these helmeted men, dirty, bearded, and feared as a fiend, bent down and spoke gentle words, proffered candy, asserted humanity.

They came, as soldiers must, to despise the war, but not the cause for which they fought. And Coca-Cola, they—rather than the company's skilled promotion machine—proclaimed as part of what they were fighting for: a symbol of the decency of the America they knew and the innocent happy times they remembered when they were growing up. It was a remarkable climax to the product's fifty years of promotional insinuation into the fabric of everyday American life, equating Coca-Cola with America itself. "The demand and longing" of the fighting men, and not sales promotion, "prompted the overseas program," as Mr. Kahn pointed out in his unpublished manuscript.

He went on to quote letters back home from the front telling of the longing, of Coca-Cola as symbol—"a little piece of home." One spoke of the "red letter day" when your two letters and six bottles of Coca-Cola arrived at mail call. The writer gave a bottle to each of his two tent-mates and kept the other four. They set the six bottles out on a table, and just looked at them. The six bottles of Coca-Cola would bring a hundred dollars apiece. "But no thank you," the letter concluded. "It is surprising what just a little thing like a Coca-Cola means to a man in the Army over here."

Another said, "I don't know what I'm saving the Coke for, but I sure hate to drink it. I guess it keeps my morale up just to have it and look at it."

War correspondent Ernie Pyle wrote about a GI in Italy who raffled off a single bottle of Coca-Cola to raise $4,000 for a fund to aid survivors of slain buddies.

There is much lore, too, of how the bottles were used as implements of warfare: as emergency insulators for jerry-made electric rigs, as bombs dropped on Japanese air strips to deflate tires and thereby bombing runs. Mr. Kahn tells of a besieged group of forty-three aviation engineers who, for fifty-five days after Pearl Harbor, defended the strategic Canton Island Base with an arsenal of forty rifles, seven pistols, and "a helluva lot of Coca-Cola bottles." No mention is made in company literature of that other use of bottles—as containers for Molotov cocktails, filled with kerosene and thrown with a lit fuse as an incendiary weapon (no more than there is of subsequent employment of Molotov cocktails in domestic American rioting, with *The New York Review of Books*, in a fit of radical chic irresponsibility and inanity, running on its front page an illustrated set of instructions on how to construct one).

But the main role was as symbol. "After spending six months and not being able to purchase so much as a bar of soap, I started through the chow line to find they were passing out Coca-Colas . . ." reads a cherished letter in the company archives from a GI who was in the Pacific Theater. "I can truthfully say that I haven't seen smiles spread over a bunch of boys' faces as they did when they saw the Coca-Cola in this God-forsaken place."

And another on why the writer was fighting: "It's the girl friend back home in a drugstore over a Coke, or the jukebox and the summer weather. It's the lights suddenly twinkling on the highway as you drive along, or shining out from some village by the wayside."

We may look back from our own disillusioned perspective on these homesick words of love of a way of life and scorn the men who fought World War II for being so shallow and so lacking in cultural nurture as to be able to hold up nothing more than a commercial product, a five-cent soft drink, as the highest order of the civilization for which they fought. We may do that, but—knowing what the drink had made itself come to mean to America and conceding that decency back then was not dead in the land—it won't wash.

Our fighting men went on to win the war on the ground in Europe, and

The pause that refreshes

DRINK
Coca-Cola

"It's the girl friend back home in a drugstore over a Coke. . . ." (Promotion calendar, 1940.)

from the air over Japan in earth's most awesome, ominous moment. General Jonathan M. Wainwright, come home to a hero's welcome in the spring of 1946, sat in a box seat in Washington, D.C., watching the grand old American game of baseball, and was photographed eating a hot dog and drinking a bottle of ice-cold Coca-Cola. And the boys were back home, too. Coca-Cola's domestic distribution system could crank up again. And the war had brought more prosperity. Americans no longer needed twice as much for a nickel too. That was a reminder of unpleasantness past. Now they wanted the quality drink. Coca-Cola, with its winning ways, would continue its winning streak in postwar America.

But that was only the half of it. There had been all of that talk by GIs in every part of the world about their feeling for Coca-Cola, and all of their drinking of it in every part of the world and, more importantly for the purposes of The Coca-Cola Company, all of their sharing of it with the people of foreign lands. The result of all that provided the company with a new market to go after, a new territory: *the rest of the world*. And there was even a nucleus for the means of production—those bottling plants scattered around the globe.

Mr. Kahn, in his unpublished manuscript, summed up what the overseas campaign had, all unplanned, accomplished: "Coca-Cola became the Global High-Sign. Though the company was prepared to write off loss, the program paid. It made friends, and customers for home consumption, of eleven million GIs. It did sampling and expansion jobs abroad which would have taken twenty-five years and millions of dollars."

John Talley, citing the same gains, summed it up in a different way, using Confederate General Nathan B. Forrest's famous phrase: "We got there fustest with the mostest."

The moment that the Allied victory was announced from Berlin, Max Keith walked out of his office in Essen and went to the telegraph company to send this cable to Robert W. Woodruff:

COCA-COLA GMBH SURVIVES. PLEASE SEND THE AUDITORS.

Mr. Woodruff must have smiled to read that. He and his hard-working company stood ready now to go out and win the world.

VIII

Oh, So You Have It Here, Too?

Coca-Cola was poised at the end of World War II to take the world. The story, over the ensuing years, of just how it did that brings us into our own times, and these are not necessarily happy ones. The nation which reached the height of its idealism in World War II has, since then, seen so many of its ideals betrayed in the high places of both its government and its businesses. Everyone and everything successful now is suspect, and among the least approved are the multinational corporations. So, in following the story of Coca-Cola, we are no longer savoring the simple and innocent quaintness of Dr. Pemberton and his brass kettle. We are rather seeking perspective in a world made small enough by jet-speed travel to be "the territory" for Coca-Cola—but at a time when treachery is a hallmark of agencies involved in international matters, from the CIA to United Nations debate. How fares the company's pure and single-minded quest for success in a world made cynical by the march of unhappy events?

International Expansion During the Candler Era

Perhaps it is important that Coca-Cola is not one of the postwar, Johnny-come-lately multinationals. We know that giving Coca-Cola to the rest of the world had been at least a glimmer in the mind of Asa Candler during his grand days. As far back as 1896, he had told his directors: "We are firmly convinced that wherever there are people and soda fountains, Coca-Cola will, by its now universally recognized merit, win its way quickly to the front rank of popular-

The Coca-Cola trademark in various languages around the world.

Buddhist monks drinking Coca-Cola.

Spanish dancers at a cultural festival sponsored by Coca-Cola.

ity." And there was that fine time of near-hubris when he told his sons to go forth to foreign lands so that they might map out new conquests.

During the Candler era, soda fountain and bottling efforts of varying degrees of success were put into operation first in Canada, in 1900, then in Cuba, Jamaica, Germany, Hawaii, Bermuda, Mexico, Puerto Rico, the Philippines, France, and England.

The first effort in Great Britain was quite small. Charles Howard Candler, looking for those new conquests, took along a gallon of syrup on his trip to Europe in 1900 and gave samples of it to restaurant owners and confectioners in several countries. When he reached London, he discovered an American by the name of John T. Ralphs actually operating a soda fountain. Mr. Candler introduced Mr. Ralphs to the drink and Mr. Ralphs, like so many of his colleagues in America, was enthralled and ordered five gallons of syrup on the spot.

A more ambitious, if not altogether propitious, beginning was made in France by a native of that land who we may know only by his first initial and surname, G. Delcroix. With World War I doughboys in his country, G. Delcroix apparently had the same inspiration that struck Robert W. Woodruff so fortunately at the outset of World War II—that of getting Coca-Cola to American fighting men. Only G. Delcroix had this splendid idea, not at the outset of World War I, but after it was all over.

The Coca-Cola Bottler, of February 1929, carried an account of his setting up a stand to sell Coca-Colas at a U. S. Army camp in Bordeaux in the spring of 1919. "When the troops found out they were about to get some real Coca-Cola, there was great enthusiasm," the account said. Some, in their hurry to renew acquaintances with their old friend, Coca-Cola, did not even bother to wait for their change. "What the hell is a franc as compared to a bottle of Coke?" one soldier is supposed to have exclaimed.

G. Delcroix must have been very pleased at his prospects. But as his luck would have it, the camp was rapidly broken for the troops to go home, so that his business there was "of short duration." Undaunted, he set about trying to get proprietors of Paris cafes interested in Coca-Cola. One of those whom he approached was an American. "Get the hell out of here," the man said. "That's what made the States dry, and that's why I am over here."

But his efforts met with some success. The *Bottler* showed a photograph of a Paris cafe front with a Coca-Cola sign. There were two soda fountains then in the city and it is assumed G. Delcroix was able to sell some syrup to them. And, the article said, he expanded into Château-Thierry, Rheims, and Soissons, confident that "the American tourist will see the familiar sign from home" and react as he or she would have at home.

The unsigned author of the article was a partner at the beginning with G. Delcroix, and told how that gentleman himself responded to the American drink. The first quaff G. Delcroix had of Coca-Cola, he found too sweet for his taste. The second seemed just right. The third wasn't sweet enough. The unsigned article concluded: "I have spent more than twenty years in foreign countries and I firmly believe its [Coca-Cola's] popularity in the United States can be largely duplicated abroad."

That was perspicacious but, alas, G. Delcroix was not to be the instrument of such success in France. A small collection of correspondence among the company archives' treasures between him and Charles Howard Candler during 1921 (when Mr. Candler was company president at the time of "souring") records his struggles. On February 2, he reported difficulty renting a horse and cart for deliveries, necessitating his making deliveries in a bag which was "quite unsatisfactory." Indeed, "sales instead of increasing have rather fallen down." So he bought a brand-new Ford chassis from an army camp with room for twenty-four cases. Mr. Candler wrote back approving his "good judgment in the furtherance of the sale of Coca-Cola," but cautioned him to "continue your policy of conservative expenditure of funds."

On May 12, G. Delcroix reported sales resistance still strong among cafe owners but spoke hopefully of getting a liquor salesman who knew the owners to take Coca-Cola on as a sideline. Then he said that he was sorry his cash balance was still low and asked "another $1,000 to be forwarded to me." Mr. Candler sent the money along with the wish that G. Delcroix would be able now "to more promptly get our goods introduced and going among the cafe owners."

A last letter dated August 4, 1921, from G. Delcroix is full of woe. The Coca-Cola Company for France had still not been registered. "Yesterday I have been informed by Mr. Donald Harper's office that the French Office for Foreign Societies had returned the documents for the reason that the seal of the Company do not appear where it ought. Mr. Donald Harper is sending back these documents to our lawyers in the States so that the seal of the Company be stamped where required. Of course it will take some time for these papers to go to the States and come back."

And: "The amount of the sales is gradually increasing, but it is still very far of what it ought to be." Further: "I cabled once and wrote twice to the Coca-Cola Company at Montreal asking them to send me a certificate of origine for . . . advertising matter and received no answer. I wired them anew this morning. Without a certificate of origine the custom duties to pay are so high that it would be five or six times the value of the goods." Finally: "The syrup which we are using here is somewhat old, but as I have been drinking of this same Coca-Cola day after day it is difficult for me to say if it has exactly the same taste that it has two years ago when we received it . . ." *meaning he had not been able to get rid of a barrelful in two years, even with his daily dipping into it.*

International Expansion Under Woodruff's Leadership

Robert W. Woodruff had journeyed to Europe in 1925, only two years after he took over, to study market possibilities. The next year, he set up a foreign department to oversee and perhaps straighten out such ventures as the one in France and to develop others. That same year, a syrup concentrate, still in use today, was developed to facilitate expansion ventures and cut shipping costs.

Mr. Woodruff put his chemists to work on developing a beet sugar suitable for Coca-Cola, and this accomplished—the drink no longer dependent on cane sugar alone—concentrate plants could be set up in all parts of the world.

The foreign department, meanwhile, began selling syrup through export firms and brought out, in 1927, an export bottle, green with a red, white, and green paper label, for high-priced Coca-Cola on board luxury liners.

By 1929, there were sixty-four bottling plants in twenty-eight countries, so The Coca-Cola Company could count itself, along with Ford Motor Company and the makers of Singer Sewing Machines, among the very first American firms doing a multinational business.

To build it further, Mr. Woodruff set up The Coca-Cola Export Corporation in 1930, and during the 1930s it oversaw foreign expansion, including some in Europe by subsidiary companies. When World War II broke out, Coca-Cola was established on three continents other than our own: Europe, Asia (including China), and South America.

Establishing Coca-Cola in Germany

Among the most successful of these early outposts was the one in Germany under the money-minded Max Keith. Here again emerges the Coca-Cola story of slow beginnings, hard work, and great faith on the part of a remarkable man, leading eventually to success. In this case, however, there was a first, fast beginning that fell apart. Ray Rivington Powers, a friend of Mr. Woodruff's from the South, went into Germany in, of all years, 1929, with a large fleet of trucks, expecting to do business on the southern scale, only to flounder in southern-style defeat. "A crashing failure" is the way H. Burke Nicholson, Jr., an overseas pioneer, described it.

Claus Halle, German-born, the company vice-president who worked under Max Keith, said that, to this day, old-time, jolly German bottlers recall how Mr. Powers would say to them in broken German: "If you continue to sell Coca-Cola the way we tell you, then one day you'll be one of the richest men in your community and you'll probably have a villa in Florida." They chuckle over the villa in Florida and, of course, over how right Mr. Powers was about their (if not his) becoming rich.

His failure was not for want of effort. Max Keith once told how Mr. Powers set out with an oversized briefcase containing a metal box with ten Coca-Cola bottles on ice. He would stand in front of a department store and expertly work a yo-yo until a little crowd gathered to watch. Then he would say: "The yo-yo is something everybody knows about. But here"—opening the briefcase and dramatically drawing out an ice-cold bottle of Coca-Cola—"is something that not everybody does," and would hand the bottles out as samples. But such "imaginative" merchandising could not overcome the "hard obstacles" he was up against, trying to sell beer-drinking Germans "this dark drink in a bottle that had to be ice-cold," as Mr. Halle put it.

Mr. Powers sought a German partner. For a time, a warehouse and moving company in Essen had a 30,000-Reichsmark investment in his enterprise. However, the owners were happy to get out after a short time, Mr. Halle said, but the present owners would be a lot happier if they had stayed in. Having lost his own investment of $5,000 by 1930, Mr. Powers put his company in bankruptcy and faded from the scene.

The company was taken over by the Export Corporation as one of its subsidiaries, and, in 1933, was fortunate enough to attract the talents of Herr Keith.

In the interview with Hunter Bell, Herr Keith said that when he came aboard, the company had one six-spout, semiautomatic bottling plant in Essen, an old Chevrolet truck, and one route salesman whom "I had to fire frequently because he often drank too much. This means when he went into a pub to try to sell Coca-Cola, he had to get beer or some liqueur before the pub owner would even permit him to talk about his business. So when he had visited too many customers, he came home completely drunk at night."

Somehow, beer-drinking Germans had to be lured to the sweet, nonalcoholic beverage. "It required hard work," Herr Keith told Hunter Bell. "We had to win customer by customer, consumer by consumer. There was no other way out." But sales grew enough in 1933 for Herr Keith to experience some "long days" in the bottlng plant, from 8 A.M. to 4 A.M., producing four hundred to five hundred cases for the trade.

Herr Keith set up a price structure that permitted a profit margin for wholesalers and most of his distribution was through them. Of the wholesalers, Herr Keith said: "The people we got into the business were not people with money or capital of any sort. Secondly, people who had capital could not trust our business and would not invest money into a soft-drink business because it was very low grade—a small man's business. As a consequence, most of them were only willing and able to operate as wholesalers for Coca-Cola, but not in a position to establish a bottling plant."

Then he added: "I must say that I believe a large portion of the success was due to the fact that most of the people we took into our organization were poor, had no money, or were bankrupt, failed during the depression years, and were out to make their living in some way. They got enthusiastic about the possibilities of Coca-Cola and worked day and night, Sundays, any day. They made Coca-Cola move in Germany."

The wholesalers would arrive at the plant at 3 or 4 A.M. to load cases onto their old trucks, horse-drawn wagons, or three-wheel pushcarts. "Peter Herdt, our wholesaler in Offenbach, started with a pushcart," Herr Keith remembered. He would push it eight miles to a plant in Frankfort in the early morning, load twelve to fifteen cases on it, and push it eight miles back. When he sold out, he would make the slow round trip again in the afternoon. "He is dead now," Herr Keith said, "but his son has one of our biggest bottling operations in the territory."

Through the wholesalers, the drink spread into the countryside surrounding Essen. Warehouses were set up in Cologne and Koblenz. Herr Keith would accompany new wholesalers on calls to taverns and stores because they "did not have the courage to go 'round with this funny drink and try to make new customers." He showed them how. The taverns were the best outlets because they had refrigeration for beer. Breweries weren't too happy about the interloper Coca-Cola being sneaked into the refrigerators. Other soft drinks were served warm. But Herr Keith persisted in having Coca-Cola served properly.

He persisted too in a variation of the old Candler-era tactic of sampling. He outfitted his salesmen with briefcases like Mr. Powers used, and they would begin each sales talk to a retailer by giving him a sample bottle of ice-cold Coca-Cola. The salesmen called the briefcases *seufzertasche*, [case of many sighs]. "They were just exhausted by carrying the briefcase all day long. But that was what I insisted on," Max Keith explained.

He used all the varieties of point-of-sale advertising and sampled youth rallies, bicycle races, and the like, by selling the product, rather than giving it away. Always, the samples had to be properly cold. Said Herr Keith: "Again and again, there were people who said, '*No, I don't want Coca-Cola. I had it already and yah! blah! I would not touch it.*' But finally we could persuade them and after they had a sip of it fresh, ice cold: '*That was entirely different from what I got before.*'" What they got, incidentally, in the sample bottles was a Coca-Cola with four more cubic centimeters of sugar than the standard drink. Germany was supplied with syrup by the Canadian company and, as Herr Keith said, Eugene Kelly (the Canadian president and another overseas giant) "liked a sweet drink."

From Herr Keith's concerted efforts, sales jumped during his first year, 1933, to 111,336 cases from the previous year's 62,695. The second plant opened in Frankfort in 1934 to further increase sales.

When Coca-Cola was sold at the 1938 Olympics (a major breakthrough even though a tag was on each bottle at the insistence of Nazi health authorities warning of the caffeine content), a Berlin plant with a forty-spout semiautomatic filler supplied the international crowd. Mr. Halle said when he went to work for the company in Essen in 1950, many Germans told him they first heard of and had Coca-Cola at the 1938 Olympics.

Business had built all through the 1930s so that "our budget for 1939 was five million cases, and it was only due to the war that we sold only approximately 4.5 million cases." Then Max Keith qualified: "But the business was profitable and all along the line from when I started I managed to make a little money."

Other Prewar International Expansion Efforts

H. Burke Nicholson, Jr., described similar slow starts with not nearly so spectacular growth in Great Britain and other European countries during the 1930s. His father, who was to be president of the Export company and later of all The Coca-Cola Company, started out in Canada under Eugene Kelly in 1933. At that time, Mr. Nicholson said (and few writers have remembered this), the Canadian company was in charge of European operations, and Mr. Kelly traveled twice a year to supervise and check up on the continental operations.

Yet another of Coca-Cola's strong men, Mr. Kelly was described by Mr.

Nicholson as having been "dedicated, handsome, and eccentric." He had a glass eye, and company people, of course, said it was the one that looked warmest when anybody talked about increasing the budget. Max Keith testified to Mr. Kelly's frugality. "I remember well," he told Hunter Bell, "that we had more than six hundred customers before they permitted me to buy a second truck. More than six hundred customers to supply from one truck!"

The elder Mr. Nicholson was sent to run the British operation in 1934, and his son worked on trucks in London during vacations from the London School of Economics. In those days, sale of a thousand cases on a warm summer's day was considered a good record, indeed. In the drear winters, days of zero sales were recorded. There were a few soda fountains near theaters and department stores frequented by tourists, but most of the business was in small confectionery shops where, often, there was no refrigeration. When war came, Coca-Cola had twenty truck routes in London, Mr. Nicholson said. Bottling was done in small plants not fully automated.

The operation in France after G. Delcroix's day remained small. Belgium was a little better, under Carl West, and Norway had one bottler. Herr Keith's German operation was by far the leader in Europe.

John C. Staton, the cooler designer, told about opening up another part of the world before the war. Mr. Kelly, an enthusiastic backer of the cooler concept, had taken Mr. Staton into the Canadian operation, and then sent him in 1938 to establish plants in Australia. Mr. Staton worked there with the same precision as on the cooler, surveying each city to determine if there were enough outlets with proper refrigeration to warrant going in. He had two firm rules to which he attributed the eventual success in Australia. One was that the drink had to be properly refrigerated. The other was that it should not be sold for more than five cents. When war came, there were four plants in Australia and two in New Zealand.

Thus in scattered and mainly small operations was the Coca-Cola multinational business functioning when World War II opened the way for rapid growth of existing plants and vast expansion into new territory. But Mr. Nicholson said it is superficial to say that the war was the reason for Coca-Cola's going worldwide. Certainly the GIs as, in Max Keith's term, "missionaries," helped, by giving international glamor to the drink's name. But Mr. Woodruff had decided by the late 1920s, in Mr. Nicholson's view, on an international course. "My father and people like Max Keith worked very hard in the 1930s. The war to us was an interruption. When it was over, we went on with what we had long since decided to do and were determined to do."

Post World War II International Expansion

The postwar overseas expansion was built on a tradition established before the war that was essentially a repetition of the early growth of the company in America: one of slow beginnings, hard work, application of proven principles, and building success.

Mr. Nicholson said that the first years after the war were mainly devoted to re-establishing the previous businesses. The big expansion in Europe came in the 1950s. Max Keith's wartime work had been, of course, a great help in preparing the way for re-establishing operations in Europe. Herr Keith himself spoke with justifiable pride of the wartime achievement: "We kept the bottlers alive. We kept the bottler organizations alive. And we were prepared to resume also our bottlers' business right after the war. Mr. West started up right after the war, bottling for the U. S. Army forces in Belgium."

Herr Keith said his German operation had to continue living on Fanta sales until 1949 because there was still no sugar available. On October 3 of that year, he was able, with Keith shrewdness, to supply retailers with one case of proper Coca-Cola for every three cases of Fanta they bought. Lee Talley (brother of John, later company president) happened to be on a trip to Frankfort and made a courtesy telephone call to Herr Keith in Essen on the night before Coca-Cola production was to begin again—October 3, 1949. Mr. Talley said he hoped he could get by to visit. "That's wonderful," Herr Keith replied, "because I want you to cut a ribbon tomorrow morning. We are starting with the Coca-Cola business again!"

And so Mr. Talley did cut the ribbon and had the pleasure of standing beside Max Keith, survivor of all these early struggles and all the harrowing years of the war, as he proudly watched his trucks carrying his beloved Coca-Cola out to the public once more. "Coca-Cola *ist wieder da!*" signs on the trucks proclaimed. Coca-Cola is back again.

Claus Halle described what it was like to work for this great old warrior (a Scottish ancestor of Herr Keith came to Germany as a soldier of fortune). Like Mr. Woodruff, he had a remarkable ability to listen and to find weak points in an argument as well as build on strong ones. He had little English when he started out but could always make himself understood by his American compatriots. "He said to me once, 'If you think clearly, you can always make yourself understood.'"

He was a tough man to work for. His wartime experiences had made him suspicious of everyone. He had his associates eat lunch with him every day, but it was not a standing appointment. Herr Keith called every morning with the invitation. One dared not be late. When once Mr. Halle couldn't get rid of a visitor and was five minutes late, he tried to explain that he couldn't be rude to the visitor—an important banker. Max Keith growled, "Why? Do we owe his bank anything?"

Herr Keith ate fast and his associates were expected not to finish lunch after he did. He said people worked like they ate, so one had to beware of becoming known as a slow eater. The executives would, at the lunches, ask Herr Keith questions about his war experiences in the hope of getting him to talk so they could avoid indigestion.

Once, Herr Keith had a restaurant cook up a full breakfast every ten minutes for more than an hour so that one could be served to Robert W. Woodruff the moment he got off his train for a visit and walked into the restaurant. Do things like that when your boss comes, Herr Keith told Mr. Hale, perfecting anything you have control over. "Then you'll have his full attention and you won't have a disgruntled boss who has complaints."

Yes, Mr. Halle affirmed, Herr Keith was tough. "When I had my twentieth anniversary with the company, Mr. John Talley, then president of Export, said actually I should have credit for thirty years because of the ten years I worked closely under Max Keith." He laughed, but then said seriously: "But it was an honor to work for him. I wouldn't be where I am had it not been for those ten years."

From Herr Keith's trucks, 233,000 cases were sold the last few months of 1949. By 1952, the figure was twenty million, and by 1965 it was a hundred million. The postwar years for the already established overseas companies were like the 1900s for the Candler operation when rapid sales and expansion followed the early struggles.

Mr. Halle detailed what postwar expansion efforts were like in Germany. After six months of training, he set out in 1950 to help new bottlers open up their areas. The people with capital were coming to Coca-Cola now; GIs had helped its prestige, as had the growth of the business itself. Mr. Halle described it as virgin territory where some people, despite the GIs, had never heard of Coca-Cola. Some merchants thought he was proferring a brand of cigarettes. But by the time-honored methods, he and the bottlers made sure that all would come to know and love Coca-Cola.

By 1960, the bottling territories of Germany had all been taken, under ten-year contracts with an option to renew on good performance. The time had come for vertical expansion. Mr. Halle was named to head up a special blitz group of twenty-five to thirty men with fifteen trucks, which traveled from plant to plant to show the owners how to do a complete merchandising campaign. Herr Keith's idea, of course, the campaigns included heavy use of signs, sampling at factories, as well as searching out new outlets. They were remarkably successful, as Coca-Cola continued its German growth through the next decade and a half. (Mr. Halle became sales manager for all of Germany, then area manager for Central Europe, then in 1975 the first non-American to be president of the Export Corporation. A reorganization, entailed by business growth of all of Coca-Cola, the next year placed him in his present position of responsibility for one third of the world.)

In 1947, Mr. Nicholson went to Amsterdam where he had the plant and fleet rebuilt from surplus military equipment, started up production, and then successfully sought other bottlers in Holland. "I enjoyed it there," he said. "I enjoyed everywhere I worked. If I could have afforded it, I would have worked for nothing." (His son is in the business, a third-generation overseas man.)

Mr. Nicholson next sought bottlers for Switzerland, requiring, as in Holland, able management and adequate capital, status in the community and "a determination to succeed." He found such men. The company's reputation was established. They didn't come knocking on the door, but when Mr. Nicholson sought, he would find enough takers to have a choice.

He did this elsewhere in Europe, and it was a great satisfaction for him to

participate in many plant openings in various countries. Usually, he stayed in a country long enough to see Coca-Cola move from zero to leadership. During the 1950s, it was not unusual to start fifteen or twenty plants a year. From 1954 on, Max Keith was in charge of all Europe and Mr. Nicholson was his deputy. They operated out of Luxembourg where they persuaded authorities not to tax the company on profits earned in other nations. The notion was passed into law and as a result many multinational firms came to operate out of Brussels, too.

Similar re-establishing of old companies and plants in addition to expansion into new territory went on in other parts of the world. In Japan, where Coca-Cola was unknown before the GI occupation, the drink caught on immediately after the war, and, typically, the Japanese developed extremely high-speed bottling machinery. China was lost to Coca-Cola with the communist regime there. South Africa had a mature operation even before the war, and from there the drink moved upward across the rest of the continent. The business also built and spread in South America and Australia during, as well as after, the war years.

Probably the favorite plant-opening memory Mr. Nicholson has is one when he stood in the snow on a June midnight with the sun shining. This was in Norvik, Norway, two hundred miles north of the Arctic Circle. Mr. Nicholson wanted to push on up to Halifax to see if there were bottling opportunities farther north, but his pilot assured him that the weather would not permit.

Mr. Nicholson also recalled with delight the bottler in Iceland, yet another strong Coca-Cola figure–the late Mr. Djon Bjorn Olaffson, whose achievements, beyond having the highest per capita Coca-Cola sales of any in the world, included having been a delegate to NATO and minister of commerce in his country.

International Leadership of James A. Farley

So Coca-Cola spread to the far reaches of the earth. And still the saga was one of hard work, canny business ability, and extraordinary people like Mr. Olaffson–an international fable of work-ethic virtue finding its reward . . . and a lot of Coca-Cola class.

Consider the man who served as president of the Export Corporation through the years of greatest expansion, yet another genial soul, James A. Farley, master politician and Postmaster General under President Franklin Delano

Roosevelt. Mr. Farley resigned in protest, when Mr. Roosevelt decided to run for a third term, and accepted the position with Export in 1940. Many companies had sought his services, but Mr. Farley, in an interview in 1975 (the year before his death) with Hunter Bell, gave his rationale for joining Coca-Cola:

"It would be understood that if I went there, I wasn't going with a company where the political influence I was supposed to have would interfere with my association with the company. Because they did not need any political influence; they had a very successful business which had operated down through the years." The remuneration was not as much as others had offered. But he would not be a kept man, or be expected to operate in Washington.

His theater of operations was around the world, and it was connections from his political past rather than any overt power-politics influence which made him invaluable in opening doors for negotiations with government leaders about setting up plants in various countries.

An example was Brazil. Mr. Farley knew then Foreign Minister Oswaldo Aranha and, through him, set up an appointment in early 1941 with President Getúlio Vargas. After the amenities, President Vargas suggested they get down to business.

"So we went over and sat on a bench—a regular, ordinary wooden bench. Mr. Nicholson [the younger] was of course with me. We told General Vargas the story of Coca-Cola. How in whatever country we went into business, all the people who were employed there—were nationals. We'd buy trucks there; we'd buy our sugar there; we'd buy everything we could there. . . ." They worked out a deal, and only after that did Mr. Farley present General Vargas a letter of introduction from President Roosevelt. That made a "great impression" on General Vargas, not using Roosevelt's name. In the aftermath, John C. Staton opened up Brazil, making his methodical surveys and applying his two rules.

Mr. Farley traveled continuously over the world (recalling a stop once in the Fiji Islands where it was hotter than anywhere else he had ever been) until 1972 when a heart attack slowed him down. Mr. Nicholson, and subsequently others, traveled with him to be at his elbow to answer technical questions once Mr. Farley got the door open. Mr. Halle recalled the time, early in his career, when Mr. Farley visited the Essen plant for the twenty-fifth anniversary of Coca-Cola GMBH. Max Keith wanted someone with English to drive the honor guest around and had Mr. Halle fitted out in a tailor-made suit (his first) of a dark material. Mr. Halle felt honored until the sales manager asked him his hat size. Only then did Mr. Halle realize they were going to get him a chauffeur's cap to go with his dark suit! He told them several sizes too large so that the cap, when it arrived, came down over his eyes and could be discarded.

After the heart attack, Mr. Farley would go to one country and telephone from there to bottlers in surrounding ones, in order to cut down on traveling yet keep in touch. They appreciated this, and it meant much to him. It strengthened the bond between them. Mr. Farley said, in all his travels, he never in the world found a bottler who wasn't "doing the job to the best of his ability." Mr. Halle served as an honorary pallbearer at Mr. Farley's funeral in 1976, and felt humbly "that I represented all of his foreign friends."

Coca-Cola Makes the Cover of Time *Magazine*

Thus, the Coca-Cola family extended over the earth. *Time* magazine, in acknowledgment, carried a cover story on May 15, 1950, about the multinational operation. Entailed was one more Woodruff coup. The editors wanted to put Mr. Woodruff on the cover. With his usual modesty and shunning of publicity, he said no, the story was about the product, not him. So the cover had an Artzybasheff drawing of an eclipsed red disk holding a bottle of ice-cold Coca-Cola to the mouth of the globe drawn as a round face, which was quite nice exposure for the drink.

The *Time* story showed how, in an entirely legitimate manner, Coca-Cola people were re-enacting around the world the things they had been doing all along in America. It described how field men recommended to new bottlers plant size and machinery needed, including water-purification equipment, in addition to instructing them in such fundamentals as not letting advertising be "competitive, offensive, tricky or brash." And it told how bottling-plant salesmen were trained, as they were in the States, with morality plays pitting the good Coca-Cola salesmen against the forces of evil personified by a competitor's salesman.

Salesmen were also told to look their best. "Greet the dealer with a smile. Show interest. Be courteous. Be honest. Keep promises. Make change. Thank the dealer." Have a slide rule to compute profit at any given time. "Don't leave your sign for the dealer to put up. He might give it away to one of his friends." Keep your truck in perfect order. Drive carefully so as not to frighten pedestrian potential customers.

A *Time* reporter went on the rounds with one of the salesmen in Milan,

Coca-Cola bottlers using the canals of Venice to make deliveries.

TIME

THE WEEKLY NEWSMAGAZINE

WORLD & FRIEND
Love that piaster, that lira, that tickey, and that American way of life.

Italy; his truck carried a sign on the rearview mirror: "Hair combed? Shaved? Uniform clean and neat? Shoes shined? Friendly smile?" The man explained to the reporter at the outset: "I have a position of responsibility. Now you will see everywhere we go today, the people will not call me just 'Pretti' or 'Come here, Pretti.' Instead they will say, 'Signor Pretti,' for I am the representative of Coca-Cola."

Later that day, Signor Pretti sympathized with the daughter of a small shop owner whose fiancé had been drafted—proving himself to be the ideal salesman, worldly in an expensive restaurant, and earthy in a worker's eating place. When a cabdriver spoke with disdain of the product, Signor Pretti won him over by saying, "Ah, but you must try Coca-Cola in the wine."

Conflicts in International Market Areas

The *Time* story noted, though, that not always was the going smooth overseas. In France, two extremes—conservative winegrowers and the Communist party—combined to get a bill passed by the Assembly allowing the health minister to ban Coca-Cola. This the good gentleman did not do, probably at the behest of some one or more charming and persuasive Coca-Cola representative.

In Switzerland, big breweries spread so many rumors about Coca-Cola that, according to John Talley, the company was finally called before a magistrate to prove that the drink had less caffeine than tea or coffee. The judge finally ruled that the drink could be harmful if someone drank *sixty* gallons of it at a sitting! Breweries in other countries opposed Coca-Cola too until, seeing they couldn't lick it, they joined forces to sell it.

A few misguided Coca-Cola people, during the early European efforts, bragged about conquering the soft-drink market, causing the soft-drink industries in several countries to become quite hostile. According to Mr. Nicholson, it was a serious public relations problem. The solution was to show how Coca-Cola, wherever it went, helped the whole industry, upgrading it from low status to one of prestige.

However, another problem was the recurring waves of anti-American feeling in one country or another over the years, with resultant drops in sales and sometimes violence against plants. According to Mr. Halle, there was very little to be done about it, except ride it out. Occasionally local ingenuity would prevail, as in India when the United States came down on the side of Pakistan during the conflict in 1965 between those two countries. All the plants in India had big showcase front windows, and the owners feared irate patriots would throw rocks or bombs through them. So "our Indian friends had a great idea." They went to the authorities and offered the plants as places for blood-donor stations and were able to put big signs in all those big windows saying, "Come in here and give blood for our fighting heroes." Trucks had signs identifying the plants as blood-donor stations. No plant was damaged, and only one truck—it had no sign.

An unsuccessful effort was to be made in the Indian parliament in 1971 to stop Coca-Cola from taking profits out of the country. Then in 1977, the Indian Government demanded that foreign equity shares in that country's syrup plant operation be reduced to 40 per cent. Export agreed on condition it continue to be in charge of quality control. When India rejected this, Export charged that this amounted to the unthinkable—a sharing of "trade secrets," including the secret formula, with Merchandise 7X.

By far, the worst overseas setback was imposition of the Arab boycott on the drink in 1967. By various accounts, the Export Corporation, along with all businesses, was given notice by the Arabs that it would be boycotted if it operated in Israel. Export turned down a request from Israeli citizens for a bottling franchise on grounds they didn't have sufficient capital. Subsequently, the B'nai B'rith organization in America put pressure on Export, and, in unfriendly interpretations of what went on in the minds of Export officials, a choice was made to keep the American Jewish market and forgo the Arab one. This would have represented a peculiar business judgment since Arab population was more than one hundred million at the time, compared with a worldwide Jewish population of only thirteen million.

John Talley, who was president of Export at the time, said he was caught between B'nai B'rith's accusing him of playing footsy with the Arabs and the Arabs threatening the boycott. He said he told both sides that "we don't play

Coca-Cola delivery via animal carrier in Morocco.

COURTESY OF THE COCA-COLA COMPANY

Ethiopian "pretty girl" picture.

politics" and asserted that a franchise was given to an Israeli citizen as soon as he proved he had sufficient capital.

The man who got the Israel franchise. Abraham Feinberg, is quoted in *Up Against the Corporate Wall*, by S. Prakash Sethi (Prentice-Hall, Inc., 1971) as saying serious negotiations with Coca-Cola were underway a week before B'nai B'rith made public its campaign of pressure. He had been seeking a franchise considerably earlier than that. Mr. Feinberg said he would not have accepted the franchise "if I believed Coca-Cola bows to Arab boycott threats."

Board Chairman Paul Austin said in an interview that to accede to the boycott would have been contrary to basic company policy. Himself a strong advocate of free trade, Mr. Austin said the only course for the company was to try through negotiations, then ongoing, to get the Arabs to lift the boycott.

Coca-Cola is big in South Africa, and the policy of keeping out of politics serves it well in that troubled land. But if Coca-Cola were to frontally fight apartheid there, it would not likely continue to do business under the present regime. We have the ugly example of business involved in politics of another land when International Telephone and Telegraph played a role in toppling a democratic government in Chile. The world overall would seem safer if these supercompanies, more wealthy and more powerful than some of the nations in which they operate, do not interfere in the internal affairs of sovereign states so as to change the course of their history. J. Paul Austin's view of the role of business in the affairs of nations is that business should, mainly by improving economies, provide the people and leaders of those nations with motivation for sane courses of action, particularly as regards avoiding warfare. And there is no evidence of The Coca-Cola Company's having gone beyond that kind of indirect approach to the internal affairs of other countries.

There is the evidence, though—in a report prepared by the Arnold and Porter law firm for The Coca-Cola Company in 1977—of $1.3 million in "illegal or improper" payments made since 1971, most of them in foreign lands. These included $60,000 for "government approvals," $140,000 for political contributions, $380,000 for approvals of price increases, $95,000 for tax and other legal disputes, $98,000 for "termination of employees," $165,000 for "efforts to obtain favorable business treatment and good will," and $145,000 for "efforts to expedite routine governmental matters in foreign countries, including customs clearances, where such facilitating payments are customary."

The report declared that neither board chairman Austin nor president Smith knew the payments were going on. Further, "neither improper payments nor improper business practices are normal and accepted business practice within the company," and all such activity had been halted. Finally, "the transactions found to be illegal or improper were small, both individually and in the aggregate, and were not material in relation to the company's overall operations."

This was the worst hint of anything illegal in the overseas story. The company made no public effort to defend the payments as business, as is usually done. The report had been preceded by an admission in 1976 that such payments had been going on. This was after the Securities Exchange Commission encouraged such confessions, hinting that it would be lenient with contrite companies.

The best we may say here is that at least Coca-Cola didn't try to weasel out and, with Mr. Dietz, hope that Mr. Candler's fine example of handling the cocaine problem was still being followed.

In the Middle East, Coca-Cola lost what had developed into a thriving business. And the Arab world lost what had been a developing technology of water sanitation and desalination of sea water which might have been used to reclaim deserts for agriculture. Board Chairman Austin was guardedly optimistic about conversations he had with President Anwar el-Sadat of Egypt in 1977 toward lifting of the boycott and resumption of water-technology aid in the Mideast by Coca-Cola.

Mr. Austin also discussed in an interview that other overseas embarrassment—the capture of the Russian market by Pepsi-Cola when its friend, Richard M. Nixon, was President. He said he had been in discussion with Soviet leaders for six or seven years, and that they had become "very definitely interested" in having Coca-Cola for the masses. But, unfortunately for that wish and for The Coca-Cola Company, Russian leaders signed that contract with "another soft drink company," giving it exclusive right to sell in the Soviet Union. Since then,

Russian authorities have been meticulous in observing the conditions of the contract, "though it turned out not to be what they want." The contract runs to 1984, the year made prematurely famous by author George Orwell.

In the meantime, there have been discussions of an instant tea plant in Russia and of development of a nutritious drink from whey. The Russians are quite interested in the latter, Mr. Austin said. He has also approached the leaders about servicing the 1980 Olympics to be held in their country, arguing that the Olympic complex would amount to an enclave, not covered by the Pepsi-Cola contract. He pushed the point vigorously that Coca-Cola has serviced every Olympics since the 1928 games in Brussels and brings to the job considerable know-how. The answer so far has at least not been no.

Coca-Cola has, of course, penetrated into other Iron Curtain countries. Mr. Halle was involved in the negotiations with Poland, Czechoslovakia, and Hungary. (The drink is also in Bulgaria and Yugoslavia.) Mr. Halle got off to a good start with officials in the first three countries by knowing his geography well enough not to refer to them as Eastern Europeans. Prague is farther west than Vienna, and the people of all three countries have Central European backgrounds.

It was in the 1960s that Mr. Halle helped establish plants run as socialist enterprises in the three countries. It was like Germany in the 1950s all over again, starting from scratch. With Coca-Cola came a heightening of standards for other soft drinks and a higher technology for the industry. The socialist countries see this upgrading as a main advantage, he said, along with having Coca-Cola to sell to tourists they seek to attract.

Mr. Nicholson told about his work in socialist countries, including Finland where another breakthrough was made by servicing the Olympics Games there in 1952. The drinks for the games were given to the country's War Wounded Association which used the proceeds for charitable purposes. When an agreement for bottling was reached, Mr. Nicholson wrote authorities, as was his custom, for a copy of their health laws regarding beverages. He was startled to receive an ancient document which began, "We, Alexander II, Czar of all the Russias and Grand Duke of Finland, do hereby decree . . ."

The trade with the socialist countries is one of barter, and a problem this raises is to find ways of converting the goods received into cash. This is one of the many constant preoccupations for company president, J. Lucian Smith.

The Coca-Cola Trading Company was set up as a subsidiary to develop methods for taking goods from one country and selling them in another to build up trade credits. Its worldwide operations are said to be in advance of similar efforts by socialist countries.

Another of Mr. Smith's tasks, as chief operational officer, is to keep up with what is going on in bottling plants around the world so that if a mistake is made in Athens, Greece, it won't be repeated in Hong Kong. Similarly, if an efficiency-increasing breakthrough is made in one place, news of it needs to be relayed to other places over the globe.

Think, said Mr. Smith, of the number of retail outlets in the world—

millions of them in Coca-Cola territory. "Somebody from a Coca-Cola plant calls on each of these millions once a week, sometimes once a day. We work on ways to improve the efficiency of that, and get it communicated. We are dealing with thousands of individual bottlers in different locales in 137 countries."

The Coca-Cola "Image" Abroad

Coca-Cola people like to point out their interest also in bettering the lands where the drink is sold, "paying its social rent," in Mr. Austin's phrase. This includes the introduction of its water technology and its work on nutritious drinks—the latter especially of interest to underdeveloped nations with much malnutrition among their populaces. Coca-Cola bottlers sponsor elaborate sports programs for young people in the many lands, including tennis, motor sports, auto racing, swimming, and soccer.

Coca-Cola-sponsored soccer competition in Sao Paulo, Brazil.

These are ways in which the company tries to avoid the appearance of the "ugly American" in foreign countries and to offset American intellectuals' denunciation of "exploitative," giant multinational corporations. But the best thing Coca-Cola has going for its international image harks back to some of the magic of the early days of the company.

The favorite and most frequently told of all the anecdotes Coca-Cola people have to relate is about the World War II German POW who, upon marching down a troopship's gangplank at New York Harbor, espied the familiar red-and-white sign and remarked, "Oh, I see you have Coca-Cola here, too."

The reason Coca-Cola people like this story so much is that it sums up the biggest secret of the drink's success abroad. *People of other lands tend to regard it as theirs because their own people produce it.* When Charles Howard Candler spoke of the advantage to the company of "allowing Coca-Cola to be bottled in hundreds of communities by persons native to and respected in those communities, who themselves profited greatly by the energy and initiative which they put into the promotion of Coca-Cola," he was of course speaking of the bottling family then growing up in America. But his words apply equally to the bottling family of the world. Wherever possible, bottlers are native to the land and, of course, at the discrimination of the company recruiters, respected in their communities. Mr. Candler's policy of letting other businesses profit from supplying the bottlers is also adhered to around the world and is a boost to the economy of each country where the drink is bottled.

The franchise system works as well worldwide as it does in America, and Coca-Cola ingratiates itself into the cultural fabric of each country through the indigenous bottlers. The same advertising campaigns, for example, are used worldwide, but indigenous company people provide the local variations in language and appearance needed to make the ads work.

Not all bottling franchises are in indigenous hands, particularly in underdeveloped countries; for example, those in Africa. But Mr. Austin contends the effort is to encourage local people to put capital accumulated from Coca-Cola operations into their own bottling efforts. And overall, the franchise system does work with the same old magic of the early days in America.

It is an ideal system, Claus Halle affirms. "It gives everyone in the system the advantages of being part of a huge enterprise. At the same time, you preserve the local character of the business. Our kind of business can only be done by someone who really knows his fellow countrymen."

Interestingly, no other multinational industries have tried to emulate Coca-Cola's franchise system. Mr. Austin said he couldn't understand why. "If the parent companies had had to invest what the bottlers did, we wouldn't have been able to expand." This is as true internationally as it was in the days of Messrs. Thomas and Whitehead.

Mr. Austin described another advantage the company has in its international operations. Coca-Cola is a nonessential product, if ever there was one. And a nonessential management team must, in Mr. Austin's terms, be comprised of "real aces, real pros." They must be extrasensitive about how a government might react to any action. They must constantly try to improve relations with government officials and other industries. Producers of essential goods offshore, he explained, though skilled in their business, tend to "ride a pretty high horse." But an esprit of service grew up in Coca-Cola's overseas staff which has gained for Coca-Cola, in Mr. Austin's opinion, the best international relations of any multinational corporation.

Certainly the old magic of the franchise system makes Coca-Cola essentially and significantly different from the other multinationals and goes a long way toward explaining how little of the sinister we have been able to discover in Coca-Cola's international affairs. The question remains whether in a world growing ever more ruthless and treacherous, Coca-Cola can keep it up.

Mr. Austin and others at the head of Coca-Cola see the role the company is playing in the world as a contribution to international understanding and a force for world peace. Mr. Nicholson gave two specific instances from his experience of how this might be. When he was a senior vice-president in Brussels, there were twenty-nine employees in the office representing thirteen nationalities. "We never had an incident of nationalist hostility. We were just involved in Coca-Cola."

Then when he was negotiating to bottle in some of the Iron Curtain countries, he was impressed by how good relations were with the officials involved, what good "trading partners" they were. "I've always believed in building bridges of understanding through trade," Mr. Nicholson said. "I was encouraged . . . by the human response working with men whose political system was so different and theoretically so antagonistic to ours. I still get postcards from some of them."

The *Time* cover story quoted Mr. Woodruff on the matter: "We're not selling the world short; we're playing the world long. We decided that we would live with the world, that the world would survive, that it must survive, as a decent place to live in."

In all the overseas development and expansion, Robert W. Woodruff was the guiding hand and the inspiration of the men out in the field. As do those in the States, the overseas company men pay tribute to him, their respect and fondness for him very real in their words. "Mr. Woodruff had the vision," Mr. Halle explained. "He had a warm spot in his heart for overseas. He and Max Keith were close friends." Mr. Nicholson adds: "He gave courage to us and held his hand over our heads."

Just as it had been for the Southerners in the early days, Coca-Cola became for people of so many nationalities the one sure, certain thing to hold and give loyalty to as the world grew more disenchanting.

J. Lucian Smith sought to explain this, and one thinks of Max Keith as company president Smith speaks: "Mr. Woodruff has, without knowing it, breathed sort of a religious fervor into this organization. You go into Germany and talk to the people who own the plant and then you talk to the lowest employee, and you find an attitude that transcends a commercial enterprise. It is true in Japan, Brazil, and all over the world." Then, as though it were an afterthought, "And all over the United States, too."

Australia.

America has changed probably most of all of the world's countries since World War II. Has Coca-Cola been able to avoid the sinister in its practices at home, to hold to the work-ethic morality and the old blend of southern gentility and go-getting modernism? On Mr. Smith's word, it's here as well.

IX

Coca-Cola Among the Computers and Conglomerates

During the years from World War II to the 1970s while America was undergoing great change at an accelerated, future-shock pace, The Coca-Cola Company experienced the most drastic changes in marketing approaches since Messrs. Thomas and Whitehead got the bottling contract. These innovations were vastly different from the days of the inspired improvisation of the franchise system and the magical finding from an encyclopedia of the great shape for the Coca-Cola bottle. However, for the company, it was change not so much for the worse as to the dull. And not all of the grandeur of the past was lost.

Coca-Cola Story Highlights: 1946–77

A day in 1946: Robert W. Woodruff is, for a time, neither president nor chairman of the board. A. A. Acklin had been president since 1939, but became ill in 1945 and was replaced by Mr. Woodruff. Now William J. Hobbs becomes president. He is only the sixth president since Asa G. Candler. Harrison Jones has been board chairman since 1942, but Mr. Woodruff is still very much boss of the company.

A happy day in August 1947: The sugar shortage caused by the war is ended.

Thanksgiving Day, 1950: Coca-Cola sponsors its first television program: a

Thanksgiving special, starring Edgar Bergen and Charlie McCarthy—the first live television network show. It is followed in December by a Walt Disney Christmas special. All the panoply of Coca-Cola promotion will soon reflect the influence of this all-powerful new medium.

April 9, 1953: The two-billionth-gallon batch of Coca-Cola syrup is produced at one of the plants. The advertising budget for the year is $30 million for the first time.

December 31, 1954: All of the parent bottling companies, but the Thomas one, having been acquired, the owned parent companies are merged with The Coca-Cola Company.

January 1, 1955: Under the company's rule of mandatory retirement at age sixty-five, Robert W. Woodruff theoretically steps down as boss. He remains, however, chairman of the company's finance committee and is still very much the boss of the company. H. B. Nicholson, Sr., moves from president to board chairman and William E. Robinson is named president.

A momentous day of change in 1955: For the first time ever, Coca-Cola is sold in bottles other than the good old six-and-one-half-ounce size. Now people drink Coca-Cola from the larger king-size and family-size bottles. The bottling family, made unhappy during the postwar years by its nemesis, Pepsi-Cola, with its aggressive marketing of various-sized bottles, is happy once again.

Another day of change in momentous 1955: Dispensers capable of pouring a premix preparation of Coca-Cola are set up throughout the nation and soon around the world. These include vending machines which pour a paper cupful of ice-cold Coca-Cola; counter units; and small carry-pack units. The company now has many new outlets.

Another day in 1955: At soda fountains and over lunch counters, enthusiastic drinkers of Coca-Cola can now have a twelve-ounce glass of it, paying, of course, twice as much to get it.

March 31, 1956: A sad day for the memory of Bill D'Arcy and Archie Lee, as The McCann-Erickson advertising agency replaces D'Arcy in the guidance of the company's tremendous promotion efforts.

March 16, 1959: A Coca-Cola syrup plant produces the third billionth gooey gallon the world has known. It took fifty-eight years for the world to drink up the Coca-Cola made from the first billion gallons of syrup, but only nine for swallowing down drinks from the second billionth. Now this third billionth has gone down in only six. The advertising budget, aimed at narrowing the gap even more, goes over the $40 million mark.

Another day in 1959: Another big change, as people in several test-market areas in New England and California may now buy Coca-Cola in twelve-ounce, flat-top cans and take them wherever they will without paying a deposit. Soon all the world will have the cans and, to the consternation of environmentalists, add them to the world's accumulation of unsightly litter.

A dire October day in 1960: A triumphant Fidel Castro and his revolutionary government seize all of the Coca-Cola business in Cuba. Non-Cuban executives and those Cuban ones who so desire are transferred to other overseas positions. Years later, in 1977, J. Paul Austin is to journey to Cuba. His policy of never divulging contents of conversations with heads of state gives rise to press speculation that the trip was a secret mission for his friend, Jimmy Carter—which he denies. Other speculation is that Coca-Cola might be allowed to return to the little country that was the first outpost of the drink beyond American shores.

Another happy bottler's day in 1960: A line of flavored drinks, the first ever for

Coca-Cola to produce, is placed on the market. The drinks are called Fanta—Herr Keith's trademark.

One more day of momentous change in 1960: The Minute Maid Corporation is merged with The Coca-Cola Company, which means that the company is now in the business of producing and selling products other than soft drinks. These include frozen citrus juice concentrates and ades under the trademarks, Minute Maid and Snow Crop; a line of nonfrozen fruit drinks called Hi C; and instant coffee and tea products made by a branch of Tenco which sells them to chain food stores and other outlets to be marketed under their own labels. Tenco supplies instant coffee for automatic vending machines under its own trademark. All of the products, it should be noted, are beverages.

February 1, 1961: The bottlers have yet another new product to rattle along their filling lines and sell—Sprite, a drink not unlike 7-UP. To come later is Mr. Pibb, not unlike Dr. Pepper. Both are to be produced in diet versions.

May 2, 1961: Lee Talley, already president of the company, is named chairman of the board, becoming the first person to hold both jobs simultaneously.

A day in June of 1961: Coke drinkers in Glasgow, Montana, become the first to try out a twelve-ounce bottle that is in the familiar shape but does not require a deposit. Again, the "woods would become full of them" as people in Baltimore during December were to try out a sixteen-ounce one-way bottle, with both to become available to all.

May 1963: Yet another new drink is sent down the filler lines—TAB, a low-calorie, sugarless beverage for dieters and diabetics.

June 6, 1963: The fourth billion gallon of syrup is turned out; the time required for the world to guzzle its supply of Coca-Cola cut from six to four years.

A day in 1964: Again celebrated by Coca-Cola, but frowned upon by environmentalists, as lift-top cans and bottle caps are provided for a world of fast-moving, convenience-seeking consumers.

May 8, 1964: Duncan Foods Company is merged with The Coca-Cola Company, giving the company a widely advertised line of coffees to sell through its ever-growing distribution systems. Again, Coca-Cola sticks to beverages in its diversification. The merger brings into the company, for a time, the strong figure of Charles W. Duncan, Jr., who heads up the Duncan operation.

February 1966: The bottlers have another drink to make happy those who avoid sugar—Fresca, a citrus-flavored diet beverage.

July 1966: The fifth billion gallon of syrup has been produced, all of its drinks of Coca-Cola having been consumed in only three years.

August 7, 1967: The Coca-Cola Company Foods Division is set up to handle the Minute Maid and Duncan operations. J. Lucian Smith is named president of the division.

The happy ending of 1967: Company sales total more than $1 billion while profits exceed $100 million—two fine more firsts.

January 1969: The world again has consumed enough Coca-Colas to use up another billion gallons of syrup, the sixth. It has taken but a few months short of the three years required to use up the previous billion gallons.

A day later in 1969: TAB and Fresca are sold to the sugar-conscious public in a reformulated version. The Food and Drug Administration ordered cyclamates, feared as a cause of cancer, out of all food and drink products. TAB and Fresca now contain saccharin which, in 1977, was to come under suspicion, also as a carcinogen, as Congress tried to decide whether to halt a proposed FDA ban on it. The FDA was also to begin, in 1977, a series of studies on whether caffeine in such products as Coke might be harmful to the nervous systems of young children.

September 1969: The bottlers hail yet another new drink, Simba, with a tart citrus flavor.

October 11, 1969: The bottling family gathers in Atlanta for a four-day national convention. Here, they are presented with a brand-new marketing program for Coca-Cola with redesigned graphics, even on the bottle, and a new slogan, "It's the Real Thing"—an inferential message derogatory of the nemesis, Pepsi.

A day late in 1969: The Coca-Cola Company acquires yet another beverage, man's first. It bought the Belmont Springs Water Company, Inc., producer of natural spring water and processed water for home and commercial use.

A day early in 1970: The company acquires a firm that produces technology dear to Coca-Cola's heart. This is Aqua-Chem, Inc., manufacturer of those desalting machines important in negotiations with foreign countries. Aqua-Chem also turns out machinery pleasing to environmentalists—solid waste incineration equipment and pollution-control equipment for purification of water, including industrial waste water. In addition, it makes packaged steam and hot water incinerators.

May 5, 1970: J. Paul Austin is named both president of the company and chairman of the board of directors. He has emerged as the apparent next strong leader of Coca-Cola after Asa Candler and Robert Woodruff.

Later in 1970: The bottlers now have beverages for the happy hour, a line of mixers called Santiba. And they introduce Samson, a protein beverage produced in Surinam.

January 1971: The time taken for the world to consume Cokes made from a billion gallons of syrup has been reduced to two years. The billion-gallon marks are then to come with such frequency that the company ceases to record and celebrate the dates after this seventh one.

A day in 1971: Charles W. Duncan, Jr., is named president of The Coca-Cola Company and is, perhaps, a contender for the next strong leader position. However, he leaves the company and a year later is named to serve as deputy defense secretary in President Carter's administration.

Later in 1971: The bottlers are only too happy to open up glass package recycling centers in their plants around the country, as Coca-Cola seeks to make further amends with environmentalists.

Year's end, 1971: Coca-Cola is, by now, the most widely distributed trademarked product in the history of the world. The company has recorded profits of 167.8 million dollars for the year.

And company history after that marks steady increases of the profits figure:

1972—$190.1 million.

1973—$214.9 million.

1974—$195.9 million, the drop attributed to a change in accounting procedures.

1975—$239.3 million.

1976—$284.9 million. Revenues that year rose 5.6 per cent, from $2,872,839,737 in 1975 to $3,032,829,056.

A footnote to the history of Coca-Cola: During a truncated civil war in 1977 in the African nation of Zaïre, President Mobutu Sese Seko was reported to have turned the tide of battle by ordering an emergency shipment of Coca-Cola from the United States. This, supplementing locally produced bottles of ice-cold Coca-Cola, so refreshed his forces, including bands of four-foot pygmies with poison-dipped arrowheads made from beer (not Coke) cans, that they were able to rout a ragtag army of two thousand exiles who seemed close to taking the country's copper belt against a force of twenty-five thousand troops (not counting the pygmies). Company officials in Atlanta had no comment to make on this interesting episode in the grand and ongoing drama of Coca-Cola success.

And an update: In January 1977, The Coca-Cola Company acquired another firm producing yet another kind of beverage, the Taylor Wine Company, as Asa Candler must surely have turned over in his grave. Later in the year, the company bought Sterling Vineyards of Calistoga, California, and the Monterey Vineyard of Gonzales, California. Also in 1977, Coca-Cola perfected a thirty-two-ounce "Easy-Goer," its first plastic bottle. The Food and Drug Administration held one ingredient in the composition of an earlier prototype of the bottle to be a possible cause of cancer.

Coca-Cola Undergoes Diversification

Those years of big change for Coca-Cola were ones of moving with the times, making the decisions and taking the forms that business generally was doing in the frenetic 1950s, '60s and '70s. In the process, The Coca-Cola Company became not only multinational, but a conglomerate as well—the latter form of business only a little less looked upon with suspicion than the former.

Had Coca-Cola lost its soul in the process, its southern-influenced code of gentlemanly behavior? Can a company keep its soul when all those around it are losing theirs? America was changing during the years after World War II, and American business was struggling against an ever-increasing inflation that the best minds of business and government have been unable to halt. Technology was improving as rapidly as history was changing, and the cold calculations of the computer were to rule over most human concerns in business as well as most other walks of life. We entered into the age of the bookkeeper, his fine-lined, balance-sheet mentality projected now to the lightning-fast and infinitely variable computations of mechanical brains. So business had one machine to make its mean decisions and other machines to produce more and more, better and faster. But the more money made, the less it was worth—producing the need to make even more. Money could be invested in acquisitions of new companies and these would not only provide more revenue but also a balance system: if one company was temporarily doing badly, the others could make up for it.

Robert W. Woodruff had, as one more of his principles during the prewar years when he saved the company, the dictum that The Coca-Cola Company would produce only one product at a single price, the five-cent Coca-Cola. He pushed that concept, handed down from Asa Candler, to its ultimate. But caught in the business currents of postwar America, the company finally had to abandon it. What did Mr. Woodruff think as diversification started during the year his so-called retirement began on January 1? "You can count on it," assured one of his colleagues. "Since it happened, he approved it." So the winner Woodruff remained flexible and could, as Asa Candler could not, keep moving with the times—just as he had done to make World War II the staging area for the international drive.

The Pepsi-Cola Threat

Along with business trends of the times, another force compelled the drastic change in company policy. The nemesis Pepsi-Cola, after a time of floundering with its outmoded lower-price image and forced by inflation to charge seven cents for twice as much, began a comeback. This was in 1950 when Alfred N. Steele took over at Pepsi-Cola. The late Mr. Steele, from all accounts a flamboyant and ebullient, think-big, ad man, had previously come from the D'Arcy agency to work for Coca-Cola in Atlanta. His style clashed with the orderly decorum on North Avenue and soon incurred Mr. Woodruff's disapproval. So Mr. Steele was sent off in exile to some remote company outpost. From there, he was only too happy to accept an offer of the Pepsi presidency, bringing along some turncoat Coke middle-management men with all their soft-drink know-how.

According to *Fortune* magazine ("The Competition That Refreshes" by Alvin Toffler, May 1961), Pepsi's profits had declined from $6,300,000 in 1946 to $2,100,000 in 1949, the year before Mr. Steele took over. He and his colleagues began overhauling the company's merchandising system, doing such familiar-sounding things as standardizing trucks, uniforms, and—more importantly—the bottle (eliminating paper labels for an embossed trademark) as well as the drink itself, reducing the sugar in it. They went after the take-home market, advertising a "light refreshment" reduced in calories. With happy results there, Mr. Steele then went after the vending-machine market and, for this, produced a six-and-one-half-ounce, an eight-ounce, and a ten-ounce bottle, in addition to the twice-as-much, twelve-ounce one. This also worked. Between 1950 and 1955, Pepsi sales increased 131 per cent.

All of this, of course, made the Coca-Cola bottling family very, very unhappy, and its members strongly urged the company to compete with a variety of bottle sizes. So, the company began field tests on the ten-ounce king size and twelve-ounce family size in late 1954. But pressure from some bottlers was so great that the tests were never finished and two new bottles were handed over to the bottling family in early 1955. (Some members though, according to the *Fortune* article, were not happy about the break with tradition, feeling that "bringing out another bottle was like being unfaithful to your wife.")

As a mark of how deeply Coca-Cola is imbedded in American folklore, one of those jokes about two men on a deserted island has it that a particular two, who had been on their island since the 1940s, saw one morning in the late 1950s a king-size Coca-Cola bottle washing in on a wave. "My God," said one, picking up the familiar shape. "We've shrunk."

The break was made not only on the bottle but, with the new sizes, on the price. Soon bottle sizes of both Pepsi and Coke would proliferate and price structures would frequently change, so that it was no longer possible to tell what you were getting twice as much of for how much. (Coca-Cola people like to point out though, with arithmetic to prove it, that one can, amid today's inflation, by shopping the supermarket sales, occasionally buy Coca-Cola in bottles as cheaply as when the six-and-one-halfer sold six to a carton for twenty-five cents. At that price, one paid .064 cents an ounce. Seek, say the Coca-Cola people, and when you find a bottle on sale at that price per ounce, you have Coca-Cola at preinflation cost.)

Increasing the Variety of Coca-Cola-Produced Beverages

The move to other drinks was compelled by the same forces of competition and ever-spiraling inflation. On the point of inflation, the company more than the bottlers felt the need to diversify. It was still stuck with the old syrup price to bottlers, and the best of Mr. Woodruff's economizing and efficiency-increasing could only keep up with the inroads of inflation, no longer increasing profits. The wholesale prices of the new drinks and then the beverages that

were added were not, of course, frozen—they could rise along with the price of everything else, and keep profits constantly increasing.

J. Lucian Smith, the company president in 1977, commented, in an interview on the Coke syrup price situation, that "it's been quite a feat to maintain our margins in the face of enormous inflation," adding that "our technical people have done fantastic jobs in increasing efficiency in production of the syrup, buying and processing sugar, and transporting syrup and sugar." But he said that the company faces the end of that road. The company and the bottlers now "have a common interest" in getting the syrup price structure revised. Presumably it would be along the lines of the price to overseas bottlers, based on cost of manufacture and distribution. That would come, he explained, once another problem with the federal government is cleared up. (The Federal Trade Commission began an action in 1970 against the exclusive territory clause of the franchise contracts, saying it is in restraint of trade. The company won preliminary actions both in federal court and before an FTC administrative law judge, but had yet to get a ruling from the full commission.)

We have noted that all of Coca-Cola's diversification has been in the beverage business, including a good old drink of water. Both Mr. Smith and board chairman J. Paul Austin indicated that would continue to be the policy. Mr. Austin in an interview, confirmed that the company would not run out and buy everything in sight, as some conglomerates have done. "We have diversified in an area where we have competence," he explained. "We would say: *Suppose this thing goes sour?* Do we have the expertise in this room which could fix up an electronics company? Not a chance. An aerospace industry? Not a chance. But anything that is handled in supermarket chains, we can do with our eyes shut." This makes good business sense, as does the comment one official made about reports in 1977 that Pepsi-Cola contemplated buying out the Pizza Hut chain: "We're not about to compete with those of our customers who also sell pizza."

About the move to wine, company president Smith emphasized it was, in part, an attempt to cash in on a market trend which showed Americans switching from hard liquor to wines. The wine industry also has the potential of helping with the problem of converting foreign currency, he explained, since many of the countries in which Coca-Cola does business are heavy producers of wine. The wine acquisitions and others expected to be made would provide such countries with a handy American-outlet distribution system.

Nonetheless, some staunch stockholders took the same position Asa Candler would have taken about the wine: they sold their stock. Mr. Smith said the company "regretted" it. But most stockholders swallowed the idea as one more in keeping with the company's basic diversification policy. Wine is, after all, a beverage, too.

So, much of the onus of the conglomerate in the public's wary eye does not apply to Coca-Cola. It is not a "great monolithic octopus gobbling everything up," as one company official feared many people might think.

Coca-Cola had merely changed with the times. If fault were to be found, it would be more nearly with the times. Consider, for example, the necessity brought about by diversification to name new drinks, contrive trademarks, and design bottles for them. Would the same magic manifest itself in these important steps as it had in the beginning with Coca-Cola?

TAB

An article in *Atlanta* magazine ("Coca-Cola's Project Alpha" by Bill Diehl, May 1963) tells how TAB got its name. The company's research department had determined that the name should be a short one, between three and six letters. "To simplify the process" of finding an appropriate short word, an IBM 1401 Computer was programmed to print all possible four-letter combinations containing a vowel. A total of 250,000 words spewed out of the computer. Then human minds mulled over these to reduce the number to six hundred possible choices. These were checked against existing trademarks to reduce the number further, to twenty-four. One of these, TABB, with the second B dropped was, for whatever human reason, chosen. (TAB is a little suggestive—if one thinks of tablet—of the medicinal.)

It is to sigh and think back to the happy, spontaneous, and logical selection by Mr. Robinson of the far superior name of the nondietetic cola drink. And sigh again to remember how he sat down, wrote out, and then perfected the famous trademark. Here is how they went about designing a trademark for TAB in 1960, according to an article in *Sky* magazine ("The Business Behind the Coke Bottle" by Tom Walker, January 1973). The designers started with classic block capital letters. Then they changed the "a" to lower case to achieve informality. And then they extended the "T" to make the trademark easy to remember. The article continued that a twist-around 'a' was employed to draw attention to the name and make it further easy to remember. An arrow was used to point down on the bottle to the slogan. (And how many of us, to this day, know what that slogan is?)

Sigh once more and think back to Mr. Thomas's classic specifications for a Coca-Cola bottle and the serendipitous magic of the use of the cacao nut's shape to get just what he wanted. Compare that to the rather wordy specifications which Robert Sidney Dickens, designer of the TAB bottle, had to work with, as quoted in the *Atlanta* magazine article: "We must design a bottle which will make a lasting impression on both the public and packaging industry. Aesthetically it must imply the same high quality customers have come to expect of all products from The Coca-Cola Company. That this drink is both tasty and easy on the diet must be implicit in the design. The package must be completely new, it must have a shape with high remember value, it must have an identity all its own, it must be a new concept in glass packaging. And, most importantly, it must have the same dimensions as other packages used by our bottlers and fit all existing machinery for bottling and vending these products. In other words it must be unique but the same." Uh-huh.

Fanta

In all the maze of diversification, we have recognized an old friend, Fanta, and that is somehow comforting. But the Fanta line of fruit-flavored drinks has no kinship except by name with that whey-based concoction Max Keith put together in the expedience of sugarless wartime years. Claus Halle described Herr Keith's Fanta as clear and light, somewhat resembling vermouth, and possessing "a very pleasant herb flavor." Dr. Orville May, the chief chemist who was in on the development of the Fanta fruit flavors, was not so charitable in his description of the taste of the original Fanta.

One reason Herr Keith chose Fanta as a trademark was its lack of specificity. The wily Coca-Cola man had it patented in Germany and in all the countries that Germany occupied, with probably the foresight that it might be useful as a name for something else in the future. Dr. May said that when company officials decided it would be just the thing to call the fruit-flavored drinks, enough bottles of the Keith Fanta were shipped across state lines in this country to allow the trademark to be registered here.

Dr. May went on to say that a large reason for the success of the Fanta orange and grape flavors was that Minute Maid had discovered essences of orange and grape which were used in the Fanta drinks. No one else at the time had those essences, making Fanta very superior.

Coca-Cola "Control" Despite Diversification

Diversification, nonetheless, did not destroy the *old* Coca-Cola spirit, as evidenced by the enthusiastic words of the man first put in charge of all carbonated beverages other than Coca-Cola. Ira C. Herbert, as quoted in the employee magazine, *The Refresher* for July–August 1966, said: "The decision of The Coca-Cola Company to go into new products has generated a whole new way of life. The company and bottlers together are learning to master the ability to do more than one thing in the marketplace at a time. A multiproduct organization must have the ability to move quickly—to do something even though it already is doing something else." For Mr. Herbert, this involved constant revision of operations plans, some of which might be obsolete on the very day they arrived for approval.

Resistance to substitutes continued as strong as in Asa Candler's day. Now, a trade research department fended them off, determined that people who ordered one of Coca-Cola's drinks at a fountain got that and not some other. The department was comprised of twenty-five men and women who traveled the country ordering Coca-Cola and then testing the drink they were served. It was a refined variation of the old sly practice of testing for quality control by the fountain servicemen. True to the times, it was a specialist effort now, an undercover operation with overtones of the CIA. But the old graciousness still showed. Always, Coca-Cola politely tried to get the offending dispenser to correct the situation, before taking legal action. In 1966, it took action in forty-five substitution cases, based on the work of the sleuths, and won all.

With all the diversification, the Coca-Cola drink remained the chief product with highest sales, and its syrup price, as we have discussed, was not subject to inflation. So the battle begun by Mr. Woodruff to cut costs in order to squeeze out more profit also continued apace. Lynn LaGarde, retired now, was chief engineer during the postwar years and was intimately involved in this. In an interview in his comfortable home in Atlanta's Sherwood Forest, he chuckled a Southerner's laugh at how they somehow kept winning that battle. "All those things we did because the price of the syrup to the bottler had to stay the same!"

Mr. LaGarde, whose engineering skills had previously been put to construction of shipyards, military bases, and other large projects, found himself immersed in the process of "putting a nickel drink in a bottle."

The sales department wanted a new vending machine to handle the multiplicity of new drinks and Mr. LaGarde, as John Staton had done with the first cooler, negotiated with a private manufacturer to get one built and priced properly for sale to customers at cost. Then, new bottles all had to be designed to fit the vending machines. (To test vending machines against vulnerability to people trying to get free drinks, Mr. LaGarde would place models at Georgia Tech, where they were subject to the thieving ingenuity of engineering students, and the Atlanta Federal Penitentiary, where the best of larcenous minds might have a go at them.)

"Lo and behold," Mr. LaGarde said with his laugh, "then cans came into the picture," and he had to get a dispenser that would handle cans along with bottles. For the cans and all the other new drink packages, Mr. LaGarde's responsibility was concerned with shape, configuration, and vendability.

Diversification also raised the need for bottle sorters, so Mr. LaGarde got them for the plants. Even the bottling plants themselves required design work. In the 1940s, there had been only two plant designs, one for northern locations, the other for southern ones. But Mr. LaGarde and his staff developed twenty-five different sets of plans to meet varying needs. In addition, he had the task of drawing up plans for syrup plants and the overseas concentrate plants.

Because there were more products to sell, the sales effort also had to be modernized and computerized. But it might well have been Samuel Candler Dobbs in 1911, rather than Charles W. Adams (senior vice-president) in 1967, addressing enrollees in the Fountain Sales Training School: "Gentlemen, if you really want to succeed in this business and in the world today, you must make your *own* opportunity as you go. The man who waits with hopes and prayers for some wave to toss him on the high peak of success and prosperity will find that wave is a long, long time a-comin'. . . . You and you alone as an individual must keep jumping, battling, climbing, charging and working in order to get ahead!''

Pepsi-Cola people in the 1960s were more open in pep talks about battling. Salesmen were praised at meetings as "veterans in the war against Coca-Cola," according to Mr. Toffler in *Fortune*. They were urged on as "shock troops" who "invaded" Coke markets with new "sales weapons." An executive is quoted: "You ought to hear our sales-training courses. The men are taught to go out there and hate!"

Such was not the Coca-Cola style. At the Coca-Cola sales meetings, those dramas Zeke Candler described were still enacted—morality plays with the "devil's assistant," a pretty girl, trying to lure the good Coca-Cola field supervisor away from his wife and his job. Or Eddie, an errant fountain salesman, receives encouragement from his shapely "dream girl," Mona Lisa: "Look—you've got the dispenser—gravity and pressurized equipment—inside advertising—outside advertising—promotions—you name it. You also have the merchandising 'know-how,' the experience, knowledge, and judgment to apply those things skillfully to each specific situation. . . . All you need to do is put all those things together in the right combination to fit the individual needs of a specific outlet—your customer. And that is custom merchandising.''

So inspired, the salesmen went out not to make war, but profits. "Continuing the momentum of 1961's all-time sales record, fountain salesmen blasted off to a new year with fresh fuel injected at spring meetings in Boston, New Orleans, and Los Angeles," *The Refresher* rapturously reported. "In flight pattern headed straight up, they saw 1962 objectives aimed at one destination: PROFIT. . . . The signal was GO! And the sky's the limit!"

Any time the salesmen lagged or fell into weary cynicism typical of the postwar times, they had such an orator as Lee Talley to goad them out of it: "Those impatient, stormy petrels whose faces are marred by dust and sweat and blood—who know the great enthusiasms—who know the great devotions—who constantly strive for improvement—who are prepared to try and fail and come back to try again—these are they who will reap the fruits of tomorrow—these are they who will know, in the end, the triumphs of high achievement. Let us, therefore, joy in the fray, asking no quarter and giving none.''

The times had changed and Coca-Cola had moved computerized with them, but not in lock step. The more dignified days still held in the company and its people.

But they were up against Pepsi-Cola and its strong new promotion, and they worried that Coca-Cola might seem too nostalgic, too wholesome to the magic youth market which the nemesis was trying to co-opt as the "Pepsi Generation." So Coke got an image-maker, Walter Margulies. According to *Down the Programmed Rabbit-Hole*, by Anthony Haden-Guest; (Hart-Davis, MacGibbon, London: 1972), Mr. Margulies' mission was to make the company's image less stuffy, more swinging. But it must not swing so high as to lose its quality identity.

To do this, Mr. Margulies overhauled the Coca-Cola graphics, even tampering some with the holy bottle, putting a twisting white ribbon on it for dynamism. The trademark was printed in red with a white whiplash, and the familiar red disc (sign of quality) was replaced on signs by an oblong of a redder red.

Another problem Mr. Margulies addressed was that of the omnipresent signs. They had become so omnipresent that nobody saw them any more, his research claimed. (An attempt to disguise a South Vietnam airfield to look like a North Vietnam one and thereby land a North Vietnam hijacker into the hands of his enemies was foiled, the story is told, because the disguisers were so accustomed to a Coca-Cola sign there that they didn't think to remove it. However, the hijacker did see it and wouldn't let the plane land.) The signs then would be reduced in the number of their sizes and shapes and would, over the globe, uniformly and crisply reflect market research, according to Mr. Haden-Guest.

The Omnipresent Robert W. Woodruff

So there was the crass new mingled with the good old strengths of Coca-Cola, a dilution perhaps of the fine blend of the past, but not a substitution. For, in addition to computers and image-makers, the company still had the benefit of the computations of the fine business mind of Robert W. Woodruff, the original —along with Archie Lee—Coca-Cola image-maker.

Mr. Toffler tells us, in his *Fortune* article, of an incident when Mr. Woodruff moved frontally on one of the more unpleasant aspects of modern business practice. It had been a joke, as far back as the 1931 *Fortune* article, that Coca-Cola had a floor in its headquarters building full of vice-presidents and former presidents who performed no visible functions. When William E. Robinson, who had been Steve Hannagan's partner in the public relations firm, became president in 1955, he set out to do something about this. He hired Curtis Gager, retired from General Foods, and Mr. Gager began to do what had come to be normal in the corporate world of the times. He made heads roll. "He put the fear of God into everyone there," Mr. Toffler reported. "Gager and Robinson worked the company over. Morale was terrible."

Mr. Woodruff looked upon this and upon sales figures and was not pleased. So, in May 1958, he kicked Mr. Robinson upstairs to board chairman and selected Lee Talley to run the company. Everyone felt better. Mr. Talley, as described by Mr. Toffler, "had come to Coke in 1923 . . . had pounded the pavements going from soda fountain to soda fountain tacking up Coke posters," and knew the Coca-Cola way of running a business.

It is worth noting that at the time he corrected this internal company problem, Mr. Woodruff had been retired for three years. As Mr. Toffler aptly put it, "Woodruff may have taken his hands off Coke's steering wheel, but he had never let go of the emergency brake." And he has not to this day, say the people of Coca-Cola.

J. Paul Austin, company people say, has exerted the most independence of any chief executive who has served since Mr. Woodruff's retirement—another indication that he is the next strong leader. Some believe that Mr. Woodruff had a sort of survival-of-the-fittest scheme in mind when he had that other strong figure, Charles Duncan, Jr., sharing the executive responsibility with Mr. Austin. Whatever the case, Mr. Duncan has departed the company and Mr. Austin survives.

The specific means by which Mr. Woodruff keeps a hand on the brake, or whatever, is the chairmanship of the company's finance committee. As various people have described his role in the position, he has not involved himself much with how the money is made, but he keeps a very close eye on how much is made and an even closer one on how the money is spent.

Mr. Pope T. Brock tells an interesting story about Mr. Woodruff's close watch of the inflow and outflow of money, and a disagreement he once had with one of those many people in and out of the chief executive position after his retirement.

"If it means a final showdown on who is the chief executive of the company, nobody doubts what the result will be," Mr. Brock exclaimed. "It is a very rare occasion that such a thing happens. But on one occasion, the then chief executive of the company had decided he wanted to spend a lot of money for a particular purpose, and when it reached Mr. Woodruff's finance committee, Mr. Woodruff didn't agree with it. He didn't think it was the wisest thing to do. Now I'll give you what the gossip is. I didn't personally hear it, but I learned of it from a source I would completely rely on. The chief executive of the company was thoughtless enough to drop a remark that either he or the Old Man had to go. A day or two after that, Mr. Woodruff walked into the chief executive's office. *And Mr. Woodruff didn't take his hat off.* He just remarked, 'About that money matter—in my view, it's a mistake to spend the money in that way, so it's not going to be spent, and that's the way it's going to be.' And he turned and walked out. That's the last anybody's heard of that."

Ah yes. We are contemplating now one man's having been the leader and subsequent strong influence on one company for more than half a century. And before that there was only one other leader, Asa Candler. We have already noted ways in which his gentleman-businessman influence has lingered. (George Woodruff said that he and his brother were taught Sunday school in the Inman Park Methodist Church by Mr. Candler, giving at least one direct link between the two leaders.) It is a remarkable record of longevity and continuity. No wonder Coca-Cola, in the mean world of today, is one business a little different —a multinational that gives back to other lands even as it takes profits away, and a conglomerate which has diversified in an orderly and logical manner.

There are, of course, some thorny legal and political Coca-Cola tangles to explore—and we shall. But the evidence thus far supports a finding that, in many ways, Coca-Cola has been more decent than the national and world environment in which it operates. To make such assertion is, of course, an affront to most of America's intellectuals and to the conditioned reflexes of its journalists. Big business is bad, the bigger the worse. And the quest of scholarship and journalism alike is to ferret out all the ways of such "badness" and, even if they be few, to harp on them endlessly. No longer does the balanced and objective appraisal take into account human nature and the imperfectibility of the world. Yet America is a business society and the scholars and the journalists offer no alternative to that. They are content to tear down all for the sins of some, possessed by their own response to the terrible events of the world in their lifetimes of a mentality dangerously close to nihilism.

Not so, happily, people of more ordinary pursuits. Bring up the subject of Coca-Cola with people not charged with the responsibility of informing public opinion, and they will usually respond positively, as did an Atlanta architect when I told him about this book: "How wonderful. To tell about a company that never has done anything really wrong, and has done all kinds of good that it didn't have to."

The good name of Coca-Cola has, then, survived in a time when no thing nor person nor institution is fully trusted. How? Much has to do with those signs the image-maker believed no longer needed to be seen. The promotion, all that splendid advertising down through the years, made its mark on America's mind, and we shall try to discover how.

William Allen White, the great editor who spoke to the decent instincts of middle Americans at a time when the nation was a great deal more decent than it appears now to be, summed up once the mark that Coca-Cola has made on the American mind. It is an often-told story that bears repeating.

He had earlier come to respect Coca-Cola's good name in a professional contretemps with the company. As it still does to all writers who threaten the trademark by spelling Coca-Cola or, as more often happens, Coke with a lower case "c," the company wrote Mr. White in the 1920s, gently reproaching him for the error and politely urging him not to repeat it. Mr. White, with Midwestern stubbornness, ignored the letter and several subsequent ones, continuing to write out the trademark as he "dern well pleased." Finally, the company dispatched one of its agents from Atlanta to call on Mr. White and explain in person to him the seriousness of what he was doing. Mr. White is said to have exclaimed to the Coca-Cola man, "Well, if your company thinks enough of its good name to send you all the way out here on a slow train to protect it, I'll comply with their wishes."

Later, on the occasion of his seventieth birthday, still a time of decency, Mr. White was asked to pose for a picture for *Life* magazine. He insisted on doing so in a drugstore sitting by the Coca-Cola dispenser. He explained this by saying, "Coca-Cola is such a sublimated essence of all that America stands for, a decent thing, honestly made, that I thought it would be fitting and typical to have the word, 'Coca-Cola' in a picture that portrayed the average American town."

X

Coca-Cola
Advertising Strategies

Through the years since World War II while the world was going to hell in a computerized, militarized, scandalized, terrorized handbasket, Coca-Cola was employing its awesome promotion machine to paint quite a different picture of the planet.

No unsightly hippies with long hair and hallucinatory drug habits stalked the streets of the world that Coca-Cola built with its imagery over those years—no more than did the jungle fighters of two Asian wars—nor brutal sheriffs beating down black civil rights marchers—nor assassins stalking the best of America's leadership—nor black rioters burning and looting in the nation's cities—nor terrorists the world over hijacking and bombing and otherwise holding civilization in hostage—nor, least of all, a shifty-eyed President of the United States conspiring to suborn perjury and obstruct justice.

Instead, Coca-Cola, through the little more than three decades of deterioration since 1945, was holding forth to the world a picture of itself as pleasant and rewarding—the kind of place most people would like for it to be.

Joe Jones, Mr. Woodruff's assistant, tells an anecdote about the boss that might give some insight into the psychology of such Coca-Cola promotion. He said someone asked Mr. Woodruff, after Watergate had been played out, what he thought about it all. He answered with the words he heard President Eisenhower say when someone asked *him* once what he thought of Richard M. Nixon, then his Vice-President. "Awww—" Ike growled, "why do we have to talk about that?"

The Coca-Cola ads were not failing to speak of ugly reality because of gentlemanly restraint, such as President Eisenhower showed, but were seizing upon the happiest aspects of existence for the single purpose of identifying Coca-Cola with them in people's minds.

In the late 1800s, actress Hilda Clark posed for promotion pictures appearing on the early Coca-Cola trays.

The Massengale Approach

This, we know, had been the strategy almost from the very beginning. Asa Candler and Frank M. Robinson were employing it with the elegant ladies and gentlemen on the beautifully printed posters in the 1880s and '90s. The company directly commissioned various lithograph firms to create the posters.

But when four-color advertising became available in magazines around the turn of the century, Mr. Candler soon saw he needed an advertising agency to prepare the art and copy for this challenging new medium. He chose the Massengale agency, probably because it was in Atlanta, close at hand.

The Massengale work, short-lived and now rare, increased the emphasis on the beautiful people of those bygone times, showing them most often drinking Coca-Cola in elegant surroundings, or playing at what in those days were rich people's sports—golf, tennis, and resort swimming. The happy times held out by the ads were mostly vicarious. There were also, in the 1900s, testimonials from sports heroes. They, like the elegant ladies and gentlemen and like the pictured locomotive engineer, a folk hero, were people to emulate. No matter how lowly one might be, if one spent a nickel for an ice-cold Coca-Cola, he or she was, during a brief pause, enjoying the same thing the rich and celebrated did.

The D'Arcy Approaches

The switch from Massengale to the D'Arcy agency was made in 1906, but continuity of theme was maintained: *Pleasant people in pleasant places doing pleasant things as a pleasant nation went pleasantly on its course.*

But toward the end of the 1900s and more so in the 1910s, the kind of people depicted subtly shifted. The ads began to speak directly to "women of society, the shop, or in the office" on an equal plane—"all classes, ages, and sexes," not just in acknowledgment of democracy, but of the rising American expectations of the time. In the 1910s, too, there was the beginning of direct identification of Coca-Cola with things dear to the American heart: a picture of the "old oaken bucket," with the caption: "No Such Water Nowadays"; but, of course, there was Coca-Cola. Or, the universal appeal to all womankind and all the woman-admiring male world of "Nothing Is So Suggestive of Coca-Cola Than a Beautiful, Sweet, Wholesome Womanly Woman." Oh yes.

Except for the announcement about sugar, we have no way of learning from Coca-Cola ads of the 1910s that World War I was raging—no more than any of the other mighty events of the 1900s or 1910s were reflected. On the other hand, in 1919, there was the portent of mighty Coca-Cola events to come,

A Georgia couple, chosen by Massengale Advertising Agency of Atlanta, endorsing Coca-Cola as both medicine and refreshment.

Drink

Coca-Cola

TRADE MARK
REGISTERED

NOTHING is so suggestive of Coca-Cola's own pure deliciousness as the picture of a beautiful, sweet, wholesome, womanly woman.

Demand the genuine by full name—
nicknames encourage substitution.

THE COCA-COLA CO.   ATLANTA, GA.

"Bathing suit" poster, 1922.

with "Delicious and Refreshing to the World," as well as a listing of foreign lands where Coca-Cola was then sold, including Egypt and the Orient.

In the 1920s, the pleasant nation of America, pleasantly peopled, was shown offering more and more opportunity to a rising middle class. "On with the dance!" as Coca-Cola identifies itself with the happy scene and the fine ladies and gentlemen, no longer so much for emulation as for self-recognition, on the ballroom floor. Likewise the appeal to men and women "in furs and topcoats." And: "Good Times from Nine Climes Poured into a Glass." There were also small town scenes and big city street scenes identifying Coca-Cola with the nation itself.

Pleasant people were shown drinking Coca-Cola in their pleasant homes, and readers were urged to use America's gift of the telephone to order some for *their* homes. Two pleasant men ride a fine American Pullman as a black waiter in white uniform pours them drinks of ice-cold Coca-Cola, while Americans, in their prosperity, were told they could have the same "at your club." And throughout the 1920s, pretty girls and wholesome young men in the ads enjoyed themselves playing at games once reserved for the rich, including a very pretty girl wearing a discreetly daring tank bathing suit.

It had to be good to get where it is, the ads proclaimed, and the inference to Americans of the roaring twenties was that they had to be good to get where they were, or surely soon would be. Except for a few ads in college newspapers and yearbooks—the first exclusive appeal to the youth market—flappers did not

"Bathing suit" poster, early 1930s.

flaunt their freedom in Coca-Cola's pleasant land, no more than did the stock market, at the end of the decade, destroy the rise of affluence among the middle class of America.

Depression? What depression? In Coca-Cola's 1930s it was "The Pause that Refreshes" everywhere—in Washington; in your own hometown; in picturesque New Orleans; on a "Big T.A.T. Monoplane"; aboard *Europa*, "the fastest ocean liner"; in the steel mills of Pittsburgh and Birmingham (pleasant people happily working); on the subway; on a train traversing the Oregon Trail; at the Kentucky Derby; on Eastern Transport's "giant eighteen-passenger plane"; at the ballpark or the bullring, and, as though nothing had happened at all since the 1920s, at the ballroom once more, graced by all those beautiful, pleasant people.

And to reassure everybody of the goodness of the world, there was, in 1931, the first of Haddon Sundblom's perennial Santa Clauses smiling down from billboards, *ho-ho-ho*, saying "My hat's off to the Pause that Refreshes." Pleasant people in their pleasant homes had the "When You Entertain" booklets to make home even more pleasant. (A detail of the workaday world of Coca-Cola was told by Hunter Bell. He said Archie Lee thought up the inspired promotion, but then too many of the booklets were ordered printed. So company men had to go on tours of various women's conventions to sell the surplus. They finally got rid of them.)

Then there were all those people gainfully employed, not standing hopelessly in employment lines, or doing slow-motion labor for the WPA, or glumly, grimly organizing Communist party cells in preparation for the Revolution. The very movie stars who helped depression-era Americans get their minds off their troubles smiled their own testimony of success and prosperity out of such ads. A wholesome mother and pretty daughter were shown making their

Artist Haddon Sundblom's 1942 Santa Claus poster, allowing on-the-wing hint that World War II was going on.

own attractive clothes at the sewing machine—recognition that people had to cut corners in such ways, but they were doing it so pleasantly. More typical was the sizzling steak on the grill of a fine garden fireplace in the back of the most pleasant of homes.

Coca-Cola-ad America did, as we have seen, participate fully in World War II, as the pinnacle of promotional success was reached in expressions by the fighting forces of their own identification of Coca-Cola with the country for which they were fighting. About the time of the war, a short-lived advertising symbol, the elfin face called Sprite appeared, with gray hair suggestive of older people but facial features as eternally young as Peter Pan's. Marshall Lane, a retired art director who began in the job in 1937, said that Walt Disney sketched the first Sprite, but his rendition was too fancy. Haddon Sundblom toned the drawing down, using his own face (as he did later with some of his Santa Clauses) as model. However, Sprite disappeared from the scene after people began calling him Cokie, a practice the legal department feared might lead to trademark problems. His name, of course, lives now as one of the diversification trademarks.

As soon as the war was over, ads welcomed the boys back home with paintings of happy reunion scenes: pleasant parents and wholesome ex-soldier son, pretty young wife, and beautiful baby greeting pleasant returning hero. Then the land that Coca-Cola kept building returned to normal. And there were new happy scenes: the "new arrival," part of the postwar baby boom, being admired by the pretty young mother and pleasant-faced grandmother. Coca-Cola kept on insinuating and insisting that it was the stuff of every day's moments of pleasant existence in an unthreatened, orderly, and just world.

Grim reality was acknowledged with only the slightest of hints. The silhouetted head of a helmeted soldier appeared in 1952, with no mention that he might have been serving in Korea. Similarly, a pretty WAC smiled forth the next year. But the majority of the ads were devoted to happy things, reflecting the traveling about, enthusiasm for games, the GI bill education, homebuilding, and entertaining in suburban split-levels going on during the postwar years.

The people of these pursuits were, as Coca-Cola people had always been before, all white people. In the postwar years, blacks no longer appeared even as servers of Coca-Cola. But in the early 1950s, point-of-sale advertising began to feature black personalities, including Reece "Goose" Tatum of the Harlem Globe Trotters and Atlanta's Graham Jackson, a pianist and singer who used to perform for President Roosevelt among other notables. After 1956, under McCann-Erickson direction, there was an increase in advertising directed to minority groups, including ads in magazines for blacks showing pleasant black people enjoying Coca-Cola in pleasant surroundings. In 1969, the black media carried ads about black leaders and accomplishments of the past, offering booklets about these. By 1972, integrated groups of young people appeared in yet another specialized medium—magazines appealing to the young. Later, of course, we would see on television blacks and whites, side by side with others of the world's variety of people, drinking Coca-Cola and singing a song of brotherhood.

Television's impact shows strongly in the print-media advertising after 1950. The classic magazine ads with excellent paintings, often resembling *Satur-*

Yes

"Bathing suit" poster, early 1950s.

"Women shoppers" theme in national magazine ad for fall, 1961.

What a **REFRESHING NEW FEELING**
...what a special zing...you get from Coke! The cold crisp taste and lively lift of Coca-Cola send you back shopping with zest. No wonder Coke refreshes you best!

day Evening Post covers, in addition to beautifully written captions and copy with ever-changing, ever-clever slogans, gave way to harsher graphics, with photographs replacing paintings. The literary quality that had marked the ads since the earliest D'Arcy days showed itself less, and the execution of the ads increasingly reflected that ad-agency people with a visual, not verbal, orientation were producing them.

The Saturday Evening Post, which had, over its long years of existence, presented a largely pleasant fantasyland America not unlike Coca-Cola's, was, partly by television's influence, to go out of business. Other magazines which reflected old values and aspirations, including *Life* and *Look*, also expired, giving way to *Playboy* and other publications which deal in sexual fantasy and aspiration, reflecting another departure of recent years—the sexual revolution, whose existence Coca-Cola ads discreetly ignored.

One strange twist that advertising took during the late 1950s and 1960s was away from showing the pleasant people doing pleasant things and toward showing merely things: a tennis racket or golf clubs, good things to eat. Marshall Lane, the retired art director, gave one reason for this change. Impersonal ads did not offend people with ethnic hang-ups or hatreds and, as point-of-sales signs, could be put in places serving any kind of person. That was as close as the ads would come to reflecting the enormous racial upheavals going on in America.

Anita Bryant, who began doing spot television commercials for Coke in 1960, represented the company in performances with Bob Hope in Southeast Asia, a euphemistic way *The Refresher* referred to their being in Vietnam. But more prominent was her role as the "beautiful, bouncing, and bubbling" pretty girl singer of Coke's (and other company products') praises, "projecting herself as a member of the younger married set." With Coca-Cola's usual luck, the relationship with Ms. Bryant had been broken off long before she made her contribution to national discord in 1977 by conducting a well-publicized vendetta against homosexuals who, in turn, boycotted products she was then promoting.

Homes and Flowers, Laura Lee Burroughs' three volumes, contributed to America's sense of pleasant place with phenomenal promotional success and bottles of Coca-Cola appeared, unobtrusively, in large numbers of the photographs. Wall charts and teacher's guides, with photography better than in any textbook, went from bottlers into the schools, reaching the youth market early with Coke's message of cordiality. A relief map of the United States in various sizes with historical murals was not only in schools but courthouses, fire departments, and other public places. Again, pride in America, not the terrible realities of the time, was Coca-Cola's theme.

An ad 'way back in 1912 expressed one part of Coca-Cola's reticence about reflecting big events of the day in the promotion. "The National Beverage" was proclaimed, with the admonition, "Whatever your party, whatever your politics, Pause in the mad rush of the daily struggle. . . ." Coca-Cola made no pronouncements about such an important piece of national history as the civil rights struggle (though, as we shall see, Mr. Woodruff was working behind the scenes to help his hometown of Atlanta make the transition from apartheid with grace). Sit-ins closed many southern soda fountains, but both participants in the black demonstrations and Klansmen at their hate-spewing meetings drank bottles of ice-cold Coca-Cola. The promotion, with this rather negative motive for blandness, had offended neither side.

The Strategy

However, impartial reasoning was not the main thrust of the promotional strategy. Its purpose, rather than not to offend anyone, was to make everyone feel good and positive about self and one's country, in addition to associating Coca-Cola with everything one felt good about. With such a purpose, Coca-Cola promotion over all the years shows respect for people—something which, considering how many TV commercials are condescending and how many others play upon anxiety about how one looks or smells, has become all too rare in advertising.

No one in the company nor at D'Arcy seems to have spelled out exactly what the strategy was. We only get hints. When Samuel Candler Dobbs wrote that article of his back in 1908 and talked about "claiming nothing for Coca-Cola that it did not already have, but pounding everlastingly into the public mind through printed display the words, 'Drink Coca-Cola, Delicious and Refreshing, five cents,'" he also gave this clue as to early strategy: "No effort was made to produce artistic copy, but rather strong copy, carrying with it a sales force at once convincing and compelling."

Nonetheless, the graphics of Coca-Cola advertising from the 1890s on have been of the very best of each period and media. The eye-and-ear appeal also partially contributed to pleasantness and pleasurableness. Continuity of colors has been part of the graphic effectiveness of the ads, signs, and other promotions. Red, yellow, green, and white have been the only ones over the years. However, green has given way, in the years since World War II, to more and more white. Pepsi-Cola chose the only primary color Coca-Cola had not preempted, blue—making blue anathema to Coca-Cola people today. Producers of a previous book about Coca-Cola had to redesign its jacket because an art director, ignorant of the soft-drink symbolism involved, had used blue as the main color in his design, according to archivist Wilbur Kurtz.

There were specific promotional goals in the early years, easy to spot, such as making the drink a year-round habit ("any time, anywhere," "Thirst Knows No Season") and instructing the nation in the decorum of drinking straight from the Coca-Cola bottle, with even a bride delicately lifting bottle to pretty lips.

Mainly, however, the strategy was a general, psychological one. William C. D'Arcy, in a speech to the Atlanta Ad Men's Club on December 21, 1910, as reported in the Atlanta *Journal*, explained it succinctly, saying that the essentials of the promotion were "human interest," "simplicity," and "honesty."

Mr. Woodruff is quoted in the Kahn biography on his concept of the promotion: "We've always tried to be decent in our advertising. We've tried to practice what I guess they call the soft sell. We never make claims. We've tried to do with our advertising what we always try to do with all our people inside and outside the company—to be liked."

Most of the discussions of how the team of Lee and Woodruff did what they did are elaborations of Mr. D'Arcy's brief description. Delony Sledge, the retired advertising director, said Mr. Woodruff thought of the drink as symbol, from the start. To him, it meant quality.

Just as Asa Candler pored over the proposed paintings of pretty girls to search out and eliminate any hint of impurity, Mr. Woodruff was quick to spot and dispose of anything not fully up to standards of "clean Americana," Mr. Sledge tells us. Hunter Bell, from his memory of the advertising work, described Mr. Woodruff's ideal of the pretty girl: "It was not just a girl who was a beautiful girl and not a hussy, but it was the type of girl who wouldn't develop into a hussy. A beautiful woman is always sexy, but they couldn't be flagrantly sexy, like so much advertising is today. These girls were the kind you'd like your son to have a date with."

Another of Mr. Woodruff's standards was pleasantness, Mr. Bell explained. "When we were in radio, the news broadcasts became available, and it was suggested we sponsor one. Mr. Woodruff said, 'Naw. I don't want Coca-Cola associated with some big tragedy, or some awful murder. We're going to stay away from that. We want Coca-Cola to be wholesome.'" Hence, the musical programs. "They were largely intended to give you a relaxed, positive attitude toward Coca-Cola," Mr. Sledge qualified.

Mr. Woodruff set such standards, and Mr. Lee, fully concurring with them and attuned to Mr. Woodruff's thinking, executed them. His strongest skill, according to those who worked with him, was in concepts. He wrote and edited copy as well, but often his vocabulary had to be simplified. His greatest contributions were as idea man, thinking them up or seizing on inspired ones of his workers.

It is not certain whether the greatest of the slogans, "The Pause that Refreshes," was Mr. Lee's idea or one of those he seized upon. Some, including Mr. Woodruff, according to his associates, say it was Mr. Lee's brainchild. Others say he was not even in on the meeting where it came forth as a result of brainstorming. The main point, though, is that Archie Lee knew a good slogan when he saw one, and what to do with it.

Mr. Sledge likes to elaborate on why "The Pause that Refreshes," no matter who thought it up, is the perfect expression of all that Coca-Cola has tried to say in its promotion. His rather long face serious, his words slow, almost quizzical, exploring, he said:

"It was 'Delicious and Refreshing' from the start. Then it soon became apparent that delicious and refreshing was something that took place not while you were riding a hoss down the middle of the road. You were relaxing and you were enjoying yourself. So we used, 'Pause and Enjoy Yourself.' We used the word, 'pause,' in many contexts. The concept was of relaxation, escape from reality.

"The fantastic success of Coca-Cola hinges on two things. One is the cola taste, a unique taste, the first unique taste since coffee. That is a physiological thing, simply the slaking of thirst with a unique taste. The other reason is psychological—the escape from reality. Thoreau said the majority of men lead lives of quiet desperation. That's true. People seek escape from lives of quiet desperation. People seek it in all sorts of escape mechanisms. If you do it with whiskey, you cut down on your opportunities considerably. But for some reason or other, this thing Coca-Cola came along and it seemed to have all the elements of all the other escapes. And you didn't pay any penalty for it. You didn't have a hangover.

"When we advertised just the physiological part of it—'The Answer To Thirst'—we had a limited market, almost as limited as selling it as a brain tonic. But if you add the slaking of thirst to this escape from reality, by George there's no limit to your market! You answer not just thirst, but despondency, or frustration, or tension. *The Pause that Refreshes.*"

Mr. Lane, the retired art director, recalled those conferences when Mr. Lee would present campaigns to Mr. Woodruff and others of the company. Mr. Lee worked very hard, he said. Often his hands would be clammy when he arrived with his big cases of ad copy and would shake hands all around. But, as all who knew Mr. Lee agreed, the atmosphere of Coca-Cola advertising work was never, during his era, the high-pressured, frenetic thing it was in most agencies then and is even more so today. The work for Coca-Cola was relaxed, friendly, and happy.

One conference that stuck out in Mr. Lane's mind was over a fine painting of a little girl serving her mother a bottle of Coca-Cola in a pleasant back yard. Mr. Pope T. Brock was sitting in to watch out for legal problems, and he noted in the original version that the little girl had two bottles on her tray and there was no other adult in the picture. The painting was redone to show only one bottle so as not to seem to be suggesting the drink for those whom the company thought were too young for it.

Mr. Lane had to ride herd on the talented and sometimes temperamental artists who did the Coca-Cola ad paintings—including, besides Mr. Sundblom, N. C. Wyeth and Norman Rockwell. The retired art director also remembers small points of promotional strategy. He would, for example, work with artists from sketches to develop a design that would print economically in the various media. When the appeal was strongly to the youth market, Mr. Lane would see to it that, subtly, the promotion spoke also to parents of the youth who generally did the buying for such things as youth parties.

It was Mr. Lane who conceived the splendid idea of incorporating the factory whistle into World War II ads, and he received a thousand-dollar raise in pay in addition to his regular annual raise as a result. All of it was a happy experience, he said, looking back on his years as part of the promotional effort.

Mr. Dietz, in *Soda Pop*, reprints a list of thirty-five rules in force for Coca-Cola advertising preparation at D'Arcy after 1938. Some split hairs; others reflected various of the company policies and Mr. Woodruff's standards. One said: "In any illustration remember—adolescent girls or young women should be the wholesome type; not sophisticated-looking. Boys or young men should be wholesome, healthy types; not too handsome or sophisticated. Seldom show very old people, and never children under six or seven years old." (Unless, of course, they are merely serving one drink to one adult.)

Another of the rules, dating back to Mr. D'Arcy, Mr. Dobbs and Mr. Robinson, said: "Never make any exaggerated claim in copy beyond the fact that it is a 'delicious, refreshing, wholesome, pure drink—easily available.'"

Another formalized discussion of the strategy is contained in an informal collection of Coca-Cola materials in the Special Collections of the Robert W. Woodruff Library at Emory University. The document is entitled, "The Philosophy of Coca-Cola Advertising," and is apparently directed at bottlers to explain "How We Create in the Public's Mind a Favorable Attitude Toward Coca-Cola." It is not dated (it appeared before the era of television since there is no mention of that medium in it), and there is no indication of who the author might be.

It makes the point that, because the price of Coke is modest, people buy it on impulse. And: "Because there is never any telling where and when an impulse will take hold on a customer; and because we know that when this impulse does come it will be momentary; it is essential that we confront our customer with the product, well advertised, in as many widely distributed spots as possible."

The philosophy points out that such impulse buying is different from the purchase of a piano or a tombstone, usually limited one to a customer. There is no telling how much Coca-Cola a customer can be induced to drink in a single day.

"We are interested in both sides of the railroad track," the philosophy goes on, making general-interest magazines, newspapers, posters, and radio the ideal media.

The role of point-of-sale advertising is set out as reminder. Such advertising, of necessity, must be terse. It cannot give reasons why one should drink Coca-Cola. So, effectiveness of the reminder depends on how well a job of previous conditioning has been done by the "heavier" media.

Then follows an acronym spelling out factors in "good advertising." *A* for Attention: The advertising must "get in people's eyes" favorably with skill and good taste. *I* for Interest: "We must compose our advertising with the happy combination of the old and new, the commonplace and ingenious, so as to arouse interest in our message." *D* for Desire: "Well chosen words, appealing illustrations, skillfully composed and shrewdly placed advertisements" must appeal to those desires inherent in all people. *A* for Action: "A determination must be instilled in a customer strong enough to guide that person to the consumption of a Coca-Cola."

A quite lengthy section is devoted, perhaps self-servingly, to explaining to the bottlers, perhaps querulous on the question, why so much advertising was needed for Coca-Cola. One statement here gives us further insight into the reasoning of "The Pause that Refreshes" appeal. Coca-Cola is not an essential commodity, the philosophy correctly sets out. The world would not be "permanently impaired" by its removal. "True, all nature moves in a rhythm of rest and action, and momentary pauses are biologically essential. And we, in identifying ourselves with this rhythm, are to that degree essential." But such identification with "the casual pleasures of life" does not induce great forethought and planning in people to get out and buy Coca-Cola. So "if what we say is to make its impression, it must be repeated many times." All of which is saying in many words what Mr. D'Arcy said so well in very few.

Bob Hall—something of a scholar and a journalist combined, caught up in the suspecting attitude of those two professions—has seized upon the philosophy to bolster his finding of all manner of sinister implications in Coca-Cola promotion.

Writing in *Southern Exposure* ("Journey to the White House," Vol. 5, No. 1, undated but issued in 1977), Mr. Hall contends that the story of Coca-Cola "is a story of the power of men and money to control what you think, to generate a blend of *images* that captivate your imagination, that will make you think 'Coke' when you see a sign or feel tired or thirsty or a little depressed ('Coke adds life'). It is a story of the most incredible mobilization of human energy for trivial purposes since the construction of the pyramids. Think of it. The world's most highly advanced team of writers, public relations experts, psychologists, lobbyists, lawyers, sales managers, and advertising executives are focusing all their creative talents on getting young kids addicted to Coke so they'll drink it for life. It is the story of what went wrong with the American dream."

Oh my. There comes to mind William Allen White's response to the shrill and off-target attacks by the WCTU on Coca-Cola. And one thinks, also, of other things young kids have become addicted to in recent years, of dark and devious programs of our times that Coca-Cola people could have put their skills to, rather than promoting a harmless soft drink.

There is implicit in Mr. Hall's article, and others like it, the notion that Coca-Cola techniques, which made the drink a symbol of the nation, might be used to manipulate people ideologically. Like nuclear technology, the techniques are there, this reasoning goes, and might be used for evil, brain-washing purposes. Coca-Cola people would demur. They maintain that none of the promotion would ever have worked had the drink not been appealing to people, something they wanted. But then, Mr. Hall's question, is it worthy of all the effort to sell it?

Man does not live by bread alone. Out of sugar and water and other good things, Coca-Cola gave to the world, in its drink and the promotion of it, an essence of the moonbeams of southern romanticism, the frivolous and harmless myths which Southerners, when defeat most haunted them, held onto for self-satisfying, self-respecting pleasure. The most recent chapter of promotional history carried this to its ultimate.

The McKann-Ericson Approach

After Archie Lee passed from the picture, the D'Arcy agency carried on in rather uninspired fashion with the mostly visual, impersonal advertising of the times. Competition from Pepsi-Cola saw the soft-sell philosophy of Mr. Woodruff give way enough to allow comparatives to creep into the slogans:

"Matchless Flavor . . . Nothing Better," "Almost Everyone Appreciates the Best," "There's Nothing Like Coca-Cola."

The competition was part of the motivation for the move to McKann-Ericson, the company seeking new approaches and fresh inspiration from people there who had worked on overseas promotion. (D'Arcy bowed out with dignity, with an ad in *The Wall Street Journal* of April 2, 1956: "We Hand It On With Pride. . . .") The new approaches didn't come immediately from McKann-Ericson. A series of finely painted, sophisticated international scenes in 1957 was considered a dud of a campaign. Marshall Lane suggested that this was because the bottlers didn't like the ads; nobody had bothered to explain to them what they were trying to do.

The comparative slogans continued: "Be Really Refreshed," "Go Better Refreshed," "It's the Real Thing." But the ads soon chirked up. A rare humorous one appeared in 1968, a two-page spread with Coca-Cola saying, "America, Give Me Your Tired, Your Hot," and then a very long list of every kind of person that had appeared in the ads over the years, ending with "your ushers, your hippies, your high school students yearning to pass math."

That was Coke's first acknowledgment of the existence of hippies. On one other occasion, during all the traumatic years after World War II, was there reference to a big event of ongoing history. This was a happy one. When the Apollo astronauts returned from the moon, the big illuminated sign at Times Square spelled out: "Welcome Back to Earth, Home of Coca-Cola."

But then, in the midst of the horror of the Vietnam war, Coca-Cola delivered its counterpoint message explicitly with the inspired television commercial showing young people of all nations holding hands and singing: *"I'd like to build the world a home/And furnish it with love/Grow apple trees and honey bees/and snow-white turtle doves/I'd like to teach the world to sing in perfect harmony/I'd like to buy the world a Coke/And keep it company.*

"I'd like to see the world for once/All standing hand in hand/And hear them echo through the hills/For peace throughout the land/That's the song I hear/Let the world sing today/A song of peace that echoes on/And never goes away."

The song was the theme for the 1974 calendar, with a different verse for each month, and appropriate accompanying color photography. For the "I'd like to teach the world to sing in perfect harmony" phrase, a beautiful little girl with long blond hair gazed out as a butterfly hovered by her. A noncommercial version of the song made the top of the pop hit lists here and abroad. Proceeds from sales of the recording went to *UNICEF*.

The song was the inspiration of McKann-Ericson's Bill Backer, perhaps an heir of Frank Robinson and Archie Lee's status. A musician himself, he was, according to company president J. Lucian Smith, "in close touch with the youth of the world at a time when our country was in considerable turmoil and, as a consequence, the whole world."

Mr. Backer came up with another inspirational song in 1974 as the scandal of Watergate played itself out. "It grew out of the same feeling as the first one," Lucian Smith explained. "People were bad-mouthing America."

"Look up, America," Coca-Cola sang to the nation. *"See what you've*

got/A million blessings for the counting/More songs to sing/More bells to ring/ More of the real things.

"*Look up, America/See what we've got/Let in the sunny side of living/ Live life refreshed/ Look for the best/Look for the real things/Like Coca-Cola/ It's the real thing/Coke is.*" The singing was accompanied by quickly changing, pleasant, and inspiring scenes across the land.

It was everything the company had been saying in its ads since the 1890s to sell Coca-Cola, making people feel good about their existence.

Mr. Smith noted that Mr. Backer, creator of the two songs, had, when he was assigned creative responsibility for the ads, come to Coca-Cola headquarters in Atlanta and spent time studying the company, past and present. He was thereby able "to really understand the product and what we wanted it to be. He was born and raised in South Carolina, so he had a feeling for Coca-Cola."

A Southerner. When the nation was gaining its sad and bitter-tasting knowledge of the meaning of defeat which Southerners had had so long, there was a Southerner offering them the sum of what the people of sweet-tasting Coca-Cola had known all along about living with unpleasantness and tragedy. There is always a bright side to look to, always some moonbeams and magic and myth to hold onto—*always a pause that can refresh.*

XI

Coca-Cola Faces Life

During all those years when Coca-Cola promotion tried to turn America's face away from the unpleasantnesses of the times, there were, of course, some harsh realities that Coca-Cola, in its corporate life, had to face up to fully—matters of law, of politics and government, of public relations.

The Minute Maid Controversy

The major setback in Coca-Cola's winning streak occurred squarely in the public's eye when, in 1970, an NBC television documentary exposed the bad housing and working conditions of Minute Maid farm workers in Florida. Titled "Migrant: A White Paper," it was an attempt to update "Harvest of Shame," Edward R. Murrow's exposé on CBS of similar conditions ten years previously. The 1970 program thoroughly examined the Minute Maid situation, which was bad enough at the time, but not as bad as conditions for other migrants like those who follow the crop harvests up the Atlantic seaboard from Florida.

Coca-Cola people look back ruefully on that awful besmirching of the company's good name. What makes them angry to this day, when they recall it, is the fact that some months before the film was shot, the company had developed a thorough plan for improving conditions of the fruit pickers. Copies of the vast planning for this were sent to NBC before the documentary was completed, company spokesmen say, but no word of those good intentions was included in the documentary. One company man said he didn't blame NBC for that, but rather "a producer who was more interested in getting an Emmy Award than in doing a good job of reporting."

Company officials learned of the omission of mentioning the improvement plan through a bottler who was shown an advance screening of the show by a local station commercial salesman who somehow thought the bottler would want to be a sponsor. The company officials called on the president of NBC, told him what had happened, and asked not for a change in the documentary, but for a mention of the plan. This was done in a voice-over announcement when the documentary was aired. The producer then charged that the company had tried to bring advertising pressure on the network. And when the plan was implemented, some journalists charged that this was only because of the documentary. It was a bad episode for The Coca-Cola Company all around.

Soon after the show, J. Paul Austin appeared before a U. S. Senate subcommittee probing the migrant situation and won praise from its humanitarian chairman, then Senator Walter Mondale, for the plans to do better down in Florida.

True, The Coca-Cola Company had owned Minute Maid for nearly ten years before it, at Luke Smith's instigation, did do something about the disgraceful situation of the Florida workers. But once the company did move, to its credit, it established what most observers consider a model program, which includes home ownership at low cost and health care. Bob Hall is one observer, however, who does not regard the Florida program as a model one. In his 1977 article in *Southern Exposure* he charges the company with spending its own money to publicize its good works and insists, with little documentation, that the works are not as good as they should be. On the other hand, author Sarah Harris, in a book in progress on the migrants, finds the program generally sound.

J. Paul Austin's idea of good public relations, according to one of his associates, is "to do something good and get caught at it," rather than tooting one's own horn about the good that one is going to do. That is the general public relations policy. And it was adhered to in the case of the fruit pickers, despite urgings by the public relations department that something should be done to offset the bad publicity. After the Florida program got into operation, the NBC "Today" show aired a highly favorable segment on it, and company people comforted themselves that the "Today" show had a much larger audience than the one which viewed "Migrant." This and other publicity about the program have been initiated by the media, company spokesmen say.

Cesar Chavez, head of the United Farmworkers Union, perhaps with a view to taking advantage of the company's chagrin over the bad publicity from "Migrant," sent his organizers, including his cousin, Manuel, down to sign up the Florida workers. In 1972, after threatening a boycott of Coke, and having won the vote of workers to organize, the UFW got a union contract covering the Minute Maid workers which Mr. Chavez called the best first contract he had gotten anywhere. Since then, the company and the nation's most effective union have grappled it out, the union occasionally marching pickets in front of the decorous North Avenue headquarters and occasionally having to threaten again to use its ace in the hole—the boycott—which could do great harm to that good name the company cherishes.

It is interesting to note that this one public relations gaff, in part the result of the failure to act sooner on the plight of the fruit pickers, in part a piece of unfair reporting, is the only major domestic hint of scandal regarding The Coca-Cola Company through all its years of operation. And the confession of faulty payments overseas remains the single scandal in the foreign operations. Either the canny people of Coca-Cola have been awfully good at hiding wrong-doing or, as seems more likely, the company just had to be untypically good for a giant American corporation to get where it is.

Coca-Cola's Influence over Georgia's Government

On the whole, the record on relations with government is similarly good. The lobbying that The Coca-Cola Company has done with the state and federal governments seems to have been restricted for the most part to seeking its own best interests in matters of taxation.

With state governments, this was back in the 1920s and 1930s mostly a matter of fending off sporadic movements in one state or another to impose a special tax on soft drinks, usually a penny levy. Ben Fortson, Georgia's venerable secretary of state, recalls with a rueful grin the time he was a freshman legislator in the late 1930s and tried to help out his political friend, then Governor Ed Rivers. Governor Rivers had been injudicious enough to suggest a sales tax as a solution to the state government's depression-weakened financial structure, and had been widely denounced in Georgia politics as "Sales-tax Eddy."

To take the heat off his friend, young legislator Fortson proposed as an alternative to a sales tax, a penny tax on soft drinks, reasoning that it was a tax on a luxury. The roof fell in on his proposal. "There was no big pressure from Coca-Cola," Mr. Fortson said with a laugh. "All they had to do was say no, and that was the end of it."

Red Hall, the retired hard-working Coca-Cola fountain serviceman, described one way the company was able to exert such strong influence on state legislators. Coca-Cola had the allegiance in each state of the close-knit Retail Drug Association—all those profitmaking sellers of Coca-Cola over the soda fountain. "If you needed help to fight a soft-drink tax, that was the place to go. They could help you whip it every time." In every city and every hamlet, the druggists could "grab a legislator by the coattail and say, 'Look here, we don't want this.'"

Representative John W. Greer of Atlanta, who has served in the Georgia Legislature since the late 1930s and has been a pillar of integrity in a body not always noted for that quality, recalls the time of Ben Fortson's unpopular suggestion and cited another force the politicians had to contend with—the family of Coca-Cola bottlers in many towns and cities of each state. The bottler in Fort Valley, Georgia, was a big backer of Governor Rivers at the time of the suggestion, "and he raised hell with Ed Rivers about it," Representative Greer remembered with a laugh.

Other than the soft-drink tax, Coca-Cola just didn't have anything to lobby for, Representative Greer maintained. "I don't remember anything else over the years. He was in the legislature in 1950 when Georgians finally did ratify a constitutional amendment levying a 3 per cent sales tax. Then Governor Herman Talmadge could escape the opprobrium Sales-tax Eddy had heaped on him by proposing the tax as a way to finance for Georgians, ever-wistful that things might be better for their young, great improvement in the education system. (His education program was also a too-little, too-late effort to comply with the Supreme Court's separate but equal requirement for segregated schools, soon to be toppled.)

Representative Greer contends that Coca-Cola pressure had nothing to do with the fact that the sales tax imposed back then (and still in effect) exempted purchases of less than fifteen cents, as do most others in southern states which rely so heavily on this most regressive means of taxation. Representative Greer insisted that the concern of Georgia legislators was that they not add to the cost of things that children buy. "There were so many things that chillun bought—candy bars and chewing gum and things like that—which were under fifteen cents, we just started the bracket at fifteen cents."

Of course, an ice-cold bottle of Coca-Cola fit that category of things that "chillun" liked. The company probably did not feel the need to apply pressure in the matter. Its feelings about the soft-drink tax were well known and, as we have seen, quite well respected.

"All these years that I've been in politics, I've never known The Coca-Cola Company to take what you'd call any selfish, big-interest point for themselves," Representative Greer continued. The company and bottlers were always generous to provide free cases of the drink for charitable gatherings—even for political ones, making certain it was equally generous to all sides in politics. However, recent federal campaign statutes have ended this sort of beneficence.

Individuals of the company might back a candidate for governor with campaign contributions, Representative Greer pointed out, but the company itself never took political positions. With all the bottlers and their varying, often-at-odds, political loyalties, it couldn't afford to.

The Coca-Cola Company, Representative Greer summed it up, just never has been one to try to run the state, as Georgia Power Company is sometimes accused of doing. No Coca-Cola lobbyist had ever asked him to do one thing. The company's government relations people never hang around the legislature, as do representatives of other large and small businesses in the state.

"There's nothing Coca-Cola needs from us, as long as folks keep getting thirsty. They don't ask for a law saying people have got to get thirsty. They don't need it. They're different from other big companies. They're just nice people. They've just been good citizens."

What, Representative Greer was asked, about the Coca-Cola bank, the Trust Company of Georgia? He replied that it was interested in the same things other banks were—interest-rate legislation and a bill, as was passed recently, allowing large banks to buy small local banks and run them by their local name, rather than as a branch bank.

But the Trust Company does not use strong-arm tactics, Representative

Greer declared, no more than does the Coca-Cola law firm of King and Spalding, which also represents most other large businesses in Georgia. Every state has such a law firm. Its political influence derives from power and wealth exercised not so much in lobbying as through the knowledge politicians have of what such a firm wants them to do.

Charles Kirbo, a partner in King and Spalding, commented about its role, in an article by Larry Woods in *Juris Doctor* (May 1977), having to do with the firm's connections to President Carter and former King and Spalding partner, Attorney General Griffin Bell. Said Mr. Kirbo anent these political connections: "We have a continuous string of litigation that comes through here from all over the world. People don't select lawyers with political skills to handle lawsuits. They want lawyers who've had experience and success in trying cases."

The brief exile of the corporate headquarters in Delaware is interesting for the insight it gives into Coca-Cola's relationship with Georgia state government. The company, along with many other corporations and stock-owning individuals, fled the state in 1938. Ol' Gene Talmadge had ordered his tax gatherers to enforce an ancient law—honored theretofore only in the breach—which called for property taxes to be paid on what amounted to the total assets of a company or individual, including stocks. The law applied only to companies incorporated outside of Georgia.

As Mr. Brock pointed out, no company could operate under such an onerous tax. Coca-Cola had been set up as a Delaware corporation at the time of sale and reorganization in 1919. So Delaware was a natural selection for the headquarters in exile. But the arrangement was cumbersome, communication and transportation back in the 1930s and 1940s not being what they are today.

It would be fifteen years before the law was changed to end the inequitable tax burden on foreign corporations. Mr. Brock tells us that it was Hughes Spalding, Sr., (son of Uncle Jack Spalding, a founder of the firm of King and Spalding) who persuaded Ol' Gene's son, Herman Talmadge (while he was serving as governor in 1953), to get the law rewritten.

The change of the archaic law not only allowed many companies like Coca-Cola to come back home, but also opened the way for a vast amount of industrialization that occurred during the 1960s and continues today, with considerable activity in luring sophisticated manufacturing firms from other lands.

After the law was changed, attorneys for The Coca-Cola Company filed an application for domestication in Georgia in Atlanta's Fulton Superior Court on September 8, 1953. At that time, the new law required companies seeking such domestication to pay a registration fee of 10 cents per share of outstanding stock. Under the levy, Coca-Cola would have had to pay $50,000 on its five million shares. But in a special session called by Governor Talmadge, the Georgia Legislature passed a law on December 15, 1953, setting a $5,000 ceiling on the registration fee.

Secretary of State Fortson, when he received an application to his office for domestication from Coca-Cola, declared it his opinion that the company was not covered by the $5,000 ceiling because it had made the required Superior Court application in September, before the law was passed. But when he asked for a legal opinion on the matter from then Attorney General Eugene Cook, that worthy declared that the company was covered by the ceiling because it had prudently waited until December 18, four days after the ceiling law was passed, to make application to the state. And the new law specifically held that the date of filing with the state was the one which determined whether a company was covered by the ceiling or not. It was as though Coca-Cola's attorneys knew that such a law might be passed, saving their company a good $45,000. Attorneys for Rich's Department Store, according to Mr. Fortson, lacking in such wisdom and foresight, filed with the state before the crucial December 14 date, and had to pay a $94,000 registration fee.

It was friendship in high places, such as that of Mr. Spalding with Governor Talmadge, rather than pressure and lobbying, that marked Coca-Cola's successes at getting done by governments that which has been needed by the company.

Coca-Cola's Governmental Influence Outside Georgia

A long-time observer of political events in both Atlanta and Washington pointed out that Coca-Cola's main needs in Washington have had to do with federal taxation. "There is no telling how many highly technical amendments helpful to Coca-Cola's domestic and foreign operations Herman Talmadge (as a U. S. senator since 1955) has put into tax bills over the years," this person said.

Senator Talmadge's predecessor, the late Walter F. George, interceded in 1941 when the Congress itself was considering the unthinkable to Coca-Cola, a federal soft-drink tax. Such a measure was passed in the House, but Senator George persuaded the Senate Finance Committee not to approve it. Senator George and Mr. Woodruff were good friends.

But the observer said the company accomplished its purposes without resort to shady practices. About the most it could be accused of would be the friendly gesture of offering transportation on company planes to various political friends in high places, planes that just happened to be going to places the politicians needed to get to.

The late Ed Forio, a vice-president who served in many capacities at Coca-Cola, was, for a time, political liaison man. *The Refresher*, January–February 1966, in a story about him, gave his credo for such work: "Make friends before you need them. Dig a well before you're thirsty. It ain't what you don't know that causes you trouble. It's what you know for sure that just ain't so."

Much has been made in our suspicious times of board chairman Austin's friendship in the highest place, that with President Jimmy Carter dating back to when he was governor of Georgia. A story in the Washington *Post* of April 18, 1977, noted that Mr. Austin used to sponsor prayer breakfasts at the governor's mansion, and that Coca-Colas were provided for Governor Carter's political barbecues. One of the first acts of the Carter presidency, the story reports, was replacement at the White House mess hall of Pepsi-Cola machines—the only ones that had been allowed under President Richard Nixon—with Coca-Cola machines, the only kind found there now under President Carter. Perhaps, the story went on ironically, the Coca-Cola bottle would replace the bald eagle as the chief symbol of America, and the 1886 date of Coca-Cola's birth would become a national holiday.

Coca-Cola friendship with Presidents began as far back as Hoover, deepened with Roosevelt who had ties to Georgia through Warm Springs, and, of course, reached its warmest glow during Eisenhower's two terms. Robert Woodruff had been friends with General Eisenhower before World War II, when the two played golf together at the Augusta National course and hunted together at Ichauway.

According to the biography by Mr. Kahn, the only direct request Mr. Woodruff ever made of his friend, the President, was that a 2.5 cent coin be minted so that in the battle against inflation, Coca-Cola might not have to raise the price to a full dime. He quickly dropped the matter when treasury officials opposed such a coin.

Inscribed photographs of subsequent Presidents hang in Mr. Woodruff's office (even one signed by President Nixon, relegated to a hallway in Mr. Woodruff's suite). However, President Nixon was not a friend to Coca-Cola while in office. His friend was Pepsi-Cola board chairmen Donald M. Kendall whom President Nixon helped to get the exclusive contract in Russia. No one at Coca-Cola gloats over Nixon having been Pepsi's President, but probably some in their secret hearts nurture the uncharitable sentiment.

Having a friend in the White House can't hurt a big multinational corporation. But are we to assume, as surely some might, that President Carter's interest in trying to find a solution to the powder-keg situation of Arab and Israeli hostility is partially designed to get Coke back into the Arab world? Or that friendly U.S. overtures to Communist Russia and Castro's Cuba are but foreign policy efforts which, in part, are concerned with getting Coca-Cola into those lands? One could as soon argue that President Roosevelt declared war on Germany in order that Coca-Cola might win its way into Europe, or that General Marshall invaded North Africa just so General Eisenhower might issue his order for bottling plants to be sent there.

Obviously, having President Carter for a friend serves Coca-Cola's interest much as the prestige and power of King and Spalding work upon lowlier politicians in Georgia. Knowing how the President might feel about Coca-Cola can be expected to influence the actions of bureaucrats and congressmen handling the proposed saccharin ban, or Federal Trade Commission officials charged with deciding whether the exclusive bottler territories amount to restraint of trade.

President Luke Smith said of the saccharin situation (at the time the hottest problem Coke had) that the effort would be to try to inform Congress as well as the Food and Drug Administration of a different point of view about whether saccharin might cause cancer. "We have a lot of information, based on findings of the company's own scientists and from 'contacts' with eminent scientists through the world." The entire soft-drink industry joined in the battle to save saccharin, along with other industries using it in products.

Similarly, Mr. Smith affirmed that other soft-drink firms using the franchise system were standing solidly together on the exclusive territory question, hoping for a favorable decision from the Federal Trade Commission.

That case is ironic in the light of past praise by a former noted trustbuster for the company's and Mr. Woodruff's dedication to competitive free enterprise. Thurman W. Arnold, former U. S. Assistant Attorney General, said once of Mr. Woodruff: "In the world of industrial tycoons, he understood the danger of monopoly and the benefits of competition more than any other man I ever knew. He built Coca-Cola into the pattern of industrial development which has been, and I think will be, a model for future big business to follow."

And of the company, a 1953 comment by Mr. Arnold is often cited by Coca-Cola people: "When, as head of the Antitrust Division, I tried to explain to businessmen the competitive economic ideal of the Sherman Antitrust Act, they challenged me to name one big American business that violated neither the letter nor the spirit of our antitrust laws. It was a fair question. I answered by describing The Coca-Cola Company. Since then I have learned more about Coca-Cola, and I am convinced that this corporation represents the emerging pattern of our future free market economy."

Mr. Brock cited one instance where company instinct served well in the matter of avoiding a restraint-of-trade situation. He said that in the early 1930s when Pepsi-Cola was floundering near bankruptcy, The Coca-Cola Company might have bought the business out for probably as low as $3,000. But, he said, the company did not take advantage of the opportunity to rid itself of a competitor and had never tried to buy out any soft-drink business.

"As things developed later on," Mr. Brock asserted, "The Coca-Cola Company was very wise in not reaching for those other soft-drink companies. The developments we've had in the antitrust laws would have brought great trouble to The Coca-Cola Company if it had absorbed all those cola companies which it could have done."

More recently, one of the nation's better social commentators, Calvin Trillin (in "Reflections: Remembrance of Moderates Past" in *The New Yorker*, March 21, 1977) seized upon the actions of members of the King and Spalding law firm in the desegregation of Georgia schools as a sinister intrusion of business into the due process of justice, trying to slow down implementation of the Supreme Court's decree. And this, of course, led him to question the fitness of Griffin Bell to serve as attorney general. (He was one of the King and Spalding figures involved in the action.)

The perhaps familiar history is worth review. Ernest Vandiver, from the small town of Lavonia, was governor in 1960, when it became apparent that the superstructure of unconstitutional law the state had thrown up as a bulwark against desegregation would soon be struck down. These laws had been passed under Mr. Vandiver's predecessor, Marvin Griffin, one of those southern politicians gifted at raising racial ire in whites and deluding them about such a matter as that superstructure of faulty law.

The white people of the state had been led to believe they didn't have to desegregate schools, regardless of what the Supreme Court said. Mr. Vandiver and his executive secretary, Griffin Bell, knew that they had to or cease to operate public schools. Mr. Vandiver is a gentleman. (His wife, Betty, was beloved in middle-class Ansley Park for sending her young to the public Spring Street School and leading the PTA there.) But he had indulged himself in the requisite racial campaign oratory, saying not one, "no, not one" black child should enter a white school while he was governor. That was mild talk in those fervid days. But it put Governor Vandiver and his executive secretary in a tight place.

To get out of that tight place, Mr. Bell conceived the plan of sending a blue-ribbon commission of distinguished citizens across the state to communicate gently to Georgians the choice they faced—desegregated schools or no schools. We have noted that Georgians wistfully look to public schools as the way for their children out of the mire of southern defeat. Mr. Vandiver and Mr. Bell were confident that once white Georgians understood what the choice was, they would opt for the schools.

Mr. Woodruff was in on the selection of members of the commission and, of course, was able to persuade those selected to serve. John A. Sibley, then Trust Company president and former member of King and Spalding, was named chairman of the commission which also included members of the Georgia Legislature. Our friend Representative Greer was secretary of the body.

He recalled that he and Mr. Sibley debated about where to hold the first hearing. (Ostensibly, the commission was a fact-finding group, to sound out Georgians on the desegregation question.) Mr. Sibley suggested it might be better to begin in Atlanta where most members were well known. Representative Greer said no, let's start in Sumter County. Southwest Georgia was the state's most racist area. They would find out the worst at the beginning.

We get the feel of those times (and the South's tragic past before them) from one recollection of Mr. Greer's. When they had arranged with the sheriff to hold the hearing in the courthouse in Americus, with separate rows of seats for blacks instead of seating them as customary in a small separate balcony, a state senator from southwest Georgia approached Representative Greer in some consternation. "What's this about having all these niggers in here?"

Representative Greer replied that they were to testify. The senator had voted for the law setting the commission up that way. Didn't he remember?

The senator was shocked. "Hell, I didn't know that's what it called for. I thought we was just votin' for us white folks to get together and decide, and then we'd tell the niggers what to do."

As it turned out, the commission was well received in Americus and its hearing was unmarred by hostility or violence. The same was true in the dozen or so other places it went. Representative Greer attributed much of this to Mr. Sibley's standing in the state, the respect people had for him, and to Mr. Sibley's manner of presiding over the hearings—"with good judgment and humor." Mr.

Sibley, to this day, is an impressive and compelling personality. His presence at the hearings was an important one.

The hearings received full coverage in newspapers and on television. The people of Georgia got the message of the choice they faced. The commission issued a lengthy report urging that the law be changed so schools could be kept open. The law was so changed and Georgia complied peacefully with the desegregation ruling.

However, Mr. Trillin contends that the purpose of the King and Spalding involvement in this important piece of Georgia history was to avoid violence and chaos harmful to Coca-Cola and other big business, but to do so with as much delay as possible of actual desegregation. The interpretation ignores not only the temper of the times, but historical fact. The effect of the Sibley Commission's work was to move Georgia from a defiant policy of no desegregation to one of gradual compliance, the pattern eventually to be adopted by all southern states and one that was encouraged by the Supreme Court itself when it spoke of "deliberate" speed in the radical restructuring of southern racial mores.

Mr. Sibley's motivation to do his civic duty in the matter may have been strictly and coldly a business one. But to sit in his impressive presence and hear him tell how he approached the hearings is to hear something more human come through. He had been raised in rural Georgia, knew and understood country people. He did not think of the whites as rednecks and had respect for the blacks. That is the spirit in which he approached the people who spoke out at the hearings. It might just be that Mr. Sibley acted in the matter out of the same kind of love for his state that Mr. Woodruff has. And maybe somebody so suspect as to serve as an Attorney General of the United States might have acted out of similar motivation, with even love of country as part of the reason for his taking his suspect office.

Nonetheless, the King and Spalding connection to President Carter and the friendship of Paul Austin with the President still remain under suspicious scrutiny. The generally favorable article by Larry Woods in *Juris Doctor* on King and Spalding points out that the firm gave up a lucrative contract handling Atlanta municipal bonds rather than accede to Mayor Maynard Jackson's policy that they work with a black firm in a "joint venture." A person close to the company was quoted as saying it wanted nothing to do with joint venture after an ugly name-calling episode occurred between two other businesses involved in such a venture.

As for Mr. Austin's friendship with Mr. Carter, we have the former's word for it that he has no intention of being a "hanger-on" at the White House. Every President, he remarked, has such hangers-on, but Mr. Carter has fewer than any in recent times.

"I had known Jimmy several years. I hold him in high regard. I think he is extra-intelligent." Then from a man who holds a formidable responsibility as the head of modern-day worldwide Coca-Cola, and who is known as a genius at delegating authority, a sobering thought about the American presidency and, inferentially, the future of the country: "The only question in anybody's mind is not about Jimmy Carter, but about whether that job can be managed by anybody. It is such a tremendous undertaking."

Wilbur Kurtz, with ever an alert eye out for Coca-Cola lore, points with pride in a happier direction, regarding Mr. Carter, to a passage in the President's autobiography, *Why Not the Best?* (Nashville: Broadman, 1975), which tells how he worried that flat feet might cause him to be turned down by the U. S. Naval Academy. So, to correct the condition, he underwent long periods of exercise during which he stood on, yes, two Coca-Cola bottles. And, Mr. Kurtz confides, while Mr. Carter was governor, Mr. Kurtz was invited to the Governor's Mansion one evening to discuss a common interest—Mr. Carter collects bottles, including Coca-Cola ones.

But these are grim times and such trivia no longer holds the charm that it did when Mr. Eisenhower was Coca-Cola's friend in the White House. Then, nobody raised a suspicious eyebrow or saw anything sinister when the President called his friend Robert W. Woodruff, inviting him to come up for a game of golf because he was feeling low and wanted to play someone he knew he could beat.

Coca-Cola's Influence on Atlanta Government

Of all the relationships of the company with governments, the most interesting has been with the city of Atlanta, beginning in those grand old days when Asa Candler was head of the Atlanta AAA, president of the Chamber of Commerce, and later the millionaire mayor of the city. Robert W. Woodruff, over the years, took an even more active role as a civic leader, but in a quieter way, behind the scenes.

Floyd Hunter in his *Community Power Structure*, (University of North Carolina Press, 1953), the book which provided the term "power structure" to be much abused in the language, was writing about Atlanta (without naming the city) in his description of an all-pervasive alliance between a city's political and business leadership. He disguised identities and some incidents, but Robert Woodruff is recognizable as the most powerful and most influential member of the old Atlanta power structure.

Former Mayor Ivan Allen, Jr., tells a droll story about the considerable influence Mr. Woodruff has on other Atlantans in roles of big business leadership. (Mr. Allen, in addition to being mayor, plays such a role himself, having inherited his father's office-supply firm that dates back to Mr. Candler's days.)

A group of distinguished business leaders were gathered for a meeting of the board of the prestigious Atlanta Commerce Club. Toward the end of business, the manager of the club's elegant dining room raised a question. Turtleneck shirts had become fashionable, and he wanted to know if it would be proper to allow men wearing them under their suit coats to enter the dining room in violation of a rule requiring ties as well as coats.

Richard M. Rich, then president of the large Rich's Department Store chain, spoke up to say that his stores had sold thousands of the turtleneck shirts and that he felt they were quite acceptable. Rolland Maxwell, then president of Davison's, another large department store chain, expressed his agreement. Mr. Rich thereupon made a motion that the turtleneck shirts be acceptable dining room wear, and Mr. Maxwell seconded it.

At this point, Mr. Woodruff (who by this stage of his life was hard of hearing) turned to Mr. Allen and grunted, "What're y'all talking about?" Mr. Allen who always made it a point to sit on Mr. Woodruff's left where he wears a hearing aid, shouted into the hearing aid, "Turtleneck shirts."

Mr. Woodruff frowned and growled, "I don't like 'em." Whereupon Mr. Rich made a motion to withdraw his motion, and Mr. Maxwell quickly seconded it. "He was always a quiet influence like that," Mr. Allen said with a chuckle.

This quiet influence began as far back as the administration of James L. Key in the early 1930s. But it became much stronger when Mr. Woodruff's boyhood friend and former employee (as a bookkeeper while attending law school at night), the late William B. Hartsfield, took office in 1937. On the last day of his long tenure, in 1962, Mayor Hartsfield confided to me: "I have never taken an action as mayor but what I would consider the effect of any national publicity about it on The Coca-Cola Company here in Atlanta and my good friend Bob Woodruff."

A large portrait of Mr. Woodruff hung in the mayor's office while Mr. Hartsfield was mayor, and he would always offer guests a bottle of ice-cold Coca-Cola and would pose with distinguished visitors for newspaper photographs in front of the portrait, Coca-Cola bottles in hand.

When serious problems arose, Mayor Hartsfield took them to Mr. Woodruff who would invite other business leaders to lunch to discuss the situation. The most volatile problems the city faced under Mayor Hartsfield were those attendant on the sit-ins of 1960 and 1961, and the desegregation of schools in 1961.

Herbert T. Jenkins, who was chief of police under Mayor Hartsfield, recalled in an interview just how greatly Mayor Hartsfield relied on Mr. Woodruff's counsel during the times of racial crisis. Chief Jenkins recalled that the mayor and the late Ralph McGill, editor of the Atlanta *Constitution*, would confer daily with Mr. Woodruff about how to handle emergencies and guide public policy. There were "very responsible black leaders" who helped on their side of town, the retired chief added.

"Mayor Hartsfield would say to me this is what we are going to do, and this is how we're going to do it. If I raised any questions, he would say, 'I have discussed it with Mr. Woodruff.' And that would settle it."

Atlanta's municipal government handled the sit-ins as well as any in the South. Police made arrests only at the request of proprietors of places where demonstrations occurred. There was no serious police violence.

When court-ordered school desegregation finally came, with a handful of black youngsters scattered through several high schools, Mayor Hartsfield and advisor Woodruff saw themselves as setting a model of peaceable compliance for the rest of the South to follow, Chief Jenkins observed.

Mayor Hartsfield, under the tutelage of image-maker Woodruff, used the occasion to promote Atlanta's image with the hordes of national newspeople who came to cover the event. They were accustomed, at such occurrences, to find ugliness and violence on the part of elements of the whites as well as unco-operativeness and hostility from city officials. In Atlanta, they saw heavy and quiet police protection that prevented the gathering of crowds and acts of violence. From Mayor Hartsfield and his school officials, they received complete co-operation with frequent briefings and backgroundings in a well-equipped, commodious, air-conditioned press room specially set up at City Hall.

The bulbous-nosed Mayor Hartsfield, with laughing eyes behind gold-rimmed glasses, told them and they told the world (and the rest of the South where other cities would follow the lead) that Atlanta was "a city too busy to hate."

Did some Coca-Cola ad man, by chance, think up that inspired slogan? Chief Jenkins was asked. No, he replied, that was strictly Mayor Hartsfield's. It came to him spontaneously, the chief recalled—like the time some press agent brought a horse into the mayor's office, and Mr. Hartsfield remarked it was the first time he'd ever had a whole horse in there. But certainly, Chief Jenkins averred, the mayor, through the years, had followed Coca-Cola's example of excellent public relations and promotion, just as he had followed the advice of his friend, Bob Woodruff. "Atlanta is a better place to live and raise children because Mr. Woodruff lived here," Chief Jenkins concluded.

Mr. Woodruff's quiet influence was to be felt later in another kind of matter involving the black movement. After Dr. Martin Luther King, Jr., received the Nobel Peace Prize, a group of distinguished black and white Atlantans organized a banquet in honor of their fellow Atlantan. But the ugliness of the times intruded, in the form of rumor-mongering by FBI agents in the city about Dr. King's private life, with the result that many on the blue-ribbon list of invited guests were declining to buy tickets to the banquet. The organizers, according to Chief Jenkins, went to Mr. Woodruff with this problem and he gave his blessing to their putting the word out that he was for the banquet and would attend if nobody else did. Soon, the occasion was sold out.

Ivan Allen, Jr., who succeeded mayor Hartsfield, relied on Mr. Woodruff's counsel, too. Himself a member of the power structure, his administration was the ultimate and consummate joining of business and government in directing the city's course, with much business development and downtown construction occurring.

Former Mayor Allen described the worst crisis during his term in office—the terrible day when Dr. King was assassinated in Memphis. "Atlanta was in agony. It was the home and the Alma Mater of Dr. King." He and Chief Jenkins, not yet retired, put every effort and energy into preserving the peace that day and night, so that Atlanta was spared the rioting which occurred in many other places.

When he got back to his office at 2 A.M. of that tense night, a phone call came in from Joe Jones, Mr. Woodruff's assistant, Mr. Woodruff had been in President Johnson's office when news of the assassination came and was anxious to hear from Mayor Allen how things were in Atlanta. Mayor Allen told him of the strenuous, successful efforts to keep the peace.

"When I got through, Mr. Woodruff said, 'That's fine. I think you've done pretty well. But you've got to start thinking about tomorrow.'

"Well, frankly, I hadn't thought of anything but that night. But Mr. Woodruff said, for the next three or four days Atlanta would be the center of attention for the world. All the news media would be here and this would probably be the largest funeral ever held in the South.

"These things had not yet penetrated to most of us. He outlined to me very carefully what the very difficult conditions would be that we'd have to cope with. He impressed on me the need for considered action and thought, which hadn't come to me before that.

"His final words to me were, 'Ivan, there are a great number of things that you may have to do in the way of major expenditures and everything else which may not be legal for the city to do. But everything must be done in order that the funeral and the events leading up to it are handled in the proper fashion. Nothing must happen in Atlanta that is not absolutely right. No matter what it costs, it will be taken care of. You understand what I'm telling you?'

"I said yes, I understood. What he was doing, he was giving me a blank check."

Mr. Allen declined to say how much he drew on that blank check or for what purposes. But "everything worked out fine," and just might not have, had it not been for citizen Woodruff. "He had the capacity to think ahead at a time of turmoil, and the willingness to see that everything was done right."

Carl Sanders, former governor, recalled in Mr. Kahn's Woodruff biography the crisis in 1966 when black people were in turmoil and near to riot in Atlanta. People were urging Governor Sanders to call out the National Guard. He sought Mr. Woodruff's counsel, as he had often done on other matters previously. Mr. Woodruff advised force as an absolutely last resort. "Here was a man I had confided in who gave me the assurance I needed that my judgment was right." And rioting was averted without the use of force.

Through the years, Mr. Woodruff has bestowed vast amounts of money on Atlanta charities and institutions, including Emory University, carrying that tradition started by Mr. Candler to an ultimate. Among his gifts have been ones of land to the city for a large downtown park (in front of Trust Company of Georgia, like a fine green, tree-lined yard) and several smaller parks.

Some of these gifts have occurred during the term of Maynard Jackson, Atlanta's first black mayor. The natural question to Mayor Jackson was whether or not the advisory relationship had continued into his administration which began in 1973. His reply was that he had met with Mr. Woodruff only three or four times, twice over lunch to discuss civic matters. But he attributed the infrequency to a general slowing of Mr. Woodruff's activities. "The person I have had the most continuous positive contacts with has been J. Paul Austin. He has been a real friend of the city, and a real supporter of mine."

He and Mr. Austin have worked closely together in a co-operative venture of the Business Round Table and the U. S. Council of Mayors to bring mayors of important cities together with important industrialists to address urban problems. Mr. Austin has also supported efforts to establish Atlanta's reputation as an international city.

On a more personal level, Mayor Jackson told how he had made a controversial decision early in his term and called several of his top business supporters to tell them about it in advance of a public announcement. "Mr. Austin asked, 'Are you quite sure of what you're doing?' I said yes. He said, 'Then I'm with you all the way.' "

Mayor Jackson added that it had been "very pleasing" to him as mayor, and during the four years he was vice-mayor, to have a cordial relationship with the people of Coca-Cola. The company had made a dramatic gesture of faith in the inner city by putting its big new office building at the North Avenue site rather than out in some suburban office park, he pointed out. A large building formerly used by Carling Brewery had been bought to house the syrup factory, and that building is just inside the city limits.

"The Coca-Cola Company," Mayor Jackson affirmed, "has been a superb citizen, both corporate and personal, of Atlanta."

And so that tradition continues of a personal and corporate bond that began in Asa Candler's days. "Power structure" became a pejorative term during the social struggles of the 1960s, so that city governments said to be run by the power structure were suspect as paternalistic and manipulative. But to have lived in a wisely led Atlanta during the years of turmoil in the 1950s and 1960s; to see it prospering and more or less healthily growing in the 1970s, with a black mayor and thoroughly integrated City Council in the heart of the deep South; to see a Georgian able to move from the new enlightenment of the state to the White House—are all causes at least to question once more the general assumption that all business is badly motivated.

Coca-Cola company people, like Mr. Montgomery's bottling company employees, are encouraged to be active in civic and charitable activities of the city, giving much of their time and energy. The bond is more than corporate. Mr. Woodruff, writing Ivan Allen a blank check to prevent Atlanta's name from being sullied before the world, was not acting out of profit motivation. Coca-Cola would have survived any disgrace. Atlanta might not have. Mr. Woodruff acted out of love for his city.

XII

Robert Winship Woodruff: The Man with a Cigar ... an Enigma

The men who have worked under Mr. Woodruff pay him sincere tribute when they recall their years with the company. Theirs is not the cant of organization men, but a strangely searching kind of awed recounting of an extraordinary human being's influence on the way they worked and upon their own humanity "I don't say this to scratch his back, and I certainly don't have anything to gain by saying it," is the type of remark the retired men would make and then go on to relate how Mr. Woodruff did this or said that, making all the difference. Their words were searching because they seemed unsure of what it was about their boss that made working for him such a satisfying and successful experience.

One of the *Fortune* magazine articles ("Bob Woodruff of Coca-Cola," September 1945), in trying to capture what in his personality was so effective, pointed out that Coca-Cola's soft-sell advertising was but a variation of Mr. Woodruff's "own intuitive method of handling people. . . . Bob dominates the company in somewhat the same unobtrusive way. He carries almost to an extreme the common executive policy of delegating functions to men with special talents. He has a private elevator in his Atlanta office, and to lesser employees is the Enigma, the Man with a Cigar. . . . He seldom issues an order, or signs a contract or even a memo. . . . But he is . . . the man who makes the decisions and pulls the strings. He may be an enigma to employees, but people who amount to anything in Coca-Cola are ceaselessly aware of him. He expects them all to keep up with him, and sometimes they cannot. His energy is inexhaustible,

Robert Winship Woodruff.

as was his father's, and likewise supercharged by discontent. Things you worry about don't happen if you worry enough, Bob tells his friends. 'The world belongs to the discontented.'"

Part of our own effort to resolve the enigma of Mr. Woodruff will be to see him not only through the eyes of those who knew him, but through their attitudes as well. J. W. (Joe) Jones tells a story about that *Fortune* article which shows the attitudes toward Mr. Woodruff back when it was written.

The writer assigned to do the story was rebuffed by Mr. Woodruff, who didn't consider himself important—only the company and Coca-Cola. *Fortune* had done an article recently on the company. So there was nothing to talk about. The writer said nevertheless he had to carry out the assignment.

To which, as Mr. Jones tells it, Mr. Woodruff replied: "Of course, I can't stop you. But I will not co-operate. I will not talk to you. As a matter of fact, I think I'll call up Harry and suggest he cancel your assignment."

But the reporter was prepared: "Well, Mr. Woodruff, Mr. Luce anticipated what your reaction to this might be. He left San Francisco this morning on a boat to China."

A part of enigma is the variety of the views. We know of Mr. Woodruff's gentleness, politeness, consideration of others, and of his quietness—an almost inarticulate sparseness of speech. Of this, Mr. Brock remarked: "He could get more done just by sitting and saying nothing. Everybody gets the idea of what he prefers." And yet at another point, Mr. Brock would say, "Mr. Woodruff has the most extraordinary amount of social energy of any man I ever knew." He spoke of social contacts in and out of the company, and of "social courtesies to people of minor importance in the company," inviting them down to Ichauway for one of the famous hunts.

"I never saw him lose his temper," said one close associate. "Or be discourteous, not even to someone he didn't like. If he is displeased, you know from the way he is quiet. You can be the smartest person under the sun, but if he doesn't like you, he won't let you work for him."

Zeke Candler, the retired fountain serviceman, told a story about brevity in a pronouncement from the boss. Shortly after the famed change of the sales department to a service one, Mr. Candler asked Mr. Woodruff just what did he want the servicemen to do—how far should they go to help the customers? The answer he got was as all-encompassing as it was brief. "Do the needful," said Mr. Woodruff gently.

Perhaps Mr. Woodruff's sparing use of speech was formed as a boyhood habit. Joe Jones recalled that old Ernest Woodruff once advised his boy: "Don't get enamored of your own voice. You can go down to the courthouse and hire a fellow for five dollars to make a better speech than you can. Devote your time to something else."

And then there are appraisals which speak as though of an entirely different person. The trustbuster Thurman Arnold: "Bob Woodruff is one of our nation's great industrial leaders. But he differs from most of his influential and conservative peers. He will make his mark in history not because of the wealth and prestige he achieved but because of his independent thinking. He never went along with the crowd. He had a conception of competitive society which many of his fellows in industry would have thought bordered on the radical. He was never deceived by slogans, nor was he influenced by pecuniary self-interest when that self-interest seemed to be opposed to the public welfare. He understood and appreciated original people and original ideas."

(The *Fortune* article Mr. Woodruff didn't want written said that some in 1945 thought him a liberal, some a conservative. He, of course, wouldn't say.)

Ralph Cordiner, retired president of General Electric: "Woodruff's unique. I've never known another businessman in his pattern, and I've been exposed to a great many of them. He has a singular feel for what parts must go together to make the whole."

The *Fortune* article described Mr. Woodruff's decision-making process and it apparently involved considerable articulateness. He would ask searching questions and make cut-through comments, would smoke out motives and errors, then make his decision. He consulted as many people as he could, including his black chauffeur, Lawrence Calhoun. "Has he asked you yet?" Joe Jones would say to the chauffeur when some big decision was pending. "No, sir. Not yet. But he will."

The decisions were not made the way a Ph.D. would make one, the article noted. "A Ph.D. would make two columns: why he should do something, why he shouldn't, weigh them and decide. Mr. Woodruff will look at the two columns, put his finger on one reason, and say that's why he'll do it."

Mr. Kahn in the biography quotes the late company president Burke Nicholson, Sr., as saying: "I wouldn't be surprised if Coca-Cola isn't a reflection of Woodruff. Bob has no specific talents. He's not a technical man nor an advertising man. He is fumbling in his talk, and when he tells you something is wrong and you ask him why, he simply can't explain, though he nearly always turns out to have been right."

In contrast to Mr. Nicholson's remark about lack of specific talent, Mr. John A. Sibley declared, "Robert Woodruff has more diversity of talent than any man I've ever known. With most people, if one is a good salesman, you don't expect him to be a good financier. If he's good at details, you don't expect him to be good on overall policy. Mr. Woodruff was a combination of all those things, and that enabled him to accomplish a great deal through other men because he had the ability to guide them in fields they were supposed to be experts in. Yet he was superior in each particular field. So he was able to accomplish things through men that a lesser man would have failed with. . . . He understood the people with whom he worked, and could get them to work extraordinarily well."

How? he was asked, and after a long, long pause, said: "He could motivate people because he saw in them their strengths and their weaknesses. He developed personal relationships that made people not only want to succeed themselves, but feel a part of his own success." To that, company president Luke Smith would add: "He believes in human dignity and self-respect."

Some of the men he inspired were not all that good, as Mr. Kahn was quick to point out. He would not fire incompetents, but try to make them less incompetent, "to do better than their natural talents justified." Mr. Brock's slowly intoned view is a little different.

"He is a man of great patience, tolerance. He is the slowest man to throw people out I ever saw. He would put up with more foolishness, rather than destroy a fellow by throwing him out on his ear." Instead, he would transfer such fellows around and about the company, hoping perhaps they might go away on their own accord.

For all of these things, Mr. Kahn tells us that Mr. Woodruff dominates any group he is with, cannot be happy unless he does so, and, on the hunts at Ichauway, though he entertains his guests like royalty, puts them through a grueling schedule of his making which sounds downright unbearable.

During those years when he refused to fly, the chauffeur, Lawrence Calhoun, had to tear around the country, night and day, going as far away as California, to meet Mr. Woodruff's train with the car polished and ready to carry him about in whatever city it might be. However, not even the loyal Mr. Calhoun could keep up the pace when Mr. Woodruff finally decided to move with the times and accept aviation. His first flight was in a DC-3 in 1952. After that, planes were to be a "salvation."

Obviously, a complex individual, Robert W. Woodruff.

An Atlanta man was quoted in the *Fortune* article regarding the winner's early years as a salesman: "His personality is so gratifying that men actually *like* to be outsmarted by him." His personality—a distinctive, maybe even eccentric one—was part of it. Another—his intellect.

The reason he dropped out of college to father Ernest's disappointment was, according to Mr. Kahn's biography, that he got the reputation of being a bad student because he wouldn't accept things on authority. He would demand to know why, and how did the professor know. Finally he asked himself if college was doing him any good, and decided definitely not.

In all of the remarkable career that followed, the decision in the 1920s to build the overseas market has been hailed by many as the most visionary use of his intellect. Joe Jones notes that Mr. Woodruff disparages that notion. "As I have often heard him express it, there wasn't any great vision. How can you have vision about something you don't know anything about? He says it wasn't vision. He was just curious. He was curious about how Coca-Cola would do in Europe, how it would do anywhere that people get thirsty." Mr. Woodruff thought the drink would do best in England where he sent Mr. Nicholson to toil. However, it turned out, of course, that it did best in Germany, under Max Keith's inspired guidance.

Is this but another expression of Woodruff modesty? We know he took that trip to Europe two years after becoming company president to study prospects there. Curiosity or great vision? It is a semantic question, but the enigma remains.

Another of Joe Jones's stories provides a better insight. It has to do with the time, in the late 1940s, that the company wanted a new portrait of Mr.

Woodruff and commissioned the Russian painter Elizabeth Shoumatoff to do it. (It was she who was at work on the portrait of President Roosevelt when he died.) Mr. Woodruff stopped by her studio in Atlanta after work for posing sessions. These were pleasant interludes. The two would chat while the artist made her sketches, Mr. Woodruff sipping a cocktail.

When, at last, the portrait was completed and presented to Mr. Woodruff, he told Mrs. Shoumatoff bluntly, "This won't do. This is not acceptable." She was near tears. Why on earth won't it do? she asked. The portrait, Mr. Woodruff argued, made him look too pleasant. ("He likes to think of himself as being tough," Mr. Jones explained.) "This isn't me," Mr. Woodruff said to the distraught artist. "This is some other fellow."

"But, Mr. Woodruff," she replied, "this is the person that I know from your coming here to pose."

Mr. Woodruff was adamant, so Mrs. Shoumatoff did another portrait showing him more composed, tougher. What, Mr. Jones was asked, became of the first portrait? He laughed. "I'll tell you what happened to it. I bought it for Mrs. Woodruff. She liked it. She said, 'This is the Bob I know.'"

So, of course, he was many things to many people, to the extent that he himself wasn't fully aware of all the facets of his personality.

Mr. Woodruff suffered two strokes a week apart in 1972. They affected his right side so that he now walks with a cane. Prior to that, his hearing had deteriorated. This is a congenital condition, Mr. Jones explained, pointing to a painting in Mr. Woodruff's office of his grandfather, Joseph Winship, holding an ear horn. The problem is with the nerves and cannot be remedied.

In the years since the stroke, Mr. Woodruff has continued to come to his executive suite daily, when in Atlanta, has continued to travel in this country and abroad, and has continued to have friends down to Ichauway for hunts, though he cannot handle a gun any more. He goes with the hunters on the dog wagon and sometimes has one of his horses saddled for a brief ride.

His office hours since the stroke have been usually from 10 A.M. until about four in the afternoon, though sometimes he shows up as early as eight forty-five. In his hard-driving days, he would work from nine to six or later, and on Saturdays.

He never complains, said an associate of many years, never turns down an appointment because he feels bad, never says, "I can't do it."

Company president Smith quoted what Mr. Woodruff says about being toward the end of his life. "Remember that line in a song called 'Old Man River' —'Tired of living and feared of dying?' I want everybody around here to know I ain't feared of dying, but I sho ain't tired of living."

During one of his typical mornings at the office in 1977, nearing then the age of eighty-eight, Mr. Woodruff greeted me. Joe Jones had called an hour earlier to say with quiet pleasure, "The gentleman will see you this morning." The gentleman rose from behind his plain desk and moved—a tall, erect figure, his face paunchy, lined with age, yet handsome, the eyes alert, shrewd—to shake hands, commenting on my good grip. The conversation was brief. Mr. Woodruff spoke of old friends, most of them gone now. "Pope Brock and John Sibley are the only two people I know older'n me." He spoke of Ichauway, of his inability to hunt any more, demonstrating with his cane that lifting a gun causes him a balance problem.

He showed, with a smile of pride, a letter from Sanford S. Atwood, retiring as president of Emory University, thanking Mr. Woodruff for his many beneficences to Emory, while Mr. Atwood was president, and reporting the success of efforts to carry out Mr. Woodruff's suggestion that the school find new sources of contribution.

Mrs. Lucille Huffman, Mr. Woodruff's secretary for many years, brought in a stock market report, and he studied it before grunting that maybe things were looking better. Then he chuckled and spoke of the attempt by India to get the Coca-Cola secret ingredients. "They want our formula." Joe Jones, at his side, chuckled too. "I don't think we need worry about their getting it."

The visit soon ended. In the reception room, Mrs. Huffman, an older Coca-Cola girl, pretty and beautifully dressed, showed me a little plaque on the wall which she said expressed much of what Mr. Woodruff believes in. It is entitled, "A Short Course in Human Relations," and says:

The six most important words: "I admit I made a mistake."
The five most important words: "You did a good job."
The four most important words: "What is your opinion?"
The three most important words: "If you please."
The two most important words: "Thank you."
The one most important word: "We."
The least important word: "I."

(When Mrs. Huffman reached retirement age some years ago, Mr. Woodruff asked her to stay on with him as long as he was able to come to the office. Each year, the board of directors votes that she may stay on for another year. Once she wrote Mr. Woodruff a note [she imparts information to him mostly by notes] saying that if he felt she weren't doing her job well enough, to let her know. She would stop any time. He tossed the note away, growling that it had been a waste of time for her to write it.)

The paneled walls of Mr. Woodruff's spacious office and reception room are decked with photographs of his many friends, as is the long hall leading into the Woodruff suite. Of those in the office and reception room, Mrs. Huffman noted, "Most of the people are dead now. It's sad to think of. They were associates of his."

The many faces look down from the past of all those years of Woodruff and Coca-Cola success, men who shared that with him, other men successful in their own right: J. C. Penney; Senator Walter F. George; Judge Thurman Arnold; Colonel Bob Jones of the legal battles; his son, Bobby Jones, the great grand-slam Atlanta golfer whom Mr. Woodruff admired for his quality-control game; Ike and Mr. Woodruff each drinking a Coca-Cola; Bernard Gimbel; Henry Ford II.

Laughing down is the good, plain face of Dr. Richard C. Gresham, dead now too, who was a classmate at GMA and became a Baptist minister. As Joe

Robert Winship Woodruff.

Jones put it, "Dr. Gresham appointed himself in charge of Mr. Woodruff's soul." About once a month, the preacher would write a private sermon for Mr. Woodruff's eyes only, and special ones for important occasions in his friend's life, whether of tragedy or good fortune. Mr. Woodruff valued them. He is not a churchgoer, but often speaks of God and immortality. On his desk is an old Bible with his name engraved in gold. He doesn't read it, an associate reported, but refers to it often. We do not know what he made of the words another man of the cloth, Methodist Bishop William R. Cannon, once spoke in prayer at some occasion at Emory University: "We are thankful that Thou has sent us Thy son, Robert W. Woodruff."

Here is Mr. Bradley from Columbus; and here Benjamin Fairless; and Chief Jenkins in his uniform in younger days, looking like a movie star; and another valued advisor, the late great Atlanta newspaper editor, Ralph McGill. Ernest Woodruff stares proudly down; and Ty Cobb, a rambunctious man Mr. Woodruff admired for his baseball skill, grins. Here is O. B. Keeler, the late sportswriter, another good friend; and here, a photograph made October 12, 1973, not long before his death, of Max Keith standing at the Dusseldorf Airport. Here Charles Elliott, the outdoors writer and hunting companion; and the elder Mr. Nicholson and Mr. Sibley. And here, near his desk, a small photograph of the late Mrs. Woodruff, a beautiful, serene face. On another wall the two of them, Bob and Nell, happy faces, on horseback side by side at their Colorado ranch. (Childless, they were a devoted couple. She loved the outdoors as much as he. At Ichauway, she was in charge. "You can't be the boss everywhere," she told her husband. "So I'll take over that job down here.")

On a wall opposite several other photographs of President Eisenhower is a grouping of inscribed ones from his Democrat President friends: Harry Truman, John F. Kennedy, Lyndon B. Johnson, and Jimmy Carter, the latter saying: "To my good friend and fellow peanut farmer, Bob Woodruff," signed in 1977, the year Mr. Carter took office.

Mr. Woodruff has always liked to have his friends around him, never eating alone the lunches prepared in his suite and served in a dining room with the wide plank floors of a country house like Ichauway and hunting-lodge-type furniture. He invites Coca-Cola people, high and low, to join him. He never travels alone and always has had company for dinner, even before his wife died.

"People love him," one of his associates said simply. "Men and women. Men do for him, not for a pat on the back, but to make him happy. It is genuine, from their hearts." This has been specially evident since Mrs. Woodruff died in 1968. "They go to his apartment to see him in the evening. To let him know they are thinking about him. So he won't be lonesome. He doesn't know half of what they say. But it makes him happy to have them."

Scattered about his office are gifts his people have given him, often trinkets, like some plastic roses Delony Sledge sent one birthday with a note saying the flowers might be phony, but not the sentiment. If Mrs. Huffman moves one or another of these, Mr. Woodruff notices it and wants to know where it is.

In the office, too, are mementos of another of his interests, golf. Here, the Woodruff winning ways did not work. He just wasn't very good at the game. "Golf," Ralph McGill once said, "is his hair shirt." Many are the tales about this. One of the best is in the Kahn biography, about the time Mr. Woodruff was in

England and his friend Bobby Jones invited him to play at St. Andrews, the site years before of one of Jones's grand-slam victories. Mr. Woodruff showed up, game and determined. But word had spread about Bobby Jones's being there, so as he and Mr. Woodruff walked out to the first tee, a crowd of three thousand was on hand to follow their game. Mr. Woodruff looked about him, aghast, and quietly withdrew from the match.

At one time, Mr. and Mrs. Woodruff maintained six homes in different parts of the country, including the 4,600-acre TE ranch in Cody, Wyoming, formerly the home of Mr. Woodruff's boyhood hero, Buffalo Bill. When the ranch was sold after Mrs. Woodruff's death, among livestock retained was a palomino horse named Silver. Mr. Woodruff had seen Silver perform once at a rodeo. Among the horse's tricks was the act of drinking a bottle of Coca-Cola. Mr. Woodruff bought the horse on the spot and hired his trainer. The people in charge of Silver at Ichauway, where he was moved, swore that he would have nothing to do with a bottle of *that other drink*.

Ichauway

Great is the lore about Ichauway, the strenuous pace of the hunts, the good drinking and eating and poker in the evenings, the summons often after midnight to a slumbering guest to come join Mr. Woodruff in quiet talk as he puffed on his pipe before the fireplace.

Charles Elliott, the outdoorsman friend, as well as writer about hunting and fishing, has captured the flavor of the plantation and considerable of Mr. Woodruff's complex personality in a book, *Ichauway Plantation*, privately printed in 1974 by the company. In it, he quotes a letter treasured by Mr. Woodruff from a first-time guest, Max Gardner, former governor of North Carolina and ambassador to the Court of St. James.

"Dear Bob," it reads. "I'm back at Shelby with a full night's sleep to my credit, with no fox hunt up to midnight last night, no turkey shoot at 3:30 this morning, no dove shoot at 7:00, no long horseback ride to the luncheon rendezvous, no quail shoot this afternoon—and with no arrangement about the kind of horse I should ride tomorrow, nor when I should shoot skeet or how much of the plantation I should inspect with you on another fresh horse—with all these in mind and a firm determination to sleep and rest for a week, I want to thank you from the bottom of my heart for your dogmatic hospitality." Edgar Bergen and Morton Downey, through their advertising connections with the company, were among celebrities put through such strenuous paces.

We catch a small glimpse of Mr. Woodruff's heart in a story of Mr. Elliott's about the attitude his plantation workers had toward him. One of these, a dog handler, rushed up to Mr. Elliott on a hunt and asked if he had an extra bird. Mr. Elliott replied that, as bad a shot as he was, every bird was extra. The handler said, "Mr. Woodruff done shot at a bird he said fell, but I didn't see it. I can't go back to him unless I carry him a dove." Mr. Elliott went on to explain that this was not kowtowing to the boss. The man knew Mr. Woodruff couldn't stand the thought of the bird's struggling off crippled.

Bob Woodruff often said the only justification for hunting was the great pleasure it gave to the horses and dogs involved. And there are, of course, many stories of noble bird dogs and Labrador retrievers over the years at Ichauway. Mr. Elliott tells one about a pointer named Duke who, within two minutes after the start of a hunt, had come to a staunch point. Mr. Woodruff and his hunting companion flushed a huge covey of quail and both men shot twice without ruffling a feather. Duke held his point, but turned his head looking first at his owner and then at the guest. "If ever I saw a look of indignity on anyone's face," Mr. Woodruff said, "that is what we got from that old pointer." When the signal was given to break point, old Duke walked with great deliberation and dignity back to the dog wagon and lay down with his head on his paws. As much as he loved to hunt, he would have no part of it any more that day.

(Mr. Elliott may be forgiven, in his interest to pass on a good story, for not pointing out that there hardly breathes a bird hunter in South Georgia who doesn't tell that same story about some one or another of his favorite bird dogs.)

He tells a gentler story about an extraordinary dog, Chinquapin Dan, who lived to be thirteen. Mr. Woodruff hunted him in his last years, though he was slow and feeble, because the dog loved it so. In his last year, ailing and barely able to get about, Dan was always taken out and allowed to point at least one covey of quail. Mr. Woodruff would shoot so that the bird would fall near him, to spare him having to travel far to retrieve it.

Mr. Elliott also speaks of the devotion of a personal servant, Luther Cain, Jr., a gentleman's gentleman ever alert to the comfort and well-being of Mr. Woodruff. "Mr. Woodruff," Mr. Elliott then writes with as much insight as we shall have about his effect on those who worked for him, "is so supersensitive to what is right and what is wrong that a man feels he has achieved some of this perception when he makes a move, however large or small, that merits a pat on the back from the Boss. I have no idea whether this correctly sums it up—I do know that Mr. Woodruff inspires extra effort among all those who know him."

At hunting as at all else, Mr. Elliott tells us, Mr. Woodruff was fiercely competitive. He figured the odds "by a careful analysis of facts, figures, personalities and projections based on past performances." Mr. Woodruff, he went on, often said that it's not enough for a man to see from one hill to the next. "He must be able to see over the hill into the valley and even into the next valley beyond."

Ichauway has been, through the years since Mr. Woodruff bought it in partnership with his friend Walter White in 1928, more than a hunting preserve. It is a working plantation with some six thousand acres under cultivation. The other twenty-four thousand are woodland, providing the game crop. In the early days, Mr. Elliott wrote, the plantation farm work was done by some fifty families of black sharecroppers who had occupied the land under previous owners. An innovation and change of South Georgia custom that Mr. Woodruff insisted on when he took over was to see that their children got to the nearest public schools and, for those with a predisposition, to college. The old mule-plowing sharecropping has given way to a system of contract farming with operators cultivating large tracts using modern farm machinery. The main crops are corn, peanuts, and soybeans, with pastureland for cattle. The bird crop, Mr. Elliott assures us, exists in its natural state, feeding some off the spillage of the other crops, but not—as at some hunting preserves—raised tame and turned loose to be easy targets for slaughter.

We speak here though of a situation to which some powerful stereotypes are attached. A southwest Georgia sharecrop plantation is descended from that least pleasant memory of the Old South—the slave plantation. Where the owner of such an enterprise is not exploitative of his labor, he stands then to be called paternalistic.

Much in the lore about Ichauway has to do with the singing at night of spirituals by a choir of black workers. Ike would call from Washington, and request, "Put my choir on," and Mr. Woodruff would hold the phone so his friend could hear the beauty of blended voices singing, "Just a Closer Walk with Thee." Mr. Woodruff's own favorites were "The Lord's a Battle-ax," "Yonder Comes Day," "What You Gonna Do When the World's on Fire?" He would join in the singing and would, often, move away by himself to cry quietly, expressing the emotion the beautiful music aroused in him, remembering his departed mother.

Well we all know about this kind of paternalistic and patronizing relationship between the rich white massah and the lowly Negro menials. Baker County, where Ichauway is located, was a fearful outpost of the civil rights movement in the early 1960s. "Bad Baker" it was called, because of the tradition and everyday reality there of fierce repression of black rights, including the desire to vote. It was the daredevil and possibly foolhardy delight of civil rights workers in the area to sneak reporters and other molders of opinion on to Ichauway and show them the spectacle of a graveyard for deceased hunting dogs, with rows of marble tombstones with tile portraits of each dog. All this opulent spending for dead dogs, the civil rights workers would snort, when, all through the countryside, crushing poverty existed among living black human beings.

Well might they have put their energies better into organizing demonstrations at Ichauway. They might have forced Coca-Cola, with its sensitivity to publicity, to exerting itself in behalf of their goals. But this seems not to have occurred to them. They did try to organize some of the plantation workers, but found them staunch in their loyalty to Mr. Woodruff—a mark, the civil rights workers felt and many today would agree, of their debasement.

Only the northern writer, psychiatrist Robert Coles has had the courage to tell of the good in such a relationship as that between Mr. Woodruff and the plantation workers, a good that Southerners know about but find difficult to explain. There is the spirit of *noblesse oblige* and the genuine respect for, and immersion in the strong and beautiful, agrarian Negro culture, handed down from the days when slaves formed it as an assertion of their humanity. There is also a joy in a way of life, the timeless satisfaction of farm life, the excitement of the hunt.

Mr. Woodruff has always paid his workers well, seen to their special needs, and enjoyed close personal friendships with them. He came up at a time (born in 1889) when the memory of slave days was fresh in the South and most of white sentiment was regret that they were gone. Even as late as 1945, a writer in so respectable a magazine as *Fortune* would refer, in the natural idiom of the day, to "girls" in the choir "with newspapers decorously folded over their knees."

One of Mr. Woodruff's acts to better the lot of the Ichauway workers got him started on his long and until recently secretive, yet spectacular, course of giving his wealth to worthy causes. When he first bought the plantation, a worker came up to meet the new boss, in Charles Elliott's version of the story. After the greeting was done, the worker was taken by a seizure of severe shaking. "What in the world is the matter with that fellow?" Mr. Woodruff demanded. Malaria, he was told. Many of the workers had it. Sixty per cent of the population of Baker County had it.

Mr. Woodruff forthwith ordered a barrel of quinine pills and spread word among the workers they were available. Through ads in the local paper, he also offered them to other residents of the county. The pills only relieved the ravaging symptoms of the disease. So, in 1937, Mr. Woodruff arranged with Emory University, working through the United States Public Health Department, to set up a $250,000 field-station program for treatment of the disease and elimination of malaria-bearing mosquitoes in the area. Doctors went to the people of Baker County with free medication not only for malaria but also for hookworm and pellagra, equally widespread. They isolated the malaria-bearing strain of mosquito and worked to eliminate it. The station remained in operation until 1957, at which time no person in Baker County had malaria, and very few had either of the other diseases.

The Philanthropist

Mr. Woodruff, in his early philanthropy, seemed to be doing the needful in situations directly affecting him. The mother he loved so died of cancer in that same year of 1937. Mr. Woodruff, having learned that Atlanta had no private facility for treatment of the disease, donated $50,000 to Emory for a Robert Winship Memorial Clinic for cancer diagnosis and treatment. Joe Jones pointed out that cancer was not mentioned in polite society back then. And generally in the South only the rich, by going to places like the Mayo Clinic, and the poor, at charity hospitals, could get cancer treatment. Mr. Woodruff's idea was to make it available to people of the middle class.

Mr. Woodruff contributed a great deal of money to the clinic over the years, as well as toward making up deficits in the budget of the university hospital. Finally, in 1952, he asked Emory to come up with a plan whereby the hospital might operate at a profit. Boisfeuillet Jones, then an Emory vice-president, developed the plan which was essentially an extension of the way the cancer clinic had operated. Physicians on the medical school faculty were established in a multiservice medical clinic, on a part-time basis, with profits from the clinic, named after his mother, Emily Winship Woodruff, accruing to the school. In all, Mr. Woodruff has given more than $100 million for the clinic, as well as much money to other Emory projects.

Here, as in the relation to Atlanta civic and government affairs, Mr. Woodruff was continuing, on a far grander scale, a tradition begun by Asa Candler. Mr. Candler's motivation for gifts to Emory were largely, we may recall, religious. Mr. Woodruff's motivation was described by his friend, the late Ralph McGill: "He is affected by people in distress everywhere."

Emory is but one of many schools he has given to, and education but one of many areas of Atlanta life his money has enhanced. Always, the announcements of his gifts would say they came from an "anonymous donor." For a time, the anonymity was real. But, by the 1960s when the pace of Woodruff philanthropy was ever-increasing, Mr. Woodruff was the world's most well-known anonymous donor.

The pretense at anonymity prevented grateful institutions from naming buildings or other things for him. At Emory, however, the recently constructed, excellent library building is called the Robert Winship Woodruff Library. (The old one, now used for classrooms, was named after Asa Candler.) University officials were able to so honor Mr. Woodruff because the library is one of the few projects on the campus he did not contribute to. He is said to have commented that it seemed strange to name a library after someone who seldom reads and who, as a student, used libraries as places to nap.

Mr. Kahn tells another story about the Emory gifts. In 1956, Mr. Woodruff was serving on a panel trying to determine how to distribute a Ford Foundation grant of $90 million for medical schools. Spokesmen for such an institution as Harvard were urging that the money should go to schools already at a peak of excellence. Mr. Woodruff argued it should be used to build others to such a peak. And he told them not to think this was to benefit Emory. "Don't worry about Emory," he asserted. "I can take care of Emory myself."

Boisfeuillet Jones (and let us here, with Mr. Kahn, acknowledge the proliferation of Joneses in the Coca-Cola story, and smile over the rhyming appearance of Bo Jones and Joe Jones), after a stint as an assistant secretary of health in the Kennedy and Johnson administrations, went to work for Mr. Woodruff as a foundation official in 1964. A quiet, sort of quintessential Emory type, Bo Jones smiled and said Mr. Woodruff probably thought it would be more economical to have him managing gifts of his money, rather than spending it at Emory.

He explained the cluster of five foundations which Mr. Woodruff, in varying degrees of responsibility, is involved with. The Emily and Ernest Woodruff Foundation was established by Mr. Woodruff's parents. With assests of $170 million, it is the largest and its interests are projects of regional significance, like the Emory clinic. Mr. Woodruff is chairman of the board.

Then there are three bottler-family foundations on whose boards Mr. Woodruff serves. They are the Lettie Pate Whitehead Foundation, set up by her and Joseph B. Whitehead's sons, mainly to provide college scholarships to poor Christian southern girls (white having recently been removed as a requirement); the Joseph B. Whitehead Foundation, with interest in youth activities in the Atlanta area, with much giving to Boys' Clubs; the Lettie Pate Evans (she remarried) Foundation with a program of gifts to institutions, mostly educational, in Georgia and Virginia.

Finally, there is Mr. Woodruff's own foundation, Trebor (Robert spelled backward), an all-purpose philanthropic fund. So the Woodruff giving encompasses a complex set of institutions, some with fixed programs in their charters, others with money to do the needful in virtually any area. Administration of the foundations is co-ordinated, with Mr. Woodruff and Bo Jones generally in charge and Joe Jones at the helm of the Woodruff Foundation.

Various figures have been projected from without the foundations of just how much money they have poured into worthy projects. An Atlanta newspaper story in 1977 estimated it at more than $200 million. But Bo Jones said the total amount of giving has never been toted up. However, he pointed, also, toward another benefit to Atlanta whose net value can't be counted. The Woodruff stamp of approval with a gift to a project assures many more donations by other philanthropic sources.

A few of the more spectacular gifts have been $8 million toward construction of the Atlanta Memorial Arts Center and $10 million for its endowment; $9 million for purchase of a square city block for the downtown Central City Park and $3 million to enlarge it; other gifts of land for smaller parks, one also downtown, another in Buckhead; $1 million toward purchase of a block on Auburn Avenue to be part of the Martin Luther King, Jr., memorial; $3,700,000 for purchase of the Hartford Insurance Company Building downtown to house private charitable agencies near the seat of city, county, state, and federal governments.

In 1977, the anonymous donor allowed his name to be made public as the giver of $4 million to the state toward purchase of Ossabow Island off the Georgia coast so it could be preserved in its natural state. The state put up $4 million and the owners of the island donated a $7 million cut in price to avoid having the beautiful place fall into the hands of commercial developers.

Also in 1977, as anonymous donor, Mr. Woodruff gave $400,000 toward a $1.8 million goal to retire the mortgage and thereby save, as a landmark, the old Fox Theater. Bottler Arthur Montgomery was general chairman of the fund-raising drive.

The big gifts have made the news, but to sit in Bo Jones's office and go over a few of the long lists of smaller gifts to many institutions is to get the real feel of the Woodruff and bottling-family beneficences. A lot of money over the years has gone to southern black colleges.

The arts center was Mr. Woodruff's idea and he persisted with it after voters turned down a bond issue to provide matching funds for a more elaborate cultural development. The center is a memorial to the 122 Atlanta cultural and civic leaders killed in a plane crash in Orly, France, in 1962, on their way home from a cultural tour of Europe. Many were among Mr. Woodruff's wide circle of friends.

A tale is told of a crisis in Bo Jones's life when he was among those accompanying Mr. Woodruff to the grand opening of the arts center and the group was given a guided tour of the big new building. The tour reached the commissary for the center's art school and there, before Bo Jones's horrified eyes stood the blue-and-white nemesis, a Pepsi-Cola machine. Bo Jones did some nimble footwork to guide Mr. Woodruff out of there before he saw the desecration, and the next day, of course, the concessionaire replaced the Pepsi machine with a familiar red-and-white one.

Mr. Woodruff is also noted for acts of personal generosity to his friends, ranging from his regular lists for Christmas and anniversary gifts to such things as a trip to Europe or an oil portrait of a loved one. Mrs. Huffman each year has the task of buying Christmas gifts for every man, woman, and child at Ichauway—clothing mostly for the men and women, candy for the children. An up-to-date list of clothing sizes of the adults is kept.

Red Hall noted another customary Woodruff gift. When twice in his life Mr. Hall was in a hospital, each morning there would come one perfect, long-stemmed rose from Mr. Woodruff. Mr. Hall recalled a reversal of gift-giving on Mr. Woodruff. On the occasion of his fifty-fourth anniversary with the company, someone sent him a big bouquet of roses. Who were they from? Mr. Hall asked. "I don't know," the boss grunted, a little sheepishly. Mr. Hall asked Mrs. Huffman. She smiled and said, "An anonymous donor."

Joe Jones said that Mr. Woodruff runs his charitable enterprise much as he ran the company. It has not been a committee endeavor. Mr. Woodruff consults others, then makes up his mind. On a construction project, he calls in an engineer and architect and says this is what I want. Tell me how to do it. Invariably they will come back and say it can't be done, Joe Jones said wryly. "He'd say, 'I told you this is what I want. You've got to do it. Get it done.' He can be very forceful."

Bo Jones told sort of the philosophy behind Mr. Woodruff's giving. "He says he's a businessman. But he's also a humanitarian in the best sense of the word. He's quite interested in helping people help themselves and in helping people who are otherwise helpless. Improving the quality of life is the essence of his philosophy of giving. He wants the good life for those who can earn it and for those who can't." The concept is not unlike the one that everybody connected with Coca-Cola should profit from it.

Mr. Woodruff's charity begins and, for the most part, ends at home, benefiting Atlanta mainly and not extending outside the South. (An exception was money given toward development of the polio vaccine.) This is a mark not of provinciality (for he is an international citizen), but probably just his awareness of the largeness of need in the South and the small number of persons with means to help meet it.

Another not well-known effort of his has been toward correcting that situation through building up business in the South. This he has done mainly through memberships on boards of large national corporations which he began to accept in the mid-1940s. It has been his practice to invite these various boards to meet in Atlanta with a view to acquainting the big businessmen on them with the virtues of the South as a place to locate. "He wanted them to get acquainted with the South," Joe Jones explained, "to know the people and the attractions, the services available here. He wanted to show them that the stereotypes of Southerners are not true, that Southerners have talent and can be trained."

Mr. Jones recalled a meeting in the 1950s of the board of General Electric in Atlanta. Things were done in grand style, with the members transported on a special Southern Railway train that stopped off in North Georgia to let them view power installations there. There was a big barbecue and the Woodruffs entertained the guests in their home. At that time, Joe Jones recalled, GE had plants in only two southern states. Now it has twenty-three in the South.

This was but an extension of an influence exerted by Mr. Woodruff that was noticeable as far back as the days of Colonel Jack Spalding, founder of the law firm. "The work of men like Bob Woodruff," he is quoted in the Kahn biography, "going into the North to produce business and opportunity for the South, taking southern men north and bringing northern men south, has done more to wipe out sectional lines than all the oratory since 1865." Now that process goes on worldwide, as Coca-Cola, with the international apparatus Mr. Woodruff secured for it, intermingles the peoples of the world in a business pursuit.

How much awareness might Mr. Woodruff have of all that he has done? We are up once more against the enigma. Luke Smith told us that Mr. Woodruff genuinely does not know how much he has accomplsihed, that he says all he did was to save the company. "He doesn't think he has done enough. He is not aware of the contribution he has made to the world. Somebody asked him if he'd like to lead his life over again. He said, 'Heavens no. There's no way I could be this lucky again.' "

Ralph McGill tried once to tell Mr. Woodruff what he had meant to the world and to his many friends. It was in 1947 and two things occurred simultaneously in Mr. Woodruff's life. Students at Emory had dedicated their yearbook to him—a gesture which meant much to Mr. Woodruff. Then his brother, Henry, died. The bad balanced against the good. Mr. Woodruff was baffled about life's meaning and turned to Mr. McGill. That good man wrote his friend these words:

"You have learned that the bell tolls for you and you have answered it in a measure greater than was required of you. You have given of your wealth and, more important, of yourself. Men and women who have never heard, and will never hear, your name will suffer less and live longer, more useful lives because of the fact that you long ago sent to know for whom the bell tolls and learned the answer. It is for that that many persons love you and have an affection for you which makes them watch over you and pray for you and wish good things for you."

In an inner hall of the Woodruff suite at company headquarters, framed certificates of recognition of Mr. Woodruff are proudly hung. They are few in number because it has been only in the last three years that he would allow his name to be associated with his good works. They are not from well-known organizations. One is jokingly from a cigar company in appreciation of his appreciation of cigars. Another is from the Georgia Sheriff Association, another the Governor's Award in Arts, another from the Kappa Alpha Order. There is an Outdoor Recreation Achievement Award from the U. S. Department of Interior, and a few others.

Mr. Woodruff will gaze on these when he comes in or is leaving his office and, occasionally, will have Mrs. Huffman rearrange the order in which they are hung.

What manner of man this? Larger than life, he has lived beyond the age of heroes, even of the nonhero, into our own troubled time of no heroes. He has, from the start, been at ease, sure of himself, among the most mighty of the nation and the world. But he is greatly moved by the dedication of a college yearbook to him and was pleased to be persuaded to accept, in 1974, the Shining Light Award presented by WSB Radio and the Atlanta Gas Light Company.

He gazes on the little collection of certificates. And the enigma remains. Or does it? He is, after all, man, not myth. Following my informal visit with Mr. Woodruff, Joe Jones agreed to put to him a question from me. A few days later, I received a typed-out answer.

The question had been prompted by something Luke Smith had said about Mr. Woodruff—how he hoped Mr. Woodruff's influence would be around Coca-Cola for a long, long time to come, and how he and Mr. Austin take every opportunity to expose "the next generation of managers" to Mr. Woodruff, so that they might "absorb his character."

My question: What would Mr. Woodruff advise such young people, or any young person, starting out in today's tough and vastly complicated business world? Here is the answer I received:

"As a suggestion for young people starting out in the business world today, I would underscore the same basic rules which seem to me to have prevailed certainly through my lifetime.

"They should acquire all the knowledge possible about their chosen field as well as a general understanding of the economics of business. They should establish for themselves personal goals of loyalty and integrity. They should develop traits of curiosity and inquisitiveness about their business and others. They should present a favorable appearance—in their behavior, in the clothes they wear, in the way they talk. Energy and ambition are requisite—be willing to 'take off your coat and go to work.' Under all circumstances they should maintain a sense of humor. If they can mix these qualities with a touch of humility, their opportunities for advancement are significantly increased. R. W. Woodruff 8-15-77."

It was, of course, good advice. But if one were to go back and read it again, as I did, one would find that Mr. Woodruff, whether meaning to or not, had described himself better than any of the many words that have been written of him, or stories told about him.

XIII

A Pause that Refreshes

Through the history of Coca-Cola, there runs a thread of stories about bees. In the biography of his father, Charles Howard Candler tells the first one: "During the summer months when most manufacture took place, the doors and windows of the basement had to be kept open because of the heat. Mr. William T. Healey, who lived on the northeast corner of Ivy and Auburn, had a good many bees, and it was not uncommon for them, in search of sweetness, to join Sam Willard and George Curtright when Coca-Cola was being made to sample the product. Numbers of them would be caught in the open strainers when the barrels and kegs were being filled. Sam has said, 'We often wished for an opportunity to try out Mr. Healey's honey, but he was not inclined to be neighborly with the factory people.'"

Archivist Wilbur Kurtz recalled that his first company assignment was to open up a number of old crates stored near the syrup factory to discover what was in them, then dispatch the contents to appropriate parts of the headquarters building. The work was hot and interrupted more than once by bees stinging Mr. Kurtz on various parts of his portly frame. "Ever since the first manufacture, we've had those goddamn bees," he growled with uncharacteristic ferocity. He had been told that the syrup kills bees who sip it, but that must have been wishful thinking. "Every time I smell the syrup," Mr. Kurtz sighed, "it reminds me of that awful work and those damned bees."

John Talley picked up the thread in his story about a problem encountered in Germany just after World War II. The TOs were shipping syrup in fifty-gallon wooden barrels to plants around the country so the troops could keep getting Coca-Cola. But the war had destroyed most warehouse space and there was nowhere to hold the barrels pending shipment. So the TOs loaded them on trains and sent them to a plant, say, in Nuremberg. If no syrup were needed at the moment, the people there would send the shipment on to Frankfort, and so on, creating a *traveling warehouse* which often held the barrels for weeks. Inevitably, some of the barrels would leak, causing the sweet smell of Coca-Cola syrup to emanate from the boxcars and attract bees.

A lady from a countryside through which the traveling warehouses passed showed up one morning quite irate at the quartermaster office. She kept bees and was very proud of her honey, famous in the locale. But her bees had been sipping nectar from the Coca-Cola syrup, making the honey taste *strange*. Indeed, she lamented, it ruined her honey, and the U.S. authorities should pay her damages.

The quartermaster officer countered, or so Mr. Talley would have us believe: "You shouldn't get any damages. You ought to ask a higher price for your honey if it tastes like Coca-Cola."

Lynn LaGarde had bitter memories, like Mr. Kurtz, of the bees "stinging the hell out of me." But today when one smells the strange, sweet smell of the syrup on gentle winds wafting from company headquarters, it is with the knowledge that bees no longer feast on it. A company spokesman explained: the way they used to get to the syrup was in the cooperage plant when emptied barrels stood open with a residue in the bottom. The cooperage operation, of course, ended when Mr. LaGarde's staff developed the stainless-steel drums, and then the tankers.

An Increase in Profits, but a Decline in Coca-Cola "Style"

Somehow that seems sad—a symbol of how the great growth of Coca-Cola has cut it off from simple things, from something so basic in nature as the nuisance of those damn bees. At least you could cuss them and slap them away, or cover your face and retreat from them. Not so with the nameless frustrations and pressures people in business feel today.

Delony Sledge talked in his slow, quizzical way about how things changed during the period of great growth after World War II. When he first came with the company in the 1930s, there were only about two hundred employees in the entire headquarters building. Now there are more than two thousand. In his early years, all the offices had glass walls with wainscoting bases. Everybody could see everybody else. This wasn't for the purpose of checking to see that everyone was working, Mr. Sledge explained. It imparted an atmosphere of openness, giving a carefree feeling to the offices.

Then there began to be more secrecy. Executives built themselves "intimate little niches" and shut themselves in, working behind closed doors, far less accessible to their employees.

"In my department, I was the last to take my windows out. I was the last to leave my door wide open," Mr. Sledge continued. If somebody wanted to talk about work or personal problems, he would invite the person in, then "listen and listen and listen."

"I'd say, 'Look, there ain't a goddamn thing I can do about that. But I'll listen to you. I'll cry with you. I'll punch your TS card.'" Then the person would say he appreciated being heard. Talking it out made him feel better.

But, he went on, that kind of thing ate up a lot of time. Sometimes "you put yourself into a position where you can't do what you think ought to be done; or if you do, it's such a traumatic experience for you that you reduce your efficiency. It teaches you to be more impersonal, to withdraw from the intimate. That does something to you. It dehumanizes you."

Another problem Mr. Sledge experienced, deriving from intimate contact with employees, is that when you know a man well, know his wife, his children, and understand that he could never make it somewhere else, you find yourself keeping deadwood on the staff. "Or you hire a hatchet man to do what you don't have the guts to do yourself." We've already noted that Mr. Woodruff suffered from the same dilemma.

Wilbur Kurtz described another kind of deterioration that came during the 1960s—a cooling of the public's great love for Coca-Cola as a symbol of America. He attributed it to disillusionment over Vietnam and a general anti-establishment mood across the country. As far back as 1961, the company made a survey to determine what it meant to people that Coca-Cola was celebrating its seventy-fifth birthday. The general consensus was, "So what?" Mr. Kurtz shook his bald head sadly.

Part of it was the way the country had changed. Part was the way Coca-Cola had to change with the times and business trends. Hunter Bell mused over how the latter affected the bottling family. In the early days, a man could come into his plant in the morning, start up his soaker, load it, clean and sterilize the bottles, prior to their being filled by a Dixie filler and then loaded into his truck. Only at this point, the man "switched hats" and went out to sell those filled bottles for the rest of the morning. Whereupon, he came back to the plant, attended to office work, or went out again to put up signs all afternoon. It was a good one-man business, a good living, making the bottler and his plant an integral, important part of a town's existence as the plant grew and expanded.

Then came the technological advances that made it possible to bottle faster and faster, with the resulting trend to consolidate plants, letting one big plant serve a territory that a dozen small ones once did. That meant sales warehouses in a town instead of the landmark of a bottling plant.

(People used to bring their children to the bottling plant to watch the bottles wobble and dance along the filling lines. "Now all you see is a big transport truck coming in with hundreds of cases to be unloaded in a warehouse," Mr. Bell regrets.)

Arthur Montgomery, the Atlanta bottler, who has three plants now serving what seven used to, told of another change that has made the bottling family less happy. "I doubt that there's a working day in the year that somebody in our plant is not dealing with the Internal Revenue Service, or the Occupational Safety and Health Agency, or some other government agency. It's just a never-ending thing. It's very unfortunate." Mr. Montgomery's laugh was ironic. "I'd hate to think I'd have to start over in this set of circumstances."

Even the grand promotion machine is not what it used to be. Company president Luke Smith said that he and Paul Austin nowadays just give general approval of the theme and thrust of an ad campaign. No longer does top management go over each ad to be certain of quality and good taste, the way Mr. Candler and Mr. Woodruff did—making sure that the pretty girls were just the right type. "The company's gotten too big for that," Mr. Smith explained. "Way too big."

Jean Stafford touched on deterioration in a nostalgic story in *Esquire* (December 1975), citing the myths her generation had about Coca-Cola and various unorthodox uses the drink has been put to. (The uses included basting hams and defrosting windshields.) She also told of seeing the late Louisiana governor, Earl Long, put Coca-Cola to *four simultaneous uses* while making a stump speech once in hot and humid Alexandria, Louisiana. He used the familiar bottle to gesticulate as he spoke. He drank from it to cool his throat. He poured from it onto his handkerchief to mop his sweated brow. And he had, within it, a slug of Southern Comfort bourbon "to keep his oratory zinging.") Ms. Stafford's complaint was over the new containers—cans and shapeless bottles with screw-off caps. She wrote that company representatives she met agreed with her that the old six-and-one-half-ounce bottle was eminently preferable. "But stiff competition had made it necessary for them to knuckle under and toady to a generation that had been bamboozled by their plagiarists."

Perhaps the saddest part of deterioration has been the decline of the soda fountain. During the postwar years, the promotion boosted them inordinately as the "world's friendliest club," with pleasant pictures of pleasant people in the familiar, pleasant setting of marble-topped counter, bent-cane tables and chairs, or dark-wood booths. But, by the end of the 1960s, few drugstores operated one. What happened to them?

Hunter Bell recalled how he took his English bride down to visit his hometown of Dawson in southwest Georgia. She was enthralled with the practice there of parking in front of the drugstore and getting a curb-service Coca-Cola. The soda fountain was a social institution back then. People would pick up their mail at the post office, then stop in at the drugstore to drink a Coke and chat or gossip with friends. Mr. Bell's view is that fast-food franchises catering to the fast-paced life of modern Americans did the fountains in. People have come to think of Coca-Cola utilitarianly, as refreshment only, no longer as part of a focal point for sociability.

Red Hall thinks that a lot of the fountains were closed in the South because of integration: to avoid the hubbub of demonstrations and out of fear (as it turned out unwarranted) that white Southerners would not patronize an integrated eating-and-drinking place. Mr. Hall saved a few fountains in the Atlanta area by talking the owners out of closing. "They'd say, I don't want a bunch of blacks in here. I'd say, you've been serving 'em ice cream cones and Cokes in paper cups all these years. If you take your soda fountain out, you'll just be catering to sick folks." Then he would toss in the clincher, dating to Samuel Candler Dobbs's day, that "seven out of ten people who come in for a Coca-Cola will buy something else as well."

Dr. Marvin Roberts, Jr., is one of those in the Atlanta area who kept the fountain open in his Northside Pharmacy on Peachtree Road, out beyond Buckhead. He and his late father opened the store there in 1941, his father having previously been a partner in Winder and Roberts, once a famous drugstore name in Buckhead.

An "Alchemist" soda-fountain dispenser, typical of the ornate ones used in drugstores of the early 1900s.

Seated at, not a bent-cane, but a plastic table among many in front of the, not marble, but wooden soda fountain, bedecked with plastic signs and menu displays, designed more for fast-food places than a drugstore, Dr. Roberts explained why he kept his fountain. Part of it was Red Hall's reasoning about people buying other things. The fountain is in the middle of his big store, with merchandise appealingly visible to the customers. Many druggists closed the fountains because they kept separate books on them and saw that salaries and overhead reached a point where they just weren't profitable. However, Dr. Roberts doesn't keep separate records, and his fountain may operate at a loss. But it brings people in to buy those other things, he points out, and, besides, he enjoys socializing with them.

He remembered with pleasure how, earlier, he had a big after-church trade on Sundays—families coming in, dressed in their finest. And the fountain was a family gathering place in the evenings. So he kept it open until 11 P.M. Now it closes at nine.

The biggest business it does is serving lunch to office workers from the surrounding area. Prices are reasonable: a ham sandwich for $1.05 and a cheese-burger for 85¢. And Jim Hays, his cook, has a special every day—the favorite, a good barbecued pork sandwich with Brunswick stew.

The lunch crowd was coming in, people standing in line to give their orders at one end of the counter and pick up their food and Cokes (among other beverages) at the other end. Two boys, about twelve, sat at one of the tables sipping through straws from enormous glasses of Coke. Jim Hays took a moment to play peep-eye with a toddler at a table with his shopper mama.

Coca-Cola had been a good friend to druggists over the years, Dr. Roberts affirmed. The store just wouldn't be the same without the soda fountain. "It wouldn't be as personal. It would be like a chain store. What we've got to sell is personal service."

Dr. Carroll Hitchcock told the sad story of why he closed his fountain in Hitchcock and Simmons' Pharmacy in Buckhead in 1969, and then sold out to enter semiretirement in 1973. The big shopping centers with their supermarkets ended the trade from women grocery-shopping nearer by. Then the city started

A typical soda fountain in the 1920s.

prohibiting on-street parking, which didn't help. And, Dr. Hitchcock said, with a sorrowful shake of his head, "I hate to say it about young people. But they would gang up and raise so much cain in the store, nobody else wanted to be there. It used to be you could control them. If one acted up, you'd just tell him to get out. Do that today, and they'll wreck your place."

Dr. Hitchcock had proudly bought the store in 1939. The stainless-steel soda fountain had sixteen stools. There were four booths and four tables with four chairs each. All were usually filled up. The fountain used twelve to sixteen gallons of Coca-Cola syrup a week, enough for four hundred glasses a day.

Dr. Hitchcock recalled with pleasure, too, the after-church crowds, and the folks coming in during the week to socialize. "I knew everybody. It was a pleasure at that time to operate."

He shook his head at the memory. He had come to Atlanta as a young man from White Plains, Georgia, where his father had a mercantile store, to seek his fortune. He went to work for Dr. Thomas Cox in his drugstore at Highland and St. Charles avenues (it is still there), and worked his way through pharmacy school. Then Dr. Cox opened the Buckhead store, but it was losing money. So he offered Dr. Hitchcock the opportunity to manage it better and buy it from the proceeds. He had it paid for within a year. That took hard work, long hours. But Dr. Hitchcock was young and could take it. He worked seven days a week, from 7 A.M. to 11 P.M. or midnight. He shook his head again. "It was good while it lasted. But today—the small drugstore is just out." He works part-time as a pharmacist in a large store. It has no soda fountain.

So the Times Have Changed

One might almost say that America is no longer a fit place for so civilized a social institution as the soda fountain. To keep on succeeding, Coca-Cola had to change in the ways that we have seen. What has happened to America, to Americans, in a technology-ruled society, may be traced in the evolution of the Coke dispensers.

There was that fine one Mr. Staton put together, with the bottles alluringly on display in their yellow crates. You opened the top, reached down into the chopped-up, ice-wagon ice, and pulled out your beaded bottle, then handed your nickel to the storekeeper or filling station operator personally. More than likely you also got to chat with him while you drank your ice-cold Coca-Cola.

Then the top-opening machines were rigged out with metal tracks which would open at the end when you deposited a nickel and you guided the bottle out of its icy nest. The proprietor didn't have to fool with you unless you needed change from him.

Then came the automatic dispensers. Some of the early ones had a little glass window so you could at least see the bottle inside, its visual allurement. But soon they were all as we know them today: tall red machines, like upended coffins, which give no visual or tactile temptation, no delight, and no personal

Evolution of the soda-fountain dispenser for drugstores: from urn (center) to hand-drawn (right) to automatic (left).

dealing with anybody. You put your quarter in and plop, like something off an assembly line, your impersonal Coke comes out.

However, there was a humanizing spirit alive in the Coca-Cola organization, even while technology wrought its changes on things and people. Delony Sledge described it with feeling. "It has been said that this wasn't a business. It was a religion. And during those days, by God, it was a religion. In most instances today, where you've got people who've been in this business ten or fifteen years, it's a religion now. You don't get that out of a General Motors. You don't get that out of IBM. There is something that is personalized. You can't personalize an automobile. You can't personalize a computer. You can have the greatest respect for it. But, by God, you can't love it. You can't idealize it.

"The product has some kind of a strange characteristic. There again, I think it's a symbolism. I don't know why. I've spent up to now fifty years trying to figure it out. I don't know what it is about Coca-Cola—except to say it has a direct appeal to the best and the happiest side of a man's life. You look at that bottle or glass of Coca-Cola or that sign and you find yourself dreaming of once upon a time on a picnic, or once upon a time at a wedding. There's that symbolism, and that dedication in people. It does something to them. I think that to some degree it was the type of person that we had. We didn't have many bastards. We had good guys. They had an interest in maintaining the symbolism of this product.

"Don't misunderstand me. They were human. We didn't have any strange, dedicated religionists, or people tiresome about it. They and their wives were good, fine Americans, mothers and fathers of good girls and boys. And they were Southerners—the men who ran this business. Now I have a reputation for being a professional Southerner. And I am very proud of it—am not ever going to make any apologies for it. There is a marked difference, even today, between that kind of person, a Southerner, and people anywhere else in the country. There is something in the southern philosophy that makes southern men and their southern wives represent more easily and more perfectly the symbols of this product and the pleasure that you identify with this product."

Mr. Sledge was saying that, in style, as well as integrity, the company still has it—that idiosyncratic something that made it magic during its years of early success and great growth. Luke Smith confided that Robert W. Woodruff has expressed concern that the company not lose its style.

"One day, Mr. Woodruff called me in and said, 'I don't want this company to get impersonal. It's gotten so big. I don't want it to get impersonal, to start pushing people around. That ain't the way we made this company. No.' "

It is difficult today to know, at the sprawling headquarters building, how much of the old spirit remains. There is a relaxed feel to the surface of things. In the spacious reception room of the world headquarters building, like a big hotel lobby, with comfortable furniture and telephones for use by guests, the faces one sees—company people, visiting bottlers, salesmen from other firms, people from over the world—have a relaxed look. The women behind the big marble receptionist's desk are pretty Coca-Cola girls. In an adjoining room are displays of company history: a portrait of Dr. Pemberton, with almond eyes gazing down, and there are others of Frank Robinson, Asa Candler, and Robert W. Woodruff, Mr. Woodruff with cigar in hand.

For visitors, there is a mystifying security system. One signs a sheet at the receptionist's desk designating what person he will visit and the time of day, then is given a badge with his name on it. When the visit is over, one turns the badge in, but is not required to sign out. If the visit is to Chairman J. Paul Austin in the executive suite in the older building next door, one signs in but does not get a badge. The middle-aged Coca-Cola girl there smiles and explains that Mr. Austin does not believe in the system. Small wonder.

Coca-Cola people nod or smile or speak as they pass you in the hall. Often it is a pretty girl secretary with a tray, bearing the familiar-shaped bottles for her boss and some guest. Since the diversification, Coca-Cola people are able to offer coffee, orange juice, and other noncola beverages, which is fortunate for a visitor calling on several Coca-Cola people in a day, because the offer is always made. In the days when Mr. Kahn wrote *Big Drink*, such a visitor had either to turn down Coca-Cola frequently, to the disappointment of genial Coca-Cola people, or be surfeited with pauses that refresh.

Atmosphere in the various offices is relaxed, genial. On one day in the small section occupied by public relations personnel, there is a flurry of activity as the

The current home of The Coca-Cola Company—Atlanta, Georgia.

staff quickly and thoroughly prepares an obituary release on a member of the board of directors who has just died. On another day, a pretty girl secretary is rapidly rolled away in a wheelchair. People in the office speak anxiously but happily about the event. She is pregnant and, as another secretary said, "She almost stayed on the job too long."

There is a formal, yet relaxed feel to company President Smith's office. While there, as I sought an outlet to plug in a tape recorder, President Smith, finding one in an awkward corner, insisted on getting down on his hands and knees to plug the thing in.

His secretary brings two Cokes in, and we sit in chairs in front of his desk, as he explains today's division of corporate responsibility in the company. During the years since Mr. Woodruff's ostensible retirement, the role of chief executive officer has varied among the number of presidents and board chairmen. Sometimes it was the president, sometimes the chairman. Since Mr. Austin and Mr. Smith have been in those positions, Mr. Austin has been chief executive officer and Mr. Smith chief operations officer.

Mr. Smith is responsible for the daily operation of the business around the world. Mr. Austin sets policy, carries on negotiations to get Coca-Cola into other countries, is in charge of relations with the United States Government, and handles stockholder and board of directors relations.

Mr. Smith said a large part of his job is planning, including financial and marketing planning, as well as "people planning"—having the right people to move into the right jobs. "The world is a big place. You've got to have people who fit into the Japanese environment, or the East European environment, wherever." Some of this is going on all the time. It is unbelievable, Luke Smith

J. Lucian Smith, current president of The Coca-Cola Company.

noted, how much time company people spend on problems involving the governments of other nations.

In a larger, more formally furnished office, J. Paul Austin also discussed the way the company has functioned since he has been board chairman. Mr. Austin, like Mr. Woodruff, is a big man, a formidable sort of jut-jawed figure, with a tense energy. Asked how, in effect, it felt to be the new strong leader in the shadow of those previous two extremely strong leaders, Mr. Woodruff and Mr. Candler, Mr. Austin spoke of an evolutionary process.

He termed his "management style," that of a corporate lawyer, as a little different from Mr. Woodruff's who was a man of all trades. But the change in direction has been "evolutionary, not revolutionary." There was no "black Friday."

A major reorganization of the company occurred in 1976, Mr. Austin went on. "Today the company is restructured very considerably, I believe on a sound basis, to a point where anyone who has a business orientation and is reasonably industrious could step in behind me and there'd never be a bobble."

Saying he was a great believer in delegating authority, Mr. Austin pointed to his desk. "You couldn't grow the company to this size off that one desk." The new organization allows "a lot of talented people to take chunks of responsibility and go off with it."

Specifically, the new organization does away with the old division of work whereby the Export Corporation handled overseas and Coca-Cola USA operated in this country. The new plan divides all the world into three parts, with a vice-president in charge of each. Our friend Mr. Halle has his Europe, Africa, Southwest Asia and, until the falling out, India. Donald R. Keough is in charge

J. Paul Austin, current chairman, board of directors, and chief executive officer of The Coca-Cola Company.

of the United States and Central and South America. Ian R. Wilson is in charge
of Canada, the Far East, and the Pacific. Thirteen divisions carry on the work
on a worldwide basis. "The new structure," says the 1976 company annual report, "provides for direct communication and operational contact between
Atlanta-based headquarters management and strong decentralized operating
units worldwide."

Mr. Austin pinpointed delegation of authority as the heart of the new plan.
The old practice of making decisions in New York on so small a matter as a
change of price structure in Brazil is ended. The authority now lies where the
decisions have to be made. Only a change in the budget for a given area requires
a trip to Atlanta for explanations why.

Forty years ago, Mr. Austin acknowledged—and one thinks of Mr. Woodruff—the company could operate with executives who each knew a little law, a
little accounting, a little of the other skills required to do business. "Now, of
course, there just aren't that many hours in a day. You have to have a whole
corps of experts in each field to function effectively."

Coca-Cola's Future

Business Week, in an article with the ominous title of "The Graying of the
Soft Drink Industry" (May 23, 1977), told how effectively Coca-Cola was functioning in 1976 in comparison with other soft-drink firms. Sales of Coca-Cola
that year amounted to $3,032.8 million, compared with the nearest competitor,
the nemesis Pepsi-Cola's $2,727.5 million. Net income for Coca-Cola was $285
million, compared with Pepsi's $136 million.

Another set of figures in the article gives the size of the bottler family in
1976 after much consolidation in recent years. In the United States, there were
581 bottling plants, ten of them company-owned. In 134 other countries, there
were 770 plants, sixteen company-owned.

Both Mr. Smith and Mr. Austin seized on the room for expansion in the rest
of the world suggested by those figures as part of the answer to the main thrust
of the *Business Week* story—which was to the effect that the vaunted "youth
market" in America will diminish in size. In 1976, America had forty-nine million people between thirteen and twenty-four, each on the average guzzling the
equivalent of 823 cans of soft drinks a year, compared with 547 downed by
other age groups. By 1985, the magazine projected, there will be only forty-five
million of these youthful guzzlers in the United States.

The article, Mr. Smith counters, assumes Coca-Cola just does business in the
States, which, of course, is not so. More than 60 per cent of the Free World
population is outside the United States and in other countries there is no drop-
off in the birth rate. Besides, both he and Mr. Austin noted, there are statistics
that show people do not suddenly start drinking less Coca-Cola per year once
they reach the age of twenty-five. The strategy of going after the youth market
has been to win each new generation for Coca-Cola and then keep its members.
Promotion is toward that end.

In addition, there is all the vast opportunity for expansion overseas and for increasing per capita consumption in countries where the drink is already sold. The saturation point is nowhere near reached in this country, they contend, and no one knows what that point is.

"There is no plant yet anywhere in the world that has stopped growing," assured Mr. Smith.

"If per capita consumption in the rest of the United States were as high as it is in the Southeast, that alone would make Coca-Cola a much bigger business," added Mr. Austin.

He went on to speak glowingly of the magic the franchise system performs, increasing per capita consumption in the rest of the world. "It is a great tribute to the universality of Coca-Cola. We can plant its seed in a country entirely different from Western nations, and the same techniques, the same business practices, the same training methods used in Atlanta, Georgia, are just as effective in Nairobi."

Coca-Cola as "Southern" and/or "International"

This kind of talk—about increasing per capita consumption, about expanding into new territory—has ever been the coin of Coca-Cola conversation, the almost obsessive preoccupation of Coca-Cola leaders. But again, the question, Is it carried out in today's dispirited world with the same great spirit as in the past?

When the older men speak of that spirit of the past, nearly always they mention the southern origins and influence, as Delony Sledge did. Mr. Pope Brock put it this way: "Undoubtedly, the southern point of view has had a lot to do with the tone of the company. It reflected itself in the type of people they employed—good, fine clerks, stenographers, secretaries, right on up to the top— the kind of people you would want to have in your home as guests. They have been a very attractive group of people. Many have remarked it. It's not just a notion of mine. Of course there are a lot of new people now. But I hear no complaint about 'em."

Hunter Bell noted that Coca-Cola "wouldn't have been the same business if it had been started in New York. Southern people have a more relaxed way of doing business. Mr. Woodruff set the tone. He picked the people and helped them succeed."

As late as 1961, *The Refresher* magazine in an article, "Portrait of a Business in Its 75th Year," gave company credence to the notion of southern distinctiveness. "Perhaps the Southern exposure of its beginnings is responsible for the persistence of the soft answer in the Coca-Cola business. . . . The rugged realities of the marketplace have been conquered . . . in terms of hospitality, sociability, enjoyment of the pleasant things of life."

The 1931 *Fortune* article stated flatly, "Although it has emerged from the South, it is essentially a Southern drink; and the Southland will always be its homeland, no matter how far and flourishing its travels."

The generation in charge of Coca-Cola now look upon such pronounce-ments a little ambiguously. Certainly, the South has had an influence. But for men who operate and think in terms of the whole world, even national identification becomes fuzzy, let alone a regional one.

"We're proud of that," president Luke Smith said of the southern origins. But, he pointed out, all one needs to do to see that the company is truly interna-tional is to eat lunch in the headquarters building. "The other day I looked around my table. I was the only Southerner there. I was also the only native American. The others included a German, a Cuban, a South African, and an Englishman.

"It's primarily an international organization, but it's got a southern flavor. We're proud of that."

Chairman J. Paul Austin, who hails from LaGrange, Georgia, is entirely in-ternational-minded. He came up through the ranks as an overseas worker. In 1973, he was quoted by writer Anthony Haden-Guest in the *Tropic* magazine of the Miami *Herald* (August 26, 1973) as saying strongly, "We are based squarely now on the multinational concept. We will become less and less paro-chial to America, more and more oriented to the international trade."

The strength of the international trade, as we know, is that Coca-Cola, through its indigenous bottlers, is parochial to each country where it is sold. But the common interests of the worldwide bottler family in Coca-Cola matters transcends parochialism and nationalism. And Paul Austin is foremost among Coca-Cola thinkers who see this as a strong positive influence on the rela-tionships of the nations of the world—as a force for peace, and a counterforce to political tendencies toward warfare in nations across the earth.

"Any business prudently managed that goes offshore is a plus for United States foreign relations," Mr. Austin declared in an interview. "Where there is a well-positioned commercial life between businessmen of one country with busi-nessmen of another, that has to be a plus."

On the same subject, Mr. Austin has written in *Top Management Report*, published by International Management and Development Institute, Washing-ton, ("Case Study in International Development," March 1977): ". . . The soft drink industry seems to be an ideal illustration of the function international busi-ness in general can fulfill in the interdependence of nations. The Coca-Cola Company and its bottlers each depend upon the other. . . .

"There is no question that nations around the world have a vital function in fostering this interdependence. However, the reduction of international difficul-ties is a precondition of successful commerce. We must all welcome the con-certed efforts among nations to create and maintain an ongoing atmosphere where borders are at least potentially open."

Mr. Austin is a staunch advocate of free-trade worldwide and a foe of boy-cotts, including America's against Cuba. In his international business thinking, he seems as close to a kind of radicalism as Mr. Woodruff was in his national think-ing. In various public utterances, Mr. Austin builds a vision of business not only exerting an influence against world cataclysm (which would mean an end, among everything else, of profits), but also as the only means to ending the dis-parity between have and have-not classes and nations. And this, he sees as the only way to prevent the world's either being blown up or ravaged by lesser degrees of warfare.

We have come a long way from Dr. Pemberton's back-yard brass kettle. Mr. Austin holds up to us the mixture of sugar and water among other essential business concerns as a hope for world peace. Stranger things have happened. Consider the whole history of Coca-Cola's promotion—sometimes selling America on looking up from its problems and frustrations, giving to the country the comforting feel of the South's old moonbeam-and-magnolia myths, trying to help it learn to live with defeat as the South has done.

We have noted how the sinister has been sought without success in J. Paul Austin's friendship with President Jimmy Carter. Maybe we can find something hopeful in it. After all, the President was a businessman himself, the first in many years (discounting Harry Truman whose haberdashery business failed) to occupy the White House.

And Jimmy Carter is a southern businessman at that, shaped and nurtured by many of the same traditions that flavored Coca-Cola. The parallel of Carter's national political success—the first for a Southerner since the Civil War ended the South's previous strong political leadership of the nation—with Coca-Cola's spectacular success over the years is at least worth noting. Out of a tradition of defeat, here are two southern success stories, two examples of Southerners, long looked down upon by people from other parts, doing things better and with more grace and style than people in those other regions have been capable of doing.

But what about Mr. Austin's contention that businessmen may lead the world to peace? *Though wars might rage* . . . Though a nation's intellectual and journalistic leadership might wallow in disillusionment and despair . . . businessmen like J. Paul Austin of Coca-Cola or ex-peanut-farmer Jimmy Carter have had that preoccupation with business that transcends both political trouble and—as with the bottler family—nationalism. And they have had the sweet taste of success in the private sector to balance against failure in the political one.

Stranger things have happened. On the business page of the Atlanta *Journal-Constitution* (September 11, 1977), not usually notable for original thought, there appeared a quite original and thought-provoking quotation by Edith Efron, television columnist and former reporter for the New York *Times* and *Time* magazine. She said, startlingly, that an antibusiness bias in the media is part of an effort to move America to socialism.

"The expansion of scientific knowledge has left those involved in the humanities as literally cultural primitives," Ms. Efron was quoted. "The result is an attempt by those outside of industry and science to gain power over those forces of change. The media reflect this antibusiness and stop-growth bias in their coverage."

If we really should ever be faced with a choice for leadership between the gloomy people of the humanities and businessmen, the choice would not be difficult—if the businessmen were like those of The Coca-Cola Company. In the annals of American business, from the days of the robber barons through today's general muckraking tradition of writing about anybody successful, the story of Coca-Cola is, let us face it, truly *a pause that refreshes.*

Coca-Cola "Collectors"

If, amid today's complexity, one longs for the simple days of Dr. Pemberton and the comparatively simple ones that so threw Asa Candler, the magic of Coca-Cola can be found to be at work again. One has simply to attend a meeting of the Atlanta chapter of the Cola Clan, an organization of collectors of Coca-Cola memorabilia, to be transported back in time to those good old days of Coca-Cola's beginnings.

The meeting begins at 6:30 P.M. in a recreation center in suburban Decatur. On display among all these happy-looking people are Coca-Cola trays, old posters, bottles of all the different designs, including the unsatisfactory Hutchinson one, and, of course, in coolers a far more than adequate number of ice-cold ones to drink from. And at this meeting, there is cake with the Coke. It's the local chapter's first birthday and the members celebrate.

There are about fifty on hand. They spend the first hour or so having what they call a "swap meet"—bottles, trays, and all the rest changing hands. Of course, there is much vivacious chatter about Coca-Cola artifacts and history. The oldest member of the Clan, not in attendance this night, is seventy-three. Two boys of thirteen are members. One of them is John Bucholz, as wholesome-looking a lad as a boy in a Coca-Cola ad. He got started collecting two and a half years ago after having gone on one of those tours of Arthur Montgomery's bottling plant on Spring Street. He specializes in trays, bottles, and glasses, and has an assortment of glasses to swap this night.

Mrs. Mary Frances Sheridan wears a pretty red-and-white hat made of aluminum Coke cans. It was created in Florida, one of the few places where aluminum cans are produced.

After the swap meet, a business session gets underway, with much excited talk about the forthcoming third annual meeting of the national Clan to be held in Huntsville, Alabama. The Clan was organized by Bob Buffaloe of Memphis in 1974. At the first convention in Atlanta, sixty collectors were on hand. Upward of a thousand were expected to attend the third.

Someone suggests that members be sure and take the Atlanta-produced two-liter bottles to the convention to swap, since Atlanta is one of the few places where these are produced. Also mentioned is a forthcoming new price list being compiled by Cecil Munsey, author of the collectors' bible, *The Illustrated Guide to the Collectibles of Coca-Cola* (Hawthorne Books, Inc., 1972). The price list will have a stabilizing effect on the memorabilia market, Clan members say.

Business completed, there begins a long period of "show and tell," with members proudly displaying such treasures as the tray with the pretty girl wearing a big white hat, an 1899 change tray, the 1904 Lillian Nordica poster. In the midst of this, Ray Deluca chats about his specialities: Coca-Cola clocks and the red-and-white dispensing machines. He seeks the machines at old stores and in junkyards. A retired employee of The Coca-Cola Company taught him how to repair the old clocks. Mr. Deluca plans to drive to the convention with a magnetic Coca-Cola sign on the front door of his car.

The "show and tell" session is interrupted for one of several auctions of "goody bags" containing, sight-unseen, collectibles of one kind or another. The proceeds go into the Clan's treasury.

By now it is 10 P.M. and the "show and tell' session shows no sign of ending. Sometimes, a member confides, the sessions last till midnight. Coca-Cola collectors are inordinately enthusiastic about their hobby. They love nothing better than to talk with one another about it. When one collector visits another from out of town, it is not uncommon for them to sit up all night, talking Coca-Cola.

Mr. and Mrs. Claud Almond are among the most active and enthusiastic members of the Atlanta Clan. To enter their attractive home in suburban Marietta is truly to walk into the past of Coca-Cola. Every wall in virtually every room is hung with posters, calendars, and other early promotions. The Almonds specialize in paper promotions produced before 1920.

Ah, the color in those Massengale era posters—Hilda Clark in exquisite tints, so much prettier in the original than in reproductions using today's inks. Everywhere about, reminders of the past of Coca-Cola: The 1930 boy and dog poster—"Hott? Hot? Isn't it cooling, refreshing, thirst-quenching?"; one of those Japanese fans of the kind Charles Howard Candler strung around his neck; the 1906 Juanita, one of only two known to be in existence; Tyrus Cobb; a 1918 soda-fountain festoon showing three pretty girls with flowers; the World War I era poster showing a pretty girl knitting, with aircraft and ace pilots delicately drawn in the background; women of fashion at the soda fountain; an 1898 cherub, the first cut-out; a pretty girl with her Coca-Cola in hand watching a kitten drinking milk.

"That one is my favorite," said Margaret Almond, herself a Coca-Cola-type pretty woman, with a full, usually smiling, animated face. Her husband, Claud, an airline employee, is slim, quiet-spoken, but equally enthusiastic about collecting.

He shows almost reverently the treasure of treasures in their collection, a tiny soda fountain menu with three pretty little girls painted on it, saying, "We drink Coca-Cola." It was produced in 1892 or 1893, and is, as far as the Almonds know, the only one in existence. "It's priceless," Claud said. "How can you put a price on a one-of-a-kind? Anyhow, we wouldn't take anything for it."

He bought it from another collector. "I made up my mind I was going to have it." He went to the man's house bearing a valuable blue seltzer bottle that he knew the man wanted very much. He offered the bottle for the three little girls, and then sat at a table and threw money on it until finally the man said, "Sold."

But the Almonds both said dealings among Coca-Cola collectors are not usually so hard-boiled. Rather, there is generally a spirit of fun and co-operativeness. One collector knows the other's speciality and calls or writes to tell of an item on sale somewhere. Or one will buy an item of the other's speciality and swap it for one in his or hers.

The Almonds began collecting eight years ago, making them early enthusiasts for the hobby. Collecting of memorabilia began in 1966, but most of the upsurge has occurred since 1970. People used to ask the Almonds why they did it. Margaret laughed her hearty laugh. "It's pretty. We like it. We enjoy it. We enjoy everything we have."

When they started collecting, they could pick up calendars for $100 that are now worth $300 or more. Some calendars on the day's market bring $1,800. A nearly perfect Hutchinson bottle that cost $75 eight years ago, now sells for $300 or more. Claud laughed to recall the time they found, at a dealer's, an 1898 and an 1899 calendar. The man wanted $300 apiece for them. "That scared us to death. But now they are worth $1,800." The most expensive collectors' item is the Tiffany-style Coca-Cola lamp. They bring at least $3,000, compared with $1,800 when the Almonds were starting out.

The Almonds have amassed their collection mostly from buying from dealers. Some people are lucky enough to make great finds in old stores, but not them. Claud said they had gone into stores out in the country and offered to buy an old sign or clock, but the proprietors refused. "They think these things belong to The Coca-Cola Company." He laughed.

Margaret told about a drugstore owner in a small town who has one of the beautiful old urns on a shelf in the store. He won't part with it. "People enjoy looking at it," he told the Almonds.

When the Almonds' house was being built, the contractor became fascinated with their collection and designed special wall insets for prized posters, giving the Almonds as much wall space as possible to hang the various paper items on.

"When we go out," Margaret exclaims, "we can't wait to get home and see if everybody's all right. We call them by name as if they were people. We see if all the ladies are where they should be, that nothing has been bothered."

Claud adds, "If I get blue or down about something, I can just walk around and start looking, and it perks me up."

Margaret pointed to a photograph among the drawings, paintings, and posters on the wall. It is of Diva Brown, a woman who gave Asa Candler's company considerable trouble with her claim that she had bought Dr. Pemberton's formula and her stubborn if unsuccessful bringing out of imitation drinks, including a Yum-Yum, which she advertised as being made from the original formula. "I just like her," Margaret said of the chin-high, determined Victorian face. "She's so aggressive-looking."

The other good thing about Coca-Cola collecting is the relationships and friendships with other collectors. Before they got into Coca-Cola, the Almonds had collected other things—coins, bottles, Avon items. But other collectors often were not pleasant, were cut-throat. Not so Coca-Cola collectors. "They're such nice people," Margaret affirms. "They're really good people."

They enjoy helping each other find collectibles, she went on, highlighted by the pleasure it gives her and Claud to find an item that is not in the collection of collections—the Coca-Cola Museum in Elizabethtown, Kentucky. When they find such a missing item, they give it to Bill and Jan Schmidt, owners of the museum. "They are always so grateful," Margaret said. "They make you feel so good." One item they gave the Schmidts was a window display of a replica of a

Wilbur G. Kurtz, retired archivist of The Coca-Cola Company.

small town, with Coca-Cola prominently displayed. Margaret found it at a flea market, covered with soot. She and Claud washed each piece carefully, and then happily carted it off to the Schmidt's.

Margaret has, for several years, been a Coca-Cola collectibles dealer, sending out price lists of surplus items she has for sale. "It helps support our habit," Claud said with a laugh. He told how sometimes to pay for a special find, they would eat grits for a week. Margaret continued, "We'll find something and just have to have it. Claud will say all right, this is happy birthday and Merry Christmas and all the rest." She laughed. "Every day is Christmas for us."

What is there about this drink, this product, that seems to attract a better sort of people, even a better sort of memorabilia collector? Let us face it. Collectors are usually grim, single-minded, and humorless people. One thinks of Mr. Sledge's, "I don't know what it is about Coca-Cola—except to say that it has a direct appeal to the best and the happiest side of a man's life." And of a woman's, of course.

Margaret laughed to tell how The Coca-Cola Company people sort of stood back at first, not quite knowing what to make of the collectors. "They just didn't know how many of us there were." Now, though, the company has come to see the collectors as but one more bit of magic in the promotion of Coca-Cola. At this year's convention, the company was fully represented, and Wilbur Kurtz had, as a company surprise for the collectors, a specially prepared, limited edition, old-fashioned-looking Coca-Cola mirror with portraits on it of Dr. Pemberton and Asa Candler. The mirrors were on sale at cost to the collectors only, at $40 each. One thousand were made; more than half were sold at the convention.

"Mr. Kurtz is so dear," Margaret Almond exclaimed. "We just think the world of him." She told how they found a booklet, *Landmarks of Atlanta*, illustrated by Mr. Kurtz's father, who, during his lifetime, was a prominent Atlanta painter and technical advisor for the filming of *Gone With the Wind*. (Mr. Kurtz's grandfather was Captain William Fuller, one of the two Confederate officers who pursued the steam-engine, General, in the great locomotive chase between Atlanta and Chattanooga.) The Almonds gave Mr. Kurtz the booklet, with one of the drawings inevitably showing a Coca-Cola bottle and a Coca-Cola glass.

On a day shortly after the Coca-Cola Clan convention, Mr. Kurtz was looking very pleased. He showed a new addition to the memorabilia in his office, a lovely Coca-Cola pendulum clock. The Clan members had presented it to him, along with a check for $395 for Mr. Kurtz to donate to an effort to restore the Cyclorama in Atlanta, a big circular painting of the Battle of Atlanta. Mr. Kurtz said the money would go as a memorial to his father, with the stipulation that it be used to restore the canvas of the painting only.

The Clan members also presented Mr. Kurtz with a special straight-sided bottle reproduction made in an edition of one thousand specially for the convention. On the diamond-shaped label of Mr. Kurtz's bottle was inscribed: "In appreciation of Wilbur G. Kurtz Jr.'s 36 years service to The Coca-Cola Company, The Cola Clan Third Annual Convention. Huntsville, Ala., August 5, 1977."

"Yes, sir," Mr. Kurtz affirms, sipping a glass of Dr. Pemberton's beverage. "That was quite a convention. There were a hundred and fifty trading tables set up in the Von Braun Auditorium."

In the archives display room adjacent to Mr. Kurtz's office, a bottler family, the round-faced mother wearing a red-and-white Coca-Cola T-shirt, the third or fourth or whatever generation son, wholesome-looking, muses about among the memorabilia, including the very percolator that Dr. Pemberton used to brew the secret ingredients that went into the first batch of Coca-Cola syrup.

In the executive suite in the building next door, Paul Austin discusses the good news from Egypt, an agreement he and associates finally secured from President Anwar el-Sadat for Coca-Cola to invest $50 million to develop, with its water technology, citrus groves in a fifteen-million-acre tract in the desert region of Ismalia. The agreement was seen as a major breakthrough toward getting Coke off the Middle Eastern boycott blacklist. (It came only a short while before President Sadat startled the world with his peace overtures to Israel. Maybe directly, maybe indirectly, here was proof of Mr. Austin's view that enhancing a country's economy encourages its instinct for peaceful survival.)

In another office, company president Luke Smith is interrupted in a conversation by his secretary who says, "It's Mr. Woodruff." Mr. Smith smiles and says to his visitor before picking up the phone, "You asked how active he is.

COURTESY OF THE ARCHIVES, THE COCA-COLA COMPANY

Architect's drawing of the twenty-six-story office tower being built in Atlanta at North Avenue and Plum Street during 1977.

Well here it is. He's still at it." The call has to do with some effort on behalf of the Boys' Club.

In the public relations section, vice-president J. William Pruett, Jr., puts the finishing touches on a speech to be delivered by some company official at some Atlanta civic group's meeting. Helping prepare such speeches and other material for the company's busy executives is a major function of Mr. Pruett's department. Press relations, by comparison, take up less of the department's time. "We're just not in the news all that much," Mr. Pruett says.

And so the life of The Coca-Cola Company continues. Outside, the smell of the syrup is sweetly wafted on the wind. Mr. Pope T. Brock stands waiting for his bus. He wears his black fedora. People of the company know that fall has come. They have the comforting certainty of the passing of the seasons, the ongoing motion of the earth . . . and they have, too, the also comforting thought of all the Coca-Cola being swigged down at every moment over the earth as it continues, in space, to whirl.